Neo-Thomism in Action

Neo-Thomism in Action

Law and Society Reshaped by Neo-Scholastic Philosophy 1880-1960

Edited by Wim Decock, Bart Raymaekers and Peter Heyrman

Leuven University Press

Cover: Thomas Aquinas as teacher. Wall painting by Georges De Geetere in the Sacred Heart House, the professor's house near Désiré Mercier's Leo XIII Seminary in Leuven, c 1900.
[Photo Danny Brison]

© 2021 Leuven University Press/Presses universitaires de Louvain/Universitaire Pers Leuven,
Minderbroedersstraat 4, B-3000 Leuven (Belgium)

ISBN 978 94 6270 306 3
eISBN 978 94 6166 421 1
D/2021/1869/52
https://doi.org/10.11116/9789461664211
NUR: 704

GPRC
Guaranteed
Peer Reviewed
Content
www.gprc.be

CONTENTS

NEO-THOMISM,
LAW AND SOCIETY
A PROLEGOMENON TO FURTHER STUDY

WIM DECOCK

In 1946, the African American economist Abram Lincoln Harris (1899-1963) looked back critically upon seven decades of "scholastic-canonist teaching" that had sought to offer solutions for the joint problems of economic organisation and social discontent by drawing on Thomas Aquinas's philosophy.[1] Paying special attention to the scholastic economics of Heinrich Pesch (1854-1926), a German jurist and economist belonging to the Jesuit Order, Harris warned against the neo-scholastic movement's "pious hope" of re-establishing "an organic or corporate economy" against the twin threats of social Marxism and libertarian capitalism. For the sake of reinforcing solidarity, neo-scholastics such as Pesch defended a corporative economy against the "brutal self-seeking of the free capitalistic epoch".[2] And against social Marxists' desire to introduce collective ownership, they advocated the sharing of decision-making within companies rather than weakening legal titles of ownership. Yet, according to Harris, the disastrous result of scholastic-styled corporativism was "a society of monopolies".[3] Such a society falls easily prey to authoritarian regimes, with economic exchange becoming "a matter of diplomatic pressures, political coercion, and the real domination of the weak by

---

1   Harris, "The Scholastic Revival".
2   On the impact of neo-scholastic corporatism in Germany, see Hagedorn, "Kapitalismuskritische Richtungen im deutschen Katholizismus der Zwischenkriegszeit".
3   Harris, "The Scholastic Revival", 56.

the strong". Citing historical events in Italy in the 1930s, Harris concluded that the road to the corporative order was the road to fascism.[4]

Harris's engagement with Pesch's economic thought allows for at least three observations. First, the neo-scholastic tradition remained a point of reference among social scientists across the globe even after the end of the Second World War. While intellectual support for the movement gradually waned – not in the least because of cultural paradigm shifts within the Roman Catholic Church itself[5] – Thomas Aquinas and his neo-scholastic interpreters continued to be read even by their opponents. Second, the neo-scholastic tradition was perceived as anything but "scholastic" in the pejorative sense of the word. Against the misleading notion that scholastics produced mere theoretical and abstract knowledge,[6] Harris's assessment of the practical impact of neo-scholastic corporatism on economic developments in Italy prior to the Second World War clearly shows that neo-scholastic philosophy bore a close relationship to societal reality. This prompts a third observation. For several decades, neo-scholastic scholars not only debated but also shaped the organisation of society. For example, the introduction of social legislation, the rise of corporative structures and the emergence of Christian democracy in Western European countries owed much to Pope Leo XIII's encyclical on the "social question" (*Rerum novarum*, 15 May 1891).

Preparing avenues for further research, the chapters in this volume assess the societal impact of the neo-scholastic revival – a revival referred to more commonly as "neo-Thomism" or "Thomist revival", due to the emphasis by Pope Leo XIII, in his encyclical *Aeterni Patris* (4 August 1879), on the privileged status of Thomas Aquinas (1225-1274) among the medieval scholastic theologians.[7] Most contributions in this volume have been presented at a workshop convened in Leuven in October 2017 at the invitation of KADOC (Documentation and Research Centre on Religion, Culture and Society), and KU Leuven's Institute of Philosophy and Department of Roman Law and Le-

---

4   The interests of Italian Catholics and fascists converged in their promotion of a 'corporative economy', see Nelis, "The Clerical Response to a Totalitarian Political Religion", 265. But official documents such as Pope Pius XI's encyclical *Quadragesimo anno* remained silent on the question whether fascist and Catholic corporatism were fully aligned or not; cf. Chamedes, *A Twentieth-Century Crusade*, 130.

5   Bosschaert, "The International Union of Social Studies of Malines and the Catholic Cultural Turn".

6   On the early modern origins of this quite negative understanding of 'scholasticism', see Decock and Birr, *Recht und Moral in der Scholastik*, 4-5 and 9.

7   The impact of the late medieval and early modern scholastic traditions on the modern revival of scholasticism cannot be ignored, though, as the analysis of sources in Abbé Pottier's *De iure et iustitia* (1900) shows; see J.-P. Delville, "Antoine Pottier and the Neo-Thomist Roots of Social Justice", infra. Moreover, such 'neo-Thomists' as Désiré Mercier would rather refer to himself and his colleagues at the Leuven Institut supérieur de Philosophie as 'neo-scholastics', see Steel, "Thomas en de vernieuwing van de filosofie", 55.

gal History.[8] The workshop offered scholars from different disciplinary and national backgrounds the occasion to reflect upon the impact of the neo-scholastic revival movement on socio-economic policy-making from the promulgation of the encyclical *Aeterni Patris* through the post-Second World War period – decades marked by several turning points in modern European history, as Emiel Lamberts explains in his opening chapter to this volume.[9] The workshop followed an earlier conference jointly organised by KADOC, KU Leuven's Institute of Philosophy and the Department of Architecture in June 2015 which set the scene by investigating the conceptual framework of neo-Thomism and its interaction with modern strands of philosophical, theological and artistic thought.[10] As will be detailed below, the contributions collected in this volume offer pathways for further investigation into protagonists of neo-Thomist thought and action in the field of law and society, its networks, institutions, study circles, periodicals and conceptual framework.

A particular effort has been made, throughout this volume, to highlight the juridical dimension of the neo-Thomist movement. The legal nature of neo-scholastic debates on social justice is at the centre of several chapters, with Joeri De Smet discussing the impact of neo-Thomism on Leuven's Faculty of Law at the turn of the twentieth century.[11] Jurists had a great impact on the development of neo-Thomism in other faculties as well. The very beginning of the Institut supérieur de Philosophie at the Catholic University of Leuven is an illustration of the seminal role that jurists played in promoting neo-scholastic philosophy. Three out of four staff members recruited by Désiré Mercier in 1893, when the Institute expanded for the first time, held degrees in law: Maurice De Wulf (1867-1947), Simon Deploige (1868-1927), and Armand Thiéry (1868-1955).[12] Maurice De Wulf, the famous historian of medieval philosophy, obtained his doctorate in law in 1891, after prior studies in arts and philosophy. He acquired the special licentiate in Thomistic philosophy in

---

8   "Neo-Thomism in Action. Law and Society Reshaped by Neo-Scholastic Philosophy, 1880-1960", Irish College, Leuven, 8-10 October 2017. Papers presented at the conference but not included in this volume are M. Banerjee's "Thomas Aquinas, Neo-Thomism and the Trans-Nationally Entangled Emergence of the Indian Judiciary as a Politico-Theological Institution, 1973-2015", J. Chappel's "Contraception, Usury and the Formation of Modern Catholic Ethics", A. Giuliani's "What a Legal Historian can Learn from the Neo-Thomist Revival of John Poinsot's *Tractatus de signis*", and P.H. Kosicki's "Between Lublin and Louvain. Transnational Neo-Thomism and Europe's Twentieth-Century Personalist Revolution".

9   E. Lamberts, "Religious, Political and Social Settings of the Revival of Thomism (1870-1960)", see below.

10 Heynickx and Symons, eds., *What is So New About Scholasticism?*

11 J. De Smet, "Neo-Thomism at Leuven's Faculty of Law", see below.

12 Hiraux, "L'Institut supérieur de philosophie de Louvain", 24. Désiré Nys, the fourth nominee, held degrees in theology, natural sciences and Thomist philosophy, see Hiraux, "L'Institut supérieur de philosophie de Louvain", 75.

1892.[13] Simon Deploige joined Mercier's neo-Thomist team following a brief spell as a practicing lawyer at the bar of Tongeren. When Mercier left Leuven to take office as Archbishop of Mechelen in 1906, Deploige became the second president of the Institut supérieur de Philosophie. During his mandate, much energy was spent on organising public events and reaching out to the wider community.[14] The ambition of the Institute, then, was to create a new Catholic elite well-versed in neo-Thomist philosophy.[15] A major contribution to that objective was made by Armand Thiéry, albeit in his own idiosyncratic manner.[16] Besides studying arts, philosophy, theology, exact sciences, architecture and psychology, Armand Thiéry obtained a law degree, but abandoned plans to pursue a career as a lawyer in order to follow his academic interests.

Another illustration of the intimate connection between law and neo-Thomism is the fact that the first student to obtain a doctorate in Thomistic philosophy in 1885 – when Mercier's Chair of Thomistic Philosophy (1882) had not yet grown into an independent institute – was Théodore Fontaine (1858-1898), a jurist by training. The following year, Fontaine started teaching a course on social law and its relationship with the workers' question (*Le droit social dans ses rapports avec la question ouvrière*). In 1888, Fontaine was a founding member of the Société philosophique de Louvain, an influential neo-Thomist think-thank. Another co-founder was Léon de Lantsheere (1862-1912), a prominent jurist who went on to become Belgian minister of Justice (1908) and then dean of the Faculty of Law (1911).[17] In 1886 he was the second among Mercier's students to obtain the doctorate of Thomistic philosophy. Along with members of the so-called School of Liège (*École de Liège*), including Abbé Pottier (1849-1923),[18] the jurists Jules Renkin (1862-1934) and Henri Carton de Wiart (1869-1951) assisted de Lantsheere in brokering the rise of Christian democracy. Renkin, Carton de Wiart and de Lantsheere sat on the board of the journal *L'avenir social*, later to be named *La justice sociale*, which was founded in 1894. In the same year, the Société philosophique de Louvain started publishing its own journal, the *Revue néo-scolastique*. It was an important forerunner to the *Rivista di filosofia neoscolastica*, founded in 1909 by Agostino Gemelli (1878-1959), a Franciscan friar and medical doctor. The *Revue néo-scolastique* counted several jurists among its board members and provided an outlet for legal scholarship. For example, in 1913 the *Revue néo-scolastique* featured a critical article on workers' unions and the right to strike by Fernand De Visscher (1885-1964), a jurist who went on to make an ac-

13   Hiraux, "L'Institut supérieur de philosophie de Louvain", 75-76.
14   Ph. Chenaux, "The 1920s Francophone Thomistic Revival", see below.
15   De Leeuw, "Neo-Thomism and the Education of a Catholic Elite in Louvain".
16   De Raeymaeker, *M. le chanoine Armand Thiéry*.
17   Heyrman, "Léon de Lantsheere".
18   See the contribution by J.-P. Delville below and Jadoulle, "Question sociale et politique pontificale".

ademic career at the Universities of Ghent and Leuven as an expert in Roman law and archaeology.[19]

Journals served as major instruments in spreading neo-Thomist views on law and society. The debates on socio-economic issues by students gathering at the Leuven Institute of Philosophy found an outlet in two specialised journals: the *Revue Sociale Catholique* (1897) and *Revue Catholique de Droit* (1898).[20] A brief look at the composition of the editorial boards of those journals reveals just how strongly involved jurists were in neo-Thomist networks. Edouard Crahay (1872-1942), appointed as professor of sociology, constitutional law and administrative law at the University of Liège in 1895 – subsequent to obtaining his licentiate in Thomistic philosophy – joined the *Revue Catholique de Droit* as its editorial secretary.[21] The list of collaborators of the journal includes the names of both famous and lesser-known jurists who were going to occupy influential positions in society, for instance Albert Janssen (1883-1966), Ignace Sinzot (1888-1940) and Pierre Verhaegen (1873-1953).[22] The same observation applies to the *Revue Sociale Catholique*. Amongst its editorial board members one can find the likes of Henry Carton de Wiart, future minister of Justice, Cyrille van Overbergh (1866-1959), the future director general of the interior ministry, and Arthur Vermeersch (1858-1936), a professor of canon law at the Jesuit College in Leuven and the Gregorian University in Rome.[23] The editorial board also included legal practitioners such as Michel Bodeux, public prosecutor in Liège, Henry Dumortier, judge at the court of first instance in Tournai, Georges Eeckhout, a barrister in Gent, and Léon Meerens, a public notary.[24]

At the Catholic University of Leuven, jurists did not only contribute to the revival of neo-Thomism by joining study circles and journals centred around the Institut supérieur de Philosophie. A major impetus to the revival of neo-Thomist thought was brokered by Victor Brants (1856-1917), a professor at the Faculty of Law, and at the Faculty of Arts and Philosophy. Brants graduated as doctor of law in 1878 and succeeded Charles Périn as chair of political economics in 1881.[25] He taught courses on land law, the history of rural pop-

19   De Visscher, "La philosophie syndicaliste et le mythe de la grève générale". On Fernand de Visscher and his brother, see Gerkens and Genin, "Charles de Visscher (1884-1973) et Fernand de Visscher (1885-1964)".

20   Both journals merged in 1920 under a new name: *Revue Catholique Sociale et Juridique*, published by the Institute until 1925. Hiraux, "L'Institut supérieur de philosophie de Louvain", 54.

21   Mirguet, "Crahay, Edouard".

22   Compare the search results for 'Revue catholique de droit' in the ODIS-database, www.odis.be.

23   V. Genin, "Arthur Vermeersch", cf. infra.

24   For a comprehensive prosopography of the members of the editorial board of the *Revue Sociale Catholique* between 1896 and 1900, see Quaghebeur, *De Revue Sociale Catholique*.

25   Meerts, "De Leuvense hoogleraar Victor Brants: een brugfiguur in het sociaal-katholicisme"; Id., "De Leuvense hoogleraar Victor Brants: sociale ideeën tussen katholieke romantiek en realisme".

ulations, comparative labour law and comparative financial law. Along with the jurists Jules Van den Heuvel (1854-1926) and Léon Dupriez (1863-1942), Brants founded a School for Political and Social Sciences in 1892.[26] Following the innovative approach of the French engineer Frédéric Le Play (1806-1882), they promoted the integration of empirical and statistical methods into traditional socio-economic research.[27] In this sense, Brants's was different from Mercier's scholasticism.[28] More so than his colleagues at the Institut supérieur de Philosophie, Brants paid attention to the revival of the scholastic tradition in the sixteenth and seventeenth centuries, carefully studying the legal, economic and political thought of Leonardus Lessius (1554-1623).[29] Brants played a fundamental role in spreading neo-Thomist philosophy across Belgian society through influential study circles such as the Société belge d'Économie Sociale, which he founded in 1881, one year prior to the foundation of Mercier's Chair in Thomistic Philosophy. One of the co-founders of the Société belge d'Économie Sociale was Brants's friend Charles De Jace (1856-1941). De Jace went on to become a practicing lawyer and a professor of political economics, natural law and comparative labour law at the University of Liège, an institution which he led in the capacity of rector between 1921 and 1924.[30] Finally, Brants was the driver behind Leuven university's Conférence d'Économie Sociale (1885), where future leaders of the workers' movement, farmers' organisations, and entrepreneurs were imbued with neo-Thomist views on society.[31]

While the academic environment in Leuven offers a fine example of the intellectual strength of the neo-Thomist revival in Belgium and its connection with legal thought and practice, the geographical scope of this volume reaches farther than Leuven, or, for that matter, Liège. It is a truism to claim that neo-Thomism in Belgium cannot be understood without reference to international movements. For one thing, the Belgian jurists kept an eye on developments abroad, drawing on the methodology of comparative law to derive inspiration from socio-economic regulation in neighbouring countries. Victor Brants, for instance, studied German corporatist theories in his 1894 book *Le régime corporatif au XIXe siècle dans les États Germaniques: étude de législation sociale comparée*. The neo-Thomists took full advantage, then, of the rise

26 Wils, "Les intellectuels catholiques et la sociologie en Belgique", 74-75.
27 On the popularity of Le Play's comparative sociology, based on empirical observation, among Catholic jurists, see Deferme and De Maeyer, "Entre sciences sociales et politique", and Brejon de Lavergnée, "Les catholiques et Le Play".
28 Hiraux, "L'Institut supérieur de philosophie de Louvain", 43.
29 Brants, "L'économie politique et sociale dans les écrits de L. Lessius". Brants was also eager to show that Lessius, a scholastic theologian, had had a great impact on Leuven's Law Faculty in the early modern period, see Decock, *Le marché du mérite*, 15-16.
30 Halkin and Harsin, eds., *Liber memorialis: l'Université de Liège*, I, 733-737.
31 Van Molle, *Katholieken en landbouw*; Id., *Ieder voor allen*; Heyrman, *Middenstandsbeweging en beleid in België*; Gerard, ed., *De christelijke arbeidersbeweging in België*.

of comparative law as a scientific discipline.[32] For another, Belgian neo-Thomists were actively involved in international networks. Joris Helleputte (1852-1925), for instance, the engineer and architect who spearheaded the neo-Gothic movement in Belgium, was a member of the Union de Fribourg (1884-1891) before becoming a founding member of the Union de Malines in 1920.[33] The corporatist ideal to which Belgian neo-Thomists such as Helleputte adhered in the 1920s was partly inspired by attempts in Belgium to revive medieval corporatist ideas, for instance through Charles Périn's Confrérie de St.-Michel.[34] But it also drew on earlier ideas advocated by Italian, German and French scholars, e.g. Luigi Taparelli d'Azeglio (1793-1862), Matteo Liberatore (1810-1892), Wilhelm von Ketteler (1811-1877), René La Tour du Pin (1834-1924) and Albert de Mun (1841-1914).[35]

In his contribution on the revival of Thomism in France in the 1920s, Philippe Chenaux recalls the impact of French scholars on the Leuven Institut supérieur de Philosophie. Between 1920 and 1926 Jacques Maritain (1882-1973), the famous French neo-Thomist philosopher and Christian humanist, was invited to Leuven no less than seven times.[36] Chenaux also draws attention to major neo-Thomist circles in Paris, Fribourg and Rome at the time. Moreover, in 1921, Agostino Gemelli founded the Catholic University Sacro Cuore in Milan. In fact, the impact of French and Italian scholars on Belgian jurists and political economists had been tremendous already during the nineteenth century. The idea of a 'Christian economy' circulated widely in Leuven thanks to the influence of Alban de Villeneuve-Bargemon (1784-1850), Charles de Coux (1787-1864), and Matteo Liberatore (1810-1892). They inspired conservative, anti-revolutionary and ultramontane tendencies among Catholic elites in Belgium. A case in point is Charles Périn (1815-1905), student of de Coux and chair of political economics at Leuven's Faculty of Law. In his influential book *On the Wealth of Christian Nations* (*De la richesse dans les sociétés chrétiennes*, 1861) Périn promoted an ascetic philosophy of moderation, renunciation and sacrifice to reconcile the interests of workers and their bosses.[37] A letter which he wrote in 1890 to the editorial board of the French *Revue Catholique des*

32 In the French-speaking world, the Société de législation comparée, founded in 1876, provided a major stimulus for the study of foreign laws, cf. Fauvarque-Cosson, "Development of Comparative Law in France".

33 The Union de Malines obviously took the Union de Fribourg as its model, cf. Van Molle, "Croissance économique et éthique catholique", 323-327.

34 De Maeyer, "De ultramontanen en de gildenbeweging".

35 Lamberts, "De ontwikkeling van de sociaal-katholieke ideologie in België", 53-54.

36 Chenaux, "The 1920s Francophone Thomistic Revival", cf. infra. See also Id., *Entre Maurras et Maritain*, 26.

37 Stevens, "Charles Périn".

Institutions et du Droit provides further evidence of his crusade against modernism and the "godless" philosophies of liberalism and socialism.[38]

The example of Périn shows that societal challenges connected to the
demise of the *Ancien régime* led to a re-vitalisation of the scholastic tradition
among Catholic elites decades before Pope Leo XIII promoted a neo-Thomist
framework to conceive of a new Catholic socio-economic paradigm. Philippe
Boutry has convincingly argued that the origins of Pope Leo XIII's encyclical
Rerum novarum lie in his practical experience as a papal diplomat in Belgium
in the 1840s.[39] Around the same time, the intellectual revival of the scholastic tradition had begun in Belgium at the instigation of Jean-Baptiste Malou
(1809-1864), bishop of Bruges.[40] From an international perspective, the revival, long before *Aeterni Patris*, of Thomist philosophy is even more obvious.[41]
Through the foundation, in 1850, of *La Civiltà Cattolica*, a major neo-scholastic journal, the Jesuit theologians Matteo Liberatore and Luigi Taparelli d'Azeglio contributed perhaps more than anyone else to the diffusion of Thomism
around the world. But as Jakub Štofaník observes, the revival of Thomist philosophy prior to the promulgation of *Aeterni Patris* can also be witnessed in
the Czech Lands, for instance at the seminary in Brno, where the theologian
Josef Pospíšil (1845-1926) lectured Thomistic philosophy before 1879. In his
contribution on neo-Thomism in Spain, Faustino Martínez Martínez emphasises the need to read the renaissance of neo-Thomist philosophy in modern
Spain against the background of a much older tradition of scholastic constitutional thought.[42] *Aeterni Patris*, then, lent official approval to a renaissance
of scholastic, especially Thomist philosophy rather than starting a new movement.

Martínez Martínez highlights the revival of scholastic political thought
in the framework of conservative critiques on the rise of the modern state that
flourished not only at the end, but throughout the nineteenth century.[43] His
contribution indicates that 'revival' is not the best word to describe the turn
to scholastic political philosophy popular among 'Spanish Moderantists' such
as Juan Bravo Murillo (1803-1873), an influential jurist and politician. In fact,
the scholastic tradition reached its apex in early modern Spain – it suffices to

---

38   Ch. Périn, "Ni libéraux, ni socialistes", letter to the editorial board of the *Revue Catholique
     des Institutions et du Droit*, Ghlin, 20 October 1890.
39   Boutry, "L'Encyclique *Rerum Novarum*".
40   Kenis, "Movements toward Renewal".
41   See also Leinsle, *Introduction to Scholastic Theology*, 354-360 and Coreth, Neidl and
     Pfligersdorffer, eds., *Christliche Philosophie im katholischen Denken*, vol. 2.
42   Llano Torres, "Ciencia jurídica y moralismo en la España del Siglo XIX".
43   F. Martínez Martínez, "Between Gospel and Constitution: Neo-Scholastic Traces in the
     Legal World of Nineteenth-Century Spain", see below.

think of the famous 'School of Salamanca'[44] – and probably "never left these lands". Protagonists of the School of Salamanca such as Domingo de Soto (1494-1560), a Dominican friar, published treatises *On Justice and Right* (*De iustitia et iure*, 1553).[45] They took the *Secunda Secundae* of Thomas Aquinas' *Summa Theologiae* as a starting point for detailed discussions on contemporary social, economic and legal issues. Such treatises continued to be written all along the centuries.[46] Despite differences in context, they are indicative of lines of continuity between the sixteenth century renaissance of Thomism and modern neo-Thomism. For example, Abbé Pottier published a treatise *On Right and Justice* (*De iure et iustitia*) in 1900. As Mgr. Jean-Pierre Delville's analysis of his source material demonstrates, Pottier relied not just on the authority of Thomas Aquinas, but even more so on that of early modern scholastics such as Lessius.[47] As late as 1956, the Dutch neo-Thomist Willem Duynstee (1886-1986), professor of law at Nijmegen University, published a treatise *On Right and Justice* (*Over recht en rechtvaardigheid*).[48]

In the 1920s and 1930s the legacy of Thomas, early modern scholasticism and neo-Thomism ended up being vindicated by ultra-conservative forces trying to legitimate authoritarian regimes – one thinks of the Acción Española and the Action Française, in particular. Protagonists of the neo-Thomist movement such as Gemelli appear to have been lured into accepting some of the darker sides of the fascist movement.[49] Studies on the scholastic tradition received a new impetus under the dictatorship of Franco (1939-1975), but not always for scientific reasons, as Ignacio de la Rasilla, a historian of international law, has pointed out.[50] Similarly, their nostalgic hope for a return to the societal order pre-dating the French Revolution tempted some French jurists belonging to the French Association des Jurisconsultes Catholiques to join forces with the ultra-nationalist Action Française and the authoritarian Vichy régime.[51] In Germany, a couple of jurists showing interest in the scholastic tradition such as Hans Thieme (1906-2000) were linked to the national socialist movement's NSDAP. The relationship between authoritarian regimes and – at least some of – the jurists and philosophers that embraced neo-Thomism falls

---

44 Grice-Hutchinson, *The School of Salamanca*; Decock, "Spanish Scholastics on Money and Credit"; Duve, "The School of Salamanca".
45 Decock, "Domingo de Soto, *De iustitia et iure*".
46 For an overview of relevant primary sources, see Decock and Birr, *Recht und Moral in der Scholastik*, 33-57.
47 Delville, "Antoine Pottier and the Neo-Thomist Roots of Social Justice", see below.
48 Jansen, "Willem Duynstee".
49 Miccoli, "Padre Agostino Gemelli".
50 de la Rasilla del Moral, "The Fascist Mimesis of Spanish International Law". See also Id., *In the Shadow of Vitoria*, 260.
51 Fillon, "La *Revue catholique des institutions et du droit*", 217-218.

outside the scope of this volume but nevertheless deserves further scrutiny.[52] Another sensitive issue that merits a more thorough investigation is the attitude of neo-Thomists towards the colonial endeavours of the modern nation states. As far as the Belgian case is concerned, it is clear that protagonists of the neo-Thomist movement such as the Jesuits Auguste Castelein (1840-1922) and Arthur Vermeersch were concerned about the moral and legal aspects of Belgian governance in Congo, each expressing different viewpoints.[53] As a result, careful analysis is needed before an overall assessment of neo-Thomist attitudes towards colonial power is made.

More comparative research is also needed to improve our understanding of the relationship between nationalism and neo-Thomism. In his capacity as the archbishop of Mechelen during the First World War, Désiré Cardinal Mercier famously contributed to the rise of Belgian patriotic sentiment by publicly opposing German occupancy.[54] In a remarkable contribution on the role of neo-Thomism in the formation of Quebec nationalism, Kasper Swerts demonstrates how the revival of Aristotelian-Thomistic metaphysics facilitated the conceptualisation of a specific French-Canadian Catholic national identity.[55] In some ways, especially through the promotion of the virtue of patriotism (*pietas patriae*), the Church was able to reconcile traditional values with the rise of the modern state. But then again, totalitarian notions of national identity were not accepted by Rome. According to Cinzia Sulas, "the Great War highlighted the intrinsic contradictory stance of religious institutions towards modern nationalism".[56] In her article, she shows that individual contributors to neo-Thomist journals in Italy, especially *La Civiltà Cattolica*, tried to justify the war in terms of love of the homeland and the moral duty to defend the nation, which was seen as the seat of divine providence. But the Holy See was sceptical of overt patriotic feelings. Pope Benedict XV warned of the combined perils of nationalism and colonialism in making the work of religious missionaries subservient to the interests of countries rather than God.[57] In 1926, Pope Pius XI fiercely condemned the 'integral nationalism' of the Action Française

---

52 For an introduction to the (larger) topic of the relationship between fascism and Catholicism, see Pollard, "Fascism and Catholicism". See also Chamedes, *A Twentieth-Century Crusade*, 93-120, and Nelis, Morelli and Praet, eds., *Catholicism and Fascism in Europe*.

53 See the contributions by P. Heyrman and V. Genin in this volume.

54 Aubert, *Les deux premiers grands conflits du cardinal Mercier avec les autorités allemandes*; De Volder, *Kardinaal verzet*.

55 K. Swerts, "*Vetera novis augere* or *Leuven Quebec augere*: Lionel Groulx, neo-Thomism and French-Canadian nationalism", see below.

56 C. Sulas, "The Notion of War in the *Rivista di Filosofia Neo-Scolastica*, 1914-1918", see below.

57 Pollard, *The Papacy in the Age of Totalitarianism*, 114-115.

and Charles Maurras (1868-1952), its ultra-conservative, atheist and xenophobic leader.[58]

"The struggle with Leviathan", to use Emiel Lamberts words,[59] is a persistent feature of neo-scholastic engagements with socio-economic and political challenges. Its modern, neo-Thomist variant can only be fully understood when earlier developments, especially in the sixteenth century, are sufficiently accounted for. Similarly, neo-Thomism in the decades following Pope Leo XIII's *Aeterni Patris* remains difficult to understand without acknowledgment of the profound transformation of Thomism in the early modern period, particularly in the aforementioned School of Salamanca.[60] After the demise of a unified medieval Christendom following the Reformation and the rise of globally acting territorial states such as the Spanish empire, the Church had been urged, already back in the sixteenth century, to defend its own political interests and independent jurisdictional power. In the process of doing so, it heavily relied on a revival of late medieval, scholastic thought, especially Thomas Aquinas – proclaimed 'doctor of the Church' in 1567 by Pope Pius V.[61] Combined with political ideas deriving from the Roman canon legal tradition, the revival of Thomas allowed for a reinforcement of constitutionalist theories of civil power, making the legitimacy of civil authorities subject to the promotion of the common good and, at least theoretically, the consent of the people. This is particularly evident in scholastic political thought developed by Jesuits in the early modern period.[62] While the early modern scholastics contributed to strengthening the authority of secular princes, they also combatted a totalitarian understanding of civil power that undermined the interests of the Church.[63] To curb princely power, they emphasised the importance of natural law (*ius naturae*) as the ultimate criterion to evaluate the validity of man-made legislation. The scholastics claimed to be the supreme exegetes of natural law.[64]

When Pope Leo XIII reignited the doctrine of 'indirect power' of the Church, notably through his encyclical *Immortale Dei* (19 November 1885), he was not, in fact, reviving the thirteenth-century texts of Thomas Aquinas, but the reformulation of Thomistic political thought by early modern scholastics

---

58 Ph. Chenaux, "The 1920s Francophone Thomistic Revival", see below; Prévotat, *Les catholiques et l'Action française*, 359-395.

59 Lamberts, *The Struggle with Leviathan*.

60 Belda Plans, *La Escuela de Salamanca*.

61 In the early 1570s, only a couple of years later after Thomas's elevation to the rank of 'doctor of the Church', Robert Bellarmine started teaching his theology classes at the Jesuit College of Leuven on the basis of Thomas Aquinas's *Summa theologiae*. Robert Bellarmine was declared 'doctor of the Church' himself in 1931, cf. infra.

62 Höpfl, *Jesuit Political Thought*.

63 Decock, "Collaborative Legal Pluralism".

64 Id., "From Law to Paradise".

such as Martín de Azpilcueta (1492-1586), Robert Bellarmine (1542-1621) and Francisco Suárez (1548-1617).[65] Early modern scholastics rather than Thomas were the real sources of a theory on State-Church relationships that culminated into the *societas perfecta*-doctrine of the eighteenth century which was then further promoted by Roman pontiffs such as Leo XIII and Pius XI to oppose the increasingly powerful nation-states. The modern Church resented the rise of 'Leviathan' (see Lamberts), with its thirst for undivided jurisdictional power that reduced the Church to a moral authority without teeth to bite. It is not a coincidence that Bellarmine, the early modern advocate of the jurisdictional interests of the Church, was first beatified in 1923 and then canonised as a saint in 1930 by Pope Pius XI. In 1931, Bellarmine was even declared 'doctor of the Church', and hence elevated to the same rank of doctrinal dignity as Thomas Aquinas about two and a half centuries earlier. In the field of law, the struggle of the Church against totalitarian rule by the nation states became apparent in its reinforced emphasis on natural law as a check and balance on positive law. In an encyclical on the duties of Christian citizens (*Sapientiae Christianae*, 10 January 1890), Pope Leo XIII invited clergymen to evaluate state legislation, viz. positive law, on the basis of superior norms, viz. natural law.[66] Here again, Pope Leo XIII did little more than adapt the pragmatic understanding of natural law in the early modern scholastic sense to new circumstances.[67]

Inquiring whether civil legislation and man-made agreements were 'natural law-proof', so to speak, Catholic clergymen quickly bumped into the thorny issue of remuneration of workers in the age of industrial capitalism. Next to the 'struggle with Leviathan', this was certainly another major challenge that neo-Thomists sought to address. Back in 1881, Edward De Gryse (1848-1909), a professor of moral theology who went on to serve as the dean of the St Martin's Church in Kortrijk, authored a work on *Our National Law and the Revolution*.[68] In the fourth part of this seminal work, De Gryse addressed the 'social question' from the perspective of the superior norms of natural law. In 1895, he studied the employment contract (*De contractu conductionis*), paying much attention to the 'just wage'. As Kwinten Dewaele highlights, De Gryse drew on Adam Smith (1723-1790) and Pellegrino Rossi (1787-1848) to propose a market-based view of labour, but not without modifying their views. De Gryse advanced, on moral grounds, the idea of a 'family wage in abstracto', that is a wage big enough for the worker to support himself, his wife and

---

65   Tutino, *Empire of Souls*; Decock, "Martín de Azpilcueta".
66   Lamberts, "Religious, Political and Social Settings of the Revival of Thomism (1870-1960)", see below.
67   Decock, *Theologians and Contract Law*, 43.
68   *Vaderlandsch Recht en Revolutie: verhandelingen over de sociale questiën van heden*, translated into French as *Notre droit national et la Révolution* in 1885.

two children.[69] While sceptical of government intervention, he did consider employers to be under a moral obligation to provide such a sustenance wage. De Gryse did not accept the argument, popular among industrialists, that the 'liberty of labour' – introduced in 1791 through the *Décret d'Allarde* and the *Loi Le Chapelier*[70] – frustrated any such considerations for the workers and the sustenance of their families.

In all countries facing the disruptive effects of industrialisation the issue of just remuneration of the workers became central to neo-Thomist debates. This is a returning issue in many chapters collected in this volume. For example, Jo Deferme highlights Simon Deploige's natural law account of the just wage.[71] Deploige emphasised bosses' duty to offer a wage sufficiently generous to allow the worker to sustain both himself and his family. He even considered that the state should intervene if the employer failed to fulfil his moral duty. Joannes Aengenent (1873-1935), future bishop of Haarlem in the Netherlands, would follow Deploige's opinion. As Erik Sengers argues in his contribution, Aengenent advocated the view that wages should not be the mere outcome of market forces.[72] A just wage should allow the worker to support not only himself, but also his family. Aengenent's work echoed the general tendency among neo-scholastics to propose a corporative economy as a an alternative to liberalism and socialism. Aengenent's work was clearly inspired by the *Social Code* (*Code social*), the Union de Malines' 1926 official declaration on socio-economic questions. Aengenent also attached much importance to the representation of workers in company boards and the conclusion of collective agreements between workers and their bosses depending on the type of business. Often accused with socialist tendencies, Aengenent saw a role for the state in regulating labour relations, besides appealing to employers' moral duties of charity and solidarity. Compared to other neo-Thomists such as Auguste Castelein, a Jesuit theologian who followed Charles Périn's rejection of interference by state institutions, Aengenent's views sound rather progressive.

The debate on the desirability of state intervention rather than private charity in addressing the social question stirred a lot of controversy among the neo-Thomists. As Jo Deferme has shown for the Belgian case, only towards the end of the nineteenth century did a majority of the Catholic scholars and policymakers come to accept that social legislation rather than charity should play a major part in alleviating the plight of the poor.[73] Neo-Thomists such as

---

69 K. Dewaele, "Neo-Thomism and the Debates on the Just Wage in Belgium (1879-1914)", see below.
70 Stevens, "Het coalitieverbod in België (1795-1866)".
71 J. Deferme, "The Influence of Neo-Thomism on Catholic Social Policy-Making in Belgium, 1880-1914", see below.
72 E. Sengers, "Joannes Aengenent (1873-1935): A Thomist Sociologist's Call for a More Human Economy", see below.
73 Deferme, *Uit de ketens van de vrijheid*.

de Lantsheere played an important role in bring about that change of view. Along with neo-Thomists belonging to the so-called 'School of Liège', such as Abbé Pottier,[74] de Lantsheere inclined towards the opinion that the protection of workers' interests should be guaranteed by state laws, enforceable in court, rather than being left to the exclusive moral responsibility of the great industrialists. The Social Conferences of Liège (Congrès des œuvres sociales), organised in 1886, 1887 and 1890 by Mgr. Doutreloux, bishop of Liège, largely contributed to that 'state-friendly' view.[75] The Social Conferences of Liège and the contributions by Abbé Pottier, in particulier, announced the birth of the concept of 'social justice' and a new, centrist political movement that resulted in the rise of Christian democracy. However, in his contribution on Castelein, Peter Heyrman offers a concrete example of the rift that divided neo-Thomist jurists and theologians on this issue. Castelein did not believe in the efficacy, let alone desirability of government intervention to solve the social question.[76] An advisor to the Association des Patrons et Industriels Catholiques, Castelein drew on the conservative French 'School of Angers' to combat attempts at privileging government intervention over private charity to reconcile the interests of workers and their bosses.

The plurality of opinions in the debate on how best to address the social question highlights a paramount characteristic of neo-scholastic thought and action in the fields of law and society. The renewed interest in Thomas Aquinas did not result in a monolithic, or sterile intellectual movement, that sought to offer some kind of standard interpretation of Aquinas's *Summa theologiae*.[77] Thomas was certainly regarded as an interesting, and even necessary partner to guide reflections on societal problems arising from a rapidly expanding industrial revolution in a post-*ancien régime* world, where workers could no longer rely on traditional associations such as the guilds to protect their interests. But that did not mean that modern social scientists and policymakers were bound to follow Thomas in a slavish fashion, on the basis of his authority alone. After all, as Arthur Vermeersch put it, "Saint Thomas

74   Delville, "Antoine Pottier and the Neo-Thomist Roots of Social Justice", see below.
75   Gérin, *Catholiques liégeois et question sociale*, 87-101; Id., "Les écoles sociales belges et la lecture de *Rerum novarum*", 269. Among the participants of the 1886 Liège conference, one can retrieve the name of Mgr. Gaspard Mermillod (1842-1892), bishop of Fribourg, Genève and Lausanne, founder of the *Correspondance de Genève* and mentor of the Union de Fribourg, see Chenaux, "Les origines de l'Union de Fribourg".
76   P. Heyrman, "A Conservative Reading of *Rerum novarum* through a Neo-Scholastic Lens: The Jesuit Auguste Castelein (1840-1922) and the Belgian *Patrons Catholiques*", see below.
77   Compare Patrick Carey's introduction in Carey, ed., *American Catholic Religious Thought*, 49.

did not know our social condition".[78] Rajesh Heynickx and Stéphane Symons have rightfully warned against the temptation to define neo-Thomism as "a parochial project of like-minded believers".[79] The meaning of 'Thomism' has been in flux without pause.[80] The search for the 'authentic' Thomas was not the priority for the bulk of scholastic writers throughout the centuries, except perhaps for a very brief spell following the promulgation of *Aeterni Patris*.[81] But if such an attempt was ever undertaken, it certainly proved to be both elusive and short-lived.

Thomists, both in the modern and early modern era, claimed the right to think independently, albeit with respect for tradition. Just as Robert Bellarmine was less preoccupied with reviving the thirteenth-century Aquinas than transforming his arguments for the sake of defending the Church's jurisdictional interests in an age of rising political absolutism, Désiré Mercier was more interested in adjusting Thomistic texts to the challenges of his age than rediscovering an allegedly orthodox interpretation of Thomas.[82] One cannot help but make a comparison with the assessment, admittedly a bit bold, put forward by the Cambridge legal historian Peter Stein regarding the persistent yet variegated use of the Roman legal tradition throughout the centuries. Stein contends that the texts of Roman law have been revisited time and time again as "a kind of legal supermarket" in which lawyers – and, for that matter, scholastic theologians – "found what they needed at the time".[83] *Mutatis mutandis*, Stein's words can be applied to engagements with Thomistic philosophy. It is not to be expected that in the course of such a long history the meanings of even such central concepts as 'property', 'just wage' and 'freedom' should remain stable at all. By virtue of a considerate conversation with other scholastics – with whom they formed an epistemic community and *Diskursgemeinschaft*[84] beyond the boundaries of space and time – clever neo-Thomists were expected, each in their own way, to twist the intellectual heritage of the past to make it fit for the societal challenges of their age.

---

78 Chappel, "The Thomist Debate over Inequality and Property Rights", 34 (n. 44). Vermeersch's argument reminds one of Luis de Molina's (1535-1600) justification for treating of contract law in a truly systematic and elaborate manner: since Thomas had hardly touched upon the matter of contract law, he was bound to do so himself, see Decock, *Theologians and Contract Law*, 65-66.

79 Heynickx and Symons, "Into Neo-Thomism", 10.

80 Chappel, "The Thomist Debate over Inequality and Property Rights", 34.

81 McCool, *From Unity to Pluralism*.

82 Steel, "Thomas en de vernieuwing van de filosofie", 48-49.

83 Stein, *Roman Law in European History*, 2.

84 Scattola, "Zu einer europäischen Wissenschaftsgeschichte der Politik", cited and discussed in Decock and Birr, *Recht und Moral in der Scholastik*, 33-34.

BIBLIOGRAPHY

Aubert, Roger. *Les deux premiers grands conflits du cardinal Mercier avec les autorités allemandes d'occupation*. Leuven-la-Neuve: Collège Erasme, 1998.

Belda Plans, Juan. *La Escuela de Salamanca. La renovación de la teología en el siglo XVI*. Madrid: BAC, 2000.

Bosschaert, Dries. "The International Union of Social Studies of Malines and the Catholic Cultural Turn: Drafting a Moral Code at the End of the Constantinian Era". *Church History and Religious Culture*, 99 (2019), 504-523.

Boutry, Philippe. "L'Encyclique *Rerum Novarum* et le climat intellectuel des années quarante du XIXe siècle". In Philippe Boutry, ed. *Rerum novarum. Écriture, contenu et réception d'une encyclique*. Rome: École française de Rome, 1997, 69-89.

Brants, Victor. "L'économie politique et sociale dans les écrits de L. Lessius (1554-1623)". *Revue d'histoire ecclésiastique*, 13 (1912), 73-89, 302-318.

Brejon de Lavergnée, Matthieu. "Les catholiques et Le Play. Affinités sociales et tensions intellectuelles". *Les Études Sociales*, 149-150 (2009), 3-7.

Carey, Patrick W., ed. *American Catholic Religious Thought: The Shaping of a Theological and Social Tradition*. New York: Paulist Press, 1987.

Chamedes, Giuliana. *A Twentieth-Century Crusade: The Vatican's Battle to Remake Christian Europe*. Cambridge Mass.: Harvard University Press, 2019.

Chappel, James. "The Thomist Debate over Inequality and Property Rights in Depression-Era Europe". In Rajesh Heynickx and Stéphane Symons, eds. *What is So New About Scholasticism? How Neo-Thomism Helped Shape the Twentieth Century*. Berlin: De Gruyter, 2018, 21-38.

Chenaux, Philippe. "Les origines de l'Union de Fribourg". In *Rerum novarum. Écriture, contenu et réception d'une encyclique*. Rome: École française de Rome, 1997, 255-266.

Chenaux, Philippe. *Entre Maurras et Maritain. Une génération intellectuelle catholique*. Paris: Les éditions du Cerf, 1999.

Coreth, Emerich, Walter M. Neidl and Georg Pfligersdorffer, eds. *Christliche Philosophie im katholischen Denken des 19. und 20. Jahrhunderts*. Vol. 2: *Rückgriff auf scholastisches Erbe*. Graz: Styria, 1988.

Decock, Wim. "From Law to Paradise: Confessional Catholicism and Legal Scholarship". *Rechtsgeschichte – Legal History*, 18 (2011), 12-34.

Decock, Wim. *Theologians and Contract Law: The Moral Transformation of the Ius Commune (c. 1500-1650)*. Leiden-Boston: Brill-Nijhoff, 2013.

Decock, Wim. "Domingo de Soto, *De iustitia et iure*". In Serge Dauchy et al., eds. *The Formation and Transmission of Western Legal Culture: 150 Books that Made the Law in the Age of Printing*. Heidelberg: Springer, 2016, 84-86.

Decock, Wim. "Spanish Scholastics on Money and Credit: Economic, Legal and Political Aspects". In Wolfgang Ernst and David Fox, eds. *Money in the Western Legal Tradition: Middle Ages to Bretton Woods*. Oxford: Oxford University Press, 2016, 267-283.

Decock, Wim. "Collaborative Legal Pluralism. Confessors as Law Enforcers in Mercado's Advice on Economic Governance (1571)". *Rechtsgeschichte – Legal History*, 25 (2017), 103-114.

Decock, Wim. "Martín de Azpilcueta". In Rafael Domingo and Javier Martínez Torrón, eds. *Great Christian Jurists in Spanish History*. Cambridge: Cambridge University Press, 2018, 115-132.

Decock, Wim. *Le marché du mérite. Penser le droit et l'économie avec Léonard Lessius*. Brussels: Zones Sensibles, 2019.

Decock, Wim and Christiane Birr. *Recht und Moral in der Scholastik der Frühen Neuzeit, 1500-1750*. Methodica – Einführungen in die rechtshistorische Forschung, 1. Berlin: De Gruyter, 2016.

Deferme, Jo. *Uit de ketens van de vrijheid. Het debat over de sociale wetgeving in België, 1886-1914*. KADOC Studies 32. Leuven: Leuven University Press, 2007.

Deferme, Jo and Jan De Maeyer. "Entre sciences sociales et politique. La pensée leplaysienne et les milieux catholiques belges". *Les Études Sociales*, 149-150 (2009), 147-166.

De Gryse, Edward. *Vaderlandsch Recht en Revolutie: verhandelingen over de sociale questiën van heden*. Roeselare: Demeester, 1881. Translated into French as *Notre droit national et la Révolution* in 1885.

De Leeuw, Thijs. "Neo-Thomism and the Education of a Catholic Elite in Louvain, 1880-1914". *Trajecta*, 21 (2012), 345-372.

De Maeyer, Jan. "De ultramontanen en de gildenbeweging, 1875-1896: het aandeel van de Confrérie de St.-Michel". In Emiel Lamberts, ed. *De kruistocht tegen het liberalisme. Facetten van het ultramontanisme in België in de 19de eeuw*. KADOC Studies 2. Leuven: Leuven University Press, 1984, 222-267.

De Raeymaeker, Louis. *M. le chanoine Armand Thiéry*. S.l., 1955.

De Visscher, Fernand. "La philosophie syndicaliste et le mythe de la grève générale". *Revue néo-scolastique de philosophie*, 78 (1913), 129-163.

De Volder, Jan. *Kardinaal verzet. Mercier, de Kerk en de oorlog*. Tielt: Lannoo, 2014.

Duve, Thomas. "The School of Salamanca: A Case of Global Knowledge Production". *Max Planck Institute for European Legal History Research Paper Series*, No. 2020-12. <http://ssrn.com/abstract=3627032>.

Fauvarque-Cosson, Bénédicte. "Development of Comparative Law in France". In Mathias Reimann and Reinhard Zimmermann, eds. *The Oxford Handbook of Comparative Law*. 2nd ed. Oxford: Oxford University Press, 2019. DOI: 10.1093/oxfordhb/9780198810230.013.2.

Fillon, Catherine. "La *Revue catholique des institutions et du droit*, le combat contre-révolutionnaire d'une société de gens de robe (1873-1906)". In Hervé Leuwers, Jean-Paul Barrière and Bernard Lefebvre, eds. *Élites et sociabilité au XIXe siècle. Héritages, identités*. Villeneuve d'Ascq: Publications de l'Institut de recherches historiques du Septentrion, 2001, 199-218.

Gerard, Emmanuel, ed. *De christelijke arbeidersbeweging in België*. KADOC Studies 11. Leuven: Leuven University Press, 1991, 2 vols.

Gérin, Paul. *Catholiques liégeois et question sociale*. Brussels: Études Sociales, 1959.

Gérin, Paul. "Les écoles sociales belges et la lecture de *Rerum novarum*". In *Rerum novarum. Écriture, contenu et réception d'une encyclique*. Rome: École française de Rome, 1997, 267-289.

Gerkens, Jean-François and Vincent Genin. "Charles de Visscher (1884-1973) et Fernand de Visscher (1885-1964) – Coryphées du droit international et du droit romain". In: *Deux-centième anniversaire des facultés de droit de Gand et Liège. Tweehonderd jaar rechtsfaculteiten Gent en Luik*. Bruges: Die Keure, 2019, 149-153.

Grice-Hutchinson, Marjorie. *The School of Salamanca: Readings in Spanish Monetary Theory (1544-1605)*. Oxford: Clarendon, 1952.

Hagedorn, Jonas. "Kapitalismuskritische Richtungen im deutschen Katholizismus der Zwischenkriegszeit. Drei Korporatismuskonzepte und ihre Relevanz für die frühe Bundesrepublik". In Matthias Casper, Karl Gabriel and Hans-Richard Reuter, eds. *Kapitalismuskritik im Christentum. Positionen und Diskurse in der Weimarer Republik und der frühen Bundesrepublik*. Frankfurt am Main: Campus Verlag, 2016, 111-141.

Halkin, Léon and Paul Harsin, eds. *Liber memorialis: l'Université de Liège de 1867 à 1935. Notices biographiques*. 1: *Faculté de Philosophie et Lettres. Faculté de Droit*. Liège: Université de Liège, 1936.

Harris, Abram Lincoln. "The Scholastic Revival: The Economics of Heinrich Pesch". *Journal of Political Economy*, 54 (1946), 38-59.

Heynickx, Rajesh and Stéphane Symons. "Into Neo-Thomism: Reading the Fabric of an Intellectual Movement". In Rajesh Heynickx and Stéphane Symons, eds. *What is So New About Scholasticism? How Neo-Thomism Helped Shape the Twentieth Century*. Berlin: De Gruyter, 2018, 7-17.

Heynickx, Rajesh and Stéphane Symons, eds. *What is So New About Scholasticism? How Neo-Thomism Helped Shape the Twentieth Century*. Berlin: De Gruyter, 2018.

Heyrman, Peter. *Middenstandsbeweging en beleid in België (1918-1940). Tussen vrijheid en regulering*. KADOC Studies 22. Leuven: Leuven University Press, 1998.

Heyrman, Peter. "Léon de Lantsheere". In Wim Decock and Janwillem Oosterhuis, eds. *Great Christian Jurists in the Low Countries*. Cambridge: Cambridge University Press, forthcoming.

Hiraux, Françoise. "L'Institut supérieur de philosophie de Louvain. Introduction historique (1889-1968)". In Françoise Mirguet and Françoise Hiraux, eds. *L'Institut supérieur de philosophie de Louvain (1889-1968). Inventaire des archives, introduction historique*. Louvain-la-Neuve: Academia Bruylant, 2008.

Höpfl, Harro. *Jesuit Political Thought: The Society of Jesus and the State, c. 1540-1630*. Cambridge: Cambridge University Press, 2004.

Jadoulle, Jean-Louis. "Question sociale et politique pontificale. L'itinéraire d'un démocrate chrétien: Antoine Pottier (1849-1923)". *Revue belge de philologie et d'histoire*, 69 (1991), 300-321.

Jansen, Corjo. "Willem Duynstee". In Wim Decock and Janwillem Oosterhuis, eds. *Great Christian Jurists in the Low Countries*. Cambridge: Cambridge University Press, forthcoming.

Kenis, Leo. "Movements toward Renewal: The Belgian Church and the Improvement of Clerical Education, 1830-50". *Dutch Review of Church History*, 82 (2003), 371-389.

Lamberts, Emiel. "De ontwikkeling van de sociaal-katholieke ideologie in België". In Emiel Lamberts, ed. *Een kantelend tijdperk. De wending van de Kerk naar het volk in Noord-West-Europa / Une époque en mutation. Le catholicisme social dans le Nord-Ouest de l'Europe / Ein Zeitalter im Umbruch. Die Wende der Kirche zum Volk im nordwestlichen Europa*. KADOC Studies 13. Leuven: Leuven University Press, 1992, 49-64.

Lamberts, Emiel. *The Struggle with Leviathan: Social Responses to the Omnipotence of the State, 1815-1965*. Leuven: Leuven University Press, 2016.

Leinsle, Ulrich. *Introduction to Scholastic Theology*. Washington DC: CUA Press, 2010.

Llano Torres, Ana. "Ciencia jurídica y moralismo en la España del Siglo XIX: La Neoescolástica". In Francisco de Paula Puy Muñoz and Salvador Rus Rufino, eds. *La Historia de la Filosofía jurídica española*. Santiago: FAB, 1998, 221-274.

McCool, Gerald A. *From Unity to Pluralism: The Internal Evolution of Thomism*. New York: Fordham University Press, 1989.

Meerts, Kristin. "De Leuvense hoogleraar Victor Brants: een brugfiguur in het sociaal-katholicisme (1856-1891)". *Bijdragen tot de geschiedenis*, 65 (1982), 197-233.

Meerts, Kristin. "De Leuvense hoogleraar Victor Brants: sociale ideeën tussen katholieke romantiek en realisme (1856-1891)". *Bijdragen tot de geschiedenis*, 66 (1983), 101-130.

Miccoli, Giovanni. "Padre Agostino Gemelli, Università cattolica e regime fascista". *Studi Storici*, 45 (2004), 609-624.

Mirguet, Françoise. "Crahay, Edouard". <https://archives.uclouvain.be/atom/index.php/archives-dedouard-crahay>.

Nelis, Jan. "The Clerical Response to a Totalitarian Political Religion: 'La Civiltà Cattolica' and Italian Fascism". *Journal of Contemporary History*, 46 (2011), 245-270.

Nelis, Jan, Anne Morelli and Danny Praet, eds. *Catholicism and Fascism in Europe 1918-1945*. Hildesheim-Zürich-New York: Olms, 2015.

Pollard, John F. "Fascism and Catholicism". In Richard J.B. Bosworth, ed. *The Oxford Handbook of Fascism and Catholicism*. Oxford: Oxford University Press, 2010. DOI: 10.1093/oxfordhb/9780199594788.013.0010.

Pollard, John. *The Papacy in the Age of Totalitarianism, 1914-1958*. Oxford: Oxford University Press, 2014.

Prévotat, Jacques. *Les catholiques et l'Action française: histoire d'une condemnation*. Paris: Fayard, 2001.

Quaghebeur, Patricia. *De Revue Sociale Catholique, 1896-1900: een gematigd-progressief wetenschappelijk tijdschrift*. Diss. lic. KU Leuven, 1984.

Rasilla del Moral, Ignacio de la. "The Fascist Mimesis of Spanish International Law and its Vitorian Aftermath, 1939-1953". *Journal of the History of International Law*, 14 (2012), 207-236.

Rasilla del Moral, Ignacio de la. *In the Shadow of Vitoria: A History of International Law in Spain (1770-1953)*. Leiden-Boston: Brill-Nijhoff, 2017.

Scattola, Merio. "Zu einer europäischen Wissenschaftsgeschichte der Politik". In Christina Antenhofer et al., eds. *Werkstatt politische Kommunikation. Netzwerke, Orte und Sprachen des Politischen*. Göttingen: V&R Unipress, 2010, 23-54.

Steel, Carlos. "Thomas en de vernieuwing van de filosofie. Beschouwingen bij het Thomisme van Mercier". *Tijdschrift voor Filosofie*, 53 (1991), 44-89.

Stein, Peter. *Roman Law in European History*. Cambridge: Cambridge Press, 1999.

Stevens, Fred. "Het coalitieverbod in België (1795-1866)". In *Liber Amicorum Roger Blanpain*. Bruges: Die Keure, 1998, 395-413.

Stevens, Fred. "Charles Périn". In Wim Decock and Janwillem Oosterhuis, eds. *Great Christian Jurists in the Low Countries*. Cambridge: Cambridge University Press, forthcoming.

Tutino, Stefania. *Empire of Souls: Robert Bellarmine and the Christian Commonwealth*. Oxford: Oxford University Press, 2010.

Van Molle, Leen. *Katholieken en landbouw. Landbouwpolitiek in België, 1884-1914*. Leuven: Leuven University Press, 1989.

Van Molle, Leen. *Ieder voor allen. De Belgische Boerenbond, 1890-1990*. KADOC Studies 9. Leuven: Leuven University Press, 1990.

Van Molle, Leen. "Croissance économique et
    éthique catholique: les points de vue de
    l'Union de Malines dans les années vingt".
    In Erik Aerts et al., eds. *Studia historica oe-
    conomica. Liber amicorum Herman Van der
    Wee*. Leuven: Leuven University Press, 1993,
    317-335.
Wils, Kaat. "Les intellectuels catholiques et la
    sociologie en Belgique, 1880-1914". *Archives
    des Sciences Sociales des Religions*, 179 (2017),
    71-88.

THE LANDSCAPE
OF NEO-THOMISM

Pope Leo XIII. Marble bust by Giuseppe Luchetti, 1888.
[Leuven, Higher Institute of Philosophy; © KU Leuven, Art Patrimony – photo Bruno Vandermeulen]

RELIGIOUS, POLITICAL AND SOCIAL SETTINGS OF THE REVIVAL OF THOMISM, 1870-1960

EMIEL LAMBERTS

The revival of Thomism, which culminated in neo-Thomism, was most apparent in Catholic circles.[1] An examination of the position of the Catholic Church in European society is therefore necessary for a full understanding of the origin and development of this phenomenon. Characteristically, between 1870 and 1960, the Church adopted a defensive attitude towards many aspects of modern society and did everything in its power to safeguard its own social influence. This confrontation drove the Church to strengthen its internal cohesion. In this, neo-Thomism was of great benefit, and provided an appropriate intellectual framework.

It was under Pope Pius IX that the Catholic Church resolutely set itself in opposition to what was then called 'modernity'. This stance was forcefully formulated in the last proposition of the *Syllabus Errorum* of 1864, which stated that "the Roman Pontiff cannot reconcile himself and come to terms with progress, liberalism and modern civilisation". Thus, the impression was created that the Church was firmly placing itself outside of modernity. The proposition deserved a more nuanced interpretation, but it was undeniable that the Catholic Church was at loggerheads with the societal and intellectual patterns that had emerged in the wake of the French Revolution of 1789.[2] The Church had suffered considerably during this revolution. Its religious monopoly had been dented, its political and economic power largely broken, not only in France but in other Catholic countries also. In the bourgeois and urbanised

---

1   Coreth, Neidl and Pfligersdorffer, eds., *Christliche Philosophie im katholischen Denken*, II.
2   Christophe and Minnerath, *Le Syllabus de Pie IX*.

society that gradually emerged, the Church was driven away from the epicen-
tre of society. Enlightenment thinking undermined its religious doctrines, political liberalism challenged its social influence, while emerging nationalism
undermined its international position. The year 1870 was a turning point in
this development. The political map of Europe was redrawn by the Prussian
victory over France and the unification of Germany under the leadership of the
Protestant Prussians. With the annexation of Rome, the Kingdom of Italy put a
definitive end to the temporal power of the pope. In this predominantly Catholic country a gulf emerged between Church and State, and successive liberal
governments would pursue a pronounced anticlerical policy. Elsewhere in Europe also, the Catholic Church came under severe pressure. In Switzerland and
subsequently in the unified Germany (to a lesser extent in Austria-Hungary)
a *Kulturkampf* was waged against the Church.[3] A veritable contest was going
on during this period between the modern state and the Catholic Church. The
core values of the philosophy of the liberals, who then dominated the political
scene, were science and *Bildung*, the conditions most suitable for the progress
and development of the individual; these were completely contradicted by the
Catholic anti-modern position, which gave priority to authority, tradition and
the old social bonds. Liberals believed that the principles of liberalism permitted the state, an agent of modernisation, to act in bringing about freedom
by putting pressure on the Catholic Church, which was seen as the strongest
threat to the emancipation of the individual. This reasoning led many liberals
not only to push the Church out of public life but also to subject it to the authority of the state. They would only partially achieve their objectives because
the Catholic Church had become very resilient during the preceding decades.

Though the Church had indeed suffered greatly during the French Revolution of 1789, it had also been strengthened by it in some respects. The destructive effects of the revolution, felt across Europe in the wake of the Napo-
leonic wars, had widely undermined belief in the rational principles to which
the revolutionaries had appealed. Trusted frameworks and structures were destroyed or had lost their significance. In these circumstances religion offered
many a safe haven and gave others new meaning to their sense of identity.
Moreover, conservatives saw in religion a support for the social order. The influence of Romanticism, with its preference for emotion and the subconscious,
also had a significant impact. Religion was regarded as an autonomous, ani-
mating power, was brought openly into the public sphere and was directed towards social activism. The revolutionary period was followed by an explosion
of religious energy.[4] The Holy See succeeded in bringing the religious revival
under its control and using it for its own purposes.

3   Clark and Kaiser, *Culture Wars*.
4   McLeod, *Religion and the People of Western Europe*, 20-55; Plongeron, *Les défis de la mo-
     dernité*, 627-792.

Moreover, the impact of the papacy and the curia was furthered by events in revolutionary France. During the difficult times of persecution, the Holy See had become a refuge for the French Church. The pope emerged stronger from the revolution, and this not only in France. He extended his influence over local churches and became the main defender of their freedom from state authority, which was being increasingly asserted and was often hostile to the Church.

As a matter of course, the Catholic revival had political consequences, especially in countries where constitutional reforms had been implemented and public opinion could exert pressure on policy. Catholics wanted to withdraw from state control and demanded greater freedom for their Church. In this way the ground was prepared in some countries for a liberal Catholicism that would make use of modern liberties to bring about more independence for the Church.[5] However, the revolutionary events of 1848 in general, and especially in Rome, considerably influenced the political and religious views of the new Pope Pius IX and revived anti-liberalism in Catholic circles. The pope's primary goal became to strengthen the unity and resilience of the Church and erect a dam against the laicising and liberal culture of the time. His encyclical *Quanta Cura* and the *Syllabus Errorum* (1864) gave full expression to this tendency. All attention was focused on the battle against philosophical and political liberalism, which was then in full swing. In order to rally the Church around the chair of Peter and to better equip it for the defence of its autonomy and social influence, Pius IX took the initiative of convening an ecumenical council that would enter history as the First Vatican Council.[6] The most striking outcome of this Council was the proclamation of the dogma of papal infallibility in matters of faith and morals. It confirmed the primacy of the pope within the Church and strengthened its institutional unity at a time when nationalism was exerting a centrifugal effect and the protective environment of a Christian society was disappearing. The Church of Peter presented itself as an unshakeable pillar, a bulwark of security in a society that seemed adrift and restless.

The proclamation of the dogma of papal infallibility was perceived by many as a mockery of modern culture and contributed to the launching of the *Kulturkampf* in the next decade. On the other hand, it increased the power of the pope and made his position even more important than before. Meanwhile, the Catholic masses had been mobilised all over Europe, especially in the context of the defence of the pope's temporal power. Catholic opinion would from then on act as a shield for the papacy and was also effectively deployed against the secularisation policy of the liberal governments in various European countries.[7]

5   Gadille, ed., *Les catholiques libéraux au 19ᵉ siècle.*
6   Aubert, *Vatican I*; Martina, *Pio IX*, III, 111-232; Schatz, *Vaticanum I.*
7   Viaene, "The Roman Question".

At the end of the pontificate of Pius IX (1878), relations between the Catholic Church and modern society were then very tense, but at the same time the Church profiled itself as a formidable counterforce, intent on maintaining its societal influence as much as possible. Neo-Thomism would play a significant role in this.

Under Leo XIII (1878-1903), Thomism became the theoretical basis for a Christian concept of culture and the reconstruction of society.[8] The new pope wanted to offer a Catholic alternative to modern agnostic philosophies, especially scientism and positivism. He wanted the Church to strengthen its doctrinal unity so that it could exert an effective influence on society. A revival of neo-scholastic philosophy and especially of Thomism was perceived to be a suitable means for countering positivism, liberalism and emerging socialism. So, in order to offer an alternative to modern philosophical and political ideas, Leo XIII fell back on a medieval philosophical system.

Thomism had been undergoing a revival since the 1850s, especially in Jesuit circles in Italy (*La Civiltà Cattolica*) and Germany. It was a philosophical system that emphasised the possibilities of human reason more than did the traditionalism of Louis de Bonald and Félicité de Lamennais, which defined truth as the general consensus of humanity based on the fundamental truths of Revelation. Besides traditionalism, ontologism also had a certain following in Catholic circles. Building on the teachings of Augustine and Malebranche, it ascribed to human beings the possibility of an immediate intuition of the divine, thereby, like traditionalism, denying the value of reason. By contrast, the revived Thomism, which would gradually come to be called neo-Thomism, wanted to make faith highly rational, although it explicitly argued against scientism and positivism. It was a philosophical system in which there was not any conflict between faith and reason, as long as God was recognised as the ontological ground.

Thomism then offered useful resources for a confrontation with modern rationalist thinking, but also for a social and political ethic that could be applied to nineteenth-century society. In the footsteps of Aristotle, Aquinas saw humans as social beings who in a rational way pursued both their own personal development and the common good. The social order had to be based on the principle of authority. Governments had to create the social conditions in which every person could fully develop and at the same time bring about a consensus between citizens in order to realise the common good. Religion provided the moral beacons that gave direction to the policies of the authorities.

In the socio-economic sphere Aquinas was in favour of an economic system that would serve human beings. Not only Christian charity but also the principle of justice had to shape a dignified human society. Private property was the core of the economic order. It supported the autonomy of the person

---

8   Piolanti, *Il tomismo come filosofia cristiana nel pensiero di Leone XIII*.

and was necessary for personal development. Yet the right to property was not absolute. Worldly goods belonged to all of humanity and had to be made available to all. Superfluous property had to be used for the good of the community, and where necessary the state had to ensure this. There were elements in Aquinas' philosophical system that could support a critical attitude both to capitalism as well as collectivism. By appealing to natural law, the emphasis was put on the uniqueness and dignity of the human person, his/her self-realisation in a social context and the promotion of the common good.[9]

Shortly after his accession to the papacy, Leo XIII boosted the revival of Thomism with the encyclical *Aeterni Patris* (4 August 1879).[10] He recommended that it be included in philosophical education in the major seminaries and ecclesiastical universities in Italy.[11] Soon after that he pushed for its introduction at the university of Leuven in Belgium, which at that time was the only complete university in the world with a Catholic character. In this institution, a more modern variation of neo-Thomism would develop that engaged in dialogue with modern science.[12] Leo XIII wanted to design a solid philosophical system capable of restoring the social influence of the Church over the whole of society.[13] He presented himself as the architect of an intellectual renewal that aimed at 'the restoration of the social reign of Christ', an idea that had already penetrated militant Catholic circles in the 1870s.[14] Religion should permeate not only the lives of individuals but also society.

Neo-Thomism developed a clear vision on the place of the Church in society. It endorsed the doctrine of its indirect power over the secular order. In its world view, the Church traditionally made a distinction between spiritual and temporal power, which started from the understanding that Church and State were pursuing different objectives: the Church looked after the spiritual welfare of mankind and the state took care of the material side. Each power was autonomous in its specific area, but on matters where the two overlapped, the Church claimed precedence over the state because of its higher nature and purpose. It appropriated to itself an indirect power over the secular order in

9   Spiazzi, "La dottrina sociale di S. Tommaso".
10 Aubert, "Aspects divers du néo-thomisme sous le pontificat de Léon XIII"; "L'enciclica Aeterni Patris. Il centenario (1879-1979)"; *L'enciclica "Aeterni Patris" nell'arco di un secolo*; Aubert, "Die Enzyklika 'Aeterni Patris'".
11 Pius X would make the teaching of neo-Thomism compulsory in the major seminaries and other ecclesiastical educational institutions in Italy (29 June 1914). The canon law code of 1918 extended the measure to the whole world. It was confirmed by Pius XI in 1923 and by Pius XII in 1950.
12 Ladrière, "Cent ans de philosophie à l'Institut Supérieur de Philosophie"; "Centenaire de la fondation de l'Institut supérieur de Philosophie"; De Leeuw, "Neo-Thomism and the Education of a Catholic Elite in Louvain"; Struyker Boudier, *Wijsgerig leven in Nederland en België*, vol. V-VI.
13 Thibault, *Savoir et pouvoir*.
14 Menozzi, *Sacro Cuore*, 107-124.

everything to do with faith and morals. It had the authority to judge the legitimacy of governments and laws from that perspective. On the other hand, in exchange for some protection, the Church offered its services to governments in order to strengthen their authority, public order and social peace. The encyclical *Immortale Dei* (19 November 1885) became a virtual charter of the theory of indirect power, which was to a great degree inspired by Thomistic views. A few years later, in the encyclical *Libertas* (20 June 1888), Leo XIII emphatically reiterated that divine law should be a guide for both public and private life. In his encyclical *Sapientiae Christianae* (10 January 1890), he asserted the Church's right to judge the legitimacy of governments and laws in light of their respect for divine and natural law.

By the end of the nineteenth century, the Church was able to make a special contribution to the well-being of society through its pursuit of social peace. In Thomism it found a philosophical foundation for a community model that would act as a counterweight to both liberal capitalism and emerging socialism. Since the Commune uprising of 1871 revolutionary socialism, which put up a vigorous fight against the increasing inequality in society, had become a menacing spectre for the wealthy. Because of its anti-religious orientation, it also posed a danger to the Church. In order to cut socialism off at the pass, a social doctrine that promoted a more just society and social harmony gradually emerged in Catholic circles. Thomism would provide some fundamental ideas for this.[15] An important theoretical contribution was made by the Jesuit Luigi Taparelli d'Azeglio in *La Civiltà Cattolica*. He emphasised the sense of community, the duties and rights of natural social groupings and structures, and the principle of subsidiarity and social harmony.[16] In the 1860s, Wilhelm Emmanuel von Ketteler, the bishop of Mainz, was the first church leader to develop a more or less coherent social doctrine, based on Aristotelianism and Thomism. His basic insights were further expanded in both lay and ecclesiastical circles. They found concrete expression in the activities of the Fribourg Union (1884-1891), an influential international Catholic think tank.[17] The members of this Union explicitly based their research on the central ideas of Thomism. Their starting point was that the general well-being should be the main objective of socio-political organisation, and the principle of justice should constitute its moral foundation. The proceeds of capital and of labour had to be more equitably distributed. Professional associations would defend the material and moral interests of their members. They would constitute the basic units of a more equitable society. The Fribourg Union was in favour of a corporative system that relied on mixed occupational associations where

---

15   Spiazzi, "La dottrina sociale di S. Tommaso".

16   Rafferty, "The Thomistic Revival and the Relationship between the Jesuits and the Papacy".

17   Lamberts, *The Struggle with Leviathan*, 271-280; Misner, *Social Catholicism in Europe*, 202-208.

workers and employers would together organise production and determine working conditions, thereby bringing about social harmony. Since establishing a truly corporative regime would require a long time, social intervention by the state would be required, at least temporarily, through the introduction of protective labour legislation and compulsory social security.

Analogous ideas could be found in the papal encyclical *Rerum novarum* (1891).[18] It put particular emphasis on the dignity of the human person, who was a social being *par excellence*. It sharply criticised the existing economic order because it led to the exploitation of the working class. The excesses of capitalism had to be resisted and the economic system had to be adjusted in a more socially equitable direction. Workers had a right to a decent, fair wage and humane working conditions. In order to defend their interests in a spirit of class collaboration and not of class struggle, they should be free to organise themselves in associations, whether mixed or not. Occupational associations could play a key role in resolving social tensions. The state also had an important role to play, but only secondarily. Historically and ontologically, natural social bonds preceded the state and imposed restrictions on its role and mandate. The four most important elements of Aquinas' social ethics were laid out in the encyclical: the unity, dignity, and mystery of the human being; the naturalness of society; the primacy of the common good; and justice as the foundation of human fellowship.[19]

At the end of the nineteenth century neo-Thomism was influential mainly in ecclesiastical circles, but it also acquired social significance due to its impact on the Catholic parties and social movements that emerged in many countries in the last decades of that century.[20] They were the result of the Catholic mobilisation that had sprung up around the Roman question and against the secularisation policy of several governments. The Catholic parties still drew most of their support from the lower middle class, and often took a conservative stance in social questions, but they came increasingly under pressure from popular Christian organisations that aspired to social and democratic reforms.

The basic Thomistic ideas allowed both a more conservative and a more progressive interpretation. Conservative social Catholics emphasised the role of Christian charity in society. Charity was the bond that united human beings with God and with their fellow beings. It was the lifeblood of the social body, an indispensable means of social solidarity. There was a mutual dependence between rich and poor. Excess wealth had to benefit the poor, but the rich were free to decide for themselves what part of their abundance they wanted

18 Mayeur, "Aux origines de l'enseignement social de l'Eglise"; Boutry, ed., *'Rerum Novarum'*; Misner, *Social Catholicism in Europe*, 213-222.
19 Zagar, "Aquinas and the Social Teaching of the Church".
20 Mayeur, *Des partis catholiques à la démocratie chrétienne*; Durand, *L'Europe de la démocratie chrétienne*.

to give to the poor, to whom and when. Society formed an organic unity, a common body, but with different functions and ranks. Pius X, the successor of Leo XIII, made it clear that God had created society with inequality as a basic principle. Social patronage remained a central issue in Catholic social action. Because of that conviction, social Catholics held on for a long time to paternalistic corporations and opposed autonomous trade unions.[21] This did not prevent the gradual emergence in several countries of autonomous Christian trade unions that resolutely put the principle of justice first and promoted a more democratic system of government. Through social intervention by the state, greater social equality could be achieved.[22] Progressive social Catholics also found a suitable intellectual framework in neo-Thomism which, by making the material well-being of citizens one of the principal duties of the state, became a powerful lever for social reformism.[23]

The First World War led to the collapse of the bourgeois civilisation of the nineteenth century, which was characterised by a strong belief in reason and science, material and moral progress, the free market and free trade, the liberal constitutional state. All these achievements were now thrown into jeopardy. The war was also responsible for the Russian Revolution (1917), the rise and breakthrough of fascism and World War II. It sent many apocalyptic horsemen on their way, who would sow even more misery, death and destruction.

However, in a first phase, the World War would lead to major social and democratic reforms. The revolutionary threat emanating from Bolshevism induced the bourgeoisie to make substantial concessions to the workers' movements. Universal suffrage, the recognition of workers' organisations and an extension of social legislation were in part fruits of the terror that overwhelmed the propertied classes. Bolshevism not only forced through some concessions, it also provoked a strong defensive reaction on the right flank of the political spectrum. Fascism was already on the march in the early 1920s, and in the 1930s outflanked and even eliminated conservative and confessional parties. At the same time, it put an end to liberal constitutionalism. Only in North-Western Europe did democratic regimes survive.

The fear of Bolshevism, the crippled peace regime after World War I and the deep economic depression gave fascism an opportunity to flourish in Europe. It rested on two pillars: a groundswell of conservative ideas with strong antiliberal and antisocialist accents, and nationalism, which had been stirred up by the war. Fascism seasoned these more traditional ingredients with revolutionary principles and proclaimed the primacy of action (*Revolution von Rechts*). It wanted to build a new society based on an elitist, irrational and

---

21 Agocs, "The Road of Charity leads to the Picket Lines".
22 Misner, *Social Catholicism in Europe*, 222-318; Hiepel and Ruff, eds., *Christliche Arbeiterbewegung in Europa*; Lamberts and Pasture, "Il sindacalismo cristiano in Europa".
23 On the influence of neo-Thomism on the social positions of American Catholics, see Carey, *American Catholic Religious Thought*, VII, 71-80.

voluntarist morality of violence. It called on the masses to bring about this kind of society and was thus unambiguously populist.[24]

Political life in Europe was sharply polarised during the interwar period. On both the left (Bolshevism) and the right (fascism), totalitarian regimes set the tone. This posed a threat to the autonomy of the Catholic Church which, helped by its neo-Thomist principles, remained stubbornly opposed to the omnipotence of the state. The totalitarian currents in different European countries made the question of the authority and limits of state power very pertinent. At the Higher Institute of Philosophy in Leuven, the crucial role of a well-organised civil society was emphasised: it should act as a counterbalance to the totalitarian state.[25] In Germany too, neo-Thomist philosophers paid considerable attention to political philosophy and opposed an absolutist view of the state, but without much success.[26] The social and political influence of the Church dwindled in the fascist countries, but its social ethics stayed alive in Catholic organisations and prepared them for the social and democratic revival that would emerge after World War II.

Meanwhile, during the interwar period, neo-Thomism entered a new phase. It assumed a more open character and interacted with other philosophical approaches. Thus it came under the influence of anti-intellectual movements in France and Germany. Idealism directed more attention than before to metaphysical questions, and the issue of the relationship of philosophy to revealed religion was raised once again.[27] Neo-Thomism experienced a new momentum, particularly in France. The contribution of Jacques Maritain was very innovative. He promoted a practically-oriented philosophy, made overtures to the world of the arts, and in ethics and social philosophy sought to harmonise neo-Thomism with personalism and pluralistic democracy.[28]

After the Second World War, fascism and aggressive nationalism disappeared from the stage. A more social and democratic climate prevailed in Western European politics. In the first phase, the left especially profited from the victory over fascism. The defeat of fascism along with the important contribution of the Soviet Union to the Allied victory led to a strengthening of the socialist and communist parties. On the other hand, the disappearance of fascism and the discrediting of the conservative formations that had collaborated with it created a political vacuum on the right. Christian Democrats succeeded in filling that gap thanks to their significant involvement in the resistance movements in several countries, which had given them the required

24 Paxton, *The Anatomy of Fascism*.
25 Coreth, Neidl and Pfligersdorffer, eds., *Christliche Philosophie im katholischen Denken*, II, 546-564; Struyker Boudier, *Wijsgerig leven in Nederland en België*, VI, 140-146, 176-186.
26 Sassen and Delfgaauw, *Wijsbegeerte van onze tijd*, 280-281.
27 McInerny, *Thomism in an Age of Renewal*.
28 Chenaux, "De Mercier à Maritain"; Id., *Entre Maurras et Maritain*; Heynickx and De Maeyer, eds., *The Maritain Factor*.

democratic credibility. At the same time, influenced by the events of the war, they had come to attach more importance to individual human rights. They benefited from the Cold War between the Soviet Union and the capitalist West that began in 1947, and became the main political power on the right of the political spectrum in Western Europe in the 1950s. From that position, they would make a major contribution to the process of European integration.[29]

The Christian Democrats believed that Christian ethical principles should govern politics, both national and international. Human accountability before God militated against the deification of the state. The state should primarily serve human beings, respecting the dignity and guaranteeing the rights of each person, and it should establish a just and peaceful society. Christian Democrats, with their personalist vision based on neo-Thomism, laid great emphasis on the development of human persons in their natural social relations, such as the family, occupational associations and local communities. In general, they assigned an important role to an organised civil society and assigned only a supplementary role to the state. In order to create greater social harmony, they opted for 'neo-corporative' formulas. Overall, they attempted to connect the free market with social justice, which had to be brought about through a harmonious interplay between the state and social organisations.[30]

The social and political legacy of neo-Thomism, which had taken shape at the end of the nineteenth century, still exerted wide influence in the first decades after the Second World War. Nevertheless, the neo-Thomist construction lost its significance for a Church that, after Vatican II, no longer strove for 'the restoration of the social reign of Christ', but merely wanted to be present in the world without dominating it. Moreover, neo-Thomism slowly lost its cohesiveness and with that its demonstrable influence on the social and political system.

BIBLIOGRAPHY

Agocs, Sándor. "The Road of Charity leads to the Picket Lines: The Neo-Thomistic Revival and the Italian Catholic Labor Movement". *International Review of Social History*, 18 (1973), 28-50.

Aubert, Roger. "Aspects divers du néo-thomisme sous le pontificat de Léon XIII". In *Aspetti della cultura cattolica nell'eta di Leone XIII*. Rome: Edizioni Cinque Lune, 1961, 133-248.

Aubert, Roger. *Vatican I*. Paris: Éditions de l'Orante, 1964.

Aubert, Roger. "Die Enzyklika 'Aeterni Patris' und die Weitere päpstlichen Stellungnahmen zur christlichen Philosophie". In: Emerich Coreth, Walter M. Neidl and Georg Pfligersdorffer, eds. *Christliche Philosophie im katholischen Denken des 19. und 20. Jahrhunderts*. Graz: Styria, 1988, 310-324.

Boutry, Philippe, ed. *'Rerum Novarum'. Ecriture, contenu et réception d'une encyclique*. Rome: École Française de Rome, 1997.

Carey, Patrick W. *American Catholic Religious Thought: The Shaping of a Theological and Social Tradition*. Vol. 7: *Neo-Thomism and Catholic Culture, 1920-1960*. Milwaukee: Marquette University Press, 2004.

"Centenaire de la fondation de l'Institut supérieur de Philosophie". *Revue philosophique de Louvain*, 88 (1990), 143-310.

29 Lamberts, ed., *Christian Democracy in the European Union*; Gehler and Kaiser, eds., *Christian Democracy in Europe Since 1945*.

30 Lamberts, *The Struggle with Leviathan*, 315.

Chenaux, Philippe. "De Mercier à Maritain. Une seconde génération thomiste belge (1920-1930)". *Revue d'histoire ecclésiastique*, 92 (1997), 475-489.

Chenaux, Philippe. *Entre Maurras et Maritain. Une génération intellectuelle catholique (1920-1930)*. Paris: Cerf, 1999.

Christophe, Paul and Roland Minnerath. *Le Syllabus de Pie IX*. Paris: Cerf, 2000.

Clark, Christopher and Wolfram Kaiser. *Culture Wars: Secular-Catholic Conflict in Nineteenth-Century Europe*. Cambridge: Cambridge University Press, 2003.

Coreth, Emerich, Walter M. Neidl and Georg Pfligersdorffer, eds. *Christliche Philosophie im katholischen Denken des 19. und 20. Jahrhunderts*. Vol. 2: *Rückgriff auf scholastisches Erbe*. Graz: Styria, 1988.

De Leeuw, Thijs. "Neo-Thomism and the Education of a Catholic Elite in Louvain, 1880-1914". *Trajecta*, 21 (2012), 345-372.

Durand, Jean-Dominique. *L'Europe de la démocratie chrétienne*. Brussels: Complexe, 1995.

Gadille, Jacques, ed. *Les catholiques libéraux au 19e siècle*. Grenoble: Presses universitaires de Grenoble, 1974.

Gehler, Michael and Wolfram Kaiser, eds. *Christian Democracy in Europe Since 1945*. London: Routledge, 2004.

Heynickx, Rajesh and Jan De Maeyer, eds. *The Maritain Factor: Taking Religion into Interwar Modernism*. Leuven: Leuven University Press, 2010.

Hiepel, Claudia and Mark Ruff, eds. *Christliche Arbeiterbewegung in Europa, 1850-1950*. Stuttgart: Kohlhammer, 2003.

Ladrière, Jean. "Cent ans de philosophie à l'Institut Supérieur de Philosophie". *Revue philosophique de Louvain*, (1990) 88, 168-213.

Lamberts, Emiel, ed. *Christian Democracy in the European Union*. Leuven: Leuven University Press, 1997.

Lamberts, Emiel. *The Struggle with Leviathan: Social Responses to the Omnipotence of the State, 1815-1965*. Leuven: Leuven University Press, 2016.

Lamberts, Emiel and Patrick Pasture. "Il sindacalismo cristiano in Europa: passato, presente e prospettive future". In Walter E. Crivellin, ed. *Il sindacato nell' Europa che cambia*. Turin: Donat-Cattin, 1994, 33-56.

"L'enciclica Aeterni Patris. Il centenario (1879-1979)". *Scripta Theologica*, 11 (1979), 425-824.

L'enciclica 'Aeterni Patris' nell'arco di un secolo. Atti dell' VIII Congresso Tomistico Internazionale (8-13 Sett. 1980). Vol 1. Studi Tomistici 10. Vatican City: Libreria Editrice Vaticana, 1981.

Martina, Giacomo. *Pio IX*. Vol. 3. Rome: Pontificia Università Gregoriana, 1990.

Mayeur, Jean-Marie. *Des partis catholiques à la démocratie chrétienne, XIXe-XXe siècles*. Paris: Colin, 1980.

Mayeur, Jean-Marie. "Aux origines de l'enseignement social de l'Église". *Revue de l'Institut catholique de Paris*, 1984, 11-33.

McInerny, Ralph M. *Thomism in an Age of Renewal*. Notre Dame: University of Notre Dame Press, 1968.

McLeod, Hugh. *Religion and the People of Western Europe, 1789-1990*. Oxford: Oxford University Press, 1997.

Menozzi, Daniele. *Sacro Cuore: un culto tra devozione interiore e restaurazione cristiana della società*. Rome: Viella, 2001.

Misner, Paul. *Social Catholicism in Europe: From the Onset of Industrialization to the First World War*. New York: Crossroad, 1991.

Paxton, Robert O. *The Anatomy of Fascism*. New York: Knopf, 2004.

Plongeron, Bernard. *Les défis de la modernité (1750-1840)*. Paris: Desclée de Brouwer, 1997.

Piolanti, Antonio. *Il tomismo come filosofia cristiana nel pensiero di Leone XIII*. Vatican City: Libreria Editrice Vaticana, 1983.

Rafferty, Oliver P. "The Thomistic Revival and the Relationship between the Jesuits and the Papacy, 1878-1914". *Theological Studies*, 75 (2014), 746-773.

Sassen, Ferdinand and Bernard Delfgaauw. *Wijsbegeerte van onze tijd*. Antwerp-Amsterdam: Standaard-Boekhandel, 1957.

Schatz, Klaus. *Vaticanum I, 1869-1870*. Paderborn: Ferdinand Schöningh, 1992-1994, 3 vols.

Spiazzi, Raimondo. "La dottrina sociale di S. Tommaso ed i prinicipi fondamentali dell'umanesimo cristiano". *Seminarium*, 39 (1977), 812-854.

Struyker Boudier, Cornelis E.M. *Wijsgerig leven in Nederland en België, 1880-1980*. Vol. 5-6: *De filosofie van Leuven*. Leuven: Universitaire Pers Leuven – Baarn: Ambo, 1989.

Thibault, Pierre. *Savoir et pouvoir. Philosophie thomiste et politique cléricale au XIXe siècle*. Quebec: Presses de l'Université Laval, 1972.

Viaene, Vincent. "The Roman Question: Catholic Mobilisation and Papal Diplomacy during the Pontificate of Pius IX". In Emiel Lamberts, ed. *The Black International*. Leuven: Leuven University Press, 2002, 135-143.

Zagar, Janko. "Aquinas and the Social Teaching of the Church". *The Thomist*, 38 (1974), 826-855.

Jacques Maritain, 1920s. Photo.
[Kolbsheim (F), Cercle d'études Jacques & Raïssa Maritain]

THE 1920s FRANCOPHONE THOMISTIC REVIVAL[*]

PHILIPPE CHENAUX

"To the great outrage of Kantian and Bergsonian philosophers, and of the whole sociological school, Thomism is currently a fashionable philosophy in France and French-speaking countries." A great observer of the intellectual life of his time, the Fribourg aristocrat Gonzague de Reynold considered this 'return to the scholastic' (to borrow the title of a 1919 work by Gonzague Truc) one of the major phenomena of the about to expire decade.[1] Encouraged by Pope Leo XIII in his inaugural encyclical *Aeterni Patris* (1879), the pre-war revival of Thomism had been fruitful in ecclesiastical teachings (Paris, Leuven, Fribourg) but never managed to reach the 'secular world'.[2] Leo XIII's neo-Thomism had essentially remained a 'philosophy of seminaries' that, over the years, and under the effect of the modernist crisis, had been transformed into a rigid doctrinal system perfectly symbolised by the XXIV Theses of the Italian Jesuit Guido Mattiussi, published on the eve of the war.[3] As historian Etienne Fouilloux wrote, 1910 "Thomism" had become profoundly "anti-mod-

---

[*] This contribution is largely based on my former research on the topic. See for instance: Chenaux, *Entre Maurras et Maritain*; Id., "De Mercier à Maritain"; Id., "La seconde vague thomiste", 139-150; Id., "Circles and Institutions"; Id., "La renaissance thomiste en Suisse romande".

[1] Gonzague de Reynold, "Le retour au thomisme dans les pays de langue française", 1 (Bibliothèque nationale suisse (Berne), Papers Reynold, Ace 35-38bis).

[2] Aubert, "Aspects divers du néo-thomisme sous le pontificat de Léon XIII".

[3] Bonino, "Le fondement doctrinal du projet léonin: *Aeterni Patris* et la restauration du thomisme".

PHILIPPE CHENAUX

ern".[4] Conversely, the 1920s revival of Thomism, driven by secular mentors
such as Jacques Maritain and Etienne Gilson, resolutely intended to conquer
a modern culture that had seen its foundations (reason, progress, freedom)
shaken by war. But this 'Triumph of Saint Thomas' very quickly led to the 'trial
of scholasticism', itself a prelude to the major intellectual crisis that broke out
when in 1926 the Action Française was condemned.[5]

The places

"One of the joys of the victory – and certainly not the least of them – is for us
to believe that German philosophy, which has reigned for such a long time
over our defeated souls, will no longer have any influence over our victorious
souls." Father Emile Peillaube, dean of the Faculty of Philosophy, was quite
direct in his report at the solemn opening session of the Institut Catholique de
Paris (Catholic University of Paris) on 4 December 1918: France's victory over
Germany was no less than the victory of Catholicism over Protestantism, the
victory of Saint Thomas Aquinas over Kant.[6] This return to grace of Thomas
Aquinas' philosophy is apparent in the faculty's programmes (1919-1920)
which were predominated by Thomist inspiration in lessons by Jacques Maritain (history of modern philosophy), Father Antonin-Dalmace Sertillanges
(moral philosophy), Father F.A. Blanche (metaphysics) and Emile Peillaube
(psychology). The creation in 1920 of two new research chairs financed by the
Fondation des morts de la guerre (the foundation for war casualties), one on
natural law, entrusted to Priest Bernard Roland-Gosselin, and the other on *Jus
gentium*, assigned to Father Yves de la Brière, aimed to increase the "Faculty's
doctrinal influence" (E. Peillaube).[7] These new teachings, to which were soon
to be added those of priest Daniel Lallement in sociology, came with new instruments for the dissemination of Thomistic doctrine.

The idea behind the Société philosophique Saint-Thomas d'Aquin (Philosophical Society of Saint Thomas Aquinas), reconstituted in 1922 by Father
Peillaube, was to "group Christian scholars and philosophers" thus "spark-
ing discussions between them in order to specify the meaning and position
of various issues".[8] It is in this context that Maritain would discuss and oppose the theses defended by Maurice Blondel in "Le procès de l'intelligence"

4   Fouilloux, "La culture de l'Église catholique", 167. See also Id., *Une Église en quête en
     liberté*, 39-65.
5   Cf. Prévotat, *Les Catholiques et l'Action française*.
6   *Revue de philosophie*, 26 (1919), 226.
7   Ibid., 28 (1921), 81-86.
8   Ibid., 29 (1922), 536.

(1922).[9] The women's Thomistic Circle, a teaching and initiation association that published its own *Cahiers*, started in 1925. In the academic year 1925-26 a conference cycle "reserved for gentlemen" on the theme of "Catholic Doctrine according to Saint Thomas Aquinas" was launched, aiming to broadcast the benefits of scholasticism to a wider audience.[10] The Faculty's *Revue de Philosophie* had started to reappear in January 1919 under the auspices of Father Peillaube, and intended to embody a "living" Aristotelian and Thomistic spiritualism open to "all acquisitions of knowledge": "The peripatetic and Thomistic philosophy is not a closed system, accomplished on all points, containing only the definitive. We have to *rethink* it with a profound sense of its principles and of the progress of science."[11] Knowing the difficulties that such an orientation aroused in Rome at the beginning of the 1920s and the sharp criticism directed at Father Peillaube on the subject, the importance of the letter addressed in the name of the pope by Secretary of State and Cardinal Gasparri to the director of the *Revue* in July 1925 cannot be understated. It judged the latter to be "a reliable doctrinal journal, very much alive and adapted to the needs of the time". Beyond this ratification of perfect Thomistic orthodoxy, it tasked the journal with the mission of fighting to have "the principles and method" of Saint Thomas "penetrate all the way through to the most opposing circles, to the intelligences most stifled by current errors and biases, such as those of *falsi nominis scientia*, which combat and mock the surest and most general doctrines of the School, under the accusation of *sterile intellectualism*".[12]

The already old project of transforming the Faculty of Philosophy, canonically erected by papal brief on 15 June 1895, into a 'Special Institute of Philosophy' following the Leuven model, found new relevance during the war.[13] The invasion of Belgium had contributed to strengthening the ties with the prestigious Belgian Catholic University. In October 1914, Monsignor Baudrillart wrote to the Belgian Minister of Education "to place the Catholic University of Paris at the disposal of those teachers and students of Leuven who might want to make use of it".[14] In May 1917, rector Baudrillart went to Rome to present the project. From his numerous meetings at the Vatican (Bisleti, Billot), and in the pontifical academies (Roman College, Angelic College), he gathered the impression that the Faculty of Philosophy held little credibility and that a trip to Rome by Father Peillaube (himself a "longtime suspect", according to his interlocutors, for articles published in the *Revue*) with a view to "overhauling

9   Lecture, 25 April 1923, published under the title "L'intelligence d'après M. Maurice Blondel", Ibid., 30 (1923), 333-364, 484-511.
10 Ibid., 32 (1925), 550-555.
11 Ibid., 26 (1919), 6-7.
12 Ibid., 32 (1925), 342-344.
13 Colin, "La Faculté de philosophie dans ses publications 1900-1985".
14 *Les Carnets du Cardinal Alfred Baudrillart (1er août 1914 - 31 décembre 1918)*, 89.

the programme" seemed necessary.[15] In January 1919, the unanimous refusal by the Faculty professors, assembled under the presidency of Dean Peillaube, to accede to the request made on behalf of the bishops to 'link' their programme to that of the Faculty of Theology and to teach the theological treatise of Saint Thomas in the Faculty of Philosophy, revealed the persisting tensions between Rome and Paris. Indeed, the reason invoked was that such teachings, deemed "impossible", risked leading to "regrettable confusion" among students and to denaturing the vocation of the Faculty which was "above all to create an *intellectual* elite", and from there to "exercise real influence on the movement of ideas in France".[16]

"The catastrophe that has shaken the world is, if I am not mistaken, the logical progression of a philosophy of dislocation and ruin." In his acceptance speech to the Academy of Moral and Political Sciences, on 13 December 1919, Cardinal Mercier did not suggest any other key to understanding the events.[17] The Higher School of Philosophy reopened its doors, as did the University, in February 1919. The list of registrations for the academic year indicated a growing number of "secular students who were attracted to aspects of philosophy by dispassionate curiosity". The course programme did not show any significant changes to the teaching body, which was essentially composed of first generation 'disciples' of Cardinal Mercier: Simon Deploige (sociology), Léon Noël (psychology and logic), Maurice de Wulf (history of philosophy), Désiré Nys (cosmology), Maurice Defourny (political economics).[18] Under the presidency of Deploige, the Leuven Institute claimed to be, above all, a "teaching institution", with a duty to respond to a growing number of students concerned with "complementing their professional education with a strong grounding in philosophy".[19] In the early 1920s and bolstered by his numerous foreign contacts (notably in France), Deploige chose to make the Institute more open by organising numerous public conferences in Leuven, featuring scholars as Jacques Maritain (invited seven times between 1920 and 1926!), Father Sertillanges, but also Louis Massignon, Henri Ghéon, Henri Massis and many other observers of the Catholic revival in that period. The passing of Cardinal Mercier in 1926, followed by that of Deploige the following year, led to a scientific repositioning of the Institute, motivated by its new director, Canon Léon Noël. As the *Annals* of the Higher Institute of Philosophy ceased to be published, the *Revue néo-scolastique de Louvain* increasingly welcomed the works of Etienne Gilson or Pierre Mandonnet. The arrival of Fernand Van Steenberghen (1928) would reinforce this evolution toward a historicised Thomism and contribute

---

15 *Les Carnets du Cardinal Alfred Baudrillart (1er août 1914 - 31 décembre 1918)*, 542-561.
16 Archives de l'Institut catholique de Paris: Doctoral College of the Faculty of Philosophy, 8 January 1919 (extract from the minutes).
17 *Revue de philosophie néoscolastique de Louvain*, 22 (1920), 123.
18 *Annales de l'Institut de Philosophie*, 4 (1920), 609.
19 Ibid., 5 (1924), VIII.

to turning Leuven into one of the main research centres on the history of me-diaeval philosophy.[20]

Prior to 1914 the Faculty of Theology of the University of Fribourg had indisputably been the primary home of Thomistic studies for the Dominicans. In 1893, the foundation of the *Revue Thomiste* by two professors of the Fac-ulty, Fathers Coconnier and Mandonnet, had contributed to increasing Fri-bourg's influence in the Francophone world.[21] However, contrary to Paris and Leuven, the Swiss university, due to the country's neutral position during the conflict and above all because of the involvement of professors from no less than twelve different nations, hardly made its voice heard in the 'war of ideas', preferring to focus on humanitarian work. As holder of the chair of church history of the Faculty of Theology from its foundation in 1891, and dean of the same faculty for a number of years, Pierre Mandonnet had left his mark on the Thomism taught at Fribourg.[22] His departure to Saulchoir in 1919 left a void and seemed to confirm a certain retreat from French thinking, lamented by the *Revue des Jeunes*: "Why, in this place which, being Catholic, privileges us, should there still be so few of us as, sadly, in the whole of Switzerland, where we are not even one to three; that is three Germans".[23] The transfer to Fribourg of the journal *Divus Thomas*, founded in 1886 by Monsignor Ernst Commer and headed after the end of the war by Father Gallus Maria Manser, demon-strated the loss of influence that benefited Germany.[24] The arrival at the river Sarine of a disciple of Maritain, Priest Charles Journet, appointed professor of theology in the diocesan seminary in 1924, changed nothing in the matter.[25] Throughout this period, the Freiburg college remained largely impervious to the lure of the French Thomistic renaissance.

Established following Emile Combes' expulsion of the congregations (1904) in Saulchoir, near Kain-lez-Tournai in Belgium, the study-convent of the Province of France had experienced a 'new expansion' thanks to the 1914 war. Under the auspices of Antoine Lemonnyer, regent of studies since 1911, the School of Dominican Studies was quick to regain great dynamism, once the hostilities had ended. Under the auspices of the Lemonnyer-Mandonnet tandem, the School of Dominican Studies specialised in the historical study of Thomism. The foundation of a historical Institute of Thomistic Studies in 1920 was the first notable achievement in this domain. As Lemonnyer wrote in his report to the provincial, it responded to the order's wish not to leave to oth-ers (Leuven, Gilson), the task of "shedding new light, from a historical stand-point, on the origins, development and true meaning of the Doctrine of Saint

20   Wiercockx, "De Mercier à de Wulf".
21   Cf. Bonino, *Saint Thomas au XXème siècle.*
22   Vicaire, "Le P. Mandonnet à Fribourg".
23   Pichon, "La pensée catholique et française à Fribourg", 363.
24   Imbach, "La Faculté des Lettres. Abteilung Philosophie".
25   Chenaux, "La renaissance thomiste en Suisse romande dans les années 1920".

Thomas".[26] The professorship of the new Institute was composed of young lecturers (Roland-Gosselin, Synave, Schaff, Chenu) under the authority of Mandonnet, a master with "exceptional experience and competence". It was at his initiative, in fact, that the *Bibliothèque thomiste*, a collection bringing together historical studies on the life, writings and thoughts of the master, was launched. In 1923 and above all, a Thomist Society was founded, aiming both to deepen doctrinal teachings and provide practical public exposure. Though not formally dependent on Saulchoir, the Thomist Society was nevertheless linked to it, in part through the person of its president and the presence on its Board of a second teacher from the house (father Roland-Gosselin), but above all in the means (scientific collection, bulletin) it deployed to properly fulfil its task. Despite all of their caution, it was not long before the Fathers of Saulchoir were criticised for "sacrificing theology" to philosophy and history.[27]

The authors of the *Bulletin Thomiste*, a body of the Thomist Society published from March 1924 as a supplement to the *Revue Thomiste* following an agreement signed with the Fathers of Saint-Maximin editing the journal, also had to defend themselves against the accusation of wanting to "constitute a historic Thomism" competing with "traditional Thomism". The scathing riposte, likely from the pen of Father Chenu, then chief editor of the bulletin, took the form of a genuine advocacy for the "principle and procedures of the historic method" applied to the study of Saint Thomas whose "doctrine, albeit high, is not an 'absolute' outside the period of its inception and the centuries that have fuelled it".[28] While the bi-monthly bulletin mainly aimed to inform on "all the publications – books, reviews, official documents, texts – of interest to the study of the life, works and the doctrine of Saint Thomas Aquinas, or to the history of Thomism", it also claimed a "role of discernment" in what could be called the actuality of Thomism. "Historical reconstruction has its appeal and benefits; but, guaranteed by it, the spirit of Saint Thomas is not limited to ancient problems, and does aim to bring its benefits to the 20th century, beyond the age of the commentators."[29] After 1926, the "enthusiasm" of the young Fathers at Saulchoir, their hope that the practical thinking of Saint Thomas could open "a way to social triumph", would be added to the intellectual efforts of Jacques Maritain or Etienne Gilson to free Thomism from any reactionary and Maurassimian encumbrance.[30]

---

26   Undated report, cited in: Duval, "Aux origines de l'Institut historique d'études thomistes du Saulchoir", 433.
27   Letter from Father Provincial Louis to Father Roland-Gosselin, 23 December 1923, cited in Ibid., 438.
28   *Bulletin thomiste*, 4-6 (1927-1928), 263.
29   Ibid.
30   Dubarle, "Le temps des enthousiasmes".

The men

Jacques Maritain was indeed, along with Etienne Gilson, the central figure of the post-war Thomistic revival. One phrase, repeated as a slogan in articles and conferences, adopted by friends and derided by adversaries, suffices to express this goal of re-appropriation: "Saint Thomas, apostle for modern times". Moreover, it is not a coincidence that it was in Leuven, during a conference in January 1920 for the Higher Institute of Philosophy, that Maritain for the first time publicly examined "the conditions of the scholastic renaissance" in the modern world.[31] The expression did not yet exist as such, but the substance of the message was already present: far from ensuring the transmission of heritage, scholastic thinkers since Saint Thomas had proven unfaithful to the lessons of the master by "grossly ignoring the concerns of their times" in the scientific and philosophical domains, thereby expediting, through their self-centred attitude, the "degradation of scholasticism at the beginning of modern times". For Thomistic philosophy was to be revived "not just as a philosophy of seminaries, but as it really is: the natural philosophy of the human soul", Thomists needed to regain both a sense of being and a sense of the times. Indirectly paying tribute to what had been achieved by Leuven with regard to positive science, Maritain called for Thomists to show an interest in modern philosophy, "not to *sympathise* with doctrine but by rethinking with modern spiritual effort the problems of our times, as Saint Thomas would do". This text, revised and corrected, would constitute one of the chapters of *Antimoderne* published two years later.

Saint Thomas, apostle for modern times was in fact the title given to a conference held in Avignon (October 1923) and then repeated in several other places (Geneva, Saint-Maurice, Leuven) on the occasion of the sixth centenary of the canonisation of Saint Thomas, 'Doctor of the Church'.[32] In this text, with hints of a manifesto, Maritain repeated and specified the programme outlined in Leuven in January 1920, by showing that what had been asked of Thomists was not, as some claimed, "to redo with modern philosophers" (Descartes, Kant, Hegel, Bergson) what Aquinas "had done with Aristotle", but rather to use the principles of Thomism "with a loyalty which will never be pure and vehement enough", to "shine the light of Saint Thomas on the intellectual life of this century". Although dedicated to Cardinal Mercier, "the great restorer of Thomistic philosophy" along with Pope Leo XIII, this lesson in method marked a clear distancing from the Leuven neo-Thomism. Indeed, it was no longer a case of 'rethinking' Thomism based on contemporary problems, but rather of 'assimilating' within it the dispersed wealth that the modern world had produced in the domains of art, science and culture.

31 Maritain, "De quelques conditions de la renaissance scolastique".
32 Id., *Saint Thomas d'Aquin, apôtre des temps modernes.*

For this, the philosopher held an enviable position in the Catholic intellectual realm of the immediate post-war period.[33] Appointed professor of history of modern philosophy at the Catholic University in June 1914 by direct intervention from Rome, promoted to honorary *doctor* of philosophy by decree of the Sacrée Congrégation des Séminaires et des Universités for having been "deserving of Catholic doctrine" in May 1917, he appeared to be above any suspicion from the standpoint of Thomistic orthodoxy. His conferences on the "role of Germany in modern philosophy" during the winter of 1914/15 had been rather well-received in Roman circles. Father Thomas Pègues, professor at the Angelicum, had written to him: "Pursue your task"; you will thereby complete the work of deliverance accomplished by our soldiers on another field."[34] His lessons at the Catholic University at the end of the war, were attended by a numerous group of assiduous students for whom Thomism, according to one of them, represented "the only living current of the moment".[35]

With the *Revue Universelle*, founded in April 1920 thanks to a legacy obtained together with Charles Maurras, the philosopher was offered "a choice forum to spread the teachings of Saint Thomas far and wide".[36] "It is the first time that Thomistic philosophy enjoys such a great entry into the cultural world", his wife Raïssa noted in her *Journal*.[37] In charge of its philosophy section, Maritain published more than thirty articles and chronicles in the *Revue* between 1920 and 1927. They later became material for important books such as *Réflexions sur l'intelligence* (1924) or *Trois Réformateurs* (1925). The first one appeared in the *Bibliothèque française de philosophie* a series that he headed at the National Library. Next to the works of orthodox Thomists such as Garrigou-Lagrange or Deploige, as well as close friends as priest Charles Journet or scholar Pierre Termier, the *Bibliothèque* also published more unexpected authors, though characteristic of the spirit of the times: the orientalist René Guénon with a work on theosophy[38] and later on the German jurist Carl Schmitt with the translation of an essay on political romanticism.[39] The second one inaugurated the prestigious collection of the *Roseau d'Or*, launched by Plon in 1925 in conjunction with Henri Massis and Stanislas Fumet. Subtly blending doctrinal rigour with literary avant-gardism (Bernanos, Green, Reverdy), they would play for some time "with verve, the role of a Catholic *Nouvelle Revue Française*".[40]

---

33 Chenaux, "Circles and Institutions".
34 Bibliothèque nationale et universitaire de Strasbourg (BNU), Fonds Maritain: Letter of
    15 December 1914.
35 Ibid.: Letter from Roland Dalbiez to Jacques Maritain, 13 July 1921.
36 Ibid.: Letter from Father Pègues to Maritain, 6 May 1920.
37 Maritain, *Journal de Raïssa*, 107.
38 Guénon, *Le Théosophisme, histoire d'une pseudo-religion*.
39 Schmitt. *Romantisme politique*.
40 Chenaux, *Entre Maurras et Maritain*, 68-78.

The Thomist study circles represented a third path of influence, and doubtless the most original for the Thomism of Maritain, or at least the one which best corresponded to his desire to win over to his cause "the minds of the world and of the laity". As soon as the war ended, the philosopher and his wife had, in fact, started to gather friends and students of the Catholic University in their home in Versailles, to "examine from a closer angle, in free discussions, the doctrine of Saint Thomas, and to confront it with the problems of our times".[41] Very soon, they conceived the project of a study association in which the members, declaring their loyalty to Saint Thomas, "would vow (first temporarily and then perpetually) to devote themselves to a life of prayer". Father Réginald Garrigou-Lagrange was asked to take spiritual leadership of this circle. "It is the only way to save Thomism in the world", Maritain wrote to him in January 1922.[42] As a limited and non-commercial edition, a spiritual directory for the members was published in the issues of the Abbey of Saint-Maurice d'Agaune in Valais (Switzerland) where the Maritains had many friends.[43] This concern not to separate "spiritual life and intellectual work" was another characteristic of Maritain's Thomism: "How could regular dwelling by the soul in the superior higher spheres of contemplation possibly not give the philosopher a precious boost of strength?"[44] In the autumn of 1922 a first Thomist Study Circle retreat took place in Versailles, attended by thirty-odd people, most of them 'seculars'. From the following year onward, these retreats were regularly held in the Martitain home in Meudon, making it into one of the important seats of French Catholic intellectual life of the interwar period.[45]

Gilson's Thomism evidently did not enjoy the same popularity outside its natural sphere of influence.[46] In fact, in private, the young professor did not hide a certain annoyance at the "fanatic figures, especially the women", who followed Maritain and came to bother him.[47] His election to the Sorbonne in 1921 as lecturer in the history of mediaeval philosophy, as well as to the École Pratique des Hautes Études, had delighted all those who had hoped that with the war, Thomist doctrine could regain 'its place' in the French university.[48] In his book *Thomisme*, published in Strasbourg in 1920 and then re-published in Vrin two years later, Gilson made no secret of his intention to do something worthwhile in this regard. The restoration of Saint Thomas and of mediaeval thinkers was, to him, above all a requirement "from a historical point of view": "It is unbelievable that we might consider several centuries of philosophical

41 Maritain, *Carnet de notes*, 184.
42 BNU, Fonds Maritain: Letter of 2 January 1922.
43 Roulin, *Une abbaye dans le siècle*, 47-52.
44 Maritain, *Antimoderne*, 154.
45 Chenaux, *Entre Maurras et Maritain*, 49-68.
46 Cf. Michel, *Etienne Gilson. Une biographie intellectuelle et politique.*
47 BNU, Fonds Maritain: Letter from Roland Dalbiez to Jacques Maritain, 5 June 1923.
48 Blanche, "Saint Thomas d'Aquin en Sorbonne".

speculation as having never existed". If we then considered the history of philosophy as "one of the instruments of philosophical culture", we should have
had to admit that the thirteenth century was no "less rich in philosophical
triumphs than the era of Descartes and Leibnitz or Kant and A. Comte".

> Thomas Aquinas and Duns Scot, to choose only examples that are scarcely
> questionable, belong to a breed of thinkers who are truly worthy of that
> name. They are great philosophers, i.e. philosophers for all times, and who
> appear so even to the minds most firmly resolved not to submit to their
> authority or reason.[49]

If the intention was combative, the method used was nevertheless similar to
how his teachers at the Sorbonne (Lévy-Bruhl, Brunschvicg) had taught him.
In his eyes the study of Thomism was indeed "inseparable" from that of other
currents of mediaeval thought "often of very different inspiration" "which it
summarises and which it also sometimes opposes". He refused to choose between Saint Bonaventure (to which he also devoted a book in 1924[50]) and Saint
Thomas, "My preferences, which are no secret, do not lean towards one or the
other exclusively, but to Christian thinking, of which both are fundamental
representatives".[51]

The influence of Gilson followed the more conventional routes of university circulation. His lessons at the Sorbonne, where one could feel "the rise
of the Thomist tide" according to Roland Dalbiez[52], as well as his seminars at
the religious science section of the École Pratique des Hautes Études quickly
made him very popular among the students. The most well-known case is that
of Henri Gouhier, of which he would later say that he was "more of a son than
a student to him".[53] Having come from Auxerre, the latter first looked to Maritain as a supervisor of his thesis, before turning to Gilson who directed him
towards working on history of philosophy, a more certain route to "a professorship in the faculty".[54] "If you will allow me to give you some advice, I would
suggest you review the history of mediaeval philosophy, in order to bridge the
gap between Descartes and Saint Thomas", Gilson wrote to him in 1920.[55] His
thesis presented to the École Pratique des Hautes Études was published in
a collection of Studies on Mediaeval Philosophy led by Gilson at Vrin with
the title *La Pensée religieuse de Descartes* (1924) and became 'memorable' as

---

49   Gilson, *Le thomisme*, 5-7.
50   Id., *La philosophie de saint Bonaventure*.
51   Lefèvre, *Une heure avec …*, 1925, 70.
52   BNU, Fonds Maritain: Letter to Maritain, 29 March 1922.
53   Shook, *Etienne Gilson*, 133.
54   BNU, Fonds Maritain: Letter to Maritain, 29 September 1921.
55   Letter of 7 November 1920, in Prouvost, "Lettres d'Etienne Gilson à Henri Gouhier", 461-
     462.

Maritain himself wrote when the book came out.[56] The philosopher's participation in the World Congress of Philosophy in Oxford (1921) and more importantly that in Naples (1924) afforded him a scientific stature that transcended
national borders by supplying him with the opportunity of making many contacts.[57] In 1929, under his direction, and at the request of his Canadian friends,
the Pontifical Institute of Mediaeval Studies was created in Toronto.[58]

Gilson's relations with the Catholic Thomist circles in the twenties were
not straightforward.[59] As one of his biographers wrote, his position within this
"secular citadel" of knowledge that was the Sorbonne, "generated suspicion
on their side and apprehensiveness on his".[60] When Maritain re-edited the
work of Monsignor Simon Deploige *Le Conflit de la morale et de la sociologie*
(1923) with a preface lauding this "work, of great value, which honours the
school of Leuven", Gilson expressed his 'scepticism' as to the method used
by the author to pit Thomist ethics against Durkheimian sociology.[61] Conversely, the philosopher's repeated offers of collaboration to the Fathers of
Saulchoir, of which he claimed to "be interested in their thinking and work"
(in a letter to Father Mandonnet on 17 December 1924) never came to fruition
for the reason that "the Thomism of M.G. was not considered by some to be
absolutely.... 'pure'".[62] Referring to the second edition of his *Thomisme* (Vrin,
1923), Father Mandonnet in the *Bulletin Thomiste* criticised "the distribution
of chapters", considering it contrary to the "[philosophical] order wished for
by the Master" who recommended "in conformity with the requirements of
our nature, that we should go from that which is easiest to that which is the
most difficult".[63] To which Gilson responded that, even though the criticism
was founded "in law", the historian within him clashed with "in fact, this
difficulty – or powerlessness – to resolve to write a philosophy *ad mentem Divi
Thomae* – according to the mind of the Divine Thomas –, of which we have an
overall plan, but no specific order".[64] Several months later, Father Sertillanges
found nothing more to say about his *Saint Thomas d'Aquin* (1925): a "good and
beautiful work", concluded the eminent Dominican, "whose author all Thomists will congratulate, thanking God for this persevering assistance afforded

---

56 *Revue de philosophie*, 32 (1925), 78-86.
57 Shook, *Etienne Gilson*, 143-147.
58 Michel, *La pensée catholique en Amérique du Nord*, 37-121.
59 Prouvost, "Les relations entre philosophie et théologie chez E. Gilson et les thomistes
    contemporains".
60 Shook, *Etienne Gilson*, 138.
61 Ibid., 140-141.
62 Letter from Father Chenu to Father Provincial Louis, 18 January 1925, cited in Duval, "Aux
    origines de l'Institut historique d'études thomistes du Saulchoir", 443.
63 *Bulletin thomiste*, 1-3 (1924-1926), 132-136.
64 Letter of 17 December 1924, cited in: Prouvost, "Les relations entre philosophie et théologie
    chez E. Gilson et les thomistes contemporains", 417.

by an outstanding mind to a cause that now has a great future ahead of it".[65]
In this book, quickly sold out and republished several times, Gilson presented
Thomist ethics as "a Christian humanism", not in the sense of a "combination
in any proportion of humanism and Christianism" but attesting to "the fundamental identity of a Christianity in which all humanism would be included
and of an integral humanism which would only find its complete satisfaction
in Christianity".[66] As for Maritain, he wrote to him that he had "liked what
you said about the Christian humanism of Saint Thomas", while having reservations as to the use of the term "Christian naturalism" which he considered
"very dangerous" and riddled with Pelagian equivocation.[67] This was a singu-
lar homage, knowing what would become of this theme, by his pen, ten years
later. But was this still 'the triumph of Saint Thomas'?

The times

Henri Ghéon's play, *Triomphe de Saint Thomas d'Aquin* (1924), written on the
occasion of the sixth centenary of the Saint's canonisation and performed
for the first time in Liège on 6 March 1924, is indeed rather characteristic, by
its title and its didactic aim, of the conquering spirit of French neo-Thomism
at the beginning of the 1920s. It also illustrates the convergence that was oc-
curring, against the backdrop of the French victory and the crisis of civilisation, between Catholicism, Thomism and integral nationalism. "It is precisely
because I am Catholic, and Catholic first, that today I cry: France first! politics first!" wrote Ghéon, "the man born of war", in 1919.[68] "Blessed Aristotle,
St. Thomas and yourself, who gave us a philosophy in which there is no room
for doubt, for indecision, for detachment", he wrote addressing Maritain following the reading of his *Éléments de philosophie* in 1920.[69] A good example
of the attraction of Thomism for neo-converts of the Action Française! But the
appeal of Aquinas' philosophy did not stop at the church doors.

　　The success of a book such as *Le retour à la scolastique* (1919) by Gonzague Truc, a proclaimed unbeliever, is eloquent in this respect. The author,
as he indicates in a short preface, meant to "demonstrate that the practice of
our mediaeval doctors, especially St. Thomas [remained] indispensable to a
restoration of thought, which is becoming increasingly necessary". In the introduction, he explained how the *philosophia perennis*, after a "hefty fall", followed by an "unfair discredit", had returned to the forefront of the intellectual
scene in the nineteenth century without however "succeeding in winning over

65   *Bulletin thomiste*, 1-3 (1924-1926), 332.
66   Gilson, *Saint Thomas d'Aquin*, 7.
67   Letter of 25 November 1924, in Gilson and Maritain, *Correspondance 1923-1971*, 25-27.
68   Letter to Jacques Rivière, 3 November 1919, cited in Ghéon and Gide, *Correspondance*, I,
     116.

the layman", thanks first and foremost to French historians (Cousin, Hauréau, Rémusat) and also to two popes, the "great" Leo XIII and the "very great" Pius X. Defined as a "free philosophy, while at the same time conditioned", explaining "dogma without subservience", scholasticism was a manifestation of the "French mind". In conclusion, the author distinguished "its current apologetic *value*" from what was more interesting to him, namely its "perpetual *value* as a doctrine and a method", which made it "ever an effective remedy for a general dulling of the mind".[70] Gonzague Truc's candid hostility for Christianity (that "sorry tragedy that dispossesses us of ancient wisdom and has thrown the dark veil of Golgotha over the modern world") did not prevent him getting the vote of Thomistic circles. Whilst Father Mandonnet saw in it "a characteristic sign of changing times"[71], Canon Léon Noël of Leuven spoke of a "new phase in the history of the neo-scholastic movement".[72] Though more reserved, Maritain nevertheless recognised in this "apologia of St. Thomas by an agnostic" "an astonishing testimony to the power of attraction and properly human and rational value of the scholastic discipline".[73] As for Gilson, he appreciated the author for having "written a book that is useful and, in its essence, true": "Perhaps", he added insightfully, "it will even remain a document for historians".[74]

Having climbed very high in the years 1923-1924, the year of the sixth centenary of the canonisation and the 650th anniversary of the death of Saint Thomas, the Thomistic wave would, nevertheless, fall quickly from the middle of the decade onward. The encyclical *Studiorum ducem* (29 June 1923) constituted a form of climax by inviting "'the whole of Christendom" "to celebrate this centenary with dignity, since the honours given to Saint Thomas not only aim to glorify the Saint Doctor, but also to exalt the authority of the teaching Church". A whole series of commemorative events followed, the most significant undoubtedly being the Thomist week in Rome (17-25 November 1923) attended by both Maritain and Deploige. Somewhat unexpected a second one was organised the following year as part of the World Congress of Philosophy in Naples (5-9 May 1924). Cardinal Mercier had declined the invitation of the Pontifical Academy of Saint Thomas Aquinas, but at first accepted to give the opening speech at the Congress in Naples, before withdrawing under pressure from Rome. This illustrates how he acknowledged the "exceptional" nature of the tribute that a "secular university, surrounded by the members of a World Congress of Philosophy and in conjunction with the religious authorities, was prepared to offer to our purest scientific glory".[75]

69   BNU, Fonds Maritain: Letter of 17 July 1920.
70   Truc, *Le Retour à la Scolastique*, XVI.
71   *Revue des jeunes,* 19 (1919), 188.
72   *Revue néo-scolastique de Louvain,* 25 (1921), 216-219.
73   *Les Lettres,* 1 (1919) 4, 6-8, cited in: Maritain, *Œuvres complètes*, I, 1127-1129.
74   *Revue philosophique de la France et de l'Étranger,* 44 (1919), 322-324.
75   Aubert, "Une retombée tardive de la Question romaine".

The reaction to what might have appeared to be a provocative though "paradoxical" "offensive" of Thomist thought, "in a world that negates its fundamental principles", swiftly followed. In 1925, a lengthy tome by an associate professor of philosophy, Louis Rougier, titled *La Scolastique et le Thomisme* (Scholasticism and Thomism), had the effect of a "heavy paving stone thrown into the neo-Thomist flowerbeds".[76] The author endeavoured to show how "the unification of faith and reason" achieved by Saint Thomas and afterwards adopted by the Magisterium of the Church had only been possible by perverting Aristotle's philosophy: "the surreptitious transformation of a logical distinction posited by the Stagirite between essence and existence into a real and ontological distinction". Leaning, on the one hand, on the progress of science and, on the other, on the most recent findings of biblical exegesis, he concluded on the "radical impossibility of harmonising Aristotle with the Bible" and therefore on the historical failure of a system of thought that had wished to found dogma and faith in reason.[77] Accused of plagiarism, Rougier's book shook up the whole Thomist community. Most of them were indignant at reading the perfect Aristotelian-Thomistic orthodoxy questioned in this way.[78] Priest François-Xavier Maquart became their spokesman when he explained in the *Revue de Philosophie* that "the real Aristotle was far from resembling the caricature" proposed by Rougier. "Not only does he expressly teach human freedom and divine transcendence, but it suffices to recall what was the fundamental problem of philosophy in his era in order to grasp, in its essence, the general economy of his system and then very clearly see that if the Aristotle of history perhaps did not explicitly express the thesis of real distinction, he at least established its principles."[79] Others, compelled by Rougier's historical approach, criticised the methods without however endorsing Maquart's interpretation, who, ccording to Father Chenu in the *Bulletin Thomiste* "was far from being beyond reproach". Arguing on the basis of a study by Jacques Chevalier on the idea of creation in the thinking of Aristotle and Saint Thomas, he instead insisted on the considerable novelty of Thomist thinking in comparison to Aristotelian philosophy: "To identify them by the material concordance of their parts would be an illusion similar to those who liken man with animals".[80] Father Marie-Joseph Lagrange, the founder of the École Biblique in Jerusalem and the author of an article on this theme in the *Revue Thomiste*, expressed himself in the same vein:

---

76   Jaccard, "La mêlée thomiste en France en 1925".
77   Rougier, *La scolastique et le thomisme*, XVII-XLIII.
78   Cf. Courcier, "'La Scolastique et le Thomisme', la réception du livre de Rougier en 1925 par le milieu thomiste".
79   Maquart, "M.L. Rougier contre la scolastique et le thomisme", 544.
80   *Bulletin thomiste*, 4-6 (1927-1929), 129.

> What a mistake it is to reproach him for saying that Aristotle was not aware of the real distinction between essence and existence! This is to understand nothing of the fundamental place of the idea of creation, unknown to this pagan... I do not want our people to be paleo-Thomists, but really neo-Thomists. I threw myself into the fray, as if I were playing Blind Man's Bluff, so that we should not confuse Aristotle with the theologian Saint Thomas.[81]

Louis Rougier's trial of scholasticism had brought out the first cracks in the united front of the Thomist community of the 1920s. A few years later, the debate surrounding 'Christian philosophy' would accentuate these differences even further and finally rupture this great façade of unanimity.[82] Meanwhile, another and much more considerable event had already seriously shaken it: the pontifical condemnation of the Action Française (1926). It spoiled the 'disastrous' collusion which, thanks to the modernist crisis and the Great War, had occurred between the philosophy of Saint Thomas and the thinking of Charles Maurras. The case of the *Revue Thomiste*, torn between the Maurrassisme loyalty of Thomas Pègues and the Maritainist sympathies of Marie-Vincent Bernadot, bore witness to a phenomenon of dual allegiance that came to an end only after direct intervention by the ecclesiastical authority in the life of the journal and the transfer of its editor-in-chief to Paris to start *La Vie intellectuelle* (1928).[83] Added to this first abrupt divide was a second, more widespread and certainly less 'agonising' one, but whose effects in the long run were no less evident: the divide (or at least progressive dissociation) between Catholicism and Thomism. *Vae mihi, si non thomistizavero!* (Woe to me if I do not Thomistise!). In the early 1920s the neo-converts (starting with Henri Ghéon) had taken this motto of Maritain's literally and had come (or returned) to the Church "by the Pope's path" (Monsignor Baudrillart).[84] At the end of the decade, Charles Du Bos and Gabriel Marcel did not hesitate to take other philosophical routes (Saint Augustine notably) to bring sense and coherence to their conversion process. Does this mean, then, that Thomism was definitively marginalised after 1926? One could certainly speak of an ebb, through the combined effect, as seen previously, of external attacks and a severe internal crisis. But should it not be considered first and foremost as the decline of a certain 'anti-modern' Thomism, one that had emerged in the early years of the

---

81 Letter to Bruno de Solages, 28 August 1927, cited in: Montagnes, "Le thomisme du Père Lagrange", 504.

82 Floucat, *Pour une philosophie chrétienne*.

83 Chenaux, *Entre Maurras et Maritain*, 133-161.

84 Already quoted "Allocution du 4 décembre 1925 pour l'inauguration des conférences de la Faculté de philosophie de l'Institut catholique de Paris", *Revue de philosophie*, 32 (1925), 570.

century and for which a return to the philosophy of Aquinas was nothing more than the intellectual justification of a 'return to order' (in the intellectual, social and political domains)? This 'triumphalist' conception had its moment of glory in the wake of the war, within the context of the spiritual crisis and nationalist glorification brought about by the events. If it became marginalised after 1926, it was only to be supplanted by another, more open, Thomism, of which Maritain, Gilson, and Chenu were the major interpreters, which converged in the great current of thought referred to as 'Christian humanism'. In this sense, it is fair to speak not only of a second wave, but also of a second Thomistic Revival after the First World War, fully supportive of the Catholic intellectual renaissance of those years, with the exception that it also needed the intervention of the Roman Magisterium to come into its own.

BIBLIOGRAPHY

Aubert, Roger. "Aspects divers du néo-thomisme sous le pontificat de Léon XIII". In Giuseppe Rossini, ed. *Aspetti della cultura cattolica nell'età di Leone XIII*. Rome: Cinque Lune, 1961, 133-227.

Aubert, Roger. "Une retombée tardive de la Question romaine. La raison de l'absence du cardinal Mercier à la célébration napolitaine du 650ème anniversaire de la mort de S. Thomas d'Aquin en 1924". In *Le Cardinal Mercier (1851-1926). Un prélat d'avant-garde*. Louvain-la-Neuve: Académia, 1994, 461-471.

Blanche, F.A. "Saint Thomas d'Aquin en Sorbonne". *Revue des jeunes*, 22 (1919), 550-557.

Bonino, Serge-Thomas, ed. *Saint Thomas au XXème siècle. Actes du colloque du Centenaire de la 'Revue thomiste'*. Paris: Saint-Paul, 1995.

Bonino, Serge-Thomas. "Le fondement doctrinal du projet léonin: *Aeterni Patris* et la restauration du thomisme". In Philippe Levillain and Jean-Marie Ticchi, eds. *Le pontificat de Léon XIII: Renaissances du Saint-Siège?* Collection de l'École française de Rome, 368. Rome: École française de Rome, 2006, 267-274.

Chenaux, Philippe. "La renaissance thomiste en Suisse romande dans les années 1920". In Urs Altermatt, ed. *Schweizer Katholizismus zwischen den Weltkriegen 1920-1940*. Religion-Politik-Gesellschaft in der Schweiz, 8. Fribourg: Editions universitaires, 1994, 27-44.

Chenaux, Philippe. "De Mercier à Maritain". *Revue d'histoire ecclésiastique*, 92 (1997), 475-498.

Chenaux, Philippe. "La seconde vague thomiste". In Pierre Colin, ed. *Intellectuels chrétiens et esprit des années 1920*. Paris: Cerf, 1997, 139-167.

Chenaux, Philippe. *Entre Maurras et Maritain. Une génération intellectuelle catholique (1920-1930)*. Paris: Cerf, 1999 [2012].

Chenaux, Philippe. "Circles and Institutions: The Neo-Thomistic Infrastructure". In: Rajesh Heynickx and Jan De Maeyer, eds. *The Maritain Factor: Taking Religion into Interwar Modernism*. Leuven: Leuven University Press, 2010, 40-53.

Colin, Pierre. "La Faculté de philosophie dans ses publications 1900-1985". In *Le statut contemporain de la philosophie première. Centenaire de la Faculté de philosophie*. Paris: Beauchesne, 1996, 316-322.

Courcier, Jacques. "'La Scolastique et le Thomisme', la réception du livre de Rougier en 1925 par le milieu thomiste". *Philosophia Scientiæ. Travaux d'histoire et de philosophie des sciences*, 10 (2006) 2, 92-156.

Dubarle, Dominique. "Le temps des enthousiasmes". In *L'hommage différé au père Chenu*. Paris: Cerf, 1990, 194-206.

Duval, André. "Aux origines de l'Institut historique d'études thomistes du Saulchoir (1920 et SS.)". *Revue des sciences philosophiques et théologiques*, 75 (1991), 423-448.

Floucat, Yves. *Pour une philosophie chrétienne. Eléments d'un débat fondamental*. Paris: Téqui, 1981.

Fouilloux, Etienne. "La culture de l'Église catholique". In Jean-Marie Mayeur, ed. *Histoire du christianisme*. Vol. 12: *Guerres mondiales et totalitarismes (1914-1958)*. Paris: Desclée, 1990, 154-186.

Fouilloux, Étienne. *Une Église en quête de liberté. La pensée catholique française entre modernisme et Vatican II (1914-1962)*. Paris: DDB, 1998.

Ghéon, Henri and André Gide. *Correspondance*. Vol. 1: *1897-1903*. Paris: Gallimard, 1976.

Gilson, Etienne. *Le thomisme. Introduction au système de saint Thomas d'Aquin*. Paris: Vrin, 1922.

Gilson, Etienne. *La philosophie de saint Bonaventure*. Paris: Vrin, 1924.

Gilson, Etienne. *Saint Thomas d'Aquin*. Paris: Gabalda, 1925.

Gilson, Etienne and Jacques Maritain. *Correspondance 1923-1971*. Paris: Vrin, 1991.

Guénon, René. *Le Théosophisme, histoire d'une pseudo-religion*. Paris: Librairie nationale, 1924.

Imbach, Ruedi. "La Faculté des Lettres. Abteilung Philosophie". In Roland Ruffieux, ed. *Histoire de l'Université de Fribourg, Suisse, 1889-1989. Institutions, enseignements, recherches*. Vol. 2. Fribourg: Editions universitaires, 1991, 656-671.

Jaccard, Pierre. "La mêlée thomiste en France en 1925". *Revue de théologie et de philosophie*, 14 (1926), 49-75.

Lefèvre, Frédéric. *Une heure avec....* Paris: Gallimard, 1924-1929.

Les Carnets du Cardinal Alfred Baudrillart (1er août 1914 - 31 décembre 1918). Paris: Cerf, 1994.

L'hommage différé au père Chenu. Paris: Cerf, 1990.

Maquart, François-Xavier. "M.L. Rougier contre la scolastique et le thomisme". *Revue de philosophie*, 32 (1925), 544.

Maritain, Jacques. "De quelques conditions de la renaissance scolastique". *Annales de l'Institut de philosophie*, 4 (1920), 571-604.

Maritain, Jacques. *Antimoderne*. Paris: Revue des jeunes, 1922.

Maritain, Jacques. *Saint Thomas d'Aquin, apôtre des temps modernes*. Paris: Revue des jeunes, 1924.

Maritain, Jacques. *Journal de Raïssa*. Paris: DDB, 1963.

Maritain, Jacques. *Carnet de notes*. Paris: DDB, 1965.

Maritain, Jacques and Raïssa. *Œuvres complètes*. Paris-Fribourg: Saint-Paul - Éditions universitaires, 1984-2007, 17 vols.

Michel, Florian. *La pensée catholique en Amérique du Nord. Réseaux intellectuels et échanges culturels entre l'Europe, le Canada et les Etats-Unis (années 1920-1960)*. Paris: DDB, 2010.

Michel, Florian. *Etienne Gilson. Une biographie intellectuelle et politique*. Paris: Vrin, 2018.

Montagnes, Bernard. "Le thomisme du Père Lagrange". In: *Ordo Sapientiae et Amoris. Image et message de saint Thomas d'Aquin à travers les récentes études historiques, herméneutiques et doctrinales. Hommage au professeur Jean-Pierre Torrell OP à l'occasion de son 65ème anniversaire*. Fribourg: Editions universitaires, 1993, 487-508.

Pichon, Ch. "La pensée catholique et française à Fribourg". *Revue des jeunes*, 21 (1919), 363.

Prévotat, Jacques. *Les Catholiques et l'Action française. Histoire d'une condamnation. 1899-1939*. Paris: Fayard, 2001.

Prouvost, Géry, ed. "Lettres d'Etienne Gilson à Henri Gouhier". *Revue thomiste*, 94 (1994), 460-478.

Prouvost, Géry. "Les relations entre philosophie et théologie chez E. Gilson et les thomistes contemporains". *Revue thomiste*, 94 (1994), 413-430.

Rougier, Louis. *La scolastique et le thomisme*. Paris: Gauthier-Villars, 1925.

Roulin, Stéphanie. *Une abbaye dans le siècle. Missions et ambitions de Saint-Maurice (1870-1970)*. Neuchâtel: Editions Alphil - Presses universitaires suisses, 2019.

Schmitt, Carl. *Romantisme politique*. Paris: Librairie nationale, 1928.

Shook, Laurence K. *Etienne Gilson*. Milan: Jaca Book, 1991.

Toda, Michel. *Henri Massis, un témoin de la droite intellectuelle*. Paris: Plon, 1987.

Truc, Gonzague. *Le Retour à la Scolastique*. Paris: La Renaissance du Livre, 1919.

Vicaire, Marie-Humbert. "Le P. Mandonnet à Fribourg". *Nova et Vetera*, 13 (1938) 2, 158-168.

Wierockx, Robert. "De Mercier à de Wulf. Débuts de l'Ecole de Louvain". In: Ruedi Imbach, ed. *Gli studi di filosofia medievale fra Otto e Novecento. Contributo a un bilancio storiografico*. Rome: Storia e letteratura, 1991, 75-95.

Simon Deploige. Painting (oil on canvas) by Louis Buisseret, 1939.
[Leuven, Higher Institute of Philosophy; © KU Leuven, Art Patrimony – photo Bruno Vandermeulen]

NEO-THOMISM AT LEUVEN'S FACULTY OF LAW

JOERI DE SMET

The reader would be forgiven for thinking that neo-Thomism and a law faculty make for strange bedfellows. The history of the Catholic University of Leuven, however, provides evidence to the contrary. This essay offers a brief but reliable overview of the pre-war academics at Leuven's Law Faculty who were inspired by neo-Thomism.

My analysis focuses on the period between 1880 and 1914. This time frame immediately follows Pope Leo XIII's encyclical *Aeterni Patris*, launching the revival of scholastic discourse at universities around the world and in Leuven specifically. The unprecedented collision of the Catholic faith with the social sciences indeed prompted a change of course, an effort to which some of Leuven's legal scholars contributed from the 1880s onwards. Historian Lode Wils writes that Belgium found itself at a turning point in the 1884-1885, partly because of Pope Leo XIII's influence.[1] Although he mainly refers to the national elections of 1884, shifting the political initiative in the Belgian Parliament from the Liberals to the Catholic Party, this was also the period in which the Catholic social Congresses in Liège were organised (1886, 1887 and 1890). At these gatherings, and in Belgian public life at large, the famous *question ouvrière*[2] was discussed at length. It would enthral many of Leuven's legal scholars for decades, far beyond the reach of this chapter. Indeed, my contribution

---

1   Wils, "België in de negentiende eeuw", 52-53.
2   Or 'question sociale'. In Dutch: 'sociale kwestie' or 'arbeidersvraagstuk'. This term covers many aspects of workers' living conditions in the wake of the Industrial Revolution, and the way society responded to those challenges.

is limited to the period until 1914. The outbreak of the First World War would prove to be one of the fault lines in the history of the Catholic University of Leuven. Not only was the city devastated by the occupying German army, resulting in huge material and human losses, the academic community also saw many of its members tied up in or even killed during the war.[3]

As to this text's particular scope, there are two reasons for the special attention paid to Leuven's Law Faculty. The first is that the Chair of Political Economy remained in the faculty until 1950.[4] This Chair was of utmost importance in the development of Catholic social teaching in Leuven. The second reason is the impact of the Law Faculty on contemporary political life in Belgium. Its pre-war professors were hugely influential in the Catholic Party, not in the least when it came to the *question ouvrière*. For these two reasons, studying the extent to which neo-Thomism was present at the faculty is more than appropriate.

This text is structured as follows. First, I will give a brief overview of two legal academics who were instrumental in providing the context in which neo-Thomism would later flourish: Charles Périn and Victor Brants. Then, I discuss the four protagonists of neo-Thomism at the Law Faculty: Théodore Fontaine, Léon de Lantsheere, Simon Deploige and Maurice Defourny. I offer a biographical overview of each and outline their main activities and standpoints, all of which will be wrapped up in an overarching conclusion.

Catholic social teaching at the Law Faculty

Catholic social teaching was represented at the Law Faculty by professors who, while trained as lawyers, concentrated on political economy. They can be seen as precursors to neo-Thomism, as this doctrine only made its way into Leuven's academic life with the establishment of Désiré Mercier's Chair

3   Some striking statistics from the time of the Great War: in the 1913-1914 academic year, 2880 students were registered, 680 of whom were at the Law Faculty. 199 students, 61 of them lawyers-to-be, of this generation would lose their lives on the battlefield, during the fire of Leuven and because of war-related illness. The first post-war yearbook contains a list of the students who lost their lives during the war which takes up 62 pages and gives an overview of the name, place of birth, field of study and cause of death (where possible) of each student. See *Annuaire de l'Université catholique de Louvain*, 1915-1919, 259-322. In the following footnotes, the university's yearbooks will be referred to as *Annuaire* with the relevant year and page number. About the fate of Leuven's Law Faculty during the war, see also Waelkens, Stevens and Snaet, *Geschiedenis van de Leuvense rechtsfaculteit*, 204.
4   Only at that point a Faculty of Economics and Social Sciences was established, which would later be split down the middle. See Waelkens, Stevens and Snaet, *Geschiedenis van de Leuvense rechtsfaculteit*, 189-190. The lawyer and philosopher Victor Brants (cf. infra) was instrumental in starting the two corresponding 'Schools' within the Law Faculty, both of which would gain independence in 1950.

of Thomist Philosophy in 1882. We introduce two key players of Catholic social teaching in Leuven: Charles Périn and his student and successor Victor
Brants. Their biographical overview is by no means exhaustive and the reader
can find more information on both elsewhere in this book.

Charles Périn (1815-1905) was a pioneer at the Law Faculty and found himself part of an academic community which was still regaining its standing.[5]
The old Catholic University of Leuven (often referred to as the Old University of
Leuven or Studium Generale Lovaniense) had been shut down by the French
revolutionaries in 1797 and its successor only saw the light of day in 1834, first
in Mechelen, one year later back in Leuven. It was in this context that Périn
succeeded Charles de Coux[6], his former teacher[7], as Chair of Political Economy, after a brief stint just teaching *le droit public* and *le droit administratif*.[8] He
was known for his ultramontane views and maintained good relations with
Pope Pius XI.[9] Périn also became president of the Confrérie de St.-Michel, an
association of lay ultramontanists.[10] In 1878, he and his supporters proposed
a change to Belgium's constitution allowing it to become an explicitly Catholic
state.[11] Only a couple of years later, in 1881, the tide had turned for Périn: a
scandal forced him to resign.[12] He subsequently turned his view to France and
did not participate in the Liège congresses.[13] However, he did not stop writing.
In 1892, for example, he published a brief note on fair wages.[14]

Périn's socio-economic thinking fused capitalist influences with conservative Catholicism, as an antithesis to liberalism and socialism.[15] The *question
ouvrière* would not be solved by protective social legislation, so he contend-

5   For an extensive overview, see Stevens, "Charles Périn". As evidence of Périn's influence
     at the time, see also P. Heyrman, "A Conservative Reading of *Rerum novarum* through a
     Neo-Scholastic Lens: the Jesuit Auguste Castelein (1840-1922) and the Belgian *Patrons
     Catholiques*", elsewhere in this book.
6   About him, see "Charles de Coux".
7   They would go on to correspond for years, often about Périn's works. The latter's archive
     contains letters between them from 1833 until 1864, the year of de Coux's death. Dumont
     and Louant, *Inventaire des papiers Charles Périn*, 10, nos. 100-101.
8   Brants, "Notice sur Charles Périn ", xvii.
9   Dumont and Louant, *Inventaire des papiers Charles Périn*, 5. Two papal letters were sent in
     praise of Périn's works, being *Les libertés populaires* (1861) and *Lois de la société chré-
     tienne* (1871).
10   Lamberts, "Joseph de Hemptinne", 88-89.
11   Id., "Het ultramontanisme in België", 53.
12   Some of Périn's letters, in which he was very critical of the Belgian bishops and Cardinal
     Deschamps in particular, were published. An audience with Pope Leo XIII did not bear
     fruit.
13   De Maeyer, "De ultramontanen en de gildenbeweging", 245.
14   See K. Dewaele, "Neothomism and the Debates on the Just Wage in Belgium (1879-1914)",
     elsewhere in this book.
15   Brants, "Notice sur Charles Périn", xxiii.

ed.[16] Only faith-based renunciation on behalf of the ruling classes, their charitable efforts and voluntary patronage toward the workers, would restore social
harmony.[17] Together with other members of the Confrérie de St.-Michel Périn
also developed a relatively modest[18] corporatist model of society, independent
of the German, Bismarckian model.[19]

Périn's student, Victor Brants (1856-1917), had been teaching for several
years at the Leuven School of Agriculture, of which he was one of the founders[20], when he took over the Chair of Political Economy in 1881.[21] He would
retain this post until his death. In 1883, he became professor at the Faculty
of Arts and Philosophy and taught a wide variety of courses, i.a. modern and
contemporary history, statistics, *Le droit rural*, *L'économie sociale au point
de vue des intérêts agricoles*, *Histoire des classes rurales*, *Législation ouvrière
comparée*, *Le régime du crédit* and *Le crédit et la spéculation dans la législation
comparée*.[22] Respected by his peers for his extensive intellectual horizon, he
is said to have reached a bibliography of 176 works.[23] As the global cataclysm
of World War I struck Leuven, Brants fled to Brussels, where he would teach
classes that the public could attend free of charge until mere weeks before his
death.[24]

At the risk of grossly oversimplifying Brants' work and impact, it can be
said that his thinking evolved in the following way. Early in his career, Brants
was a clear student of Périn, whose influence is mainly visible until around
1885.[25] This was not in the least caused by the fact that both had studied the
French sociologist Frédéric Le Play, whose approach clearly inspired the Société Belge d'Economie Sociale (1881).[26] In the period 1885-1890 Brants grad-

---

16   Brants, "Notice sur Charles Périn", xxx. For this view, he was criticised during his life and
     after his death: Van Dievoet et al., eds., *Lovanium docet*, 160.
17   Brants, "Notice sur Charles Périn", xxii.
18   The workers' role was mainly limited to being consulted about production processes. See
     De Maeyer, "De ultramontanen en de gildenbeweging", 239.
19   Brants, "Notice sur Charles Périn", xxxvi. Brants himself was much more familiar with the
     German style of corporatism: in 1894, he wrote the work *Le régime corporatif au XIXe siècle
     dans les états Germaniques: étude de législation sociale comparée*.
20   Starting in 1878, at which point he had received doctoral titles in both philosophy and law.
     Van Dievoet et al., eds., *Lovanium docet*, 181.
21   *Annuaire* 1882, 13.
22   *Annuaire* 1880, 13; 1881, 13; 1882, 13; 1895, 50; 1896, 50; 1897, 52. See also Van Dievoet et
     al., eds., *Lovanium docet*, 181.
23   Terlinden, "M. le prof. Brants", 440.
24   Ibid., 447-448.
25   Meerts, "De Leuvense hoogleraar Victor Brants: sociale ideeën", 104. That is not to say that
     Brants echoed Périn's ideas. For instance, he stayed closer to *Rerum novarum* than Périn
     ever did.
26   Terlinden, "M. le prof. Brants", 442. One notable member of the Société was Auguste Cas-
     telein: see P. Heyrman, "A Conservative Reading of *Rerum novarum* through a Neo-Scho-
     lastic Lens: the Jesuit Auguste Castelein (1840-1922) and the Belgian *Patrons Catholiques*",
     elsewhere in this book.

ually distanced himself from the conservative teachings of Périn and his associates. He developed a more nuanced and realistic view on social issues, although he remained firmly convinced that solving the *question ouvrière* above-all required a moral and religious restoration. This evolution is at least partly due to the fact that Brants, following his more conservative teacher Le Play, observed society as it was and induced his findings from there.[27] From the 1890s onwards Brants would moderately advocate social legislation.[28] His corporatist views on social relations and how they could be embedded in law were largely inspired by the example of the Germanic countries.[29]

The neo-Thomist thinkers at the Law Faculty

The first neo-Thomist: Théodore Fontaine (1858-1898)

The life and work of Théodore Fontaine, born in Tienen on 21 December 1858, was tragically short.[30] Nevertheless, his influence on the Law Faculty and the university are considerable. The first reason is that after receiving his degree as Doctor of Laws he became Désiré Mercier's first Doctor in Thomist Philosophy in 1885. Mercier's professorship in this discipline had only been established three years prior. Two days before defending his doctoral thesis, Fontaine had already been awarded the title of *Licencié en philosophie de saint Thomas*.[31] His thesis was entitled *La Sensation et la pensée* and received critical acclaim.[32] This was evidenced by the fact that Mercier gave a copy of it to Leo XIII when visiting Rome in 1885.[33] Fontaine thus put Thomism in the limelight again in Leuven, only six years after *Aeterni Patris* and before the Institut supérieur de philosophie was founded (in 1889).

The second reason why Fontaine merits mentioning is that he became responsible for the new course *Le droit social dans ses rapports avec la question ouvrière* in 1886.[34] This course had seen the light of day under the influence of then-rector Pieraerts.[35] The "first neo-Thomist" immediately applied his knowledge to a topical matter: "It was a happy initiative to study the serious problems of social life in the light of philosophical principles",

27   Deferme and De Maeyer, "Entre sciences sociales et politique", 154.
28   And his voice was heard, as he was involved with the Commission du Travail, established by the Belgian government as a reaction to the *question ouvrière*, from its inception.
29   Meerts, "De Leuvense hoogleraar Victor Brants: een brugfiguur", 198. Quite remarkably, his contemporary Terlinden remains silent about any radical shifts in Brants' thinking.
30   Abts, "Théodore Fontaine".
31   De Raeymaeker, "Les origines de l'Institut supérieur de philosophie, 523, note 30.
32   De Wulf, "Nécrologie: M. Th. Fontaine".
33   De Raeymaeker, "Les origines de l'Institut supérieur de philosophie", 528.
34   *Annuaire* 1887, 15 and 214.
35   De Wulf, "Nécrologie: M. Th. Fontaine", 452, note 3.

so stated Maurice De Wulf (1867-1947) in Fontaine's obituary in 1898.[36] After his untimely death, Simon Deploige, another scholar at the forefront of the Leuven neo-Thomist movement (cf. infra), would take over the course.[37] As of 1889 Fontaine also taught moral philosophy. Typical for the neo-Thomist scholars of the Law Faculty, Fontaine crossed faculty borders: he also joined the Faculty of Arts and Sciences and became secretary of the Higher Institute of Philosophy in 1890. Two years earlier Fontaine had co-founded the Société Philosophique de Louvain, becoming its first secretary. Membership was reserved to former students of Thomist philosophy, i.e. those having at least the degree of *Licencié*. Léon de Lantsheere (cf. infra) was another founding member and Simon Deploige would join the society two years later. In 1894, this society founded a new journal, providing a forum for the members' common academic thread: the *Revue néo-scolastique*.[38] By that time, however, the story of Theodore Fontaine had almost reached its conclusion. One year prior, in 1893, he resigned from his academic functions for health reasons.[39] He died in Lachy (France) on 19 August 1898, just shy of forty years old.

The minister: Léon de Lantsheere (1862-1912)

Léon de Lantsheere was born on 23 September 1862 in Brussels.[40] He studied in Leuven. Having shown an initial interest in mathematics, he ultimately studied law, but never left his former passion behind.[41] He graduated as Doctor in Law and *Licencié en philosophie selon saint Thomas* in 1885. One year later, he became Doctor in Thomist Philosophy, the second one graduating under Mercier's supervision. His dissertation was entitled *Du bien au point de vue ontologique et moral*.[42]

---

36   De Wulf, "Nécrologie: M. Th. Fontaine", 452.
37   Waelkens et al., eds., *Geschiedenis van de Leuvense rechtsfaculteit*, 184.
38   De Raeymaeker, "Les origines de l'Institut supérieur de philosophie", 524-526.
39   Strikingly, the university's *Annuaires* are completely silent about his departure and later death. According to De Raeymaeker, this is due to a disagreement Mercier and then-rector Abbeloos had about the direction which the School of Saint Thomas – the later Institut Supérieur – ought to take. De Raeymaeker, "Les origines de l'Institut supérieur de philosophie", 553-554.
40   Vynck, "Léon de Lantsheere". On de Lantsheere, see also Heyrman, "Léon de Lantsheere".
41   Ladeuze, "Discours", xxxii-xxxiii.
42   Ibid., xxxiii; De Raeymaeker, "Les origines de l'Institut supérieur de philosophie", 523-524, note 30. Contrary to Ladeuze, De Raeymaeker writes that de Lantsheere only received his degree of *licencié* in 1886, a few months before being awarded the title of Doctor in Thomist Philosophy.

Afterwards, de Lantsheere joined the bar of the Brussels Court of Appeal.[43] One year later, in 1889, he started his political career as a member for the Catholic Party of the Provincial Council of Brabant and as a member of the High Council of the Congo. In 1900 he was elected as representative for Brussels in the Belgian Chamber of Representatives, a position he would keep until his death.[44] Contrary to Théodore Fontaine, he first took an academic post in the Leuven Higher Institute of Philosophy (in 1892, as *conférencier*)[45] before becoming a professor at the Law Faculty (in 1895).[46] He taught the courses *Le droit penal* and *Les institutions civiles comparées*. The latter one was part of the curriculum at the School for Political and Social Sciences, focusing alternately on the topics of family and property.[47] De Lantsheere was elected dean of the Law Faculty between 1903 and 1905. In the following years he became a key figure in the political debate on the future of Congo Free State. De Lantsheere would write the report of the special parliamentary commission on the issue, preparing the administrative and legal takeover of the Congo by the Belgian state on 18 October 1908.[48]

In the subsequent years de Lantsheere reached his political zenith as Belgian Minister of Justice (1908-1911) a position that also his father Théophile, since 1905 Governor of the National Bank of Belgium, had held in 1871-1878. In his eulogy, the Leuven Rector Ladeuze quoted the law of 12 August 1911 as his major accomplishment, a long-awaited text granting legal personality to the two private universities of Belgium, the Catholic one in Leuven and the Free University of Brussels.[49] After his term as Minister of Justice, de Lantsheere returned to the Law Faculty, where he immediately became Dean again. This new impetus for his academic career, however, was only short-lived. De Lantsheere died unexpectedly on 26 August 1912 in Asse, then aged 49.

Mathematics, as mentioned before, was only one discipline in which de Lantsheere was well-versed. Ladeuze states that he was active in "philosophy, law, mathematics, Assyrian language and culture, the origin of Christianity,

---

43 Waelkens, Stevens and Snaet, *Geschiedenis van de Leuvense rechtsfaculteit*, 185 and 195. Stevens first writes that he already went to Brussels in 1880, but that seems hard to believe, as that was the year in which he started studying law. As is said on page 195, this must have been 1888.

44 Vynck, "Léon de Lantsheere".

45 De Raeymaeker, "Les origines de l'Institut supérieur de philosophie", 523-524, note 30. According to Stevens, this was only in 1893 and de Lantsheere kept this position only for ten years: Waelkens, Stevens and Snaet, *Geschiedenis van de Leuvense rechtsfaculteit*, 185.

46 Vynck, "Léon de Lantsheere".

47 *Annuaire* 1896, 40 and 50; 1897, 52; Waelkens, Stevens and Snaet, *Geschiedenis van de Leuvense rechtsfaculteit*, 185.

48 Waelkens, Stevens and Snaet, *Geschiedenis van de Leuvense rechtsfaculteit*, 195-196.

49 Ladeuze, "Discours", xxxv; Waelkens, Stevens and Snaet, *Geschiedenis van de Leuvense rechtsfaculteit*, 195.

mediaeval Arabic philosophers, modern literature and history of art".[50] He also published on the history and language of the Hittites and Amorites and on Babylonian law. He spoke Persian, but, remarkably, no Dutch.[51]

De Lantsheere's conferences at the Higher Institute display his broad philosophical interest. Either he discussed the works of (early) modern philosophers such as Descartes, Kant, Spinoza and Hegel, or he dealt with overarching topics such as the classification of the sciences, the history of philosophy or sociology.[52] At the Institute, he was particularly renowned as an expert of Kantianism that he had studied as part of his dissertation.[53] De Lantsheere was also involved in the Belgian celebration of the centenary of the French liberal Catholic Charles Forbes René de Montalembert. He spoke at this meeting in February 1912, as did Cardinal Mercier and the French politician Henry Cochin.[54]

As mentioned above, de Lantsheere was the second doctoral student in Thomist Philosophy of Mercier. In his dissertation, *Du bien au point de vue ontologique et moral*, he describes the parallels between neo-Thomism and Kantianism, although he remains faithful to the former.[55] Descamps paints a picture of de Lantsheere as being "resolved to contribute, by word and deed, to the defense of Thomistic philosophy". Maurice De Wulf, in his obituary, writes that de Lantsheere's dissertation predicted a conflict between two worlds: "in the last twenty-six years [between de Lantsheere's dissertation and his death], Kantianism has gained considerable ground, and Thomism, whose unceasing progress is well known, is tending more and more to become the philosophy of Catholic spiritualists". Also, according to Stevens, de Lantsheere's legal thinking and teaching drew much inspiration from his philosophical education.[56] He for instance applied the method of speculative sociology as it was studied at the Higher Institute of Philosophy.[57] These sociological insights also underpinned his article "L'origine de la peine au point de vue sociologique".[58]

From a neo-Thomist perspective, de Lantsheere combatted both eighteenth-century natural law (as did his colleague Deploige, cf. infra) and positivism. His objection against the former was that it assumed an idealised situ-

50   Ladeuze, "Discours", xxxiii.
51   Waelkens, Stevens and Snaet, *Geschiedenis van de Leuvense rechtsfaculteit*, 185-186. See his *De la race et la langue des Hittites* (1891), *Hittites et Amorites* (1887) and *Le droit à Babylone et l'évolution juridique* (1894)
52   Descamps, "Léon de Lantsheere", xxxix.
53   Van Dievoet et al., eds., *Lovanium docet*, 187.
54   Descamps, "Léon de Lantsheere", xlviii. De Lantsheere's speech, *Montalembert et les temps modernes*, was published in *Montalembert: discours prononcés à la manifestation organisée à Bruxelles à l'occasion du centenaire de Montalembert* (1913).
55   Ibid., xxxix-xl.
56   Waelkens, Stevens and Snaet, *Geschiedenis van de Leuvense rechtsfaculteit*, 185.
57   Van Dievoet et al., eds., *Lovanium docet*, 187.
58   De Lantsheere, "L'origine de la peine au point de vue sociologique".

ation which contrasted starkly with the law as it existed, while he reproached the latter for relativising all legal concepts and rules, and only dealing with legal evolution and change. In his article "L'évolution moderne du droit naturel", he argues that every legal system has some rules which are wholly contingent, but that there is always a fundamental legal order, as well as *biens juridiques* which ought to be respected.[59]

De Lantsheere's social commitment is demonstrated, first of all, in his political work. He belonged to the so-called '*jeune droite*', the Christian Democrat faction of the Catholic Party. Together with Henri Carton de Wiart and Jules Renkin, he was a member of the editorial staff of the Christian Democrat journal *L'Avenir Social*, later renamed *La justice sociale*.[60] The *Jeune droite* brought itself in the limelight by i.a. supporting the socialists in Parliament to pass the bill that regulated working hours for miners.[61]

Unsurprisingly, de Lantsheere's neo-Thomist background was reflected in his social thinking. One example of this is the article "Le pain volé", in which he shone a Thomist light on property rights.[62] The outcome was a relatively progressive view on a just distribution of property.[63] De Lantsheere was also involved in the Société d'Economie Sociale, of which Victor Brants was the president. To its members, he delivered a reportedly very personal speech on "La personnification civile" that was later published in the *Revue sociale Catholique*.

The priest: Simon Deploige (1868-1927)[64]

Simon Deploige was born in Tongeren on 15 October 1868.[65] In 1884 he registered at the university in Leuven, then just 16 years old, and became a Doctor in Philosophy and Arts in 1888. He was awarded the degree of Doctor in Law in

---

59 Descamps, "Léon de Lantsheere", xli; De Lantsheere, "L'Evolution moderne du droit naturel".
60 Van Dievoet et al., eds., *Lovanium doce*, 187; Schokkaert, "La justice sociale".
61 Deferme, "de Lantsheere, Léon", 121-122.
62 See K. Dewaele, "Neothomism and the Debates on the Just Wage in Belgium (1879-1914)", elsewhere in this book.
63 Van Dievoet et al., eds., *Lovanium docet*, 187.
64 Guy Deploige, a relative of Simon Deploige who does genealogical research, has self-published a book about the latter: <http://www.deploige.be/boek%20Mgr%20Deploige.PDF>. It is an impressive biography, including an abundance of photographs and references to Deploige's letters, and can also be found in the library of the Higher Institute of Philosophy in Leuven. A large part of it seems based on the eulogy by Defourny, "Mgr. Simon Deploige" (*Annuaire* 1927-1929) – the text also shows that this eulogy was consulted. However, in the following, I will not cite the book, as there is no way to judge the quality of the work or its underlying research. It still more than deserves mentioning and can be a good reference work for the reader with a specific interest in Deploige.
65 Meeussen, "Simon Deploige".

1889, becoming *Licencié en philosophie thomiste* in the spring of 1890.[66] Maurice Defourny (cf. infra) admiringly remarked that Deploige had concluded his studies at the age of 22, concluding a curriculum which in ordinary circumstances should have taken him eight years.[67] After his studies he registered as a lawyer at the Tongeren Bar, where he would stay until 1893. In those years Deploige was asked to conduct an international study on the practice of plebiscite. This political assignment was linked to the then debate on whether or not referenda ought to be introduced in the Belgian Constitution. Deploige made a study trip to Switzerland and published several contributions on the topic. He was clearly not in favour of referenda, finding them only useful in states that had neither king nor president. Belgium, obviously, was a bad fit.[68]

During his time at the Tongeren Bar, Deploige was offered a Chair of Comparative Constitutional Law at the State University of Liège, founded by King William I of the United Kingdom of the Netherlands in 1817. Deploige refused, apparently because he wanted to remain independent from public authority.[69] His return to academia, however, followed soon after. In 1893 Mercier asked him to become one of the first four staff members of the Leuven Higher Institute of Philosophy, as a representative of the Law Faculty.[70] The others were Maurice De Wulf, Armand Thiéry and Désiré Nys. They hailed from the Faculties of Philosophy and Arts, Medicine and Sciences respectively.[71] In Leuven, Deploige taught the courses *Législation rurale* and *Le droit social dans ses rapports avec la question ouvrière* until 1906.[72] In 1903, a Chair of Social Economy was established, with Deploige as its first holder. From then on he taught a corresponding course on the history of economic and political doctrines.[73] The chair's purpose was to enable research on the *question ouvrière* in the spirit of *Rerum novarum*.[74] Later, Deploige also taught natural law and social philosophy.[75]

While working at the university, Deploige was also trained as a priest. He was ordained in Liège in 1896. When Mercier became archbishop in 1906, Deploige succeeded him as president of the Higher Institute of Philosophy. In 1912, he became Honorary Prelate of Pope Benedict XV, earning him the title of *Monseigneur*. Deploige made full use of his close relationship with the pope when World War I broke out. One month before witnessing the devastation of

---

66   According to De Raeymaeker, Deploige achieved that degree one year later, i.e. in March 1891. De Raeymaeker, "Les origines de l'Institut supérieur de philosophie", 524, note 30.
67   Defourny, "Mgr. Simon Deploige", xc.
68   Ibid., xci-xciii.
69   Ibid., xciv.
70   *Kardinaal Mercier, stichter van het Hoger instituut voor wijsbegeerte*, 23.
71   De Raeymaeker, "Les origines de l'Institut supérieur de philosophie", 557.
72   Defourny, "Mgr. Simon Deploige", xciv.
73   Meeussen, "Simon Deploige".
74   Wils, *Het verdriet van Leuven*, 101.
75   *Annuaire* 1927-1929, 13.

Leuven in August 1914, he had had the prescience to establish a field hospital at the Higher Institute, anticipating the German invasion. In December of that year he was sent to Rome as an envoy of the Belgian government-in-exile in Le Havre. There, he reported on the German atrocities in Belgium to Pope Benedict. Defourny observes that Deploige's efforts bore fruit: twice in 1915, the Vatican condemned the German destruction of Belgium.[76] Immediately after his mission to Vatican City, Deploige was sent to Spain, accompanied by lawyer Valentin Brifaut. The country had remained neutral and showed no interest in condemning the German invasion in Belgium.[77] At least part of Deploige's task was to "discredit the German propaganda".[78] In the meantime, he remained in contact with Pope Benedict XV.[79] He returned with a manifesto entitled *A Belgica*. It contained an unconditional condemnation of "the assault on Belgium" (Defourny's words) and was signed by more than 500 prominent Spanish Catholics.[80]

Still during the war, in 1917, Deploige founded Le Foyer du Soldat Belge in Lourdes. Its purpose was to provide holidays for war-weary soldiers. After the war, Deploige not only resumed his academic duties but also became a driving force behind the construction of a new university library. Having turned 50, he also wanted to redirect his attention to his own research. He did, however, have a brief stint in national politics as well: in 1923 he became a Provincial Senator for Limburg as the substitute of Eugène Keesen, another honorary prelate, who had died that year. He successfully stood for election in 1925.[81] In the Senate, Deploige was mainly involved in debates centring on Catholic morals and the freedom of education. He was also a member of the General Council of the Leuven university.[82] Simon Deploige died suddenly on 19 November 1927.

While still a student, Deploige had already manifested himself in the fight against socialism. One surviving anecdote recounts the time he spoke out at a congress of socialist students and assured them that cooperation between them and the Catholics would never be possible. This does not mean, however, that he can be considered as a radical ultramontanist or a social conservative following in the footsteps of Périn. Deploige was one of the founding members of the Belgian Democratic League, the cradle of the later Christian

76 Defourny, "Mgr. Simon Deploige", c.
77 Ibid., ci. According to Defourny, the Spanish policy was also due to rivalry with England (i.a. because of the classic apple of discord of Gibraltar) and France (because of discussions on border controls and France's success in Morocco).
78 Van Rompaey, *België in het Vaticaans archief*, 301.
79 A letter from Deploige to Pope Benedict, dating from 26 January 1915, was found in the Vatican Archives: Van Rompaey, *België in het Vaticaans archief*, 147, (93.V)120.
80 Defourny, "Mgr. Simon Deploige", xci.
81 This made him one of the many professors from Leuven who were involved in politics: see Waelkens, Stevens and Snaet, *Geschiedenis van de Leuvense rechtsfaculteit*, 268.
82 *Annuaire 1927-1929*, 13.

labour movement, and was part of its Central Conseil until 1895. That year, he left the Ligue due to internal disputes, following the example of his friend, founder-president Joris Helleputte.[83]

As a graduate in Thomist philosophy, Deploige was entitled to become a member of the Société Philosophique de Louvain. At the Higher Institute he also founded a Cercle d'Etudes Sociales and participated in its weekly meetings, partly because he liked interacting with the students.[84] He contributed to the Institute's *Revue catholique sociale*, from its formation in 1897 and was its editorial secretary until 1906. The *Revue* had a purpose similar to that of the later Chair of Social Economy.[85] The journal existed under its original name until 1920 and was then rebooted as *Revue catholique sociale et juridique* until 1925.[86] Deploige was also an editor of *Le mouvement sociologique*, which existed from 1900 until 1906.[87] Other periodicals in which he was involved as a collaborator or contributor were the *Revue néo-scolastique*, the *Revue catholique du droit*, the *Revue des sciences philosophiques et théologiques*, the *Comptes rendus des semaines sociales de France*, the *Revue des jeunes*, *Les lettres* and *Le correspondant*.[88]

As mentioned above, Deploige taught a course explicitly dealing with natural law.[89] Its contents were closely linked to his sociological research. His major study on this field, *Le conflit de la morale et de la sociologie*[90], openly attacked positivist and relativists scholars as Comte, Spencer, Simmel, Durkheim, Lévy-Bruhl and Duguit.[91] According to Deploige, the apparent conflict between morality and sociology particularly stemmed from the work of Lucien Lévy-Bruhl, a French anthropologist and sociologist who was influenced by Emile Durkheim. In his work *La morale et la science des mœurs*, Lévy-Bruhl had argued that the modern sociological method and the traditional theoretical method were mutually exclusive ways of observing societal phenomena. As a devoted neo-Thomist Deploige set out to save morality, above all from the claws of Durkheim.[92] According to Deploige, sociology was incapable of threatening natural law, or at least the variant of which he was

83 Defourny, "Mgr. Simon Deploige", xc.
84 Ibid., xcviii; Meeussen, "Simon Deploige".
85 Wils, *Het verdriet van Leuven*, 102.
86 Schokkaert, "Revue Sociale Catholique".
87 Van der Meijden, "Le Mouvement Sociologique".
88 Defourny, "Mgr. Simon Deploige", xcviii.
89 Confusingly, this term is often used interchangeably with 'morality' in accounts of Deploige's thinking. This is reflected in the following paragraphs.
90 Defourny, "Mgr. Simon Deploige", xcv; Wils, *Het verdriet van Leuven*, 98.
91 Defourny, "Mgr. Simon Deploige", xcv.
92 Deploige was particularly disturbed by his comparative analyses of the social function of different religions. Vanderstraeten, "Who Had Faith in Sociology?", 464; Defourny, "Mgr. Simon Deploige", xcvii-xcviii; Wils, *Het verdriet van Leuven*, 98-99; Id., "Les intellectuels catholiques et la sociologie en Belgique", 76-79.

a proponent. He aligned with sociology insofar as it criticised the abstract, eighteenth-century natural law of Rousseau and the French eclectics, a variant which did he not favour.[93] Deploige argued that his preferred natural law escaped unscathed from the attack of sociology since Thomas Aquinas himself had used observation when constructing his *scientia moralis*. The angelic doctor had also derived social rules from these observations when they disclosed certain patterns. Deploige's conclusion was clear: that what Durkheim and his associates considered as innovative had been done centuries before by Thomas Aquinas.[94] As such, Deploige not only presented Thomas Aquinas as a sociologist[95] but also asserted that Thomism was capable of incorporating the relatively young scientific discipline of sociology, or at least as Deploige understood it.

Al this does not mean that Deploige was an adversary of sociology; rather, he opposed its French positivist protagonists. In his view the new discipline could be a useful auxiliary for morality, but not a competing method.[96] He envisaged two situations in which sociology could contribute to natural law. According to Deploige, every person has a destiny to fulfil; he or she ought to use his or her talents productively under the guidance of reason and of free will. In order to reach this goal, social relations are indispensable, but these relations are historically diverse and contingent on particular circumstances. Natural law is there to make a choice between the various options. This choice can be made more accurately, or at least with more expertise, after methodically observing the aforementioned social relations and weighing their costs and benefits. This is the first contribution of sociology to natural law. The second appears once the choice has been made. Through observation and methodical analysis, sociology can then help to clarify the circumstances under which a sub-optimal situation can be changed.[97] Deploige's aversion of the French, positivist sociologists led him to the statement that not they but the German Adam Müller had developed the new discipline. Deploige wittily points out that Müller's major work was already published when Auguste Comte was only ten years old.[98]

---

93 Defourny, "Mgr. Simon Deploige", xcvii. Defourny also mentions Kant, Cousin, Jouffroy and Caro. According to Deploige, they erred because they derived societal rules from the premise of an isolated individual.
94 Wils, *Het verdriet van Leuven*, 99-100.
95 Vanderstraeten, "Who Had Faith in Sociology?", 465.
96 Defourny, "Mgr. Simon Deploige", xcv.
97 Ibid., xcvi.
98 Wils, *Het verdriet van Leuven*, 100.

The philosopher-economist: Maurice Defourny (1878-1953)

Maurice Defourny was born in Herstal on 6 November 1878. He was part of the
first generation of laymen who registered to study at Leuven's Higher Institute
of Philosophy. First, he became Doctor in Philosophy, then, in 1902, *Maître
agrégé* in Thomist philosophy. His dissertation, supervised by Deploige, was
entitled *La sociologie positive: Auguste Comte*.[99] As did Deploige, Defourny
considered the positivist Comte a useful ally in the battle against liberalism,
particularly in terms of methodology.[100] Having concluded his studies in Leuven, Defourny undertook research stays with the French sociologists Durkheim
and Tarde, and the German economists Schmoller and Wagner.[101] Despite having visited these scholars, he was firmly convinced that Catholicism remained
the main driver for the moralisation of society and that sociology ought to play
a modest role.[102] In 1903, he returned to Leuven and started teaching *Histoire
des théories sociales*, a newly created professorship at the Institute.[103] He was
also charged with the course on social economics, both at the Institute and at
the School of Agriculture. Defourny joined the Thomist Société Philosophique
de Louvain[104] and quickly climbed the academic ranks, becoming full professor in 1909.[105] In the post-war period he succeeded Victor Brants in the chair
of Political Economy[106], but continued teaching *Histoire des théories sociales*
and also became responsible for the *Conférence de philosophie sociale* at the
Institute.[107]

　　Particularly in the pre-war years Defourny was heavily involved in political and social matters. Several of his early publications focused on topical
political issues. In 1912 he became an associate of the study services of the
Ligue Démocratique Belge.[108] In addition he also published several philosophical studies, notably on Aristoteles, whose *Politika* he analysed extensively.[109]
He joined various associations and became editorial secretary of the *Revue
catholique sociale*. After the war, as his academic responsibilities increased,
Deploige was less involved in periodicals and associations. But he did coordinate the activities of the Union Internationale d'Etudes Sociales de Malines, a

99　Id., "Les intellectuels catholiques et la sociologie en Belgique", 71.
100　Ibid., 81.
101　Vynck, "Maurice Defourny"; Wils, "Les intellectuels catholiques et la sociologie en Bel-
　　gique", 76.
102　Vanderstraeten, "Who Had Faith in Sociology?", 466.
103　Ibid., 466, note 12.
104　De Raeymaeker, "Les origines de l'Institut supérieur de philosophie", 525, note 32.
105　Rousseaux, "M. Maurice Defourny", i.
106　*Annuaire* 1913, 13; 1920-1926, 14.
107　*Annuaire* 1920-1926, 14.
108　Vynck, "Maurice Defourny".
109　Leclerq and Rousseaux, "M. Maurice Defourny", iv.

structure modelled on the Union de Fribourg (1884-1891).[110] Defourny was particularly involved in the drafting of the Union de Malines' *Code Social*. At the university he replaced Deploige as president of the Cercle d'Etudes Sociales and was Dean of the Law Faculty from 1921 until 1923.[111]

Defourny, who in pre-war years had been labelled as a philosopher and political thinker, gradually became an *économiste social*.[112] The latter characterisation is appropriate, because Defourny's economic work explicitly drew from Christian philosophy and morality.[113] What is more, he stayed away from reducing the complexity of reality to a few oversimplified hypotheses.[114] Although in the post-war years he stayed further away from actual politics, he continued to study social issues, the rising tensions between labour and capital in particular. As his Leuven predecessors in political economy, he asserted that only a middle way in between the extremes of socialist collectivism and liberal individualism could restore social harmony.[115] Defourny was convinced that strengthening professional organisation and introducing innovative forms of co-management in companies would lead to economic pacification.[116] Such a vast corporatist reorganisation of both society and enterprise would require time and effort, but was definitely worth striving for.[117] To date nothing has been written about the later stages of Defourny's career. However, it is certain that at some point he was appointed Emeritus Professor. He died in 1953.

Provisional conclusion

Although it remains difficult to draw in-depth conclusions from these brief biographical overviews, some general patterns can nevertheless be identified. Ideally, these should be refined by further research on the works of these four scholars and on how neo-Thomism was disseminated at the Leuven Law Faculty through other channels. We might also gain valuable insight from research into the courses and works of those (contemporary and later) legal scholars who had no particular link to the Thomist revival but were nonetheless influenced or even trained by our protagonists.

---

110 Rousseaux, "M. Maurice Defourny", ii. The Union de Fribourg was founded in 1884 to stimulate reflection on the *question ouvrière*. Its resolutions served as the basis for the encyclical *Rerum novarum* in 1891. See Van Molle, "Croissance économique et éthique catholique", 323 and 326.
111 Vynck, "Maurice Defourny".
112 Leclerq and Rousseaux, "M. Maurice Defourny", v.
113 Rousseaux, "M. Maurice Defourny", ii-iii.
114 Leclerq and Rousseaux, "M. Maurice Defourny", v.
115 Ibid., vi.
116 Rousseaux, "M. Maurice Defourny", ii.
117 Ibid., iii.

First, it is striking to see to what extent the *question ouvrière* played a central role in the works of all the quoted scholars. A great deal of continuity can be observed, from Charles Périn (born in 1815) all the way to Maurice Defourny (born in 1878). Any answer they may be thought to have formulated went without fail in the direction of a corporatist social order. Confrontational social action was clearly nowhere to be found, even in the case of a Christian Democrat such as Léon de Lantsheere. Social mobility did not seem to be an end in itself, nor was it a means of achieving social peace. Rather, the solution lay in reconciliation, cooperation and gradual rapprochement between employers and workers. What also recurred was the argument that a Catholic inspired corporatist society offered an answer to both liberalism and socialism.

A second development that occurs during the pre-war period is the tentative emancipation of the social sciences as studied by the neo-Thomists. This is evidenced by the various holders of the chair in *L'économie politique*. Both Charles Périn and Victor Brants were trained as lawyers and taught what we would now call social sciences in addition to legal subjects. It was only Brants' successor, Maurice Defourny, educated not as a lawyer but as a philosopher, who only taught social sciences, even if he too was attached to the Faculty of Law.

A third and final trend is the integration of neo-Thomism in mainstream thinking. The first neo-Thomists were very explicit in their ambition to promote it. Defourny, in contrast, was a graduate of the Institute but evidently did not feel a pressing need to explicitly spread the neo-Thomist word. Rather, he combined his background with experience drawn from research stays at other universities (cf. supra) and developed his own views (even if he explicitly incorporated Christian philosophy and morality into his corporatist stances, reminiscent of those of his predecessors). One hypothesis for further research is therefore that, as the Institute and its body of students grew, the neo-Thomist discourse gradually became embedded in academia after World War I – after all, *Aeterni Patris* had been published almost forty years before. However, more research is needed to test this hypothesis against the actual development of neo-Thomism in Leuven.

BIBLIOGRAPHY

Abts, Johan. "Théodore Fontaine". In *ODIS*, 2016. <www.odis.be/lnk/PS_79184> (last consulted on 21 June 2017).

Abts, Johan and Sharon Vynck. "Charles Périn". In *ODIS*, 2013. <www.odis.be/lnk/PS_5768> (last consulted on 20 June 2017).

Annuaire de l'Université catholique de Louvain. Leuven: Vanlinthout en Vandezande, 1845, 1846, 1880, 1881, 1882, 1884, 1887, 1895, 1896, 1897, 1913, 1915-1919, 1920-1926 and 1927-1929.

Brants, Victor. "Notice sur Charles Périn, par V. Brants, professeur à la Faculté de Philosophie". *Annuaire de l'Université catholique de Louvain*, 1906, Appendix, xv-liii.

"Charles de Coux". In *ODIS*, 2003. <www.odis.be/lnk/PS_5967> (last consulted on 19 June 2017).

Deferme, Jo. "de Lantsheere, Léon". In *Nouvelle biographie nationale*, vol. 10. Brussels: Académie royale de Belgique, 2010, 120-122.

Deferme, Jo and Jan De Maeyer. "Entre sciences sociales et politique. La pensée leplaysienne et les milieux catholiques belges". *Les Études Sociales*, 149-150 (2009), 147-166.

Defourny, M. "Mgr. Simon Deploige, professeur à la Faculté de Droit, président de l'Institut supérieur de philosophie. Eloge funèbre prononcé par M. le professeur Defourny". *Annuaire de l'Université catholique de Louvain*, 1927-1929, Appendix, lxxxviii-cvi.

De Lantsheere, Léon. "L'Evolution moderne du droit naturel". *Revue néo-scolastique*, 4 (1897) 15, 298-306 and 4 (1898) 17, 45-59.

De Lantsheere, Léon. "L'origine de la peine au point de vue sociologique". *Annales de Sociologie et Mouvement sociologique*, 1 (1900-1901). Paris-Brussels: Société Belge de Sociologie, 1903, 311-336.

De Maeyer, Jan. "De ultramontanen en de gildenbeweging, 1875-1896: het aandeel van de Confrérie de St.-Michel". In Emiel Lamberts, ed. *De kruistocht tegen het liberalisme. Facetten van het ultramontanisme in België in de 19de eeuw.* Leuven: Leuven University Press, 1984, 222-267.

De Raeymaeker, Louis. "Les origines de l'Institut supérieur de philosophie de Louvain". *Revue Philosophique de Louvain*, 24 (1951), 505-633.

Descamps, E. "Léon de Lantsheere. Par le baron Descamps". *Annuaire de l'Université catholique de Louvain*, 1913, Appendix, xxxvii-liv.

De Wulf, Maurice. "Nécrologie: M. Th. Fontaine". *Revue néo-scolastique*, 1898, 451-452.

De Wulf, Maurice. "Nécrologie – Léon de Lantsheere". *Revue néo-scolastique*, 1912, 563-565.

Dumont, Cécile and Armand Louant. *Inventaire des papiers Charles Périn*. Brussels: Archives générales du royaume, 1986.

Genin, Vincent. "Du champ scientifique au service de l'État belge. Le droit des gens à l'Université catholique de Louvain: juristes, réseaux et doctrines au XIXe siècle". *Annales de droit de Louvain*, 75 (2015) 2, 193-213.

Gérin, Paul. "Sociaal-katholicisme en christen-democratie (1884-1904)". In Emmanuel Gerard, ed. *De christelijke arbeidersbeweging in België*. Vol. 1. Leuven: Leuven University Press, 1991, 56-113.

Heyrman, Peter. "Léon de Lantsheere". In Wim Decock and Janwillem Oosterhuis, eds. *Great Christian Jurists in the Low Countries.* Cambridge: Cambridge University Press, forthcoming.

Kardinaal Mercier, stichter van het Hoger instituut voor wijsbegeerte aan de Universiteit te Leuven: Herdenking van de honderdste verjaring van zijn geboorte 1851-1951. Leuven: Leuvense Universitaire Uitgaven, 1951.

Ladeuze, Paulin. "Discours prononcé par Mgr P. Ladeuze, Recteur magnifique de l'Université, le jeudi 29 août 1912, aux funérailles de M. le professeur L. de Lantsheere". *Annuaire de l'Université catholique de Louvain*, 1913, Appendix, xxxii-xxxvi.

Lamberts, Emiel, ed. *Kruistocht tegen het liberalisme*. Leuven: Leuven University Press, 1984.

Lamberts, Emiel. "Het ultramontanisme in België. 1830-1914". In Emiel Lamberts, ed. *Kruistocht tegen het liberalisme*. Leuven: Leuven University Press, 1984, 38-63.

Lamberts, Emiel. "Joseph de Hemptinne: een kruisvaarder in redingote". In Emiel Lamberts, ed. *Kruistocht tegen het liberalisme*. Leuven: Leuven University Press, 1984, 64-109.

Leclerq, J. and P. Rousseaux. "M. Maurice Defourny, Professeur émérite de la Faculté de Droit. Notice par MM. les Professeurs J. Leclerq et P. Rousseaux". *Annuaire de l'Université catholique de Louvain*, 1953, Appendix, iv-viii.

Meerts, Kristin. "De Leuvense hoogleraar Victor Brants: een brugfiguur in het sociaal-katholicisme (1856-1891)". *Bijdragen tot de geschiedenis*, 65 (1982), 197-233.

Meerts, Kristin. "De Leuvense hoogleraar Victor Brants: sociale ideeën tussen katholieke romantiek en realisme (1856-1891)". *Bijdragen tot de geschiedenis*, 66 (1983), 101-130.

Meeussen, Erik. "Simon Deploige". In *ODIS*, 2010. <www.odis.be/lnk/PS_4952> (last consulted on 22 June 2017).

Rousseaux, P. "M. Maurice Defourny, Professeur émérite de la Faculté de Droit. Discours prononcé aux funérailles par M. le Professeur P. Rousseaux". *Annuaire de l'Université catholique de Louvain*, 1953, Appendix, i-iii.

Schokkaert, Luc. "Revue Sociale Catholique (1897-1920) (periodiek)". In *ODIS*, 2004. <www.odis.be/lnk/PB_8177> (last consulted on 22 June 2017).

Schokkaert, Luc. "La justice sociale (1895-1902) (periodiek)". In *ODIS*, 2005. <www.odis.be/lnk/PB_4952> (last consulted on 26 June 2017).

Stevens, Fred. "Charles Périn". In Wim Decock and Janwillem Oosterhuis, eds. *Great Christian Jurists in the Low Countries.* Cambridge: Cambridge University Press, forthcoming.

Terlinden, C. "M. le prof. Brants". *Annuaire de l'Université catholique de Louvain*, 1915-1919, 436-450.

Van der Meijden, D. "Le Mouvement Sociologique (1900-[1906]) (periodiek)". In *ODIS*, 2006. <www.odis.be/lnk/PB_17707> (last consulted on 22 June 2017).

Vanderstraeten, Raf. "Who Had Faith in Sociology? Scholarly and Ideological Divergences in Belgium around 1900". *Science in Context*, 31 (2018) 4, 457-475.

Van Dievoet, Guido et al., eds. *Lovanium docet: geschiedenis van de Leuvense rechtsfaculteit (1425-1914)*. Leuven: KU Leuven Faculteit Rechtsgeleerdheid, 1988.

Van Molle, Leen. "Croissance économique et éthique catholique: les points de vue de l'Union de Malines dans les années vingt". In Erik Aerts et al., eds. *Studia historica œconomica. Liber amicorum Herman Van der Wee*. Leuven: Leuven University Press, 1993, 317-335.

Van Rompaey, Lies. *België in het Vaticaans archief. Nuntiatuur in Brussel. 1903-1916. Regestenlijst*. Leuven-Brussels-Rome: KADOC - Belgisch Historisch Instituut te Rome, 1996. <https://kadoc.kuleuven.be/db/inv/707-4.pdf> (last consulted on 9 October 2019).

"Victor Brants". In *ODIS*, 2016. <www.odis.be/lnk/PS_2174> (last consulted on 21/06/2017).

Vynck, Sharon. "Maurice Defourny". In *ODIS*, 2010. <www.odis.be/lnk/PS_19307> (last consulted on 26 June 2017).

Vynck, Sharon. "Léon de Lantsheere". In *ODIS*, 2016. <www.odis.be/lnk/PS_4919> (last consulted on 26 June 2017).

Waelkens, Laurent, Fred Stevens and Joris Snaet. *Geschiedenis van de Leuvense rechtsfaculteit*. Bruges: die Keure, 2014.

Wils, Kaat. *Het verdriet van Leuven: de reaktie op het positivisme in het Hoger Instituut voor Wijsbegeerte (1889-1914)*. Diss. Lic. KU Leuven, 1991.

Wils, Kaat. "Les intellectuels catholiques et la sociologie en Belgique, 1880-1914". *Archives de sciences sociales des religions*, 179 (2017), 71-88.

Wils, Lode. "België in de negentiende eeuw: religieus, politiek en sociaal". In Emmanuel Gerard, ed. *De christelijke arbeidersbeweging in België*. Vol. 1. Leuven: Leuven University Press, 1991, 19-55.

NATIONAL CONTEXTS AND INTERNATIONAL NETWORKS

Lionel Groulx. Photo, 1927.
[Montreal, Archives of the Université de Montréal]

VETERA NOVIS AUGERE OR *LEUVEN QUEBEC AUGERE*
LIONEL GROULX, NEO-THOMISM AND FRENCH-CANADIAN NATIONALISM

KASPER SWERTS

In the autumn of 1907 the French-Canadian nationalist historian Lionel Groulx explained to Émile Chartier – the future vice-rector of the Université de Montréal – why he had chosen to attend courses at the university of Fribourg during the summer. In legitimating his preference for Fribourg, Groulx disclosed to his friend that:

> The Faculty of Arts of Fribourg is a hundred cubits above that of Leuven. This is an observation that results from our colloquia with professors, many of whom are alumni of Leuven, from the comparison of the two programs, from the examination of the working methods and from information taken from students who have attended both universities.[1]

Groulx's fixation on the University of Leuven [Louvain] was apparent throughout the early months of 1907, when the historian was contemplating his next destination during his sojourn in Europe. In February, he conveyed to Chartier how he was "thinking about trying his luck in Leuven" and concluded a couple months later that "in all likelihood [I] will be packing my trunks for Leuven".[2] So at first glance it comes as a surprise that Groulx ultimately chose Fribourg

---

1   "La faculté des Lettres de Fribourg est à cent coudées au-dessus de celle de Louvain. C'est une constatation qui résulte de nos colloques avec les professeurs, dont beaucoup sont des anciens de Louvain, de la comparaison des deux programmes, de l'examen des méthodes de travail et de renseignements pris auprès d'élèves qui ont fréquenté les deux Universités." Huot, Lalonde-Rémillard and Trépanier, eds., *Lionel Groulx. Correspondance: 1894-1967*, 310; Trépanier, "Groulx, Lionel".
2   Ibid., 197, 263.

over Leuven, considering it was Groulx's preferred destination during the first six months of 1907. Groulx however clarified his change of mind when writing to Medard Émard, the bishop of Valleyfield, Quebec how

> After Paris, I naturally had to think of Leuven. But if, as a result of its multiple provisions, Louvain is an incomparable centre for sociological sciences, I have reason to believe that it is not as easy to find one's account for French literature there. [...] I spoke there [in Fribourg] with former professors and students of Leuven, and all of them unanimously agreed to tell me impartially that if the stay in Leuven is preferable to whoever wants to study sociology, Fribourg is infinitely better for the teaching of Greek and Latin classics, as well as for the teaching of French literature.[3]

Because of his emphasis on the professors and students who had studied at Leuven, and the comparison between both programmes, Groulx's choice for Fribourg did not necessarily constitute a rejection of Leuven. On the contrary, Fribourg and Leuven should be considered as part of a larger network which was marked by a determination to restore and revalidate the writings of the medieval philosopher Thomas Aquinas so as to address the social and political issues of the modern society. Following Pope Leo XIII's encyclical *Aeterni Patris* in 1879 – urging Catholics to "let carefully selected teachers endeavour to implant the doctrine of Thomas Aquinas in the minds of students" – this neo-Thomist or neo-scholastic resurgence had influenced myriad Catholic universities.[4] This had proven highly successful in Leuven where under the guise of the future archbishop Désiré Mercier the newly founded Higher Institute of Philosophy and the *Revue néo-scolastique* had prompted the Belgian university to one of the leading neo-Thomist centres at the end of the nineteenth century.[5] Unsurprisingly, this neo-Thomist prominence had not escaped Groulx's attention, who further rationalised his decision to Émard by commenting how in Fribourg "one is a neo-scholastic, and of a school even more orthodox than that of Leuven, since one can trace Kantian infiltrations in the work of Mgr [Désiré] Mercier".[6]

---

3   "Après Paris, je devais naturellement songer à Louvain. Mais si, par suite de ses œuvres multiples, Louvain est un centre incomparable pour les sciences sociologiques, j'ai lieu de croire qu'on n'y trouve pas aussi facilement son compte pour les lettres françaises. [...] j'ai causé là [Fribourg] avec d'anciens professeurs et élèves de Louvain, et tous se sont unanimement entendus pour m'avouer impartialement que si le séjour à Louvain est préférable à qui veut faire des études de sociologie, Fribourg l'emporte infiniment pour l'enseignement des classiques grecs et latins, comme pour celui des lettres françaises." Ibid., 412-413.

4   <https://w2.vatican.va/content/leo-xiii/en/encyclicals/documents/hf_l-xiii_enc_04081879_aeterni-patris.html>; see Mcinerny, "Thomism"; Scerri, "The Revival of Scholastic Sacramental Theology after the Publication of Aeterni Patris".

5   Aubert, "Désiré Mercier et les débuts de l'Institut de Philosophie"; De Raeymaeker, "Les origines de l'Institut supérieur de Philosophie de Louvain".

6   "on y est néo-scolastique, et d'une école encore plus orthodoxe que celle de Louvain puisqu'on trouve moyen de retracer des infiltrations kantiennes dans l'œuvre de Mgr

This short anecdote concerning Groulx – who would play a crucial role in the development of French-Canadian nationalism during the first half of the twentieth century – highlights the two major arguments this article will make. First, Groulx's reference to the Catholic University of Leuven as a leading centre in the resurgence of neo-Thomism is an indication of the influence Belgium and the neo-Thomist philosophy had on the development of nationalism in Quebec during the first half of the twentieth century. By focusing on Groulx's correspondents – and Arthur Robert in particular – it will be illustrated how intellectuals in Quebec were influenced by the writings of prominent neo-Thomists from Leuven. Secondly, it will be argued that neo-Thomism had a marked influence on the conceptualisation of nationalism in Quebec during the first half of the twentieth century. Comparing Groulx's work with the writings of the Leuven neo-Thomist chemist Désiré Nys, it will be argued that the neo-Thomist distinction between the concepts of *matter* and *form* had a profound influence on Groulx's concept of the nation. Moreover, this neo-Thomist underpinning of Groulx's writings helps to reconsider his interpretation of the notions of urbanisation and the agrarian society which have traditionally been characterised as essential to Groulx's ideology and depiction of French-Canadian nationalism. A final concluding section will reflect on the broader implications neo-Thomism can have for the study and analysis of nationalism during the first half of the twentieth century.

The Catholic University of Leuven and Quebec

In the summer of 1914, the pre-eminent leader of the French-Canadian *Nationalistes*, Henri Bourassa, urged the readers of the seminal journal *le Devoir* that "Catholics throughout the world owe Belgium a very special homage, for it offers a striking denial of the nonsense which still lingers in magazines, newspapers and free-thinking or Protestant parliaments: Catholic discipline and morality are incompatible with the material and intellectual progress of peoples".[7] Bourassa's request immediately highlights two important elements.[8] First, his remarks illustrate the pertinence of Catholicism for French-Canadian nationalism, as it also proved instrumental for the subsequent nation-

[Désiré] Mercier". Huot, Lalonde-Rémillard and Trépanier, eds., *Lionel Groulx*, 413. For more on Groulx and his sojourn in Europe, see Rouges, "L'image de l'Europe dans les écrits de Lionel Groulx".

7   "les catholiques du monde entier doivent à la Belgique un hommage tout particulier, car elle offre un éclatant démenti à cette niaiserie qui traîne encore les revues, les journaux et les parlements libres-penseurs ou protestants: la discipline et la morale catholiques sont incompatibles avec le progrès matériel et intellectuel des peuples." Bourassa, "Les syndicats chrétiens de Belgique".

8   For more on Bourassa and his importance in Canada and Quebec, see Kennedy, *Liberal Nationalisms*.

alist movement, the Action Française under Groulx's leadership.[9] Secondly, Bourassa's emphasis on Belgium and its role as vanguard in the Catholic world illustrates how French-Canadian Catholic nationalists ascribed an important role to the country as an example for the further development of their own society during this period.

This was a conclusion that was also reached by historian Yvan Lamonde. He analysed the prominence of the social question in Quebec and Belgium, and highlighted the influence the latter had on the former.[10] In the conclusion to his piece, he raised a number of questions that could be further explored, including "the Canadian social science students in Leuven".[11] This was an element that was also raised by the editors of Groulx's correspondences – Giselle Huot, Juliette Lalonde-Rémillard and Pierre Trépanier – who noticed how easily "one ignores how many students went to Leuven. One thing is certain: Belgian influences in Quebec did not dry up in 1908".[12] Due to Groulx's prolific correspondences and his own relation to Leuven, it is beneficial to emphasise the correspondents in Groulx's network who had travelled to Leuven to enrol in the social sciences, as they address Lamonde's initial question and subsequently corroborate his argument of the prevalence of Belgium on the development of the French-Canadian society during the early decades of the twentieth century. Consequently, three figures remain: Louis-Ubalde Mousseau, Émile Cloutier and Arthur Robert. From these three cases, Robert can be considered the most illustrative example of the importance of the Catholic University of Leuven – and neo-Thomism in particular – for the development of French-Canadian society.

A professor in philosophy at the Université Laval, Robert would traverse the Atlantic in 1905 for a short sojourn in Rome before enrolling at the School of Social and Political Science in Leuven, from which he would obtain a licentiate in social and political science in 1907, as would his peer Mousseau.[13] The School itself can be considered a quintessential example of the influence neo-Thomism had on the university starting from the late nineteenth century. Spurred by the social and political unrest in Belgium during the last quarter of the nineteenth century, the School relied on a number of neo-Thomists to reconcile the emerging social and political sciences with Catholic philosophy. The head of the School during Robert's sojourn for example, Léon de Lantsheere – a founding member of the *Revue néo-scolastique* – gave a seminar on 'criminal sociology' during Robert's enrolment, and other courses taught by neo-Thomists such as Victor Brants and Émile Vlierbergh illustrate the under-

---

9   See Trofimenkoff, *Action Française: French Canadian Nationalism in the Twenties.*
10   Lamonde, "La trame des relations entre la Belgique et le Québec (1830-1940)".
11   Ibid., 181.
12   Huot, Lalonde-Rémillard and Trépanier, eds., *Lionel Groulx*, 499.
13   Allaire, *Dictionnaire Biographique*, 82; *Annuaire de l'Université catholique de Louvain*, 159.

lying premise of the School to reconcile the social sciences with neo-Thomism.[14]

Unsurprisingly, Robert would continue to adhere to these two principles in his later career. Following his graduation, Robert would prove instrumental for the foundation and development of the social sciences in Quebec, becoming the first director of the École des Sciences Sociales at the Université Laval in 1932, and playing an active role in the newly founded conferences on the social sciences – the *Semaines sociales* – all the while continuing to contribute to Groulx's seminal nationalist monthly journal *Action française* during the 1920s.[15] Moreover, Robert would continue to put emphasis on the neo-Thomist philosophy that underpinned the teachings at Leuven during this time. In his course manual *Leçons de logique* (1914) for example Robert would rely heavily on the works of Désiré Mercier in order to clarify the "immortal principles of scholastic philosophy so often recommended by the popes". Robert's continued adherence to the teachings at Leuven was even more apparent in his praise for the Catholic University of Leuven's Higher Institute of Philosophy, describing how it "has shown [...] how the centuries-old doctrine of Aristotle and St. Thomas still possesses enough vitality to hold its own beside the modern scientific conquests and the doctrines received today".[16] Robert's fixation on the Institute's success to adapt the Thomistic philosophy to the modern sciences highlights how the Catholic University of Leuven at the beginning of the twentieth century was able to establish itself as a leading neo-Thomist centre, and via its Institute and the writings of its prominent members succeeded in influencing Catholic intellectuals across different disciplines and continents.

Désiré Nys and the emergence of neo-Thomist chemistry

Unsurprisingly, Robert's colleague Lionel Groulx expressed a similar attachment to the writings and teachings of the neo-Thomists from Leuven. Groulx's private library for example housed the works of different neo-Thomists associated with the Higher Institute of Philosophy, including the neo-Thomist historian Maurice De Wulf's seminal manual *Introduction à la philosophie néo-scolastique*, and Désiré Nys' *Cosmologie, ou, étude philosophique du monde inorganique*. The latter holds a peculiar place amongst the neo-Thomists in Leuven, as noticed by his colleague De Wulf who commented how "if we refer to the prevailing mentality around 1880, it might seem strange, almost abnormal, to see a young theologian-philosopher, attending the course of chemists

14 Ibid., 88.
15 Lamonde, "La trame des relations", 175; Id., *Histoire sociale des idées au Québec*; Brooks and Gagnon, *Social Scientists and Politics in Canada*, 30-34; Robert, "Aspirations du Canada français"; Harvey, *Histoire de l'École des Hautes Études Commerciales de Montréal*.
16 Robert, *Leçons de logique*, 209.

and physicists. But D. Nys was fond of the study of science."[17] Nys's affection resulted in the neo-Thomist pursuing a career in chemistry, ultimately completing his thesis under the auspice of his mentor in Leipzig, the renowned German chemist Wilhelm Ostwald.[18] Ostwald – who ultimately won the Nobel Prize for Chemistry in 1909 – would prove instrumental for Nys's conceptualisation of chemistry and his emphasis on the study of energy to reconcile neo-Thomism with chemistry and the study of the inorganic world.[19]

The basis for this importance, and a good starting point to encapsulate Nys's relevance for this analysis, is Ostwald's publication *La déroute de l'atomisme contemporain* in 1895.[20] Ostwald explained how "everywhere it is repeated, as an axiom, that only the mechanics of atoms can give the key to the physical world. Matter and motion are the two concepts to which, in the final analysis, the most complex natural phenomena are brought back. This theory can be called physical materialism."[21] Ostwald criticised this mechanistic interpretation of the natural world stating that it is "my conviction that this way of looking at things, for all its credit, is unsustainable; that this mechanical theory has not achieved its goal [...] The conclusion is obvious: it must be abandoned and replaced, as far as possible, by another, better one."[22]

The answer, according to Ostwald, was to focus on the concept of energy. He explained how "Mayer discovered the most general invariant, energy, which governs all physical forces. Always, in all their history, matter and energy remain side by side [...] they go together, matter being the vehicle, the reservoir of energy."[23] By depicting matter, the core tenet of the mechanistic theory, as a mere vehicle, Ostwald prioritised energy as the invariable guiding principle of the natural world. Consequently, this meant that matter was nothing more than an "invention" and that "the actual reality, i.e. the one that has an effect on us, is the energy".[24] Moreover, Ostwald's theory of energy as the underlying force of the natural world was not limited to the inorganic world. In his seminal work *Die Energie* (1908) Ostwald devoted a chapter to "Sociological Energetics", explaining that "social energetics plays itself out

17   "si on se reporte à la mentalité régnante aux environs de 1880, il pouvait sembler étrange, presque anormal, de voir un jeune théologien-philosophe, fréquenter le cours des chimistes et des physiciens. Mais D. Nys affectionnait l'étude des sciences." De Wulf and Renoirte, "Le Professeur Désiré Nys", 48.
18   Schaschke, "Ostwald, Friedrich Wilhelm (1853-1932)"; Bancroft, "Wilhelm Ostwald".
19   For a general analysis of the way energy played a role in 19th-century physics, see Hunt, "Electrical Theory and Practice in the Nineteenth Century".
20   The original German article was called "Die Überwindung des wissenschaftlichen Materialismus". Brenner, *Duhem: Science, réalité et apparence*, 84-87.
21   Ostwald, "La déroute de l'atomisme contemporain", 953.
22   "ma conviction que cette manière de voir, malgré tout son crédit, est insoutenable; que cette théorie mécanique n'a pas atteint son but [...] La conclusion s'impose: il faut l'abandonner et la remplacer, autant que faire se peut, par une autre meilleure." Ibid.
23   Ibid., 957.
24   Ibid., 956.

in a much greater variety of ways with humans [...] because while animals generally only have the energy of their own bodies at their disposal, humans also avail themselves of many other kinds of energy". Ostwald further related the nature of these different forms of energies in humans to the role of culture which, according to the German, "consists in ensuring the most favourable transformation coefficient for the energy to be converted".[25]

Ostwald's emphasis on energy as the guiding principle of the natural world had a clear influence on Nys, who accepted his mentor's theoretical premise. In accordance with Oswald, Nys argued that "with the energetic [...] the local movement loses the sovereign importance attributed to it by the mechanism and regains its very modest place in the midst of such diverse phenomena in the world", ultimately concluding that "it was energy that becomes the fundamental concept encompassing all the properties and transformations of matter".[26] The most important consequence however, according to Nys, was that the theory had given "physics a natural basis where science and philosophy can now be reconciled".[27] Nys's colleague De Wulf had elaborated on the importance of this convergence by specifying that neo-Thomism "aims at submitting the great leading principles of medieval scholasticism to the control of the latest results of scientific progress".[28] Consequently, emphasis was put on the importance of contemporary science to converge with the principles of philosophy; De Wulf further explained how "the great constitutive doctrines of the medieval system are RETAINED, but only after having successfully stood the double test of comparison with the conclusions of present-day science and with the teachings of contemporary systems of philosophy".[29]

This emphasis by neo-Thomists on conciliating philosophy with science led to Nys's first critique of Ostwald. The chemist argued that "although the energetists have shown wise caution in restricting the object of physics to the phenomenal reality, it is questionable whether the method employed in the study of this object is in all respects recommendable".[30] The problem, according to the chemist, was that the traditional theory of energy – and its researchers – did not incorporate philosophy in their overall methodology and ontology. As Nys explained, "energy, as we know, prohibits any investigation into the nature of the phenomena. [...] The new theory, in a word, is a method of classification, nothing more."[31] Nys criticised this method of classification, posing the question whether "is it desirable in the interest of science and phi-

---

25 Stewart, "Sociology, Culture and Energy: The Case of Wilhelm Ostwald's 'Sociological Energetics'", 341, 344.
26 Nys, "L'énergétique et la théorie scolastique (suite et fin)", 6.
27 Ibid., 8.
28 De Wulf, *Scholasticism Old and New*, 211.
29 Ibid.
30 Nys, "L'énergétique et la théorie scolastique (suite et fin)", 10.
31 Ibid.

losophy that physics should, in principle, establish such exclusivism, abstain from any bias, from any research, from any judgement on the constitution of the properties of matter? We do not believe so."[32]

Nys's belief in the pertinence of philosophy for the study of the inorganic world had extensive consequences, as it permitted him to interpret his discipline from a neo-Thomist perspective. Following this rationale, Nys explained how "the [neo-Thomist] system can be reduced to three fundamental propositions:

> 1. Simple bodies and chemical compounds are beings endowed with *substantial unity*, specifically *distinct* from one another, and naturally *extended*.
> 2. These beings possess *active and passive powers* which belong to them in virtue of their substantial essence and are indissolubly bound up with it.
> 3. They have an *inherent tendency* to realize by the exercise of their native energies certain special ends.

Moreover, Nys further elaborated on the validity of the principles by commenting how they engendered "an important corollary: the possibility, or rather the necessity of substantial transformation and, in consequence, the existence in every natural body of two constitutive principles, *matter* and *form*".[33]

Because of the neo-Thomist emphasis on the distinction between essential and contingent properties – i.e. matter and form – Nys criticised Ostwald's argument that all properties can be characterised as energy. The neo-Thomist explained how "there are two ways of classifying all the properties of matter under the 'energy' label. Either one considers certain properties as constitutive of the power of action that characterises energy and other properties, either as means of measurement or as conditions of activity. Or else, they are all regarded as constitutive elements of dynamic power, or, to use the current language, as energy factors."[34] For Nys, "The first classification and the idea on which it is based are perfectly compatible with scholastic theory; they seem to be the decal of experience. The second, on the other hand, accepted by the energetic, leads to absolute dynamism."[35] Nys's rejection of the principle of absolute dynamism – i.e. Ostwald's argument that everything, even human interactions, can be reduced to the notion of energy – highlights how the chemist's adherence to the neo-Thomist framework affected his interpretation of the discipline of chemistry. For if everything could be reduced to an absolute principle, the distinction between *matter* and *form*, and the indissoluble unity between the two notions would be rendered obsolete, and, by consequence, the neo-Thomist philosophy and framework would be considered useless for the study of chemistry and the inorganic world.

32   Nys, "L'énergétique et la théorie scolastique (suite et fin)", 10.
33   Id., "The Scholastic Theory", 73.
34   Id., "L'énergétique et la théorie scolastique (suite et fin)", 22.
35   Ibid.

Consequently, Nys maintained the distinction between essential and contingent properties, and argued that they constituted one indissoluble entity that could not be reduced to one essential element: energy. The chemist could thus conclude that "the dualism between energy and matter, which the German scholar [Ostwald] fights with extreme violence, is therefore a dualism absolutely foreign to scholastic theory."[36] By postulating that the dualism between energy and matter was non-existent in the neo-Thomist framework, Nys resolved the problem of reducing every chemical compound to a factor of energy by arguing that because of the indissoluble nature of each substance the issue becomes irrelevant, and certain properties can exist that can't be reduced to energy. Moreover, an important consequence of Nys's adherence to the neo-Thomist framework was that by stressing the indissoluble unity of a chemical compound, Nys ascribed a prominent role to the contingent, existential properties that were inextricably connected to the essential properties. The chemist contended that "so great is the imperfection of essential forms in the inorganic world that they are not only immersed, to use St. Thomas' word, in matter, but are dependent for their generation and existence upon a *determined quantity* of matter".[37] Nys would further explain this principle in the inorganic world by using a practical example, how "the atomic weights, 16 of oxygen, 32 of sulphur, 35*5 of chlorine, are so many definite masses of matter necessary for the very existence of these bodies", ultimately concluding that "here the subjection of the form to its substrate is as profound as possible; the physical impossibility of breaking it up without destroying it provides us with an evident proof".[38]

Nys's reliance on neo-Thomism had thus resulted in a conceptualisation of the inorganic world, and the role and nature of chemistry that diverged from his mentor's and led to the former's critiques on the latter. Moreover, the emphasis on the distinction between matter and form – a core principle of the neo-Thomist philosophy – and their indissoluble unity had allowed Nys to reconcile Catholicism with modern science, thereby contributing to the neo-Thomists's determination to adapt Catholicism to the trappings of the modern world. In this sense, neo-Thomism had provided Nys with the necessary framework and concepts to address the modern societal, political and scientific contexts whilst maintaining an adherence to the traditional principles and tenets of Catholicism. In a similar vein, Groulx would succeed in adapting the neo-Thomist principles so as to constitute a French-Canadian nationalism that could both pertain to its traditions and address the changing societal and political contexts.

36 Ibid., 29.
37 Nys, "The Scholastic Theory", 79.
38 Ibid.

Groulx and the *matter* and *form* of the nation

Nys's unique reconciliation of chemistry and neo-Thomism might at first glance seem unconventional for an analysis of the nationalist historian Groulx. However, by comparing two very distinct disciplines – history and chemistry – it becomes possible on the one hand to assess and highlight the neo-Thomist tenets that influenced both cases, thereby generalising their relevance, whilst on the other hand point out the specifics of the French-Canadian nationalists, and how they adapted neo-Thomist philosophy to their specific geographical and historical contexts, and their conceptualisation of nationalism.[39]

First, it is apparent that Groulx and other French-Canadian historians described the nation as prime actor in history. Groulx explained that "nationalism in itself was no artificial reaction" but that it was "the vital, natural, and therefore legitimate reaction of any people or nation that wants to live according to the laws of its spiritual interiority or deep genius".[40] Similarly, the historian Joseph-Ernest Laferrière – who had obtained a degree in history from the Catholic University of Leuven in 1912 – illustrated this notion by proclaiming that "patriotism is a precious flower bequeathed to us by our ancestors. It sprouted early on Canadian soil. It dates back to the time when a handful of Frenchmen decided to settle in this country."[41] The result was that the nation acted as the invariable guiding principle in the historical reality, this in a similar way as energy had been for Nys's conceptualisation of chemistry and the inorganic world. In addition, Groulx would further characterise this nation in the French-Canadian context, explaining how "two words express the deep substance of our being: Catholic and French".[42] Groulx's emphasis on the elements of Catholicism and Francophone culture as basis for the French-Canadian nation has been well-researched. Coined as *clerico-nationalism*, it would be the prominent type of French-Canadian nationalism during the first half of the twentieth century.[43]

Groulx however would make a further distinction between the properties that were associated with the French-Canadian nation. He explained

---

39 This is related to the general arguments on the benefits of a historical comparison. See for example Espagne, "Comparison and Transfer: A Question of Method"; Kocka, "Comparison and Beyond"; Lorenz, "Double Trouble".

40 "la réaction vitale, naturelle, donc légitime, de tout peuple ou nation qui veut vivre selon les lois de son intériorité spirituelle ou de son génie profond". Groulx, *Le nationalisme canadien-français*, 3-4.

41 "le patriotisme est une fleur précieuse que nous ont léguée nos ancêtres. Il germa de bonne heure sur le sol canadien. Il date du moment ou une poignée de Français décidèrent de se fixer au pays." Centre d'histoire de Saint-Hyacinthe, Saint-Hyacinthe, Canada, Fonds Abbe Joseph-Ernest Laferrière, CH012, Box 2, Folder CH012/000/000/032: Article "L'éducation patriotique par l'étude de notre histoire", 1933.

42 Groulx, *Le nationalisme canadien-français*, 4.

43 See Linteau, *Histoire du Québec contemporain*, 700-707; Senese, "Catholique d'abord".

how "two elements constitute nationality. The first, called by philosophers the material element, could be defined as follows: common possession of a heritage of memories, glory, traditions, ethnic and cultural similarities. The other element, the formal element, the main one, could be defined as: the will to live together because of physical and moral solidarities [...] and the will to preserve the hereditary heritage."[44] The direct reference to philosophers to describe the distinction between the *matter* and *form* of the French-Canadian nation constitutes a clear example of Groulx's accordance with neo-Thomist philosophy. Moreover, the similarity with Nys's description of chemical compounds compels us to consider Groulx's conceptualisation of the nation in light of his adherence to the neo-Thomist philosophy which subsequently allows us to re-evaluate certain aspects that have traditionally been associated with the classical designation of *clerico-nationalism*.

The major corollary that follows from Groulx's distinction between *matter* and *form* is that the French-Canadian ascribed more importance to the contingent properties than has been assumed up to now. By stressing the Catholic and Francophone properties of the nation, researchers have often presumed that he perceived the nation as a immutable whole. Groulx however refuted this idea himself, explaining how "the formula of Canadian-French nationalism" consisted of a "simple will to persevere in our being; to remain what we are". In line with his neo-Thomist distinction, Groulx warned that this volition (i.e. form) was insufficient as the nation ran the risk of remaining "in static or inert forms" and not living, "as it goes without saying, in the free blossoming of the living being".[45] Just as Nys had argued that a chemical compound – whatever its form – was dependent on its matter in order to exist in reality, so too Groulx asserted that a nation, regardless of its essential properties, required contingent properties that could entice individuals to adhere to the nation, and guarantee its survival. It is because of this emphasis on the contingent properties that it becomes possible to re-evaluate the role and prevalence of the rural or pastoral element in Groulx's conceptualisation of French-Canadian nationalism.

Researchers have traditionally stressed this element. Frédéric Boily for example specified in his analysis of Groulx's political ideology how, according to him "one of the most significant characteristics of the nation consists in its peasant aspect".[46] By designating the pastoral as a constitutive characteristic of Groulx's nationalism, researchers subsequently posed a dialectic between Groulx's fixed aspect of the pastoral and the changing societal circumstances during the first half of the twentieth century which were induced by urbanisation and industrialisation. The historian Serge Gagnon exemplified this when

---

44 Groulx, *Orientations*, 224.
45 Id., *Le nationalisme canadien-français*, 4.
46 Boily, *La pensée nationaliste de Lionel Groulx*, 26.

he explained how "as Groulx wrote, the fortress of survival, the rural families, were weakening as urbanization increased".[47] It should be noted that French-Canadian nationalists were indeed weary of the effects of urbanisation and industrialisation. Esdras Minville, a colleague of Groulx at the nationalist journal *Action française*, illustrated this anxiousness when he proclaimed that "the Canadian city is the tomb of tradition", further explaining that "it is their [French-Canadian] soul that they thus disperse with their history".[48]

The problem with positing a dialectic between the pastoral nature of French-Canadian nationalism and the changing historical circumstances, i.e. urbanisation, is that researchers presumed that the pastoral element constituted an essential property in Groulx's French-Canadian nationalism and as such was intrinsic to the nation itself. Taking into account Groulx's adherence to neo-Thomism, the pastoral should not be considered an essential property – i.e. a characteristic of the nation's *form* – but constituted an element of the nation's *matter*. As Groulx had described, the basis of the French-Canadian nation was the volition to remain Catholic and French. The pastoral traditions however – those that Minville feared were threatened by the changing societal circumstances and urbanisation – were a part of the nation's *matter* and as such were not considered as essential properties of the French-Canadian nation.

Consequently, the issue was not a dialectic between an essential pastoral French-Canadian nationalism and a contingent, urbanised context. On the contrary, Groulx acknowledged the importance of the changing contingent circumstances for the existence of the *form* – similar as Nys had acknowledged the possibility of the "subjection of the form to its substrate". The issue was then how the changing *matter* of the nation could be aligned with its essential *form* in order to guarantee its continued existence. Groulx illustrated this point when he explained how

> About eighty years ago, our people were still overwhelmingly a country people. The countryside of our country could pass for a small, closed world [...] Economic and social factors that everyone knows have radically changed and changed this situation. We now live mostly in the city; the city itself has transported its mores to the countryside; and here are all the once crumbling ramparts, and the American microbe floating everywhere in the air. So souls need special tonics; human metal can no longer be forged as it once was. Well, please tell me again: while everything was changing around us, did the school change considerably? Has it become an orderly school for national purposes, for the recovery of our lives?[49]

47 Gagnon, *Quebec and its Historians*, 120.
48 Minville, "La défense de notre capital humain", 271. For more on Minville, see Foisy-Geoffroy, "Esdras Minville et le nationalisme économique".
49 "Il y a quatre-vingts ans environ, notre peuple restait encore en grande majorité un peuple de campagnards. La campagne de chez nous pouvait passer pour un petit monde clos [...] Des facteurs économiques et sociaux que chacun connaît ont radicalement boulever-

With the traditional ramparts shattered, and the morals of the city transported to the countryside, Groulx acknowledged that the *matter* of the traditional French-Canadian nation had ceased to exist. Consequently, Groulx had deemed it imperative to adapt and transform the *matter* – the special tonics – in order to safeguard the continuation of the essential properties of the nation. This is why Groulx and other nationalists emphasised the importance of education and national history, as they believed this was instrumental to convey the essential properties of the nation and educate the youth so they were prepared to compose a new *matter* that allowed the nation's *form* to survive. Groulx's colleague Laferrière for example explained how "all self-conscious peoples have sought the support of this [social force of the cult of the past]. [...] From the past come lessons and examples, experiences and enlightenment. The past is a school of respect, pride, constancy, magnanimity, courage."[50] Groulx himself would further elaborate on the importance of educating the national principles to strengthen and prepare the youth for the contingent future when he explained how "we have a doctrine which teaches us the natural hierarchy of values, the transcendent order according to which nations must be constituted in order to live and prosper. The youth will have to be enlightened by this doctrine to learn where to focus their efforts, to provide the luminous guidelines."[51]

By adhering to Groulx's distinction between *matter* and *form* – which itself is a consequence of the neo-Thomist influence on Quebec – it has become possible to shed new light and nuance on a traditional key aspect of the conceptualisation and analysis of French-Canadian nationalism during the first half of the twentieth century. Moreover, the clear overlap between Nys's definition of neo-Thomist chemistry and Groulx's characterisation of nationalism indicates how neo-Thomism was able to be transformed and adapted to specific disciplines, historical and socio-political contexts. In addition, it shows the extent to which neo-Thomists from Leuven at the beginning of the twentieth century were successful in influencing Catholic intellectuals across the world, and

---

sé, changé cette situation. Nous vivons maintenant en grande majorité à la ville; la ville elle-même a transporté ses mœurs à la campagne ; et voici tous les remparts d'autrefois écroulés, et le microbe américain flottant partout dans l'air. Les âmes auraient donc besoin de toniques spéciaux; le métal humain ne saurait plus être forgé comme jadis. Eh bien, je vous prie encore de me le dire: pendant que tout changeait autour de nous, l'école a-t-elle considérablement changé? Est-elle devenue une école ordonnée aux fins nationales, au redressement de notre vie?" Groulx, "Pour qu'on vive", 10.

50   "tous les peuples conscients d'eux-mêmes ont recherché l'appui de cette force [sociale du culte du passé]. [...] Du passé surgissent des leçons et des exemples, des expériences et des lumières. Le passé est une école de respect, de fierté, de constance, de magnanimité, de courage." Centre d'histoire de Saint-Hyacinthe, Saint-Hyacinthe, Canada, Fonds Abbe Joseph-Ernest Laferrière, CH012, Box 2, Folder CH012/000/000/032: Article "L'éducation patriotique par l'étude de notre histoire", 1933.

51   Groulx, *Notre maître, le passé*, 8.

contributed to the debates on different diverging issues during the first half of the twentieth century. In this sense, while Groulx may have ultimately chosen to attend Fribourg during the summer of 1907 instead of the Catholic University of Leuven, the Belgian university had a lifelong influence on the French Canadian, and on his conceptualisation of French-Canadian nationalism.

Conclusion: the general pertinence of neo-Thomism for nationalism studies

Despite the eventual demise of Groulx and the substitution of a French-Canadian Catholic nationalism by a secular, Quebec nationalism during primarily the 1960s – known as the 'Quiet Revolution' – our contribution highlights the influence of the Catholic University of Leuven, and of neo-Thomist philosophy on the development of French-Canadian nationalism during the first half of the twentieth century.[52] Neo-Thomism had proven to be instrumental for Groulx in characterising and conceptualising nationalism, and in reconciling the core tenets of his perceived nation – Catholicism and Francophone culture – with the modern, urban society. It is this neo-Thomist endeavour to reconcile traditional Catholic philosophy and values with modern society and the social and political unrest that had spurned from it, that is crucial to emphasise. I believe this holds a tremendous value for the study of nationalism during the late nineteenth and early twentieth century, and for the field of nationalism studies in general.

In the field of nationalism studies, the traditional characterisation of Groulx's nationalism as *clerico-nationalism* could be considered a quintessential example of what has been designated primordial nationalism. The naturalist definition of primordialism – which has commonly been used as a template to analyse nationalist movements and historians across the world during the nineteenth and twentieth century – states that nationalism is an innate characteristic of humankind, ascribing to every person in every historical context a national identity.[53] The consequence is that primordialism entails an "ideological view of the past" in which nationalist historians trace back the origin and essential characteristics of the nation and their subsequent development throughout history.[54] It is this underlying premise of the primordial nation that neo-Thomism can help to address. As seen in this contribution,

52 The dialectic between the two forms of nationalism in Quebec has been nuanced in recent years, see Meunier and Warren, *Sortir de la 'Grande Noirceur'*; Gélinas, *La droite intellectuelle québécoise et la Révolution tranquille*; Bouchard, "L'imaginaire de la grande noirceur et de la révolution tranquille"; Pelletier, "La Révolution tranquille".
53 Özkırımlı, *Theories of Nationalism*; Guibernau and Hutchinson, *Understanding Nationalism*; Coakley, "'Primordialism' in Nationalism Studies: Theory or Ideology?".
54 Hutchinson, *Modern Nationalism*, 3, also see Berger, *Writing the Nation*.

while Groulx did ascribe certain essential properties to the French-Canadian nation – and which have been used by researchers as proof of his primordial conceptualisation of nationalism – the historian nuanced the primacy of these characteristics via neo-Thomism and the distinction between *matter* and *form*. The result was a form of nationalism that does not completely corresponds with the traditional definition of primordialism, as the neo-Thomist distinction grants nationalism a certain degree of mutability in specific historical circumstances. Moreover, the distinction subsequently ascribes the contingent factors a bigger role and influence over the essential properties than has traditionally been assumed in the primordial template, as seen by the role urbanisation and the pastoral play in Groulx's conceptualisation.

The French-Canadian case however is only one of many that could benefit from a closer analysis of the links between neo-Thomism and nationalism. Neo-Thomism's emphasis on the reconciliation of Catholicism with modernity – in addition to the success of Leuven and its Higher Institute of Philosophy – had resulted in a successful diffusion of its core tenets and principles across the Catholic world during the late nineteenth and early twentieth century. Different Catholic nationalist groups – including the Action Française in both Quebec and France – had thus been influenced by the principles and philosophy of neo-Thomism as a way to reconcile the traditional Catholic values with the modern-day society, and transforming the traditional primordial premises to allow for a nationalist movement that was both intrinsically traditional and modern. Moreover, the influence neo-Thomism had was not limited to explicit nationalist movements like Groulx's, but had far-reaching consequences for Catholics across different nations, including Belgium itself, where Désiré Mercier would vehemently oppose German occupation during the First World War, becoming a vanguard of the Belgian nation. During the war itself, Mercier drew close connections between the notion of patriotism and religion to justify the Belgian resistance against the German occupier. Describing the situation in Belgium during the first months of the First World War, Mercier posed the question "which of us does not feel that Patriotism is a sacred thing, and that a violation of national dignity is in a manner a profanation and a sacrilege?"[55]

Mercier's own adherence to the principles of nationalism illustrates how neo-Thomism and Catholicism played a key role in the conceptualisation of the nation and nationalism during the first half of the twentieth century. What this contribution has shown is that neo-Thomism and nationalism are not juxtaposed against each other, but are mutually dependent, with Catholic nationalists benefitting from a philosophy and conceptual framework that allowed them to reconcile the traditional Catholic values with the trappings of modern society. On the other hand, the adaptation of the neo-Thomist philosophy into different national contexts can help to explain its success during the late

---

55   *The Voice of Belgium*, 20. Also see Boudens, *Kardinaal Mercier en de Vlaamse Beweging*.

nineteenth and early twentieth century, as it allowed for a greater diffusion throughout the Catholic world. In conclusion, this contribution has shown that, in addition to its valuable role in the nationalist movement in Quebec during the first half of the twentieth century, neo-Thomism, and the study of it, still have myriad valuable purposes for the study of nationalism during the nineteenth and twentieth century. In this sense, following the neo-Thomist's adage of *vetera novis augere* [the old invigorates the new], it can be concluded that the Catholic University of Leuven and its neo-Thomists did not only invigorate the nationalists in Quebec, but were essential in the reconciliation of Catholicism and nationalism during the first half of the twentieth century.

BIBLIOGRAPHY

Aubert, Roger. "Désiré Mercier et les débuts de l'Institut de Philosophie". *Revue Philosophique de Louvain*, 88 (1990), 147-167.

Bancroft, Wilder. "Wilhelm Ostwald". *Science*, 1948 (1932), 454-455.

Berger, Stefan. *Writing the Nation: A Global Perspective*. London: Palgrave Macmillan, 2007.

Boily, Frédéric. *La pensée nationaliste de Lionel Groulx*. Montreal: Septentrion, 2003.

Bouchard, Gérard. "L'imaginaire de la grande noirceur et de la révolution tranquille: fictions identitaires et jeux de mémoire au Québec". *Recherches sociographiques*, 46 (2005), 411-436.

Boudens, Robrecht. *Kardinaal Mercier en de Vlaamse Beweging*. Leuven: Davidsfonds, 1975.

Bourassa, Henri. "Les syndicats chrétiens de Belgique". *Le Devoir*, 1 August 1914.

Brenner, Anastasios. *Duhem: science, réalité et apparence: la relation entre philosophie et histoire dans l'œuvre de Pierre Duhem*. Paris: Vrin, 1990.

Brooks, Stephen and Alain Gagnon. *Social Scientists and Politics in Canada: Between Clerisy and Vanguard*. Montreal: McGill-Queen's University Press, 1988.

Coakley, John. "'Primordialism' in Nationalism Studies: Theory or Ideology?" *Nations and Nationalism*, 24 (2018) 2, 327-347. <https://doi.org/10.1111/nana.12349>.

De Raeymaeker, Louis. "Les origines de l'Institut supérieur de Philosophie de Louvain". *Revue Philosophique de Louvain*, 49 (1951), 505-633.

De Wulf, Maurice. *Scholasticism Old and New: An Introduction to Scholastic Philosophy Medieval and Modern*. Dublin: Gill & Son, 1907.

De Wulf, Maurice and Fernand Renoirte. "Le Professeur Désiré Nys". *Revue néo-scolastique de philosophie*, 30 (1928), 47-57.

Espagne, Michel. "Comparison and Transfer: A Question of Method". In Matthias Middel and Lluis Roura, eds. *Transnational Challenges to National History Writing*. New York: Palgrave Macmillan, 2013, 36-53.

Foisy-Geoffroy, Dominique. "Esdras Minville et le nationalisme économique, 1923-1939". *Mens: Revue d'histoire intellectuelle de l'Amérique française*, 1 (2000), 51-68.

Gagnon, Serge. *Quebec and its Historians: 1840 to 1920*. Montreal: Harvest House, 1982.

Gavreau, Michael. *The Catholic Origins of Quebec's Quiet Revolution, 1931-1970*. Montreal: McGill-Queen's University Press, 2005.

Gélinas, Xavier. *La droite intellectuelle québécoise et la Révolution tranquille*. Quebec: Les Presses de l'Université Laval, 2007.

Groulx, Lionel. *Notre maître, le passé*. Montreal: Bibliothèque de l'Action française, 1924.

Groulx, Lionel. "Pour qu'on vive". Edited by Action Nationale (1934).

Groulx, Lionel. *Orientations, les éditions du zodiaque*. Montreal: Librairie Déom Frères, 1935.

Groulx, Lionel. *Le nationalisme canadien-français*. Ottawa, 1949.

Guibernau, Montserrat and John Hutchinson. *Understanding Nationalism*. Cambridge: Polity, 2001.

Harvey, Pierre. *Histoire de l'École des Hautes Études Commerciales de Montréal*. Vol. 2: *1926-2970*. Montreal: Éditions Québec/Amérique, 2002.

Hunt, Bruce. "Electrical Theory and Practice in the Nineteenth Century". In Mary Nye, ed. *The Cambridge History of Science*. Vol. 5: *The Modern Physical and Mathematical Sciences*. Cambridge: Cambridge University Press, 2002, 311-327.

Huot, Giselle, Juliette Lalonde-Rémillard and Pierre Trépanier, eds. *Lionel Groulx. Correspondance: 1894-1967.* Vol. 2: *Un étudiant à l'école de l'Europe: 1906-1909.* Montreal: Fides, 1993.

Hutchinson, John. *Modern Nationalism.* New York: Fontana Press, 1994.

Kennedy, James. *Liberal Nationalisms: Empire, State, and Civil Society in Scotland and Quebec.* Montreal: McGill-Queen's University Press, 2013.

Kocka, Jürgen. "Comparison and Beyond". *History and Theory*, 42 (2003), 39-44.

Lamonde, Yvan. "La trame des relations entre la Belgique et le Québec (1830-1940): La primauté de la question sociale". In: Ginette Kurgan-van Hentenryk, ed. *La question sociale en Belgique et au Canada: XIXe-XXe siècles.* Brussels: Éditions de l'Université de Bruxelles, 1988, 173-184.

Lamonde, Yvan. *Histoire sociale des idées au Québec, 1896-1929.* Montreal: Fides, 2004.

Linteau, Paul-André et al. *Histoire du Québec contemporain.* Vol. 2: *Le Québec depuis 1930.* Montreal: Boréal, 1989.

Lorenz, Chris. "Double Trouble: A Comparison of the Politics of National History in Germany and in Quebec". In Chris Lorenz and Stefan Berger, eds. *Nationalizing the Past: Historians as Nation Builders in Modern Europe.* London: Palgrave Macmillan, 2010, 49-70.

Mcinerny, Ralph. "Thomism". In: Charles Taliaferro, Paul Draper and Philip L. Quinn, eds. *A Companion to Philosophy of Religion.* Chichester: Blackwell, 2010, 189-195.

Meunier, Martin and Jean-Philippe Warren. *Sortir de la 'Grande Noirceur'. L'horizon 'Personnaliste' de la Révolution Tranquille.* Sillery: Septentrion, 2002.

Minville, Esdras. "La défense de notre capital humain – 'Le réservoir de la race'". *Action française*, 15 (1926), 258-276.

Nys, Désiré. "L'énergétique et la théorie scolastique (suite et fin)". *Revue néo-scolastique de philosophie*, 19 (1912), 5-41.

Nys, Désiré. "The Scholastic Theory: Historical Sketch". In Désiré Mercier, ed. *A Manual of Modern Scholastic Philosophy.* London: Kegan Paul, Trench, Trubner & Co, 1916, 71-126.

Ostwald, Wilhelm. "La déroute de l'atomisme contemporain". *Revue générale des sciences pures et appliquées*, 6 (1895), 953-958.

Özkırımlı, Umut. *Theories of Nationalism: A Critical Introduction.* Basingstoke: Macmillan, 2000.

Pelletier, Réjean. "La Révolution tranquille". In Gérard Daigle and Guy Rocher, eds. *Le Québec en jeu. Comprendre les grands défis.* Montreal: Les Presses de l'Université de Montréal, 1992, 609-624.

Robert, Arthur. "Aspirations du Canada français: Fondement philosophique". *Action française*, (1922), 66-81.

Robert, Arthur. *Leçons de logique.* Quebec: La librairie de l'Action sociale catholique, 1940 [1st ed. 1914].

Rouges, Nathalie. "L'image de l'Europe dans les écrits de Lionel Groulx (1906-1909)". *Revue d'histoire de l'Amérique française*, 46 (1992), 245-254.

Scerri, Hector. "The Revival of Scholastic Sacramental Theology after the Publication of Aeterni Patris". *Irish Theological Quarterly*, 77 (2012), 265-285.

Schaschke, Carl. "Ostwald, Friedrich Wilhelm (1853-1932)". In Carl Schaschke, ed. *A Dictionary of Chemical Engineering.* Oxford: Oxford University Press, 2014.

Senese, P.M. "Catholique d'abord: Catholicism and Nationalism in the Thought of Lionel Groulx". *Canadian Historical Review*, 60 (1979), 154-177.

Stewart, Janet. "Sociology, Culture and Energy: The Case of Wilhelm Ostwald's 'Sociological Energetics' – A Translation and Exposition of a Classic Text". *Cultural Sociology*, 8 (2014) 3, 333-350.

The Voice of Belgium: Being the War Utterances of Cardinal Mercier. London: Burns & Oates, 1917.

Trépanier, Pierre. "Groulx, Lionel". In Gerald Hallowell, ed. *The Oxford Companion to Canadian History.* Oxford: Oxford University Press, 2004.

Trofimenkoff, Susan Mann. *Action Française: French Canadian Nationalism in the Twenties.* Toronto: University of Toronto Press, 1975.

A group of Dominican students in the Collegium Pontificium Internationale Angelicum, Rome. Metoděj Habáň (in the 2nd row 3rd from the left) studied there from 1921 to 1928. The years spend in Rome had a central position in his formation.
[By courtesy of J. Štofaník]

RECEPTION AND ADAPTATION OF NEO-THOMISM IN EAST-CENTRAL EUROPE, BETWEEN THE INTELLECTUAL AND SOCIAL INVOLVEMENT OF THE CATHOLIC CHURCH[*]

JAKUB ŠTOFANÍK

One movement that excited the interest of the Catholic world in the nineteenth century was the revival of the philosophy of Thomas Aquinas. This scholastic philosophy appeared in new conditions and fundamentally changed the nature of Catholic philosophy as well as the face of the Church in society. Neo-Thomism as an official philosophical background and a transnational movement inside the Catholic Church was not limited to Western Europe. It was accepted and reflected even in Vienna, Prague, Budapest and Krakow, where its socio-economic dimension was particularly appealing. Neo-Thomism threw fresh light on the relationship between the common good and the good of an individual; the place of intermediary bodies in civil society as a whole; the role of the state and the nature of social justice.

This contribution will examine the transfer, development, and adaptation of neo-Thomism in East-Central Europe, namely within the territory where the Czechoslovak Republic was established in 1918. It will analyse the position of neo-Thomism and particularly its influence in the fields of law and socio-economic policy from the late nineteenth century (under the dual Austro-Hungarian monarchy) till the mid-twentieth century, when this part of Europe was already under the control of the Soviet Union. The chapter will try to answer the questions of who were the most important actors and networks in the development of neo-Thomism within Czechoslovakia. It will also focus

[*] This study was written within the scope of grant project no. 16-04364S "The Religious Life of the Industrial Working Class in the Czech Lands (1918-1939): Institutions, Religiosity and the Social Question of the Czech Science Foundation".

on the social and political dimension of this official philosophy as well as on Catholic involvement in society.

The excitement and revival of the philosophical tradition of Thomas Aquinas did not emerge in this part of Europe at the time of the papal encyclical entitled *Aeterni Patris*. The interest in this leading teacher of the Church and his philosophic legacy had already been seen far earlier.

One of the major centres of neo-Thomism in the Czech Lands was Brno, with its seminary where Professor Josef Pospíšil began to give lectures on Aristotelic-Thomistic philosophy as early as in 1876. As the founder of the revived scholastic philosophy, he established himself by publishing his book entitled *Filosofie podle zásad sv. Tomáše Akvinského* (Philosophy According to the Principles of St. Thomas Aquinas) in 1883, to be followed in the 1890s by the second volume entitled *Kosmologie podle zásad sv. Tomáše Akvinského* (Cosmology According to the Principles of St. Thomas Aquinas). One interesting aspect of these books was that the author decided to publish them in Czech, which was not only an expression of his national creed but also his contribution to the creation of Czech philosophical terminology. Pospíšil's works reflected the need to defend Christianity against the opinions of the time and met with a favourable response at home and abroad. In Rome, Pospíšil became a member of the Academy of St. Thomas Aquinas, and at home his works were also praised by the then professor of philosophy in Prague, Tomas Garrigue Masaryk (the first Czechoslovak president in 1918-1935), who described Pospíšil's writings as some of the best of Czech philosophical literature.[1] Pospíšil also influenced many of his colleagues and nurtured his ideological followers, who included, for instance, Václav Hlavatý, Josef Kachník, Josef Machota and Eugen Kadeřávek. The situation was similar in Hungary, where the neo-Thomistic philosophy was spreading from the university in Budapest and the seminary in Esztergom. To support this direction, the Society of St. Thomas was established in Budapest, and the seminary in Timisoara began to issue a specialised philosophical magazine in 1886. At the same time, Gustav Pécsi, a leading advocate of neo-scholasticism and a professor of philosophy, also established himself in Esztergom.[2]

It was to the great merit of these figures that in the mid-1880s led to neo-Thomistic philosophy being included in the curriculum at theological faculties and episcopal seminaries. Exactly these institutions represented at the time the leading structures behind the transfer and development of neo-Thomistic philosophy in East-Central Europe.

Before World War I reflections on the troublesome social issue began to strongly resonate through Catholic intellectual circles. As the basis for the revival of society and also for the critique and rejection of the revolution-

1   Pikhart, *Český novotomismus od vydání encykliky Aeterni patris do 50. let XX. století*, 21.
2   Perrier, *The Revival of Scholastic Philosophy in the Nineteenth Century*, 224.

ary spoils, the Catholic social reformers adopted the language of Thomism, through which they formulated their responses. Mediaeval scholastic philosophy was thus supposed to form a strong barrier against the changing worlds and philosophy that led mankind to the crossroads of revolution. However, it actually had the opposite effect. The Thomistic philosophy created a sort of brace – an intellectual reinforcement for various groups that rejected modern thinking and opposed individualism. Through the same Thomism and its references to public welfare, social justice, price and trade, issues concerning the temporary social and economic reality began to be discussed.[3] However, this philosophical breeding ground, originally understood as a sign of slacking and regression, generated responses to the changing world, the growing industrialisation and urbanisation, and subsequently articulated them in the language of economists and sociologists. The agenda of the Church, which should have stood up against modern society and its depravity, became the environment where these two antagonists came into contact and could engage in discussion. One emblematic representative of this branch of neo-Thomism was Bedřich Vašek, who significantly influenced the Czechoslovak Christian sociology of the entire interwar period. Vašek's conceptions on the social arrangement stemmed fully from the social teaching of the Church and he promoted their integration into the life of the Church. His best work was *Křesťanská sociologie* (Christian Sociology), published in three volumes in 1929-1933 and subsequently abridged and adapted for students of theology. It was published in shorter form as a scriptum in 1935 as *Rukojeť křesťanské sociologie* (Handbook of Christian Sociology). The book attracted great attention and was soon published in five reprints. It thus became one of the fundamental compendia to which the teaching of Christian sociology adhered across various seminaries throughout Czechoslovakia.

In his articles and books, the professor from Olomouc advocated the greatly pro-active and ostensible approach of the priesthood to social issues and questions which troubled the working class. He saw the reasons for the priesthood's involvement among the working class primarily in the need to reverse the "painful desertion of the working class from the Church"[4] and in the urgency to face its ideological adversaries among the socialists as well as liberal parties. Nor did he avoid criticising his colleagues (priests and chaplains) for the lack of action or empty phrases that were so frequent in the Catholic camp. He encouraged priests and laymen not only to further their study of the social teaching but also urged them to immediate activity and response. He reasoned using the arguments of Pope Pius XI, saying that workers themselves should be the first apostles of the working class, and called for the responsibility for holding and organising Christian social activities to be trans-

3   Mayeur, "Catholicisme intransigeant, catholicisme social, démocratie chrétienne", 489.
4   Vašek, "Sociálna úloha kňaza podľa encyklík", 98.

ferred directly to the workers.[5] Such opinions were quite extraordinary among
the leading Czechoslovak Christian social thinkers and referred rather to the
views that Social Catholicism advocated in Western Europe. However, despite
his significant influence and position, Vašek did not manage to establish these
opinions among the bishops, who consistently pushed for strong control of
social activities and community life through local parishes and chapels.

Vašek was also very pro-active outside the academic environment. He was
involved in church life as well as public life and from 1928 was a great supporter
of Catholic action, and also helped with the preparation of Catholic conven-
tions. As one of the few Catholic representatives, he also participated in the
International Congress on Social Policy, held in Prague in 1924.[6] He was also a
part of various international Christian social networks. From 1937 he was the
only Czechoslovak member of the Union internationale d'études sociales (International Union for Social Studies) which held its sessions in Malines (Mechelen), Belgium and from 1920 was the leading forum for social Catholic thinking.[7]

The period after World War I brought another change in the local neo-
Thomistic circles. It was the increasing involvement of the Dominicans in the
development of this philosophical direction. Activities of local Dominicans
were preceded by the renewal of the independent Czech Dominican province
which, in this process, took inspiration from the French provinces of the order.

The enterprises of the Dominicans are exactly what represented the im-
aginary flashpoint of neo-Thomism in the Czechoslovak environment between
the two world wars. In person, this process was represented by two Dominicans: Silvestr Braito[8] and Metoděj Habáň[9]. They both came from a humble

5   Vašek, "Sociálna úloha kňaza podľa encyklík", 101.
6   *Mezinárodní sjezd sociální politiky v Praze 1924*, 139-154.
7   Archives of the Archdiocese of Mechelen-Brussels, Van Roey VI-28: Correspondence
     between Leopold Prečan and the Belgian primate Cardinal Van Roey, 1937.
8   Silvestr Maria Braito (1898-1962) was born in Bulgaria to Italian parents who died when he
     was still a child and he was taken in by the Merhaut family, acquaintances of his parents
     who later moved to Bohemia. After the death of Mr. Merhaut he was sent to a Dominican
     orphanage in Prague, from where he joined their juvenate during his studies at grammar
     school. In 1915 he joined the Dominicans and began to study at their order seminary in
     Olomouc, later to leave for Rome. After his consecration, thanks to his talent the order
     sent him for further studies in Le Saulchoir, Belgium, which was the spiritual centre of
     the French Dominicans. There he learned about new movements focusing on the spiritual
     renewal of Catholic life in French-speaking countries. After returning from Belgium, he
     established, and for many years was the chief editor of, a revue entitled *Na hlubinu* (To the
     [Spiritual] Depth). In 1950 he was convicted and in 1960 released from prison in an amnesty.
9   Metoděj Habáň (1899-1984) was born in Moravia, graduated from the grammar schools in
     Uherské Hradiště and České Budějovice, joined the Dominican order in 1918 and was sent
     to study in Rome, where he attended the Angelicum. In 1927 he was awarded a doctorate in
     philosophy and spent a short time in Fribourg, Switzerland. After returning to Czechoslovakia
     he worked as a professor at the Faculty of Theology in Olomouc and was the head of the
     Czech Dominican province in 1938-1942. His interest centred mostly around psychology and
     aesthetics. The thinking of Jacques Maritain was a major influence on his works.

environment and as excellent students were sent to study in Belgium, Switzerland and Rome. After returning to their homeland, they focused on publishing and organisational activities. Braito began to publish a magazine in Olomouc in 1926 entitled *Na hlubinu* (To the [Spiritual] Depth), whose publication continued uninterrupted even during World War II until 1948, when it was prohibited after the Communist party seized power in the country. The *Na hlubinu* magazine strove to intensify spiritual life, promoted a rather innovative approach and openness and did not shy from exploring controversial topics from the political, cultural and social life of the time. In 1929, *Filosofická revue* (Philosophy Revue) began to be published as a quarterly with Metoděj Habáň as the editor. Most of the Thomists of the time were centred around the revue. It regularly published translations from foreign philosophers, such as Roman Ingarden, Ludwig Landgrebe, Jacques Maritain and Erich Przywara. The *Filosofická revue* tried to present the legacy of St. Thomas as part of modern philosophy and drew attention mainly to the local intellectuals.

The texts published in these magazines, however, overlapped into other sciences, such as sociology, psychology, religious studies, pedagogy, aesthetics, and also logics and the philosophy of natural sciences. Besides Braito and Habáň, significant contributors also included Reginald Dacík, Emilian Soukup and Artur Pavelka. The revues' excellent links to developments abroad in the area of Christian philosophy, and its reflection in the social sciences or literature, can be seen in reviews of diverse works by authors writing in French, Italian, German, Dutch and English. In 1927, also in Olomouc, the Dominicans established a book edition entitled Krystal, which was behind a major editorial achievement – the publication of the *Summa Theologica* by St. Thomas Aquinas in the Czech language in 1937-1940.

The Czechoslovak Thomists attracted the greatest attention both home and abroad through the International Thomist Conference held in Prague at the beginning of October 1932 at the Philosophical Faculty of Charles' University.[10] The conference organisers tried to demonstrate the dimensions of Thomistic philosophy and its ability to revitalise the receding philosophical thinking. The Czech Dominicans' foreign contacts enabled them to prepare a prestigious congress attended by leading Christian philosophers, such as Erich Przywara of Munich, René Kremer of Leuven, Régis Jolivet, Hijacint Bošković and Kazimierz Kowalski. An interesting approach to the topicality and quality of the philosophical debates at the congress was taken by the Czech philosopher Jan Patočka, then 25 years old. While articles in the Catholic media informed about the congress with considerable appreciation, Patočka published a major critique in the *Česká mysl* (Czech Mind) magazine. He considered the congress to be philosophically insufficient or even propagandistic. His critique focused mostly on Czechs attending the congress. His

---

10   Habáň, *Sborník mezinárodních tomistických konferencí v Praze 1932.*

articles in *Česká mysl* met a considerable response and led to a philosophical argument between Habáň and Patočka, later to become far more personal than an ideological conflict.[11]

The conditions after the year 1918 and the emergence of an independent Czechoslovak state were also favourable for the development of Catholic philosophy in Slovakia, in which a whole new generation of philosophers had established themselves. As a certain bridge between the Hungarian tradition and new conditions, Alexander Spesz was something of a Nestor of Slovak neo-Thomism in the interwar period. His work was followed up on by other figures, such as Štefan Faith, Pavol Beňuška, Ján Dieška and Inocent Müller. Compared to the Czech lands, the neo-Thomistic direction in Slovakia was much weaker and did not have its own publication platforms with a more apparent programme. The only exception was a short-lived revue entitled *Smer* (Direction), issued between 1941 and 1948.

What bound together these, now forgotten, neo-Thomists? The generation which made the greatest contribution to the development of neo-Thomism were mostly priests born at the end of the nineteenth century whose studies began at the time of the Austro-Hungarian Empire. They all received more than just a seminary education. The important thought-forming experience of this group stemmed from their foreign studies, which went beyond the bounds of theology (sociology, psychology, aesthetics) and usually concluded with an internship at one of the papal universities. All local neo-Thomists were priests, as neo-Thomistic circles were not able to generate any stronger lay representative, even though they tried to address the broader intellectual community through magazines.

Neo-Thomism did not remain just an official philosophy, taught at theological faculties and disseminated through professional magazines and scientific congresses. Its language became strongly established in the social teachings of the Church and was an important source of inspiration for Catholic considerations concerning the changing society.

Karl von Vogelsang established himself as the founding figure of this direction in the Austro-Hungarian Empire.[12] He even attracted attention from the young Austrian socially-focused Catholics who continued to form the Austrian social school. This group was also in touch with leading Catholic social thinkers, such as René de la Tour du Pin, who served as a French military attaché in Vienna between 1879 and 1885. Tour du Pin mediated French experience with organising the working class on the Catholic principle, as well as different kinds of sociological approach based on long-term research and analysis

---

11   Pikhart, *Český novotomismus od vydání encykliky Aeterni patris do 50. let XX. století*, 23-30.
12   Karl von Vogelsang (1818-1890), after studying in Berlin he was a Prussian state official for some time and later also a Member of Parliament. As an adult he converted from Protestantism to Catholicism and in 1864 moved to Austria, where he was active as a publicist until his death.

of the working-class environment by Frédéric Le Play, providing the Catholics in East-Central Europe with effective arguments and experience. In the intellectual field, Le Play offered material and analytical tools appropriate to the time and science, which allowed Catholics to formulate response using the scientific language of sociology.[13] In terms of organisation they drew inspiration from the French Catholics as regards new forms accentuated by the independent working-class associations.

Vogelsang also exercised a direct influence in the sphere of politics, namely on the social legislation during Taaffe's government (1879-1893). This conservative government was determined to carry out social reforms much more than its liberal predecessors. It is interesting to notice that the conservatives, with their critique of liberalism and the capitalist economy, were much closer to what was advocated by the emerging socialist movement. This closeness must be seen as being linked to a certain political calculus and efforts to squeeze out the political competition. The state social policy was seen by the conservatives as a means of eliminating the adverse consequences of the market economy and was also supposed to weaken the socialists as it would meet important requirements of the working class movement. Taaffe's social legislation was also strongly aimed against the milieu of larger entrepreneurs, who made up one of the most important groups of supporters of the liberal parties, i.e. political adversaries. If, on top of all this, the conservatives could also rely on the emerging social teaching of the Catholic Church, or support from the clerics, it is understandable that they took the opportunity to do so.

The different types of socio-economic approach formulated in the Catholic environment resounded through broad social debates and politics and had unmistakeable potential. The principles of Social Catholicism were acquired by the representatives of the Catholic camp among the ruling as well as non-ruling national group as a political strategy to gain supporters from the working class back during the time of the Austro-Hungarian Empire. However, despite Christian universalism and ideological affinity, the Catholic parties never united to form a joint bloc. The reasons behind this lack of unity could lie in the strong national character of the individual Christian parties, which was never overcome even by the transnational idea of Christian universalism. The environment of the Christian social parties established from the end of the nineteenth century was, however, linked to strong anti-Semitism through the language of Social Catholicism. These trends were most apparent in the leader of the Austrian Christian Democrats, Karl Lueger. Lueger's party in the Imperial Council called a reduction in the growing power of the Jews, the confiscation of Jewish properties and the implementation of laws that would abolish the equality of the Jews. Seeing the Jews as high capitalists, creators of cartels and a major obstacle to good Christian business, or as socialistic instigators

13   Pelletier, "Engagement intellectuel catholique et médiation du social", 30.

and revolutionists, added to the wide array of diverse allegations and traditional Catholic anti-Judaism, thanks to the Christian Socialists. The tense anti-
Semitism of the Christian Social party to a certain extent compromised the
entire Christian social project, also influencing that part of society which had
earlier been in favour of the Church's involvement in the social issue.[14]

It was not only Bedřich Vašek who acted as a meeting point between the
environment of the Thomistic philosophers and interest in the social issue in
Czechoslovakia. These issues were also the subject of great attention from the
two publication platforms, *Na hlubinu* and *Filosofická revue*. The parties involved in the development of Thomistic philosophy thus remained focused
also on contemporary issues and tried to become fully involved in the broad
social discussions.

The Christian social thinkers had a very critical view of the liberal capitalist system which they perceived as being the cause of many pathological
phenomena in society.[15] In their opinion, the liberal economy was particularly
guilty because of its selfish egoism. They rejected the concepts of monopolies
and the economic system where prices were dictated by cartels. The Catholic
environment was strongly critical of capitalism, not only as regards Christian
social reasoning but also through extensive literary activities.[16]

Articles dealing with Social Catholicism in various periodicals, however,
included more or less critical statements about the Catholic Church, mentioning that the message of the great workers' encyclical had not been fulfilled and
its requirements had not been met.[17] The priesthood was strongly encouraged
to step out of the sacristies and become fully involved among the workers.
The cause of the Church's alienation from the workers was seen in the fact
that "the Czech priesthood had long distanced itself from the workers' social
movement. In countries where the new movement was effectively and timely
influenced by the priesthood, the conditions are much better. So in Holland,
Belgium and Germany they are firmly seated as bastions of the Christian workers' organisation."[18]

Besides continuing self-education in social issues, work on introducing
workers' trade union organisations was also seen as one of a priest's duties.
The priests were called upon both to commune with their parishioners and
also to strengthen the spirit of social justice. The language used by the Catholic press in addressing its readers was considerably scientific on the one hand,
reflecting debates in the fields of sociology, the national economy and phi-

---

14   Hamannová, *Hitlerova Vídeň*, 316-323, 330.
15   Veselý, "Hospodářství a mravní zákony"; Dudáš, "Kto nesie hlavnú vinu na terajšej
     kríze?".
16   Jaksicsová, *Kultúra v dejinách – dejiny v kultúre*, 77-80, 94-96; Putna, *Česká katolická
     literatura v kontextech*, 811-823.
17   Doležal, *Český kněz*, 90-91; Škrábik, "Katolicizmus na Slovensku dnes a zajtra", 630.
18   Budař, "Kněz – politika – dělnictvo", 98.

losophy. On the other hand, it was filled with numerous parables and religious metaphors,[19] as well as the belief that the gospel is a message which should be advocated equally on the factory floor, in the mines, iron works, banks and on the boards of industrial and financial concerns.[20]

The same authors were more conciliatory towards socialism, and considered its materialism and atheism[21] to be hampering cooperation that could otherwise have been seen as beneficial. The priests who contributed to the discussion on the social involvement of the Church principally agreed with the analytical methods of the socialists and often used the same phrases or vocabulary. However, they had reservations concerning the way the socialists wanted to restore society, the class conflict and the lack of respect for the ideas of private ownership. Despite the proclamations of the higher hierarchy, priests were told "not to build barriers [against the socialists] as they are already high enough now" and also recommended not to shy away from the socialists as being unworthy of them, but to communicate with them and be very careful not to "use the arguments and arsenal of liberalism and capitalism against the socialists, as these arguments are repeated by Catholics, too, without them being convinced of their veracity".[22]

A much more critical position was formulated by the Catholic intellectuals through Christian social thought against communism. Critiques of communism often appeared in the magazines in connection with capitalism. It commented upon its hostility towards religion, the reckless exploitation of socially weaker individuals and the subversiveness of its fight against capitalism. The authority and source of information about conditions in the Soviet Union was the Russian émigré Nikolai Berdyaev and his work.[23] The fundamental arguments that Berdyaev brought to the local debate were the rejection of the messianic character of the proletariat, the dominance and ubiquity of the state and suppression of individual freedom. According to the Catholic authors, the instructed word and weapons of pro-active love needed to be used to face the Bolsheviks' propaganda.[24]

Bolshevism was depicted as a dangerous global disaster that only pretended to have an economic and social agenda to improve the living conditions of the poorest. "In their agenda the communists include love for poverty and economic justice, but Christians should not be deluded as this is merely a way and tactic to achieve a major objective: the denial of God's law and the

---

19 Bubán, "Kristus na predmestí", 4-6.
20 Doležal, *Český kněz*, 94.
21 "Hospodářský liberalismus a socialismus", 85; Gašparec, "Kapitalizmus, socializmus, stavovstvo", 94-97.
22 Kompának, "Sociálne povinnosti kňaza vyplývajúce z pápežských encyklík", 72.
23 Berďajev, "O demokracii a socialismu".
24 S., "Bolševizmus hrozí!", 859; Dacík, "Katolicismus a komunismus".
25 Ciker, "Komunizmus v Československu".

destruction of the Catholic Church."[25] However, in a series of articles as part of this Catholic struggle against communism the leading Dominican theologian Silvestr Braito formulated the mistakes that the Catholics were making, mistakes which could be ill-fated for them. He called for Catholics not to point out the dangers of Bolshevism as far as the rights of workers were concerned. According to Braito, the Catholics should give up the idea that the social issue can be resolved by offering alms, and the Church as a whole should avoid even the slightest suspicion that it leans on individuals or organisations which prey on, or abuse, workers.[26] His reasoning stemmed from the belief that the communists' most powerful weapon was the appeal of their ideas, which were all the more attractive the more others closed their eyes to the social injustice affecting hundreds of thousands of people. He also drew attention to the fact that if Christians do not decide to address social wrongdoing and inequality, "this will be addressed by those who proclaim that the rights of Christianity and belief and hope dissuade people from a radical solution".[27]

The opinions and viewpoints presented by this Dominican were not entirely alone, yet they in no way represented the predominant state of mind. The view of communism, also formulated through the dominating discussions, focused on its destructive nature, the threat it posed to society and culture, as well as the necessary feeling that society was in danger.

The socio-economic dimension of the debates that stemmed from the social teaching of the Church and neo-Thomistic philosophy also strongly appealed to the various Catholic political parties and organisations and associations linked to them.[28] The multi-national nature of Czechoslovakia was also reflected in the structure of the Catholic parties, each of which had its own priorities and political objectives.

Jan Šrámek, the head of the most influential Catholic party (CSL) and a pre-war lecturer on Christian sociology and founder of the Christian trade unions in Moravia, was very close to social topics. Similar inspirations also found their way into documents describing this party's agenda. The most important agendas from the beginning of the 1920s worked with the idea of Christian solidarism and followed up on Christian socialism, while they extended the original requirements of Social Catholicism to farmers as well as to the workers. Social Catholic teaching in CSL agenda was thus adapted to suit the heterogeneous social basis of the party. Christian solidarism was based on the need for cooperation across various social milieu. It also called for concili-

26 Braito, "Omyly v boji proti komunismu".
27 Id., "Boj proti komunismu".
28 In the interwar period the following main Catholic parties existed in Czechoslovakia: Czechoslovak People's Party (CSL), Slovak People's Party (SLS) which later included the name 'Hlinka's' and changed to HSLS, German Christian-social People's Party – Deutsche Christlichsoziale Volkspartei (DCV) and Provincial Christian-socialist Party – Országos Keresztényiszocialista Párt.

ation and cooperation between all social groups and strove to become a platform for resolving conflicts between employees and employers. The mistakes of contemporary capitalism were to be rectified by renewing the virtues of entrepreneurs. The party's agenda saw capitalism as an improper way of using private property, caused by the moral shortcomings of its owners. The agendas laid great emphasis on the division of society into estates and the need for the workers to organise themselves into trade unions.[29] The introductory chapter of the party's program entitled *Obnova lidské společnosti* (Renewal of Human Society) rejected capitalism for its individualism, greed and mammon, while at the same time denouncing socialism for its materialistic philosophy of life. After this 'obligatory round' it strove to present a sort of synthesis of the Christian teaching on human society, intended to complement the party's political agenda and reforms. The section on family discusses housing for workers, as well as educational issues and the protection of mothers. Referring to the sociologist Frédéric Le Play, the agenda concluded that the housing issue is a source of social poverty.[30] The state and municipality should be involved in this area, and should support the establishment of housing cooperatives and workers' houses. New working class quarters should be built along the lines of garden towns, with plenty of greenery and wide streets. Considerable attention was paid to the workers in the third part, which is about the estates. The political program of the CSL promoted joint associations of employers and workers to represent the organisational structure replacing the forcefully disrupted trade unions and guilds, but was not to be subjected to the exaggerated requirements of the Social Democrats, who wanted to make the worker's estate an exclusive caste to win the class conflict.[31] At the same time the agenda rejected the communist ideas regarding collective property, and on the basis of experience from post-revolutionary Russia it assumed that Bolshevism was a threat to nation's life and culture as a whole, was maintained using violent means and spread poverty, hunger and desperation instead of welfare.[32]

The significant diversity of economic and social attitudes in the agendas of the individual elements of the CSL and among its members and supporters caused serious problems, despite all the efforts to achieve mutual solidarity. These problems surfaced in numerous arguments across the whole party. The diversity of requirements was also what caused a split in the party, resulting from inner tension among the representatives of the individual social groups. One consequence of this tension was the secession of the workers' wing in the CSL in the mid-1920s.[33]

---

29 Trapl, "Charakteristika Československé strany lidové v letech", 197.
30 Stašek, *Obnova lidské společnosti*, 22.
31 Ibid., 42.
32 Ibid., 50.
33 Trapl, "Charakteristika Československé strany lidové v letech", 199.

The use of the arguments of social teaching by the Church took quite a different form in Hlinka's Slovak People's Party (HSLS) as regards its agenda and the political reality. The renewal of the social order, which was to include not only material but also mental and moral values, incorporated a strong bond between the social and national autonomistic aspect. The social issue and that of Slovak autonomy (inside of Czechoslovakia) were usually firmly interlinked in the HSLS, and represented one of the specifics of the way in which the language of Social Catholicism was used by Slovak political Catholicism. This autonomistic discourse was therefore closely tied with the search for the enemy and for anyone who harms Slovak workers, farmers, entrepreneurs or intelligentsia. Besides the allegations of big cartels, the Czechs and the central government, which exacerbated the unequal distribution of economic sources in the state, were also seen as liable by many representatives of the HSLS. Such allegations began to appear with the emergence of the Czechoslovak Republic in 1918, voiced not only by relatively radical opponents of the unified state but also by the pro-Czechoslovak representatives of the HSLS. The language and references to the social teaching of the Church in the HSLS were therefore used to emphasise and legitimise the nationally intolerant attacks against the Czech element in the economic life of Slovakia during the era of interwar Czechoslovakia, and later also against the Jewish population.

Hlinka's Slovak People's Party itself, and the organisations linked to it, were somewhat more active in promoting workers' interests than the Czech Catholic political circles. This is also evident in the direct support for strike movements and in the establishment of links to ideologically different organisations. In 1924, for instance, with the approval of the People's Party, the Christian trade unions went on strike in textile factories in Rajec and Žilina, followed later by Trenčín, together with organisations supported by the Social Democrats. The Christian trade unions and HSLS were not afraid to stand up for much stricter calls for improvements to the working conditions of the labourers, which not only boosted their membership, but also improved their overall credibility in the eyes of the workers.[34] Accepting the more radical methods and emphasising the social themes in real political life was what made the HSLS different from the Czech People's party. What caused this difference across the political representation of the two national Catholic communities? The reasons for such an interest in social issues in the HSLS must be seen in the party's mindset and its certain political calculus, rather than in its pro-worker orientation and deep enthusiasm for Social Catholicism. In the midst of this unrest, the HSLS was offered the chance to gain publicity amongst the workers, while as a political power predominantly in opposition, it did not take the risk of accepting any political responsibility. It could only gain from the support of the socially tense cases with a bit of added national drive. The

---

34 Katuninec, "Kresťanské odbory v spolupráci a konfrontácii s komunistickými odbormi", 79.

CSL, being predominantly a member of coalition governments, could not afford such involvement except with a much greater political risk, which was also why it did not engage itself in this direction. However, this support for the workers in their effort to improve their living conditions remained only an occasional activity for the HSLS, too, and was in no way distinctively reflected in the party's agenda or political activities.

As regards social teaching, what resonated most within the HSLS was the system of estates, as well as passages from social encyclicals through which the ideological or political competition could be refuted. Both of these elements immediately found their place in the circumstances after 14 March 1939 – Slovakia's declaration of independence, when it became necessary to develop and specify the ideology of the authoritative regime and the ruling party. Štefan Polakovič, the main ideologist of Hlinka's Slovak People's Party, declared his affinity to these kinds of approach and inspiration right at the beginning of his paper entitled *K základom Slovenského štátu* (On the Foundations of the Slovak state). He referred to the regime of the Slovak state as "Christian totalitarianism" and considered it an alternative to individualism as well as to non-Christian etatism.[35]

The social teaching of the Church and its perception of the estates system was also referred to by the Constitution of the Slovak Republic of 21 July 1939. Corporativism in Slovakia was closely linked with the idea of Christian and national solidarity, formulated in the preamble to the Constitution.[36] The constitution of the new state was thus supposed to follow the example given by the pope in the encyclical entitled *Quadragesimo anno*. Such a perceived affiliation with the estates was supposed to lead to "a balance between the idea of the whole and the idea of the individual" and, according to contemporary commentaries, it was "inevitably necessary that individual estates, as well as individuals, were bound together by the ribbon of social justice and Christian love".[37] Affinity in this direction was repeatedly declared by leading representatives of the state, such as the President and Catholic priest Jozef Tiso and member of the Slovak Assembly Karol Mederly. According to them, the estates system was supposed to remove the "nest and cause of conflicts, the class conflict which pitted employee against employer".[38] The estates system was inspired both by Catholic social teaching and Italian fascism. Although it did not fully establish itself during the existence of the state,[39] it was an insepara-

---

35   Polakovič, *K základom Slovenského štátu*, 19.
36   Constitutional Law dated 21 July 1939, No. 185/1939 Sl. z.
37   Gašparec, "Glosy k stavovskému zriadeniu v ústave Slovenskej republiky", 196.
38   Ibid.
39   The law on the estates system was prepared but never adopted. The German party as well as the representatives of the Holy See had major objections against its implementation. The estates system, drawn in the Constitution, therefore never came into effect and remained entirely fragmentary. For more about the stance of Vatican diplomacy regarding this issue, see Kaššovic, *V službách vlasti*, 45-49.

ble part of social discussion. The response to the Church's social teaching was also evident in the approach to ownership, where its social dimension was accentuated,[40] as well as in the social legislation intended to protect the socially disadvantaged against exploitation and in planning wages with respect to family background. Along with these apparently pro-social measures, the right to strike was reduced, as were other forms of independent protection of employee interest.[41]

This is where a rudimentary question arises. Why then did Social Catholicism not establish itself and become a real alternative to the increasingly radical courses in Slovak political Catholicism, which eventually led to its moral and political discrediting? The reasons could lie in the developments both before and after March 1939. What had not been achieved in the party's direction in the political culture of interwar Czechoslovakia was only hard to negotiate in the increasingly radical HSLS. Despite the significance given to the Christian-social ideological background in official party documents and various addresses, there was no Social-Catholic wing inside the party with any real influence on the party's direction. Representatives of these social Catholic principles and trends were mostly individuals, such as Karol Sidor or Rudolf Čavojský,[42] who very soon after the establishment of the Slovak Republic were ousted to less significant positions by the far more radical wing led by Vojtech Tuk and Alexander Mach.

Despite this, the language of Social Catholicism saw a very interesting overlap in Slovakia during the war. In its economic and social rhetoric it managed to formulate an alternative to the national socialistic direction after the Salzburg negotiations, which assumed that Slovakia would comply with the need for wartime production, the restriction of social benefits, wage cuts and restrictions on workers' right to associate. References to papal encyclicals thus lacked a philosophical as well as moral dimension. It became nothing more than a substitute symbol, through which the relevant participants tried to articulate the right for greater economic independence and the country's own social policy, one that would not be so strongly forced on them by Nazi Germany. This religious language, using references to Social Catholicism, articulated political dissatisfaction which, if pronounced directly through another language, could have had far more dangerous consequences. However, this parallel economic and social discourse, seeking support in the social teaching of the Church, had no higher moral standards. It did not question aryanisation, the transports of the Jews or the expulsion of many experts involved in the development of industry and the social system before 1939. At the time when the HSLS was becoming increasingly radical, as well as at the time of the

40 Constitutional Law dated 21 July 1939, No. 185/1939 Sl. z., Sect. 79.
41 Rákosník, *Proměny sociálního práva v Československu*, 100.
42 Sidor, *Ako sa díva Cirkev na sociálnu otázku?*; Id., "Riešenie sociálnej otázky v rámci katolíckej akcie"; Čavojský, *Spomienky kresťanského odborára*.

Slovak state during the war, the language of Social Catholicism became only a suitable ideological addendum to political Catholicism in Slovakia, being used in anti-Semitic attacks and nationally intolerant critique, which further compromised the Catholic political camp.

The language of Social Catholicism and Christian-social direction were also very appealing to the Hungarian and German Catholic parties. It actually allowed them to become active in a field which did not necessarily have a narrow nationalistic profile, and at the same time offered them an opportunity to participate in discussions about important issues in society. The overlap with the Church's social teaching and the tradition of Christian social parties also gave them legitimacy and helped to launch their activities in the newly established Czechoslovak Republic, where they were seen as nothing more than national minority parties.

From when it was first established, the Hungarian Provincial Christian Socialist Party referred to the social teaching defined in the papal encyclicals and tried to address the Slovak population, too, with only partial success. It was established on 23 November 1919 in Košice. The party was quite successful especially in the early 1920s in Eastern Slovakia and Subcarpathian Ruthenia. Its members were a relatively heterogeneous group. Entrepreneurs, wealthy farmers and rural landowners, as well as workers, inclined to the party. The accentuation of social issues and the use of language of Social Catholicism brought the party both success as well as supporters among the industrial proletariat in towns. The Provincial Christian Socialist Party (KKSS) also had its own network of trade union organisations in which workers, craftsmen and transport and public administration employees associated. From the end of the 1920s the influence of the Christian Socialist Party waned considerably and the party struggled with a lack of finances and respected leaders.[43]

The German Christian Social Party followed up on the tradition of the Austrian Christian Social Party established in the 1890s. The breakup of the Habsburg Monarchy found the German Christian Social Party in the Czech lands adopting the positions of German nationalism, unlike their Czech counterpart, which sought ways of integrating into the national life. German Catholics in the newly established Czechoslovakia then found themselves in a difficult situation. On the one hand, they had to face the wave of anti-Catholicism, to which they were also better able to respond owing to their experience from the end of the century and the Los von Rom movement. On the other hand, like the Hungarian population, they became a minority in a state which had been established against their will and whose citizens they had not wanted to become. The German Christian Social People's Party (Deutsche Christlichsoziale Volkspartei – DCV) was officially established at its convention on 2 November

---

43   Slovenský národný archív, collection: Policajné riaditeľstvo Bratislava, box 241: Správa prezídia policajného riaditeľstva (Report of the Police Directorate Presidium), 1927.

1919 in Prague, where its agenda was also approved. The editor Josef Böhr was appointed as its first chairman, and the party leadership also comprised two university professors, an economist and a theologian. The agenda was based on the principles of Christian social thinking developed in the Habsburg Monarchy by Vogelsang, Schindler and the trade union leader Leopold Kunschak in the latter half of the nineteenth century. The DCV was equally influenced by nationalist trends and supported efforts for national self-determination and the defence of German national rights. Besides national requirements, they also promoted the defence of Christian principles in schools, education and the family. The heritage of the Austrian Christian Social Party was also strongly manifested in this party in its relations with the Jewish population. They repeatedly mentioned the need to curtail the Jewish influence on the economy and proposed the adoption of the numerus clausus for their admission to secondary schools and universities, by which they veered strongly towards anti-Semitism as early as in the 1920s. They were characterised by their emphasis on Christian solidarity. They intensely advocated private ownership and at the same time drew attention to the need for the individual to be responsible to the whole. They perceived the system of estates, which would be based on mutual cooperation between the estates and was supposed to eliminate social conflicts and class conflict, as the best model for society. An important part of their agenda was dedicated to requirements such as social insurance for the disabled and ill, for the old and unemployed, equality between men and women and the provision of proper social care for children and young people. Its members were recruited mainly among the rural and urban middle class, from craftsmen and tradesmen to lower officials. Industry workers mostly opposed DVC policy, and the party's agenda only succeeded in addressing workers in some areas in North Bohemia and in the Czech-Moravian border regions. The language of the Church's social teaching was used in German political Catholicism mainly to criticise its ideological opponents, just as it was with the Czech and Slovak parties. They understood socialism not only as an economic system but also as a philosophy of life which went against the principles of Christianity because it was subjected to the material aspect of life. They denounced calls for class hatred and advocated an appeal for cooperation between the estates for the common good. During the Great Depression, the DCV focused primarily on resolving issues in the textile industry, which, together with glassmaking, was the most vulnerable industry affected by the declining demand in the early 1930s. These economic segments were also concentrated in north-eastern Bohemia, where the German Christian Social Party as well as its trade unions had a strong presence.[44]

But how did all these ideas make their way and become established among the people to whom they were mainly addressed – the workers? What did the lan-

---

44 Šebek, *Mezi křížem a národem*, 31-37, 165-166.

guage of social justice, the issues of public welfare, the price of labour and trade mean to the workers, and how did the ideas of the Catholic intellectuals succeeded in mobilising the real world beyond the gates of the factories and mines?

A good insight into this topic can clearly be obtained from the example of the Christian social trade unions. In terms of Czechoslovakia as a whole, Christian trade unions were only one of the minor players in the field of trade union organisations. If we were to look at membership figures, we could see that the Christian social trade unions accounted for approx. 134 thousand members in mid-1920s. At the end of 1933 there were some 147 thousand. Compared to the dominant Czech-Slovak Trade Unions Association, backed by the Social Democrats, the Christian trade unions managed to address only around a quarter of the Association's members in the mid-1920s, and this proportion declined in the following years.[45]

In Bohemia, Christian trade unions played only a supporting role until World War I, being closer in nature to a public initiative rather than an organisation trying to defend workers' interests, while in Moravia the situation was better owing to the activities of Jan Šrámek. From 1907 the Moravian Christian trade unions focused on establishing trade union groups in factories and tried to achieve a strong position in negotiating with employers. Thanks to this pro-active approach, the Christian social trade unions in Moravia soon managed to win over the distrustful workers and their membership increased. Even back during the Monarchy the Christian social trade unions in the Czech lands offered its members financial assistance during illness and unemployment for eight weeks, later changed to seven, free legal advice and help with finding a new job. Later they also added allowances for commuting to work and a contribution to cover funeral or moving expenses.[46]

After the establishment of Czechoslovakia, the whole Christian social trade union movement began to significantly convert into a political movement and became divided up between the national representatives of political Catholicism. The objective of creating a united platform across the Czech, Slovak, German and Hungarian Christian trade union organisations remained unfulfilled. The Christian social trade union movement in Czechoslovakia thus remained fragmented, and not even religious universalism or joint inspirations in the social teaching of the Church could unite it. The heterogeneity of this movement and the national division was further strengthened by the fact that even within the national segments there were several parallel and competing Christian workers' organisations.

But who were the ordinary members of Christian trade unions, and what were they offered by these organisations on the grounds of their statutes? Or,

---

45   In 1925 the Czech-Slovak Trade Unions Association, backed by the Social Democrats, had 574,006 members. By the end of 1933 the figure was 642,111 members. *Zprávy Státního úřadu statistického Republiky československé*, 38, 1334; *Zprávy Státního úřadu statistického Republiky československé*, 1254-1255.
46   Marek, *Čeští křesťanští sociálové*, 193.

how were the Christian trade unions and their officials presented to the outside world? Members of Christian social trade unions were for the most part
workers themselves. The dominating trade union organisations in Slovakia
and in the Czech lands had always been profiled as workers' organisations.
Also, in comparison with other trade union organisations, very few of their
members were state officials, usually around 5% of them. In other trade unions the proportion of state officials and non-worker professions used to be
much higher.[47] In the latter half of the 1920s workers in the Christian trade
unions began to play a stronger role in the trade union leadership, too. Even
though chairmanships were usually reserved for the chairmen of political parties or members of parliament, the posts of deputy chairmen and secretaries
were already beginning to be occupied by the elected workers.

The Christian social trade unions had to struggle to gain the trust not
only of the workers, but paradoxically also of employers such as the archbishopric estates in Olomouc. An illustrative example is the case of the machinist
Josef Vacl, who worked in Kroměříž (Moravia) and was also active in a Catholic
workers' association, of which he was the chairman. His superiors repeatedly
called upon him to answer the question of whether, as chairman of an association supposed to defend the interests of workers on the archbishopric estates,
he was not acting to the detriment of his employer. Vacl had to defend himself
against this strong critique and pressure by going as far as to write a letter to
the archbishop, in which he explained that his employer's interests were in
no way threatened and that the trade union he headed was a Christian organisation and pursued good goals. He also pointed out that after the 1918 coup
workers on the archbishopric estates were organised in trade unions backed
by the Social Democrats and that it was only after great effort that its members
could be convinced to believe the Christian idea. According to Vacl, it would
not be appropriate to aggravate them because of ill-considered action or defi-
ance against organising people in Christian trade unions after such an effort
to convince them.[48] Even though we do not know how that case ended, or
whether the Olomouc archbishop intervened in person, it turns out that not
even those employers who were directly linked to the Catholic Church were
necessarily happy with the activities of the Christian trade unions.

In considering the position and power of these Christian social organisations, we also have to bear in mind the fact that the motives for joining a
trade union organisation or for the frequent conversions to another, often related to the power and negotiating position of the relevant organisation in
each particular enterprise. The social benefits that membership entailed, as
well as the local distribution of power and personal reasons, could all have

47   Rákosník, "Limity působení ľudáckého odborového hnutí ve 30. letech", 95.
48   Zemský archiv v Opavě, pobočka Olomouc, collection: Arcibiskupství Olomouc, box 1144:
     Prípad Josef Vacl a jeho práce ve všeodborovém sdružení křesť. dělnictva (The case of Josef
     Vacl and his work in the All-Trade Union of Christian Workers), 1922.

played a far more important role in the decision than a person's philosophy of life or religious affinity. The efforts to gain religious members from socialist or communist trade unions, promoted through central trade union circulars, may also have been totally ineffective among workers for very down-to-earth reasons.[49] Christian workers' organisations did not lack organisational talent, but the crux of the matter was rather in the Catholics' views of striking and its use as an extreme, yet in certain cases the only effective means of defending the interests of employees. The Christian trade unions preferred negotiating. However, in doing so they could easily lose credit mainly in the eyes of those workers who had faced a stubborn employer or were in a critical financial situation that they were unable to handle.

On the other hand, we have to realise that the workers' movement was not a homogeneous entity and it was not just the dominant players that helped to form it. The Christian social trade unions, despite having organisations with fewer members, still participated in shaping the collective identity of the workers and in the development of civic society.

The objectives of Christian trade union organisations were usually formulated in their statutes as an effort to improve economic conditions, which also included a moral, educational and Christian social dimension. They considered the papal social encyclicals as the prototype and inspiration for their involvement.[50] Their language was naturally used by the whole movement in negotiating the material and social interests of workers.

The central points of the Christian social workers' movement in Czechoslovakia were also linked to the existing cultural traditions and values of the Catholic environment: family and ownership, which the Catholics considered necessary to defend. These aspects were accompanied by the declared struggle for social justice and denial of the class war, with efforts to restore religion and to fight against atheism and materialism. In the case of Slovakia in particular, an important role was played by the nationalist component through which they became opposed to the "illusion" of Marxist internationalism, Hungarian territorial revisionism, and also to the idea of Czechoslovakism.[51]

---

49 Slovenský národný archív, collection: Policajné riaditeľstvo Bratislava, box 168: Obežník
    č. 10/34 Všetkým skupinám: Odpis (Circular No. 10/34 to all groups: Write-off), Slovenské
    kresťansko-odborové združenie, 15 December 1934.
50 Archiv hlavního města Prahy, Spolkový katastr, box 765: Křesťansko-sociální svaz
    tabákových zaměstnanců v republice Československé (Christian Social Union of Tobacco
    Workers in the Czechoslovak Republic); Slovenský národný archív, collection: Policajné
    riaditeľstvo Bratislava, box 253: Stanovy a pravidlá všeodborového združenia kresťansko-
    sociálneho robotníctva Slovenského (Statues and rules for the All Trade Union of
    Christian Social Slovak Workers), Ružomberok 1925, knihtlač Lev; Ibid., box 16: Spolok
    Sdruženie katolíckych robotníkov so sídlom v Bratislave (Association of Catholic Workers'
    Association with its headquarters in Bratislave).
51 Van Duin and Poláčková, "Against the Red Industrial Terror!", 158.

While World War II disturbed the neo-Thomistic networks only marginally (the closure of universities and therefore also theological faculties in the Protectorate of Bohemia and Moravia, restrictions on the publication of magazines and books), a major disruption came after the Communist Party seized power in February 1948 and in subsequent years. Immediately after this coup, the publishing of *Na hlubinu* and *Filosofická revue* was suspended, to be followed by a ban on the entire Olomouc-based Krystal edition. Networks maintained at the level of the individual monastic communities, so important for the development and continuity of neo-Thomistic philosophy, were cut off with the dissolution of the monasteries that came at the beginning of 1950. The order seminaries and noviciates were dissolved and many of its members were put on trial or sentenced to forced labour. The 1950s brought the investigations and trials, in which many of the leading Catholic thinkers, activists and community life organisers were accused and convicted. Metoděj Habáň and Silvestr Braito were also tried. Habáň spent four years in prison for illegally continuing his monastic life, but at the end of 1950s he was allowed to return to a spiritual life in the remote Sokolov region. Silvestr Braito was arrested as part of the 'Vatican Agents' trial and sentenced to 15 years for high treason and espionage. He was released from prison in the 1960 amnesty, but died two years later and did not live to see his rehabilitation in 1968. The 1950s and the first half of 1960s were therefore marked by the fact that it was totally impossible to develop neo-Thomistic philosophy or engage in any organisational activities on a Christian basis. The theological seminaries were reduced to two, seated in Bratislava and Litoměřice, while the professorships and research conducted at the seminaries was strictly controlled by the Communist Party.

To a certain extent, citizens' involvement and their interest in wide social affairs, stemming from the social involvement of the Church, also left their own legacy. The heirs of this stream argued that the new regime should respect social justice and strengthen solidarity across individual groups of inhabitants. The mobilisation and activation of citizens around the topics of Social Catholicism before the seizure of power by the Communists was what stimulated a remarkable generation of Catholics in the period after 1948. Having survived the political trials and often many years of imprisonment or other forms of persecution, many Catholic activists followed up on this legacy in the Catholic dissent and underground Church of the 1970s and 1980s. This legacy and its social dimension in society thus survived in the samizdats and in home seminars and was incorporated into the programme of the decade of spiritual revitalisation in the 1980s. The language of Social Catholicism, which obviously continued to develop after 1945, had lost none of its appeal for the Catholic dissent and underground Church. It continued to represent an attractive recourse for argumentation, which helped to create positions and opinions against the dominant political and social power of the Communist Party.

This also provided a channel for voicing dissatisfaction and critique: critique which agreed with the necessity to resolve social issues and social tension but did not agree with the manner and means promoted by the Communist Party.

Some interesting projects were launched at the end of the 1960s, when Metoděj Habáň was engaged in dialogue between the Marxists and Christians in the philosophical seminar conducted by Milan Machovec. Habáň also helped to establish the ecumenical seminary in Jircháře, organised lectures in Prague and established foreign contacts. The promising development, however, was brought to a halt at the end of the 1960s with the new wave of persecution. Catholic philosophical efforts and any involvement thus had to continue illegally.

The reception and development of neo-Thomism in East-Central Europe pointed out several very interesting aspects. The resorting to philosophical and theological recourses, primarily seen as a manifestation of being backward and closed off, in fact created a functional platform within the Catholic Church at the end of the nineteenth century and in the early twentieth century, which provided room for it to discuss its opinions with its philosophical rivals as well as pressing topical issues, collectively referred to as the social issue. The language and arguments stemming from the neo-Thomistic tradition found their place in debates of scientific experts while fully adopting methods of analysis and address used not only in philosophy, but also in psychology, aesthetics and sociology or the national economy. The church agenda, which was supposed to stand up against modern society and its depravity, became an environment enabling these two adversaries to come into contact and engage in dialogue.

The incorporation of neo-Thomistic philosophy and its broadest overlaps into the life of individual Catholic communities, however, also encompassed a diversity of forms and intentions. The problem did not lie so much at the level of academic philosophical debates, although many times it did lead to some passionate debates (Patočka and Habáň). A much more responsive environment was in the social involvement of the Church and the language of Social Catholicism acquired by various political and interest groups. The interest of political Catholicism in the social teaching of the Church was, to a large extent, motivated solely by the fact that these kinds of approach gave to Catholic political parties grounds to criticise, refute and disqualify its own political competitors. This social discourse took on a specific form especially in the wartime Slovak state, where it acted as a support to the authoritative regime, was involved in anti-Semitic attacks and participated in the expulsion of many experts who had played a role in the development of industry and the social system before 1939.

It was also in the same arena of debates on the organisation of society that an opinion was formulated on one of the rivals to Social Catholicism in terms of its ideology and agenda. The manner in which the local Communist Party and the regime in the Soviet Union were depicted in the interwar and wartime period had a major effect on the Catholic ability to respond to changes in the regime after 1948. What the Catholics expected after the change of the regime was quite far from reality. For a long time Communism had been presented, including through Catholic social teaching, as the greatest evil and an infernal force, and most of the priests and believers expected immediate bloodshed, the closing of churches, open fighting, etc. As this did not happen, and openly hostile actions against churches did not come until several years later, the religious community did not know how to respond. Even though the churches did not approve of the regime, they were quite limited in their potential to mobilise, as it made no sense to stand up against rhetoric and efforts to improve the homeland, social reforms, and against the proclaimed efforts to ensure social justice and religious freedom. It is a paradox that the churches were actually given the necessary mobilising potential by the regime itself at the beginning of the 1950s, which saw the start of repeated violent actions against religious communities and priests and laymen put on trial. However, for the local environment this moment also meant a disruption of continuity and the dawn of neo-Thomism.

BIBLIOGRAPHY

Berďajev, Mikuláš. "O demokracii a socialismu" [On Democracy and Socialism]. *Řád*, 1932, 76-86.

Braito, Silvestr. "Boj proti komunismu" [The Struggle against Communism]. *Na Hlubinu*, (1936) 11/10, 707-709.

Braito, Silvestr. "Omyly v boji proti komunismu" [Mistakes in the Struggle against Communism]. *Na Hlubinu*, 12 (1937) 3, 208-209.

Bubán, Ján. "Kristus na predmestí" [Christ in the Suburb]. *Kultúra*, (1937) 1, 4-6.

Budař, Jan. "Kněz – politika – dělnictvo" [Priest – Politics – Working Class]. In *Časopis katolického duchovenstva*. Sursum, 1924, 96-98.

Čavojský, Rudo. *Spomienky kresťanského odborára* [Memoirs of a Christian Trade Union Official]. Bratislava: Lúč, 1996.

Ciker, Jozef. "Komunizmus v Československu" [Communism in Czechoslovakia]. *Kultúra*, (1937) 11-12, 237-241.

Dacík, Reginald. "Katolicismus a komunismus" [Catholicism and Communism]. *Na Hlubinu*, 11 (1936) 9, 627-631.

Doležal, Josef. *Český kněz* [Czech Priest]. Prague: Knihy života, 1931.

Dudáš, Andrej. "Kto nesie hlavnú vinu na terajšej kríze?" [Who is to Be Blamed for the Present Crisis?]. *Kultúra*, (1933) 2, 133-137.

Duin, Pieter van and Zuzana Poláčková. "Against the Red Industrial Terror! The Struggle of Christian Trade Unions in Austria and Czechoslovakia against Socialist Trade-Union and Workplace Domination, 1918-1925". In Lex Heerma van Voss, Patrick Pasture and Jan De Maeyer, eds. *Between Cross and Class: Comparative Histories of Christian Labour in Europe 1840-2000*. Bern-New York: Peter Lang, 2005, 127-173.

Gašparec, Ignác. "Kapitalizmus, socializmus, stavovstvo" [Capitalism, Socialism, Estates]. *Kultúra*, (1937) 5, 94-97.

Gašparec, Ignác. "Glosy k stavovskému zriadeniu v ústave Slovenskej republiky" [Notes on the System of Estates in the Constitution of the Slovak Republic]. *Kultúra*, (1939) 9, 195-197.

Habáň, Metoděj. *Sborník mezinárodních tomistických konferencí v Praze 1932* [Proceedings of the International Thomist Conference in Prague 1932]. Olomouc: Filosofická revue, 1933.

Hamannová, Brigitte. *Hitlerova Vídeň* [Hitler's Vienna]. Prague: Prostor, 2011.

"Hospodářský liberalismus a socialismus" [Economic Liberalism and Socialism]. *Filosofická revue*, (1937) 9, 84-85.

Jaksicsová, Vlasta. *Kultúra v dejinách – dejiny v kultúre: moderna a slovenský intelektuál v siločiarach prvej polovice 20. storočia* [Culture in History – History in Culture: The Modernist Movement and a Slovak Intellectual in the Contours of the First Half of the 20th Century]. Bratislava: Veda, 2012.

Kaššovic, Ján. *V službách vlasti. Spomienky na verejnú činnosť v rokoch 1939-1946* [In the Service of the Homeland: Memoirs of Public Activity in 1939-1946]. Bratislava: Ústav pamäti národa, 2012.

Katuninec, Milan. "Kresťanské odbory v spolupráci a konfrontácii s komunistickými odbormi" [Christian Trade Unions in Cooperation and Confrontation with Communist Trade Unions]. In Xénia Šuchová. *Ľudáci a komunisti: súperi? spojenci? protivníci?* Prešov: Universum, 2006, 76-88.

Kompánek, Anton. "Sociálne povinnosti kňaza vyplývajúce z pápežských encyklík" [Social Duties of Priests as Implied by the Papal Encyclicals]. *Duchovný pastier*, 18 (March 1937), 68-72.

Marek, Pavel. *Čeští křesťanští sociálové* [Czech Christian Socials]. Olomouc: Univerzita Palackého, 2011.

Mayeur, Jean-Marie. "Catholicisme intransigeant, catholicisme social, démocratie chrétienne". *Annales. Économies, Sociétés, Civilisations*, 27 (1972) 2, 483-499.

Mezinárodní sjezd sociální politiky v Praze 1924 [International Congress on Social Policy in Prague, 1924]. Prague: Nákladem Sociálního ústavu Československé republiky, 1924.

Pelletier, Denis. "Engagement intellectuel catholique et médiation du social. L'enquête monographique de Le Play à Lebret". *Mil neuf cent*, 13 (1995) 1, 25-45.

Perrier, Joseph Louis. *The Revival of Scholastic Philosophy in the Nineteenth Century*. New York: Columbia University Press, 1909.

Pikhart, Marcel. *Český novotomismus od vydání encykliky Aeterni patris do 50. let XX. století* [Czech Neo-Thomism from the Publication of the Aeterni patris Encyclical to 1950s]. Hradec Králové: Gaudeamus, 2000.

Polakovič, Štefan. *K základom Slovenského štátu: Filozofické eseje* [On the Foundations of the Slovak State: Philosophical Essays]. Turčiansky Sv. Martin: Matica slovenská, 1939.

Putna, Martin. *Česká katolická literatura v kontextech: 1918-1945* [Czech Catholic Literature in Context: 1918-1948]. Prague: Torst, 2010.

Rákosník, Jakub. "Limity působení ľudáckého odborového hnutí ve 30. letech" [Limitations on the Activities of the People's Party Trade Union Movement in the 1930s]. In Xénia Šuchová. *Ľudáci a komunisti: Súperi? Spojenci? Protivníci?* Prešov: Universum, 2006, 88-102.

Rákosník, Jakub. *Proměny sociálního práva v Československu v letech 1945-1956* [Development of Social Law in Czechoslovakia in 1945-1956]. Thesis (DPhil), Charles University Prague, 2012.

S., R. "Bolševizmus hrozí!" [Bolsehvism is Theatening!]. *Kultúra*, (1932) 12, 855-860.

Šebek, Jaroslav. *Mezi křížem a národem: politické prostředí sudetoněmeckého katolicismu v meziválečném Československu* [Between the Crucifix and the Nation: Political Environment of Sudeten German Catholicism in Interwar Czechoslovakia]. Brno: Centrum pro studium demokracie a kultury, 2006.

Sidor, Karol. "Riešenie sociálnej otázky v rámci katolíckej akcie" [Solution to the Social Issue within Catholic Action]. *Kultúra*, (1931) 9, 692-698.

Sidor, Karol. *Ako sa díva Cirkev na sociálnu otázku? Sociálny zákonník – náčrt katolíckeho sociálneho učenia* [How does the Church View the Social Issue? Social Codex – an Outline of Catholic Social Teaching]. Bratislava: Slovák, 1935.

Škrábik, Andrej. "Katolicizmus na Slovensku dnes a zajtra" [Catholicism in Slovakia Today and Tomorrow]. *Kultúra*, (1931) 9, 625-633.

Stašek, Bohumil. *Obnova lidské společnosti: Program a zásady Československé strany lidové v Čechách* [Renewal of Human Society: Agenda and Principles of the Czechoslovak People's Party in Bohemia]. Prague: Ústř. sekretariát ČSL, 1920.

Trapl, Miloš. "Charakteristika Československé strany lidové v letech 1918-1938" [Characteristics of the Czechoslovak People's Party in 1918-1938]. In Petr Fiala. *Český politický katolicismus 1848-2005*. Brno: Centrum pro studium demokracie a kultury, 2008, 177-313.

Vašek, Bedřich. "Sociálna úloha kňaza podľa encyklík" [Social Role of a Priest According to Encyclicals]. *Duchovný pastier*, 18 (April 1937), 97-102.

Veselý, Jiří Maria. "Hospodářství a mravní zákony" [Economy and Moral Laws]. *Filosofická revue*, (1940) 12, 106-111.

Zprávy Státního úřadu statistického Republiky československé [Reports of the State Statistical Office of the Czechoslovak Republic]. Prague: Státní úřad statistický, 1932.

Zprávy Státního úřadu statistického Republiky československé [Reports of the State Statistical Office of the Czechoslovak Republic]. Prague: Státní úřad statistický, 1934.

Cyrille Van Overbergh. Photo, 1910.
[Leuven, KADOC: KFA2634]

THE INFLUENCE OF NEO-THOMISM ON CATHOLIC SOCIAL POLICY-MAKING IN BELGIUM, 1880-1914

JO DEFERME

"Our times are popular. But is this a bad thing?"[1] This rhetoric question by Armand Thiéry (1868-1955), an omnipresent figure in the Leuven neo-Thomist network as a priest, theologian, experimental psychologist, philosopher, architect and professor, already illustrates how he and his friends approached the social question. They indeed considered the rising social tensions in modern, industrialised society and the ensuing demands for democratisation as an urgent issue, but one that, nonetheless and in its essence, needed to be considered within a moral framework.

In this essay I will try to illustrate how some authors that were closely connected to the Leuven Higher Institute of Philosophy (1889) and its founder Désiré-Joseph Mercier (1851-1926) reflected on social theory and policy. As the main sources for this contribution, I studied some of the Institute's periodicals, in particular the *Revue sociale catholique* (1896-1909), the *Revue néo-scolastique* (1894-1909) and the *Revue néo-scolastique de philosophie* (1910-1914). Following a brief discussion on the social challenges of the period, I will focus on how some prominent Belgian neo-Thomists approached the social question and highlight two main features: their tendency towards so-called 'middle way thinking' and their persistent reference to natural law.

---

1   Thiéry, "Le pape et la question sociale", 2.

A period of profound social challenges

Generally speaking, and particularly in the first half of the nineteenth century, Catholic intellectuals paid little attention to economic theories and social relations. From the 1850s that started to change. In that context, the revival of Thomist thinking became a major inspiration for how Catholics approached socio-economic issues, and this in several countries.[2] Highly industrialised Belgium offered an interesting context. In 1886 the country witnessed an explosion of social unrest. Following the strikes of March of that year, the Catholic government initiated several social policy initiatives. Unsurprisingly, those policy changes were accompanied by fierce ideological debates. Prominent tension fields were the conflicting views on man and society, individual liberty versus social solidarity, particular initiative versus state action, individualism versus collectivism and modernity versus tradition. A crucial issue was the gradual emergence of the idea of 'enforceability'. This entailed that social laws should be made enforceable or guaranteed, all this in contrast to non-binding forms of social action such as charity. This shift in legal theory, however, did not yet cause much friction amongst Catholics. The debate on enforceability remained largely theoretical or ideational in nature. While discussing the intellectual roots of enforceability, Belgian Catholics nonetheless zealously debated how the principle needed to be implemented in policy.

Interestingly, the canvas of Belgian political Catholicism in this period included a wide range of thoughts, often with subtle differences amongst them: neo-Thomists, leplaysian social scientists, the more progressive Christian democrats etcetera. The boundaries between those 'groups' often proved to be fairly narrow, making it hard to distinguish which strands influenced which part of social Catholic thinking. Some prominent protagonists of Belgian social-Catholicism were active in multiple 'subgroups'.[3] Generally speaking, the Christian democrats tended more towards enforceability, whereas other tendencies strived to balance traditional (charitable, corporatist ...) views with the challenges of modernity.

2   On the evolution of Catholic economic thought in general, see Almodovar and Teixiera, "The Ascent and Decline of Catholic Economic Thought", passim.

3   Quaghebeur, De Revue sociale catholique, 46, 67; Lamberts, "Van Kerk naar zuil", 114; Wils, "De verleiding van de sociologie", 158 ff.

Thomas Aquinas, Thomism, neo-scholasticism, modernity, corporatism

Belgian neo-Thomism particularly flourished at the Leuven university, and in particular at the newly established Higher Institute of Philosophy (1889), an initiative that was clearly inspired by Leo XIII's encyclical *Aeterni Patris* (1879).[4] Obviously, neo-Thomism essentially constituted an attempt to revive the ancient teachings of Thomas Aquinas. Thomas' view on man and society was inherently religious, anchored down in eternal law. Human nature was divine in origin, so consequently, humans took part in eternal law through natural law. God gave man the faculty of reason, and through reason he had discovered philosophy and science. Man had to make good use of those potentials, but without ever forgetting that they were God-given. God had created man as an embodied being, living in a corporeal reality, as a moral and social being. As to human labour, Thomas saw it as a way of actualising the potential of human nature.

Also *Aeterni Patris* stressed the mix of the human and the divine in the work of Thomas. Inspired by how the doctor Angelicus had reconciliated religion and philosophy, late-nineteenth-century neo-scholasticism enabled Catholic social thinking to find a certain connection with modern social science. Whereas the reasoning appeared similar, the historical context was of course quite different. Neo-Thomism found its starting-point above all in a critique of liberalism, socialism, positivism and other modern modes of thoughts, labelled by *Aeterni Patris* as 'false wisdoms'. Their abstract way of theorising and their belief in the makeability of man and society, so it was phrased, had engendered troublesome phantasies, deplorably detached from tradition and lived society.

Aeterni Patris considered it erroneous to oppose religion completely to natural science. On the contrary, man was created by God as a moral, reasoned and embodied being. Similarly, Mercier contrasted neo-scholasticism with the dogmatism of positivism. One should return to Thomas, so he argued, updating his views would be beneficial to the present day and age. Although dogmatism was refuted, all reflections on man and society needed to depart from a God-given reality and an organic view of society. As neo-scholasticism continued to adapt its ideas uninterruptedly, its way of thinking was presented as becoming richer every day.[5] This kind of holistic reasoning also resounded in Armand Thiéry's connection between psychology and physiology: philosophy and morals should not be considered as separate from the physiological

---

4   On the establishment of the Higher Institute, see for instance De Leeuw, "Neo-Thomism and the Education of a Catholic Elite", 352.
5   Mercier, "La philosophie néo-scolastique".

reality.[6] For some Aquinas' theory was even empirically embedded.[7] In Thomas' words, natural law was something we all know in our hearts.[8] In the discourse on social policy, this notion would become crucial, as we will learn further on.[9]

Whereas Thomism aimed at reconciling religion and philosophy, neo-Thomism strived towards a reconciliation of religion and (social) science; a reconciliation that – crucially – had to function as an alternative for modernist modes of thought. The Thomist tradition saw man as an essentially social creature. In that sense, there was an affinity with modern social science and perhaps a timid rupture with the existing liberal political culture.[10] A particular feature of Belgian neo-Thomism, according to Géry Prouvost, was its relative independence from theology. Belgian authors argued that the neo-Thomist philosopher was able to scientifically reason on its own.[11] Gerald McCool too described Belgian neo-Thomism as "less clerical in tone and less oriented towards theology".[12]

So, neo-Thomism was coined as a Catholic weapon against the excesses of Enlightenment, without brutalising liberal bourgeois society. This last element was considered important, given the perspective of social order and the preference of gradual social change. Many authors have wondered how all this was translated into the realm of social policy.[13] We argue that the shared ideal of most social Catholics lay in some kind of corporatism. Or rather, in a mixture of several distinct interpretations of this concept. According to the Leuven historian Emiel Lamberts, corporatism proved flexible enough to incorporate many different modern social tendencies.[14] In any case, corporatism would enable Belgian Catholics to develop their ideas on the meso level of society.

---

6   Thiéry, *Introduction à la psycho-physiologie*, 1-7.
7   Ashley, "The Anthropological Foundations of Natural Law", 7.
8   McInerny, "Thomistic Natural Law", 38.
9   Leo XIII, *Aeterni Patris*, passim; Elders, *The Ethics of St. Thomas Aquinas*, 209-210; see also Te Velde, "Thomas in de Lage Landen", passim; De Lantsheere, "Les caractères de la philosophie moderne", 105.
10   Boileau, *Cardinal Mercier's Philosophical Essays*, 618-626. See for instance Lamberts, "De ontwikkeling van de sociaal-katholieke ideologie in België", passim; Rezsohazy, *Origines et formation du catholicisme social*, 172; Deferme, *Uit de ketens van de vrijheid*, 156; De Leeuw, "Neo-Thomism and the Education of a Catholic Elite", 349. For similar evolutions in the Netherlands: Woldring, *De Christen-democratie*, 74, 188; on the hybrid character of neo-Thomism regarding tradition and modernity, see Heynickx, "On the Road with Maritain", passim.
11   Prouvost, *Thomas d'Aquin et les thomismes*, 46-47.
12   McCool, *The neo-Thomists*, 37-38.
13   Pouthier, "Émergence et ambiguïtés de la culture politique démocrate chrétienne", 287-290.
14   Lamberts, "De ontwikkeling van de sociaal-katholieke ideologie in België", 55-61.

The realm of ideas: the neo-Thomist views on 'modern' ideologies and modes of thought

In the three decades preceding World War I Belgium was ruled by Catholic governments uninterruptedly. Several administrative bodies were established to study and implement social legislation: a High Council of Labour in 1892, an 'Office du Travail' in 1894 and finally, in 1895, a separate Ministry of Industry and Labour.[15] Did neo-Thomism exert its influence in those bodies? Former research particularly focused on the impact of other networks and tendencies of multifaceted Belgian social Catholicism. It for instance highlighted how the so-called 'leplaysians', the adherents of the empirical and comparative sociological research approach of Frédéric Le Play (1806-1882), the members of the Société d'Economie Sociale in particular, indeed tried to appoint their representatives in the new social policy bodies.[16] Amongst these delegates, some show a clear connection to the Leuven Higher Institute and the Belgian Thomist revival. It remains, however, doubtful if there was a specific 'neo-Thomist delegation'. But even if the institutional impact of neo-scholasticism on Belgian pre-war social policy cannot be ascertained, this does not exclude a clear intellectual influence.

From an overall perspective, one of the main goals of neo-Thomism was to find an alternative for modernity. Similarly, in social policy, they sought for alternative solutions to those offered by liberalism, socialism and modernist sociology. Georges Legrand (1870-1946) offers a fine example. This lawyer, social scientist and lecturer in political economy at the Agronomic Institute in Gembloux, explicitly mentioned some prominent conservative forerunners as a source of inspiration. He for instance referred to the arguments of De Maistre and De Bonald against 'abstract' and unworldly practices such as revolution. In opposition to the modernist focus on law-making for 'the abstract human being', neo-Thomism was firmly rooted in reality. "I have already met French or Italian people, but never the universal human being", Legrand mockingly criticised any form of 'a priori social thinking', as opposed to theories aligned with tradition and natural law.[17]

The period around the turn of the century witnessed the emergence of sociology as a new science, inspired by positivism. Although that tendency was not welcomed by the neo-Thomists in general, their views somewhat differed. Mercier himself, for instance, clearly tried to offer a scientific foundation to Catholic social doctrine by opening up to positivism.[18] The *Revue*

---

15 Deferme, *Uit de ketens van de vrijheid*, 211; *Pasinomie*, 7 April 1892, 171-172.
16 On the leplaysian strand, see De Maeyer and Deferme, "Entre sciences sociales et politique", passim.
17 Legrand, "Deux précurseurs de l'idée sociale catholique en France".
18 Wils, "De verleiding van de sociologie", 158.

sociale catholique on the other hand published numerous articles displaying a far more critical position on positivism, and especially on its so-called deterministic character. Georges Legrand for instance argued that social scientists who rebelled against religious dogma, had better be consistent and should therefore also reject the dogmas of positivism.[19] In general, so wrote professor of political economy Fernand Deschamps (1868-1957), Catholics did not oppose the idea of interdependence in modern society.[20] Determinism, however, proved a bridge too far.

Leo XIII had presented the return to Thomism as a form of 'social defence', as a rejection of societal disintegration and the resulting loss of family values.[21] The Belgian neo-Thomists appeared to reason accordingly. They expressed a critical view on modernity as such and therefore also opposed the political offspring of modernity. The liberal and socialist answers to the social question were firmly rejected. Liberalism was denounced because of its social atomism and its understanding of liberty. Alternatively, Belgian neo-Thomists considered liberty as embedded in the fundamentally religious destination of man, and in the social coherence of society. Corporatism, interpreted as an illustration of an 'innate tendency towards solidarity', was presented as a valid alternative to liberal atomism.[22] But of course, corporatism was a house with many rooms. A few decades earlier, the Leuven scholar Charles Périn had developed a version of corporatism that did not completely collide with liberal values, at least not in the socio-economic field. Périn, for instance, respected the crucial liberal idea of freedom of labour. Or as Almodovar and Teixeira phrased it, he "was not entirely opposed to the doctrines of political economy".[23] At the turn of the century, however, opinions on that matter had clearly shifted. Neo-Thomist lawyer Maurice Damoiseaux even blamed Périn for having stated that the regime of free competition was inevitable and included unavoidable evils.[24]

Not only liberalism was rejected by Mercier and his pupils, but also and to an even greater extent was socialism. Let us listen to Armand Thiéry once more.[25] He considered the growing popularity of socialism as a serious problem: "In times of popular rule, anti-religion makes people believe that it is the party of the people. This is the evil!"[26] Although he explicitly spoke out against harsh individualism, Thiéry considered socialist collectivism at least

19   Legrand, "Apriorisme et évolution en science sociale".
20   Deschamps, "Quelques remarques sur la sociologie", 102-113.
21   Aubert, "Aspects divers du néo-thomisme sous le pontificat de Léon XIII", 152.
22   Noël, "Le régime corporatif"; Thiéry, "Le Pape et la Question sociale".
23   Almodovar and Teixiera, "The Ascent and Decline of Catholic Economic Thought", 71.
24   Damoiseaux, "Un économiste catholique belge", 185.
25   Thiéry is mentioned in McCool, *The neo-Thomists*, 37.
26   "En temps de règne du peuple, l'antireligion fait croire qu'elle est le parti du peuple. Voilà le mal!" Thiéry, "Le Pape et la Question sociale", 4.

as bad. Still, popular cooperation in itself was considered as something positive. Social groups had to coordinate their actions and elites were to guide that
process.[27] Socialist collectivism, however, merely replaced individual egoism
and jealousy with collective egoism and jealousy. He illustrated his ideas by
way of a study of the labour conditions at the Ghent socialist consumer cooperative Vooruit.[28]

Remarkably, several authors of the *Revue sociale catholique* rejected socialism not because of its moral reprehensibility, but rather tried to
denounce its intellectual flaws. The aforementioned Antwerp professor
Fernand Deschamps, another pupil of Mercier, would even declare socialism
to be dead. In its evolution he witnessed a clear breach with Marxism, for him
clear proof of its fundamental ideological weakness.[29] Deschamps also refuted the socialist vision of solidarity. Connecting citizens merely through the
state was unacceptable and completely unattuned with lived reality.[30] Simon
Deploige (1868-1927), one of Mercier's main collaborators and his successor as
president of Leuven's Higher Institute of Philosophy[31], disavowed collectivism
as a "banal stupidity".[32] He too rejected the socialist notion of solidarity, as it
was in his view merely based on hatred.[33]

The Belgian neo-Thomists indeed devoted a lot of attention to other
thought systems. They tried to find a compromise with the perspective of
social science, remained critical towards liberal political culture but particularly stressed the downsides of socialism. It is indeed remarkable how much
energy they invested in refuting competing political ideologies. Their alternative view on man, society and the social question was developed in much less
detail. The main protagonists of Belgian neo-Thomism usually claimed the
benefits of a middle way between liberalism and socialism, between individualism and collectivism. They welcomed a timid form of 'egalitarianism', albeit
largely limited to popular cooperation and complemented by paternalism.

---

27   Ibid., 10.
28   Thiéry, *Le travail minutaire*, 15.
29   Deschamps, "La Dissolution du Socialisme Marxiste", 249.
30   Id., "Sur un discours de M. Denis", 46.
31   De Leeuw, "Neo-Thomism and the Education of a Catholic Elite", 358; McCool, *The
      neo-Thomists*, 37.
32   Deploige, "Politique catholique et politique socialiste", 228.
33   Id., "La théorie thomiste de la propriété (suite et fin)", 301.

The social question in general: Armand Thiéry's 'besoin d'égalité'

In the 1897-1898 volume of the *Revue sociale catholique* Thiéry published an article dealing with "the pope and the social question".[34] He considered the issue as extremely serious and, crucially, a challenge that could not be solved by the state. As Catholicism had always protected the interests of the weaker citizens, a genuine solution had to be faith-based. Thiéry considered his day and age as the era of the common people. People felt in themselves a need for more equality, so he stated. This should not be considered as good or bad in itself, as it merely was a sign of the times. Thiéry, however, warned extensively that socialism would not engender constructive solutions.[35] Cooperation amongst workers, however, needed to be cherished. "Those who occupy the lowest social ranks are chagrined to find their strength and property limited; they dream of uniting to found a more perfect collective force, which would assure them a greater use of each one's efforts."[36] If the common people would learn to cooperate, the elites could limit themselves to responsible leadership and paternalism.[37] Thiéry believed that social tensions would be solved by walking a middle way in between both liberal individualism and socialist collectivism, all this rooted in popular cooperation and guided by elitist paternalism.

Theologian and priest Edward De Gryse (1848-1909) devoted a number of articles in the *Revue sociale catholique* to the emergence of 'Catholic democracy'. In his view Catholic faith and 'egalitarian' were not juxtaposed. However, the societal tendency towards more equality needed to be approached as a fact of Providence, surpassing the powers of human control and 'makeability'. When writing on the emancipation of the lower classes, De Gryse promoted a 'just paternalism'. If the industrial workforce was adamant in organising its own associations, the option of creating separate Christian labour unions looked quite valid.[38] So, similarly to Thiéry, De Gryse proposed a mixture of religious inspiration, paternalism, middle way thinking and (timid) popular emancipation through association.

---

34 Thiéry, "Le Pape et la Question sociale".
35 Ibid., 3.
36 Ibid., 9.
37 Ibid.
38 De Gryse, "La démocratie catholique", 1899-1900, 351-360.

Social policy: the idea and practice of middle way thinking

The social question pushed late-nineteenth-century Catholics towards finding new solutions, all this while avoiding those offered by liberalism or socialism. When looking at some specific examples of how Belgian neo-Thomists perceived social policy, two main characteristics come to the fore. First of all it needs to be underlined that those authors nearly always voiced the need to find balanced, middle-way approaches, avoiding the extremes and aligned with the organic evolution of society. From that period onwards, centrism would become an important and even major source of inspiration for Catholic politics, a tendency that clearly prevailed as the Christian democrat branch of Belgian Catholicism increased in importance. Secondly, it is remarkable to read how often they motivated their (sometimes innovative) social solutions by referring to natural law. Both features were clearly inspired by their desire to offer an alternative that was aligned to the reality of God's creation and thus could counter the mounting (and in their eyes abstract) modernist philosophies.

At the end of the nineteenth century, Belgian debates on social policy were dominated by the notion of '*liberté du travail*' or labour freedom. Lawyer, sociologist and civil servant Cyrille Van Overbergh (1866-1959), another key actor in the Leuven neo-Thomist network, considered it as the 'cornerstone of our economic constitution'. But he also acknowledged that it was increasingly contested as it no longer corresponded with social reality. The concept portrayed or imagined workers and employers as two equal parties that freely and individually decided on labour conditions, thus without interference by associations or the state.[39] Van Overbergh stressed how workers were hardly in a position to enter into open and fair contract negotiations and that their weaknesses were eagerly exploited by their employers.[40] He recalled how the national labour commission already in 1886 had ascertained that the practice of issuing labour contracts hardly existed in Belgium. To bring about a change, legal action was required.[41] On 10 March 1900 the Belgian parliament voted a bill on the labour contract, complementing the gaps in the Code Napoleon on the issue. The text defined some minimal requirements and listed the reciprocal obligations of both contracting parties. The bill included some remarkable moral components and urged employers and workers to treat each other with mutual respect.[42]

---

39 On 'liberté du travail': Deferme, *Uit de ketens van de vrijheid*, 28.
40 Van Overbergh, "Les unions professionnelles: Étude de philosophique sociale", 245; Id., "Le contrat de travail", 95.
41 Id., "Le contrat de travail", 95.
42 Deferme, *Uit de ketens van de vrijheid*, 262; Id., "Het ontstaan van de wet op het arbeidscontract", passim.

Three years later, in December 1903, Parliament voted its first bill on industrial accidents. This law initiated an important change in social thinking and practice, as it introduced the notion of professional hazard. That principle, in fact stating that industrial labour logically entailed accidents, was perceived by many as an open attack on the core values of liberal political culture and its emphasis on individual responsibility. Before 1903, when an industrial accident occurred, someone had to be found responsible, in most cases the individual employer or the workers involved. The bill, however, stated that accidents in industrial settings could also be due to coincidence or even '*force majeure*'.[43]

In the discussions on the issue the distinct strands of Belgian social Catholicism each displayed their own sensitivities. The leplaysians devoted a lot of attention to the question of compulsion, whereas the Brussels Christian democrats successfully promoted that accidents resulting from a so-called '*faute grave*', being serious misconduct or manifestly dangerous working conditions, needed to be extra compensated. Catholics also eagerly debated on how the new legal context needed to define individual responsibility. Authors connected to the Belgian Thomist revival movement often presented those discussions without explicitly taking position themselves. They carefully tried to disclose all arguments in the debate, aiming at finding a balance between the different stances, but mostly supported the governmental view on the matter.[44]

Social policy instigated by the idea of natural law

As we have argued, Belgian neo-Thomists, writing on how to deal with the social question, often referred to natural law and to the fact that man was created by God as a natural, moral, social and embodied being. Henceforth, they considered their own approaches to social issues as more aligned to organic reality than the rather abstract notions of modernist theories. This somewhat 'down-to-earth' inspiration appears to have enabled them to accept and promote innovative approaches to social policy. Thomas himself had stated that human behaviour was guided by rules, more specifically those of nature, in other words by reality itself. Natural law according to Thomas

43 Deferme, *Uit de ketens van de vrijheid*, 277; Id., "Het ontstaan van de notie sociaal recht", passim.
44 Beeckman, "Faute lourde – faute grave"; Prins, "Les Tribunaux Professionnels en matière d'accidents du travail"; Halleux, "Le rôle des causes fortuites sous le régime capitaliste"; Mélot, "De l'extension à l'agriculture de la loi sur la réparation des accidents du travail"; Vliebergh, "La loi du 24 décembre 1903"; Van Overbergh, "Encore les accidents du travail"; Ministère de l'Industrie et du travail, *Conseil supérieur du travail 1896-97. Accidents du travail*, 388.

was about finding what was essentially human. Therefore, laws needed to be subservient to basic human needs.[45] In the words of Leo Elders: "According to Aquinas natural law is nothing other than a participation in the eternal law present in man. Natural law is the order of our tasks and obligations as acknowledged by reason. [...] Since natural law has its roots in human nature, it is universal and permanent."[46] Similarly, the ideal of social justice also had to be in accordance with natural law: if one simply followed the laws of nature, one would unavoidably reach a context of social justice.[47] For Van Overbergh for instance, labour regulation had to be elaborated in accordance with the laws of human nature: "Under the individualist regime, the worker depends on the machine, living capital on dead capital. Catholicism dictates that it is necessary that objects are subordinate to man, that the machine is subordinate to the worker. Hence the whole admirable set of protective measures under the generic name of labour regulation appear to be the natural fruits of Christian morality."[48]

The prominent Belgian neo-Thomist philosopher Simon Deploige published several contributions in the *Revue sociale catholique*. In his essays on "Catholic and socialist politics" and on "property rights", he extensively discussed the flaws of socialism and rejected its views as far too naive and idealistic. But he also briefly outlined what could be a Catholic alternative.[49] Although Deploige admitted that, in given periods of history, property had been organised in a collective fashion, especially in agriculture, Christians were well aware that all things on earth were the creation of God and that man consequently had the natural right to appropriate them. Labour enabled man to become owner of natural resources and income.[50] Collective forms of labour (and of property) could only function properly in primitive societies. Although rejecting an all too pronounced glorification of industrial progress, Deploige considered private property as far more efficient and thus an essential component of the modern world. "Human nature is such that the exploitation of goods must be done by private initiative."[51] Private property perfectly

45 Lisska, *Aquinas' Theory of Natural Law*, 96-108; Pasnau, *Thomas Aquinas on Human Nature*, 9; see also Hoogerwerf, *Christelijke denkers over politiek*, passim; Ballin, "De virtuele eenheid van het recht", 101.
46 Elders, *The Ethics of St. Thomas Aquinas*, 209-210.
47 Solari and Corrado, "Social Justice and Economic Order", passim.
48 "Sous le régime individualiste, l'ouvrier dépend de la machine, le capital vivant du capital mort. Il faut dit le Catholicisme, que la chose soit soumise à l'homme, que la machine soit subordonnée au travailleur. De là, tout cet admirable ensemble de mesures protectrices qui, sous le nom générique de réglementation du travail, apparaissent comme les fruits naturels de la morale chrétienne." Van Overbergh, "Les courants sociologiques", 180.
49 Deploige, "Politique catholique et politique socialiste", 237.
50 Solari, "Social Economy, Private Property and Capital", passim; Deploige, "La théorie thomiste de la propriété", 73.
51 Deploige, "La théorie thomiste de la propriété (suite et fin)", 287.

accorded with existing customs and habits, and above all, it was grounded in natural law.[52] His line of thought was clearly aligned with that of Leo XIII and *Rerum novarum*.

Although Deploige acknowledged (and approved) that private property dominated the sphere of production, he also recognised that things were quite different in the realm of consumption. Natural law indeed demanded that goods were distributed in such a way that the common good was served. "It is therefore in the nature of things that the surplus of the rich should be used to support the poor", so he stated, "the selfish rich man sins against the virtue of charity".[53] Moreover, Deploige clearly asserted Thomas' position that individual property rights could be overruled when a person's survival was at stake. As regards to the role of the state in these matters, he indeed considered it a competence of public authorities to organise some forms of redistribution, especially when the elites failed to honour their charitable responsibilities.[54]

Another interesting contribution of Deploige, this time in the *Revue néo-scolastique* and responding to an essay on the matter by the Bruges bishop Gustave Waffelaert (1847-1931), dealt with the in Belgium much disputed issue of just wages. *Rerum novarum* had brought a somewhat ambiguous position on this highly controversial topic. Leo did not completely dismiss the liberal idea of wages as a result of free, negotiated consent, but added that there were other important observations, such as self-preservation. Thomas had indeed stressed that man needed a sufficient amount of physical strength to be able to exercise his labour. Aquinas had also pointed to the relationship between the usefulness of the work done and its remuneration. The salary had to be equivalent to the quantity and value of the work done.[55] Deploige asserted that when discussing the issue these Thomist principles needed to be thoroughly understood. "Man has a duty to preserve his life. Labour provides him the regular means of providing for his subsistence [...] natural justice requires that, in general, this work should also be worth at least his full subsistence."[56] Employers, according to Deploige, were obliged to provide a just salary, at least allowing the worker to survive, but preferably also sustaining his family. If the employer failed in providing a just salary, public authorities needed to intervene. This remarkable call for state intervention was, however, immediately limited. The support of workers that could not provide for their families, for instance because of illness, was no public responsibility, but one of mere Catholic charity.[57]

---

52   Deploige, "La théorie thomiste de la propriété", 71; Id., "La théorie thomiste de la propriété (suite)", 165-175.
53   Id., "La théorie thomiste de la propriété (suite et fin)", 288-289.
54   Ibid., 290-295.
55   Elders, *The Ethics of St. Thomas Aquinas*, 269-270.
56   Deploige, "Pensées d'un évêque sur le juste salaire", 57.
57   Ibid.

Workers' associations and social insurances

Also when discussing workers' associations and social insurance, the Belgian authors linked to the Thomist revival movement diligently embedded their arguments in natural law. In the spring of 1898, the Belgian parliament voted a law that granted workers' associations the possibility to obtain a legal form. The issue was widely debated, triggering discussions on individualism versus cooperation, social cooperation versus confrontation, the different relevant legal frameworks, the competences of associations, mixed versus separate workers' unions.[58] That last issue in particular, the question whether workers' associations needed to be created with or without involvement of their employers, had occupied socially involved Catholic intellectuals for decades. In his *Les libertés populaires* (1871) Charles Périn had already warned against the growing popularity of separate labour unions, the socialist ones in particular.[59] In the 1880s the leading Belgian Catholics still firmly opposed separate workers' unions. The ideas on the matter only started to shift after the third Catholic social congress in Liège (1890) and the promulgation of *Rerum novarum* (1891). Around those years some leading Christian democrats such as Arthur Verhaegen (1847-1917) started to establish separate Christian (anti-socialist) labour unions.[60] Still, even up to the Second World War, part of the Catholic public opinion kept on promoting mixed associations.[61]

The periodicals connected to the Leuven Thomist revival movement, the *Revue sociale catholique* in particular, published widely on the issue, particularly while the debate on the bill of 1898 was progressing. The *Revue* did not voice univocal stances. Authors as Ernest Dubois, Charles de Ponthière (1842-1929) and also the already quoted Georges Legrand remained reluctant and displayed a deep distrust towards confrontational syndicalism.[62] Although pleading for cooperation amongst workers, they considered mixed unions a far better lever towards social harmony.[63] But other protagonists of the Leuven neo-scholastic network, Cyrille Van Overbergh in particular, vehemently opposed the efforts of some parliamentary factions to introduce limitations to the legal recognition of workers' associations.[64] The articles dealing with the issue remained overwhelmingly technical. Van Overbergh's contribu-

---

58 Deferme, *Uit de ketens van de vrijheid*, 227.
59 Périn, *Les libertés populaires*, 81.
60 De Maeyer, *De rode baron*, 313; Righart, *De katholieke zuil in Europa*, 161; Luyten, *Ideologisch debat en politieke strijd over het corporatisme*, 22.
61 Gérin, "Sociaal-katholicisme en christen-democratie", 99.
62 Dubois, "Les Unions professionnelles devant le Parlement belge"; De Ponthière, "Unions professionnelles"; Legrand, "Chronique sociale: la discussion de la loi sur la personnification civile des unions professionnelles au Parlement belge".
63 See also: De Visscher, "La philosophie syndicaliste et le mythe de la grève générale".
64 Van Overbergh, "Les Unions professionnelles devant le Parlement belge"; Id., "La veille d'un grand débat".

tion of 1895 to the *Revue néo-scolastique*, however, offers a more theoretical approach, aligned with the writing of Aquinas and his understanding of natural law:

> Man has a natural right to improve himself. [...] If he lived alone, or if he had to seek in the family alone the means of attaining this goal, he could achieve it only in an imperfect and insufficient manner. The *raison d'être* of civil society is to make up for this inadequacy by fully providing its members with what is called the common good. [...] If, therefore, in order to achieve this fuller development, secondary groupings are necessary or useful within society, the social authority cannot oppose their constitution. It even has the duty to help them to form and develop.[65]

Van Overbergh saw civil society as deeply rooted in natural law. "Associatons", so he wrote, "are to society what organs are to the human body".[66] Consequently, it was not up to the state to decide whether or not organisations could be established. But it could indeed allow certain privileges, such as exemption from taxes. Van Overbergh referred to the freedom of association as embedded in the Belgian constitution and offered clear support to the bill proposed by the Catholic government.[67]

A somewhat related topic, that of social insurances was hardly dealt with in the periodicals linked to the Leuven neo-scholastic network. The same silence was detected on the subject of popular savings.[68] The *Revue sociale catholique* published substantially more articles on unions, industrial accidents and agricultural issues. When the topic of social insurance was touched upon, the content of the contributions remained predominantly technical.[69] Georges Legrand, for instance, instigated local authorities to stimulate retirement savings. A compulsory contribution by labourers themselves was not

---

65 "L'homme a le droit naturel de se perfectionner. [...] S'il vivait solitaire, ou s'il devait chercher dans la famille seule les moyens d'atteindre ce but, il ne pourrait le réaliser que d'une manière imparfaite et insuffisante. La raison d'être de la société civile est de suppléer à cette insuffisance en procurant pleinement à ses membres ce que l'on appelle le bien commun. [...] Si donc, pour réaliser ce développement plus complet, des groupements secondaires sont nécessaires ou utiles au sein de la société, l'autorité sociale ne peut s'opposer à leur constitution. Elle a même le devoir de les aider à se former et à se développer. [...] C'est pourquoi la société civile a le devoir de reconnaître, dans les limites du bien commun, le droit qu'ont naturellement ses membres de former des associations particulières et même d'en favoriser l'exercice." Van Overbergh, "Les unions professionnelles. Étude de philosophique sociale", 234-235.

66 Ibid., 237.

67 Ibid., 236-249.

68 Van Molle, "Spaarwezen en spaarkassen in België", 124.

69 Du Sart, "Questions de mutualité".

considered a problem.[70] The *Revue néo-scolastique* remained almost entirely silent on the subject.[71]

Conclusion

Our short survey of the writings on social issues by the major protagonists of Leuven's pre-war neo-Thomist network linked to the Higher Institute of Philosophy, allows us to draw some preliminary conclusions. Neo-scholasticism was merely one of many intellectual components nourishing the dialogue of late-nineteenth-century Catholicism with the social question. The different groups in Belgian social-Catholicism and their influence remain hard to delineate. Some elements of our analysis, however, deserve to be highlighted. Firstly we noticed how the Leuven authors involved devoted much more attention to combatting the competing 'modern' ideologies, liberalism and socialism in particular, than to disclosing their proper ideals and strategies. In their writing they expressed, be it implicitly, a strong reticence towards dogmatic or ideological thinking. As conservatives, they showed themselves adverse to modernist ideas of 'makeability' and urged to replace the unworldly, abstract ways of thinking of modernity by an organic view of society and social reality. God had created man not as an abstract being, but as a reasoned, moral, social and embodied one.

In the field of social policy, nearly all authors whose works we analysed, displayed a strong inclination towards middle way thinking. Their views on social policy and how it could be philosophically embedded remained fluid. Several of their articles mainly concerned technical issues. But nearly all their writing explicitly referred to the ideas of Thomas Aquinas and his understanding of natural law. This 'down-to-earth' inspiration, as we called it, enabled several authors to develop alternative approaches to social policy. In any case, it allowed them to distance themselves from ideas and concepts that for decades had dominated liberal bourgeois thinking in socio-economic matters, for instance linked to the freedom of labour and of salary determination. As a natural being and an embodied creature, man could indeed invoke some eternal natural rights, that not only employers but also the state had to recognise and protect. Another important input of neo-Thomism into Catholic social thinking was the way it stressed the innate nature of associations: joining forces was presented as a natural right of man. While referring to natural law, some Leuven authors even defended a certain level of state interventionism in social policy matters and pleaded for 'enforceability'. As modern industrial society had placed the individual worker in such a weak position that even his

70 Legrand, "Pensions ouvrières".
71 Deferme, *Uit de ketens van de vrijheid*, chapter 6.

natural rights were threatened, the state was obliged to intervene. So although the Leuven neo-Thomist network clearly departed its reflections on the social question while handling an essentially conservative (antisocialist and -positivist) agenda, their ideas on social policy also displayed a timidly 'modern' feel, inspired by ideas of natural law.

BIBLIOGRAPHY

Sources

Beeckman, A. "Faute lourde – faute grave". *Revue sociale catholique*, 1896-1897, 144-153.

Crahay, Edouard. "La réglementation du travail en Suisse". *Revue néo-scolastique*, 2 (1895) 5, 83-93.

Damoiseaux, Maurice. "Un économiste catholique belge". *Revue sociale catholique*, 1897-1898, 181-186.

De Gryse, Edward. "La démocratie catholique". *Revue sociale catholique*, 1899-1900, 351-360.

De Gryse, Edward. "La Démocratie catholique (suite)". *Revue sociale catholique*, 1900-1901, 5-18.

De Gryse, Edward. "La Démocratie catholique (suite et fin)". *Revue sociale catholique*, 1900-1901, 33-50.

De Gryse, Edward. "Encore la Démocratie catholique". *Revue sociale catholique*, 1900-1901, 130-143.

De Lantsheere, Léon. "Les caractères de la philosophie moderne". *Revue néo-scolastique*, 1 (1894) 2, 101-111.

Deploige, Simon. "La théorie thomiste de la propriété". *Revue néo-scolastique*, 2 (1895) 5, 61-82.

Deploige, Simon. "La théorie thomiste de la propriété (suite)". *Revue néo-scolastique*, 2 (1895) 6, 163-175.

Deploige, Simon. "La théorie thomiste de la propriété (suite et fin)". *Revue néo-scolastique*, 2 (1895) 7, 286-301.

Deploige, Simon. "'Politique catholique et politique socialiste". *Revue sociale catholique*, 1897-1898, 225-237.

Deploige, Simon. "Pensées d'un évêque sur le juste salaire". *Revue néo-scolastique*, 8 (1901) 29, 55-57.

De Ponthière, Charles. "Unions professionnelles". *Revue sociale catholique*, 1 (1896-1897), 242-251.

Deschamps, Fernand. "Sur un discours de M. Denis". *Revue sociale catholique*, 1897-1898, 41-48.

Deschamps, Fernand. "La Dissolution du Socialisme Marxiste". *Revue sociale catholique*, 1898-1899, 235-249.

Deschamps, Fernand. "Quelques remarques sur la sociologie". *Revue sociale catholique*, 1901-1902, 101-115.

De Visscher, Fernand. "La philosophie syndicaliste et le mythe de la grève générale". *Revue néo-scolastique de philosophie*, 20 (1913) 78, 129-163.

Dubois, Ernest. "Les Unions professionnelles devant le Parlement belge". *Revue sociale catholique*, 1 (1896-1897), 79-87.

Du Sart, Raoul. "Questions de mutualité". *Revue sociale catholique*, 1903-1904, 132-137.

Halleux, J. "Le rôle des causes fortuites sous le régime capitaliste". *Revue sociale catholique*, 2 (1897-98), 129-135.

Legrand, Georges. "Chronique sociale: la discussion de la loi sur la personnification civile des unions professionnelles au Parlement belge". *Revue sociale catholique*, 2 (1897-1898), 58-61.

Legrand, Georges. "Pensions ouvrières". *Revue sociale catholique*, 2 (1897-1898), 342-345.

Legrand, Georges. "Chronique sociale: la politique sociale de Bismarck". *Revue sociale catholique*, 2 (1897-1898), 345-347.

Legrand, Georges. "Deux précurseurs de l'idée sociale catholique en France: de Maistre et de Bonald". *Revue néo-scolastique*, 7 (1900) 25, 58-77.

Legrand, Georges. "Apriorisme et évolution en science sociale". *Revue sociale catholique*, 1903-1904, 18-22.

Leo XIII. *Aeterni patris. Encyclical of Pope Leo XIII on the restoration of Christian philosophy.* <www.vatican.va>.

Leo XIII. *Rerum Novarum. Encyclical of Pope Leo XIII on capital and labor.* <www.vatican.va>.

Leo XIII. "Brefs de SS Léon XIII relatifs à la fondation d'un Institut supérieur de Philosophie à l'Université Catholique de Louvain". *Revue néo-scolastique*, 1 (1894) 1, 76-84.

Mélot, A. "De l'extension à l'agriculture de la loi sur la réparation des accidents du travail". *Revue sociale catholique*, 1902-1903, 65-80.

Mercier, Désiré. "La philosophie néo-scolastique". Revue néo-scolastique, 1 (1894) 1, 5-18.

Mercier, Désiré. "Le bilan philosophique du XIXe siècle". Revue néo-scolastique, 7 (1900) 25, 5-32.

Mercier, Désiré. "Le bilan philosophique du XIXe siècle". Revue néo-scolastique, 7 (1900) 27, 315-329.

Ministère de l'Industrie et du travail. Conseil supérieur du travail 1896-97. Accidents du travail. Brussels: Weissenbruch, 1897.

Noël. "Le régime corporatif". Revue sociale catholique, 1896-1897, 299-307.

Périn, Charles. Les libertés populaires. Paris: Lecoffre, 1871.

Pius XI. "Quadragesimo anno. Encycliek van Z.H. Pius XI over het herstel der sociale orde en haar vervolmaking volgens de wet van het evangelie. Bij gelegenheid van het 40-jarig jubilé van het verschijnen der Encycliek van Leo XIII Rerum Novarum". In Georges Rutten. De sociale leer der Kerk samengevat in de wereldbrieven Rerum Novarum en Quadragesimo Anno. Antwerp: Geloofsverdediging, 1932, 305-397.

Prins, Adolphe. "Les Tribunaux Professionnels en matière d'accidents du travail". Revue sociale catholique, 1 (1896-1897), 193-205.

Thiéry, Armand. Introduction à la psycho-physiologie. Leuven: Polleunis & Ceuterick, 1895.

Thiéry, Armand. Le travail minutaire et l'affaire des salaires au Vooruit. Leuven: ISP, 1896.

Thiéry, Armand. "Le Pape et la Question sociale". Revue sociale catholique, 1897-1898, 1-11.

Van Overbergh, Cyrille. "Les unions professionnelles. Étude de philosophique sociale". Revue néo-scolastique, 2 (1895) 7, 233-256.

Van Overbergh, Cyrille. "Le contrat de travail". Revue néo-scolastique, 3 (1896) 9, 92-97.

Van Overbergh, Cyrille. "Les Unions professionnelles devant le Parlement belge". Revue sociale catholique, 1 (1896-1897), 5-18.

Van Overbergh, Cyrille. "La veille d'un grand débat". Revue sociale catholique, 1896-1897, 321-332.

Van Overbergh, Cyrille. "Encore les accidents du travail". Revue sociale catholique, 1900-1901, 277-288.

Van Overbergh, Cyrille. "Les courants sociologiques du XIXe siècle". Revue néo-scolastique, 7 (1900) 26, 173-189.

Vliebergh, Emiel. "La loi du 24 décembre 1903 sur les accidents du travail et sa première application à l'agriculture". Revue sociale catholique, 1906-1907, 97-112.

Literature

Almodovar, António and Pedro Teixeira. "The Ascent and Decline of Catholic Economic Thought". History of Political Economy, 40 (2008), 63-86.

Ashley, Benedict M. "The Anthropological Foundations of the Natural Law". In John Goyette et al., eds. St. Thomas Aquinas and the Natural Law Tradition. Washington: Catholic University of America Press, 2004, 3-16.

Aubert, Roger. "Aspects divers du néo-thomisme sous le pontificat de Léon XIII". In: Giuseppe Rossini. Aspetti della cultura cattolica nell'età di Leone XIII. Rome: Cinque Lune, 1961, 133-227.

Ballin, Ernst Hirsch. "De virtuele eenheid van het recht". In: Rudi te Velde, ed. Homo sapiens. Nijmegen: Valkhof Pers, 2017, 98-121.

Berstein, Serge, ed. Les cultures politiques en France. Paris: Seuil, 1999.

Billiet, Jaak, ed. Tussen bescherming en verovering. Sociologen en historici over zuilvorming. Leuven: Leuven University Press, 1988.

Boileau, David A., ed. Cardinal Mercier's Philosophical Essays: A Study in Neo-Thomism. Leuven: Peeters, 2002.

Bushlack, Thomas J. Politics for a Pilgrim Church. A Thomistic Theory of Civic Virtue. Cambridge: Eerdmans, 2015.

Deferme, Jo. Uit de ketens van de vrijheid. Het debat over de sociale politiek in België 1886-1914. Leuven, Leuven University Press, 2007.

Deferme, Jo. "Het ontstaan van de wet op het arbeidscontract (10 maart 1900) in het kader van de uitbouw van de sociale wetgeving". In Bruno Debaenst, ed. Van status tot contract: de arbeidsovereenkomst in België vanuit rechtshistorisch perspectief. Bruges: Die Keure, 2013, 85-100.

Deferme, Jo. "Het ontstaan van de notie sociaal recht. Visies van politici 1886-1914". In Bruno Debaenst, ed. De Belle Epoque van het Belgisch recht 1870-1914. Bruges: Die Keure, 2016, 21-36.

Deferme, Jo. "The Influence of the Catholic Socio-Political Theory on the Foundations of the Belgian Welfare State: The Case of Subsidized Liberty". In Jan De Maeyer and Vincent Viaene, eds. World Views and Wordly Wisdom. Leuven: Leuven University Press, 2016, 89-104.

De Leeuw, Thijs. "Neo-Thomism and the Education of a Catholic Elite in Louvain 1880-1914". Trajecta, 21 (2012), 345-372.

De Maeyer, Jan. *De rode baron. Arthur Verhaegen 1847-1917*. Leuven: Leuven University Press, 1994.

De Maeyer, Jan and Jo Deferme. "Entre sciences sociales et politique. La pensée leplaysienne et les milieus catholiques belges". *Les Etudes Sociales*, (2009) 149-150, 147-166.

Elders, Leo J. *The Ethics of St Thomas Aquinas*. Oxford: Peter Lang, 2005.

Gerard, Emmanuel, ed. *De christelijke arbeidersbeweging in België*. Leuven: Leuven University Press, 1991.

Gérin, Paul. "Sociaal-katholicisme en christen-democratie (1884-1904)". In: Emmanuel Gerard, ed. *De christelijke arbeidersbeweging in België*. Leuven: Leuven University Press, 1991, 56-113.

Goyette, John et al., eds. *St. Thomas Aquinas and the Natural Law Tradition: Contemporary Perspectives*. Washington: Catholic University of America Press, 2004.

Heynickx, Rajesh. "On the Road with Maritain". In Rajesh Heynickx and Jan De Maeyer, eds. *The Maritain Factor: Taking Religion into Interwar Modernism*. Leuven: Leuven University Press, 2010, 7-25.

Heynickx, Rajesh and Jan De Maeyer, eds. *The Maritain Factor. Taking Religion into Interwar Modernism*. Leuven: Leuven University Press, 2010.

Hoogerwerf, Andries. *Christelijke denkers over politiek. Een oogst van 20 eeuwen*. Baarn: Ten Have, 1999.

Lamberts, Emiel. "Van Kerk naar zuil: de ontwikkeling van het katholiek organisatiewezen in België". In Jaak Billiet, ed. *Tussen bescherming en verovering*. Leuven: Leuven University Press, 1988, 83-133.

Lamberts, Emiel. "De ontwikkeling van de sociaal-katholieke ideologie in België". In Emiel Lamberts, ed. *Een kantelend tijdperk. De wending van de Kerk naar het volk in Noord-West-Europa / Une époque en mutation. Le catholicisme social dans le Nord-Ouest de l'Europe / Ein Zeitalter im Umbruch. Die Wende der Kirche zum Volk im nordwestlichen Europa*. Leuven: Leuven University Press, 1992, 48-63.

Lisska, Anthony J. *Aquinas's Theory of Natural Law: An Analytic Reconstruction*. Oxford: Clarendon, 1996.

Luyten, Dirk. *Ideologisch debat en politieke strijd over het corporatisme tijdens het interbellum in België*. Brussels: Koninklijke Academie voor Wetenschappen, Letteren en Schone Kunsten, 1996.

McCool, Gerald. *From Unity to Pluralism: The Internal Evolution of Thomism*. New York: Fordham University Press, 1989.

McCool, Gerald. *The neo-Thomists*. Milwaukee: Marquette University Press, 1994.

McInerny, Ralph. "Thomistic Natural Law and Aristotelian Philosophy". In John Goyette et al., eds. *St. Thomas Aquinas and the Natural Law Tradition*. Washington: Catholic University of America Press, 2004, 25-41.

Mikluščàk, Pavel. "Subsidiarität in der katholischen Kirche". In Peter Blickle, Thomas O. Hüglin and Dieter Wyduckel, eds. *Subsidiarität als rechtliches und politisches Ordnungsprinzip in Kirche, Staat und Gesellschaft*. Berlin: Duncker & Humblot, 2002, 25-36.

Millon-Delsol, Chantal. *L'État subsidiaire*. Paris: PUF, 1992.

Millon-Delsol, Chantal. *Le principe de subsidiarité*. Paris: PUF, 1993.

Pasnau, Robert. *Thomas Aquinas on Human Nature*. Cambridge: Cambridge University Press, 2002.

Pouthier, Jean-Luc. "Émergence et ambiguïtés de la culture politique démocrate chrétienne". In Serge Berstein, ed. *Les cultures politiques en France*. Paris: Seuil, 1999, 285-314.

Prouvost, Géry. *Thomas d'Aquin et les thomismes*. Paris: Éditions du Cerf, 1996.

Quaghebeur, Patricia. *De Revue sociale catholique (1896-1900): een gematigd-progressief wetenschappelijk tijdschrift*. Diss. Lic. KU Leuven, 1984.

Rezsohazy, Rudolf. *Origines et formation du catholicisme social en Belgique*. Leuven: Publications universitaires de Louvain, 1958.

Righart, Hans. *De katholieke zuil in Europa. Het ontstaan van verzuiling onder katholieken in Oostenrijk, Zwitserland, België en Nederland*. Meppel: Boom, 1986.

Solari, Stephano and Daniele Corrado. "Social Justice and Economic Order According to Natural Law". *Journal of Markets and Morality*, 12 (2009) 1, 47-62.

Solari, Stephano. "3) On neo-Thomism". FEBEA interview online, 9 April 2015.

Solari, Stephano. "4) Neo-Thomism, Social Economy and Marginalism". FEBEA interview online, 9 April 2015.

Solari, Stephano. "5) Social Economy, Private Property and Capital". FEBEA interview online, 9 April 2015.

Te Velde, Rudi, ed. *Homo sapiens. Thomas van Aquino en de vraag naar de mens*. Nijmegen: Valkhof, 2017.

Te Velde, Rudi. "De vraag naar de mens". In Rudi te Velde, ed. *Homo sapiens*. Nijmegen: Valkhof, 2017, 11-32.

Te Velde, Rudi. "Thomas in de Lage Landen. Het neothomisme in Nederland". In Rudi te Velde, ed. *Homo sapiens*. Nijmegen: Valkhof, 2017, 182-198.

Van Molle, Leen. "Spaarwezen en spaarkassen in België. Op zoek naar meer sociale zekerheid voor doelgroepen". In August Van Put et al., eds. *De Belgische spaarbanken. Geschiedenis, recht, economische funktie en instellingen*. Tielt: Lannoo, 1986, 121-159.

Van Put, August et al., eds. *De Belgische spaarbanken. Geschiedenis, recht, economische funktie en instellingen*. Tielt: Lannoo, 1986.

Wils, Kaat. "De verleiding van de sociologie. Belgische en Nederlandse katholieken en het positivisme (1880-1914)". *Trajecta*, 6 (1997) 2, 156-173.

Woldring, Henk E.S. *De Christen-democratie. Een kritisch onderzoek naar haar politieke filosofie*. Utrecht: Het Spectrum, 1996.

Antonio Cánovas del Castillo. Painting (oil on canvas) by Ricardo de Madrazo, 1896. [Madrid, Palacio de las Cortes]

BETWEEN GOSPEL AND CONSTITUTION
NEO-SCHOLASTIC TRACES IN THE LEGAL WORLD OF NINETEENTH-CENTURY SPAIN

FAUSTINO MARTÍNEZ MARTÍNEZ

The project of 'jovial modernity' has been described by Peter Sloterdijk as grounded in a kinetic utopia inciting a continuous process of mobilisation across different spheres. These dynamics become particularly apparent in that specific social, political, juridical and religious context that we generally label as the Old Regime (*Ancien Régime*). In that period, and linked to all categories quoted above, new concepts were proclaimed and at the same time defined: plastic arts, the credit system, mechanical engineering, the state, scientific research and jurisprudence or the law. This last notion was closely connected to state power, not only as a compendium of its power and nourishing role but also as a result of its strenuous efforts to survive. Indeed, the state exists because the law helps it to exist, imperatively and co-actively. This ever-growing state and its administration, based on public intervention and taxes, continuously discovered new fields on which it could lay its hands with regulatory desire. In law it found its most fulfilled reflection and most qualified instrument to carry out its vocation. It was its preferred tool, the vehicle through which it instructed itself and others. As the state became larger and stronger, more solid and robust, the state-serving law was increasingly present. That same modernity, however, also engendered interesting limits to state power: it was no longer allowed to operate with absolute freedom, discretion or arbitrariness. Through a global construction of justice and again referring to Sloterdijk, the idea emerged that humans hold and can exercise innate and inalienable rights.[1]

This conjunction of state with natural rights obviously ended up by crystallising, after the liberal revolutions, in a new construction, combining but also balancing the ambitions of the state with the desire to limit its impact by recognising and guaranteeing the rights and freedoms of its citizens. This edifice is generally referred to as a 'constitution', while the concept 'constitutionalism' is used to define the doctrine explaining how these capital texts, endowed with irresistible force and the ability to modify the political and social landscape, should be built and function. No other legal texts in the history of mankind, with the code accompanying a constitution as a major exception, had a similar impact. A constitution simultaneously ambitions to create power, to divide it and to guarantee rights, precisely because the division of state power across different organic instances with delimited functions offers a first and crucial lever towards guaranteeing rights. A constitution can operate as a pledge of rights and freedoms because it simultaneously arms the guardianship of the state and limits its power by creating it under the law and by offering it rules of conduct.

This radical liberal approach, however, would never fully mature. The French revolutionary regime, although outlining it at certain very punctual moments, never materialised it. The conservative reaction initiated from 1795 onwards tried to reconcile the 'old world' with the revolutionary one. It tried to avoid both the most extreme absolutism and the risks of a continued revolution, both exclusive monarchical sovereignty and unlimited national sovereignty (equally omnipotent and dangerous), both the grittier despotic and most pronounced democratic tendencies. Established rule strove towards *le juste milieu*, balancing order and freedom, but clearly opting in favour of the former. France grew to be an interesting doctrinal guide for Europe. But throughout the nineteenth century, England, or in any case the peculiar way in which French politicians read the English constitution, dominated constitutional thinking and scholarship. A wave of moderate liberalism infused post-Napoleonic Europe with the idea of balanced powers, with a Crown operating as a 'watchmaker', an increasingly powerful government, two legislative chambers to capture all political and social sensitivities, a small judiciary power bound by law enforcement and very few political rights and freedoms, but always respecting and protecting the two primal civil rights being security-liberty and property.[2] This was particularly the case in Spain. Indeed, this 'old' country was not an exception on the contemporary European scene, although it displayed a proper rhythm and timing. Doctrinally, politically speaking and particularly from a constitutional point of view the era remained quite moder-

---

[1] Sloterdijk, "El Antropoceno", 14-17. The Catholic counterpoint was studied by Carpintero Benítez, "La modernidad jurídica y los católicos".

[2] Starzinger, *The Politics of the Center*; Craiutu, *Liberalism under Siege*; Id., *A Virtue for Courageous Minds*; and, at last, Rosanvallon, *El momento Guizot*.

ate.[3] Authors sought balance and moderation; extremism was rejected. *In medio virtus* remained the motto. Therefore, we will speak of shared sovereignty, of an absent constituent power and of a founding power remaining difficult to locate. We will highlight a predominantly monarchical model, incorporating aristocratic and democratic elements, looking back on history, tradition and customary law, without excluding national singularities. Although this model may not be characterised as immutable, it remained reluctant to unjustified changes and ungenerous in rights and liberties. It embraced the defence of civil rights, but left scarce margin for political ones, conceived more like duties or functions of citizenship than as optional acts in the positive sense. In short, when studying Spain, we need to deal with a constitutional model referring more to institutions than to citizens, more to powers than to individuals, more to duties than to rights. It found its backdrop and intellectual substrate in Catholicism, usually accompanied by the adjective 'state' or 'national'. In sum, religion offers a perfect explanation of Spain's nineteenth-century constitutional identity, a gateway to access the prevalent political lines of the ideological currents that supported it.

The way in which the concept 'constitution' was used in nineteenth-century Spain and across continental Europe, is a clear reflection of these ideas. It was seen as a non-essential and instrumental notion, a text designed to organise government without taking into account its provenance in the nation or the people. In this way the understanding of the concept approached the views of the ideologues of the doctrinal and moderate movement, rooted in France but extending all over Europe. For them, these references merely offered alibis, excuses and irrelevant arguments: the constitution was 'given', already made, constituted and received, ready to be put into practice. In that perspec-

---

3   As a general framework: Díez del Corral, *El Liberalismo Doctrinario*. For a more detailed and topical characterisation of that doctrinal constitutional world: Matteucci, *Organización del poder y libertad*; Álvarez Alonso, *Lecciones de Historia del Constitucionalismo*; Fioravanti, *Constitución*; Artola Gallego, *Constitucionalismo en la historia*. We will use the terms 'moderate' and 'conservative' interchangeably. In a certain sense both qualifiers are relatively close. We must bear in mind that the Spanish Moderate Party (officially the Partido Monárquico-Constitucional) was replaced after the *Restauración* (from 1874 onwards) by the Conservative Party. The latter was the logical and final evolution of the first one, the final accomplishment of doctrinal and moderate liberalism. However, in my view, 'moderate' has a very deep political connotation that refers to the search of political balance in the relationships between the two main actors of the constitutional process: Monarchy and Parliament. The notion 'conservative' has a more social connotation as it seeks to defend and protect the already formed society. We can therefore agree that the word 'moderate' is predominant in Spain until 1874 and that from that date 'conservative' takes its place. As mentioned above, every conservative is moderate, but not every moderate is conservative. In any case both notions refer the nineteenth-century parliamentary, rational and civilised right, the authentically liberal right. For this Spanish liberal experience: Gómez Ochoa, "El liberalismo conservador español"; Suárez Cortina, ed., *Las máscaras de la libertad*; Romeo Mateo and Sierra, eds., *La España liberal, 1833-1874*; Sánchez García, "El liberalismo español".

tive such legal texts displayed an inherent power, knowing or identifying its authors(s) was a secondary concern. Notwithstanding this generalisation we need, of course, to acknowledge that not all European countries reached 'the constitutional world' following perfectly defined rules and clearly marked and determined stages. Their past and traditions but also the influences they underwent and the ideological currents and novelties they experienced played a role of importance. Indeed, nineteenth-century constitutionalism showed a marked national component, it was adapted to the political climate of each country or kingdom. Spain was not isolated. In this context constitutional impulses were developed in more dynamic and radical liberal currents but also in praiseworthy inertia and resistance that paralysed any revolutionary drift. The Spanish constitutions since 1812 until 1876 offered not more than a particular reading of how liberal ideas were perceived in different political units, always seeking to avoid breakdowns or drastic ruptures. It particularly strived towards a soft, calm and quiet transition, combining or trying to combine what existed and functioned with other elements that could engender benefits, advantages or improvements in politics and administration. In short, it sought a balance between the old and the new world.[4]

The construction of liberal Spain and the Spanish liberal nation from this moderate and conservative point of view, is the main object of our analysis. While showing the specificity of Spain in constitutional matters and highlighting the different thought flows that supported it, the impact of neo-scholasticism becomes manifestly apparent. Building a nation was both a political and constitutional task, the two perspectives remained closely entwined in nineteenth-century Spain. The constitution was considered as a basic pillar of the state, although not the only one. It had an aura of omnipresence as it was linked to the prevailing ideas of stability, certainty and continuity, interconnecting past and present values. If we want to understand its vicissitudes, we inevitably have to look at the Spanish 'constitutional world' and identify what were the ideological elements that determined and surrounded it. In this conglomerate religion occupies a decisive position and with it all the connected values, principles and categories, with neo-scholastic thought as a pre-eminent source.[5]

4　　On the Spanish constitutional perspective: Sevilla Andrés, "El poder constituyente en España"; Alejandre García, *Temas de Historia del Derecho*; Sánchez Agesta, *Historia del Constitucionalismo español*; Fernández Segado, *Las Constituciones históricas españolas*; Clavero, *Evolución histórica del constitucionalismo español*; Id., *Manual de historia constitucional de España*; Solé Tura and Aja, *Constituciones y períodos constituyentes en España*; Varela Suanzes-Carpegna, *Política y Constitución en España*; Torres del Moral, *Constitucionalismo histórico español*; Tomás Villarroya, *Breve historia del constitucionalismo español*; Pérez-Prendes, *Escritos de historia constitucional española*. See also the most recent (and posthumous) work of Varela Suanzes-Carpegna, *Historia constitucional de España*.
5　　For the idea of Spain in the nineteenth century: Álvarez Junco, *Mater Dolorosa*; Álvarez Junco and De la Fuente Monge, *El relato nacional*. For a reconstruction of this idea based on literary sources, Andreu Miralles, *El descubrimiento de España*.

In the beginning there was liberalism ...

Let us, therefore, start with one of the most conspicuous representatives of the moderate thought within that peculiar current that we generically characterise as Spanish liberalism.[6] In 1858, almost six years after his abrupt departure from power, Juan Bravo Murillo (1803-1873) was appointed president of the Congreso de los Diputados, a political position with high symbolic significance.[7] In that same year and returning to the political front as leader of the Moderate Party, he pronounced his idea of society and state in a famous speech, popularly known as his 'political testament'. This text perfectly outlines what it meant to be moderate and conservative in Spain during the second half of the nineteenth century. Bravo Murillo remained open and loyal to his principles and values, his beliefs; he always professed the same ideology. As a right-wing member of the Moderate Party, he positioned himself close to Throne and Altar, far from parliamentarianism and from national or popular ideas on sovereignty. After offering various reflections on the purpose of political power, he concluded his political testament by exposing the salient essence of his ideology: private property. For him this was a fundamental right, even preceding and completely conditioning freedom, a notion that in his view predominantly referred to personal security and the vocation to create and formalise a supposed national will. In Bravo Murillo's worldview society was nothing more than an association of proprietors. The broad property rights that they shared could only be restricted according to their wishes and criteria and therefore offered them full protection. The main vocation of the state was the protection of society, its constituent owners and their sacred rights. Without them the state apparatus would be unable to survive and to sustain itself, it would be forced to recognise its inadequacy and undeniable defeat.[8]

This text is, indeed, one of the best synthetic exhibitions of the moderate and conservative world that Bravo Murillo represented as no other. The ideology of the Moderate and Conservative Party, of conservatism and of conservative government agglutinated around the Throne-Monarchy-Religion triad, so closely linked to Spain and its history. Any, even a minimal alteration in this triple design would change the essence of the nation and its political constitution. It would modify Spain's integrity and substantiality. As a convinced supporter of legality and an enemy of arbitrariness, but also clearly departing from the idea

6   Vallespín, ed., *Historia de la Teoría Política*, vol. 3. For the concrete Spanish experience, from the point of view of history of political thought, Abellán, *Historia Crítica del Pensamiento Español*, vol. 4; Antón and Caminal, eds., *Pensamiento político en la España contemporánea*; Menéndez Alzamora and Robles Egea, eds., *Pensamiento político en la España contemporánea*.

7   Pro Ruíz, *Bravo Murillo*.

8   Macpherson, *La teoría del individualismo posesivo*; Varela Suanzes-Carpegna, ed., *Propiedad e Historia del Derecho*; and, recently, Martínez Pérez, *Posesión, dominio y Registro*.

that man's creations are never good and perfect (attributes only corresponding to God), Bravo Murillo criticised socialism as incompatible with society, even as its antithesis. The main reason was its inconsistency with property, a fundamental constituent of society. Property and the ensuing society were the work of God and should not perish. Bravo Murillo continuously advocated his love for the social order, the preservation of society, the Throne and the country's institutions. Of course, he acknowledged the existing, often innate inequalities. They needed to be combatted through the charitable efforts of the rich and the resignation of the poor, without touching at the given social order or the established powers. He pursued a strong and durable governance consolidating order, tranquillity and stability. To this purpose, government disposed of three separate instruments: religion, the administration of justice and its armed forces. These instruments too needed to be understood in close relation to property (rights). Hence Bravo Murillo's criticism of the *Desamortización*[9], for its undeniable opposition against religion and the institutional Church. He showed a determined commitment to the legal and physical defence of property rights in pursuit of social stability. Bravo Murillo considered property as the basis of everything, the natural right by excellence. It could be threatened, questioned, criticised, attacked, limited, but never destroyed. It had always been there and would always remain. In order to guarantee an optimal functioning of the social system, the tensions between politics and administration needed to be lifted. The first needed to serve the second: politics was merely a tool, administration the purpose. The former was based on improvisation, gest and trial; the latter implied regularity, constancy and security. While fleetingly referring to the purposes of society and of constitutions, Bravo Murillo concluded that this destiny did not imply hierarchy, but consistent succession, tranquillity, individual freedom, security of men and their property, the well-being of citizens, peace and public order. This is what should be offered to society, what the state should provide and what should be collected in a constitution. Only in this manner a stable, firm and robust government was possible, achieving peace and tranquillity.[10] As regards to the instruments applied, Bravo Murillo already accepted some nuances. His design required a strong Throne, with rules perfectly subjected to law, not despotic neither arbitrary, nor absolute. After all, without the Throne, in particular the Isabel II dynasty, there would only be chaos.[11]

9   Political and economic process that consisted in the nationalisation of properties called 'amortizadas' or 'en manos muertas'. The properties of the Church and other ecclesiastical institutions were to be sold in public auction to the highest bidder. Developed by progressive governments, its main objective was to reduce the immense public debt of the state in the nineteenth century as a result of several wars and a harsh and continuous economic crisis.
10   Sierra, "La sociedad es antes que el individuo".
11   Bravo Murillo, "Mi testamento y mis codicilos políticos", I, 74-113. And see also the selection of texts by Bravo Murillo, collected by Comellas, *Política y Administración en la España Isabelina*.

This reflection by Bravo Murillo offers a mature expression of the authoritarian and conservative trends of Spanish Moderantism. This was, however, not the most traditional current of Spanish conservatism nor was it the most predominant or triumphant. At its side there were two other factions in Spain's liberal building. The so-called *doctrinarios*, the most balanced and pragmatic, formed a clear majority and were also the most successful. Under their great leader, General Ramón María Narváez (1799-1868), they often partook in government. The left wing of liberalism, the so-called *puritanos*, was close to the Progressive Party, with Joaquín Francisco Pacheco (1808-1865) as the most famous protagonist. Besides other topics such as elections and local autonomy, these different liberal factions particularly discussed the question of sovereignty. It was defined as national by the *puritanos*, as shared with the Crown by the *doctrinarios*, and as exclusively monarchical by the conservatives.

Nonetheless, it is Moderantist conservatism that interests us the most, mainly because with Juan Bravo Murillo, Manuel de la Pezuela y Ceballos, Marquis of Viluma (1797-1872), Jaime Balmes (1810-1848) and after 1848 also Juan Donoso Cortés (1809-1853) as its main protagonists and supported by the anti-liberal aristocracy and the more conservatives generals, it remained culturally interlinked with Spain's political past, demonstrating the lack of interruption between the old and the new. Moderantism clearly opted for a strong and solid monarchy and defended the union between the two social models conserved and represented within Spain's bicameral parliament. The old society had its place in the Senado composed by aristocracies of all kinds (political, administrative, ecclesiastical, economic, scientific, academic and nobility itself). The new society was heard through the Congreso de los Diputados, where the newborn commercial, political, administrative bourgeoisie was represented. Moreover, its proponents found clear assistance in Catholicism and sustenance in neo-scholasticism. For them, the rupture that they experienced in 1833 could be closed by means of the marriage between Isabel II and Montemolín, healing the wounds of the past and preparing Spain for the future. This royal union was for them the perfect way to restitute dynastic rule. Not surprisingly this line in Spanish conservatism would evolve towards 'neo-Catholicism' in the second half of the nineteenth century. Oscillating between Carlism and liberalism it constantly sought recourse in scholastic thought, blossoming so abundantly in the Spanish territory. What separated this conservative Moderantism from Carlism, equally monarchical and Catholic, was its gradual acceptance of the parliamentary regime and of a limited set of rights and freedoms.

After the abdication of Isabel II in 1869, the rapprochement with Carlism became inevitable, leading to the Comunión Católico-Monárquica. The transition of conservative Moderantism towards more traditional stances was facilitated because also the Carlist views of the *Restauración* referred to neo-Catholic ideas and concepts. Juan Vazquez de Mella (1861-1928) for instance defended the *fueros* and privileges in the best traditionalist tradition, interlinking both religious, political and socio-democratic arguments.[12] He pleaded for Catholic unity, defended the Catholic monarchy, and made a remarkably anti-centralist, maybe even federalist case for municipal, regional and *foral* freedom.[13] The religious argumentation of these conservative Spanish liberals must be emphasised. Hence their repeated references to papal authority in Rome and their rejection of everything that could be labelled as modern. The *Syllabus* of Pope Pius IX was for them a compendium of their ideology, clearly listing everything they defended or should exhaustibly attack. Their success in the political arena remained limited, except for their support to the dominant (but more moderate) conservative block, the so-called *doctrinarios* led by Narváez. Later on they moved without reservations to Canovism, a political current lead by Antonio Cánovas del Castillo (1828-1897) and his Conservative Party, the main ideologue and architect of the *Restauración*.[14] Despite their small political impact, these purest Spanish Conservatives, at first within the Moderate Party and later inside the Conservative Party too, showed a remarkable and durable cultural influence dominating the multifaceted academic and editorial circles of the country until the first third of the twentieth century.

12 The *fueros* were the legal texts, usually anonymous and officially confirmed or recognised by the king or the lords, where the medieval law was collected, full of privileges, franchises and immunities. In some territories, such as the Basque Country or Navarra, but less intense in Catalonia, Aragon and Valencia, whose legal order had been eliminated at the beginning of the eighteenth century after the War of Succession, the *fueros* were considered an essential part of the historical constitution that had been broken by the kings of Castile and subsequently by the Spanish nation. They recollected the idea of covenant and the limitations of royal power. In the nineteenth century the *fueros* were considered as deposits of freedoms, not in an individual but a collective sense, linked to the different territories. They were the expression of the particular and glorious past that had remained absent in the liberal project of a centralised and uniform Spain. Carlism would strongly support these historical claims, just as it did with religion, threatened by the freedom of conscience and belief. Hence its particular roots in the Basque Provinces and in Navarra. These *fueros* retained certain influence in the field of private law (inheritances, marriage economic systems, family law, particular contracts and community forms of property), while their role in public law was abolished. On these issues, see the overview of Sánchez-Arcilla, *Historia del Derecho*, I, 207-240 and 292-302.

13 As mentioned above these foral freedoms were presented not as individual or natural rights, but as collective and territorial privileges, particularly referring to taxation and military service. Their origin was the history, the past, the tradition, not the human nature or a rational system. Given their strong attack against equality and unity, they were totally incompatible with the new liberal world. For that reason they were eliminated by a national act of 16 August 1841 for Navarra (the so-called *Ley Paccionada*) and then by a new national act on 21 July 1876 for the Basque Provinces. See also Sánchez-Arcilla, *Historia del Derecho*, I, 1.050-1.055.

14 During this period (1874-1923) the conservative political program was implemented by a strong government composed of two main factions, namely the conservative Canovas, on the right and the liberal Sagasta, on the left. This government intensely collaborated with the Crown, dominated Parliament and controlled elections.

Conservative Moderantism was, of course, not properly neo-Catholic, as it applied a great dose of pragmatism. But it openly referred to neo-scholastic philosophy and pleaded for its implementation, somewhat in line with how Fray Ceferino González (1831-1894) advocated not only the restauration and rebirth of Thomism, but also its flexible adaptation. Neo-scholasticism and conservative Moderantism shared the same ideological base, their reflections on the three previously mentioned pillars of Spanish society coincided. The ideal political regime was the monarchy, there were no alternatives. Spain was Catholic, its governing powers needed to relentlessly support this religious creed. Finally, the administration had to limit itself to managing the given world without introducing major changes. These same views prevailed in all moderate and progressive factions of Hispanic liberalism, except for its far left side where democrats and republicans would make their appearance.[15]

The foundations of Moderantism: Crown, Nation and Religion

When Moderantism took the reins of power after the death of Ferdinand VII in 1833, it advocated a shy, romantic and somewhat sentimental and superficial liberalism, short of aspirations. While parliamentarianism was reduced to a minimum in response to the Carlist threat, liberalism was decidedly defined in economic terms, offering space for the growth of a new property-based and re-sourceful bourgeoisie.[16] Abandoning absolutism was the main objective, not a project leading to a radically liberal world. With Francisco Martínez de la Rosa (1787-1862) as its main architect, a kind of contract was concluded between the nobility, the army and the bourgeoisie to move towards a parliamentary regime, but all this not too hasty and avoiding excesses. The *Estatuto Real* (1834), as it was drafted by the aforementioned Francisco Martínez de la Rosa, Nicolás María Garelli (1777-1860) and Javier de Burgos (1778-1848), served just that purpose. De Burgos in particular strived towards a reform of the Spanish administration, but all this maintaining the hegemony, the undisputed sovereignty of the Crown. The new constitutional text asserted it as the dominant political institution. Government and the prime minister or *presidente del Consejo de Ministros* emerged as new executive powers, linked to the bicameral parliament, with an aristocratic Estamento de Próceres and a common Estamento de Procuradores. The judiciary was designed in a traditional way and would only change slowly, without much attention to the rights and freedoms of the citizens. Although the more conservative wing of the Moderate Party

15   Artola Gallego, *El modelo constitucional español del siglo XIX*.
16   Jover Zamora, *Historia Social de España*; Tuñón de Lara, *La España del siglo XIX*; Id., ed., *Historia de España*, vol. 8; *Historia General de España y América*, vol. 14; Artola Gallego, *Partidos y programas políticos*, vol. 1; *Historia de España Menéndez Pidal*, vol. 34; Carr, *España*; Burdiel, *Isabel II*.

was quite satisfied with the text, the *Estatuto Real* did not at all answer the wishes of its more moderate and progressive factions.[17] As a result the reform, modification or simple abrogation of the new constitution became a political item almost immediately after its proclamation. Already in 1836, the *Estatuto Real* was again repealed. Seeking inspiration in the (mythical) Constitution of Cadiz (1812) Spanish progressive and moderate factions found a new, somewhat natural and satisfactory compromise in the Constitution of 1837.

Meanwhile, and somewhat outside the constitutional arena, public opinion in Spain was clearly evolving, spurred on by books and newspapers, political debating clubs, pamphlets and other socialising instruments. All political factions and currents embraced a minimal set of views that we can label as liberal: political capacity of the individual citizen with freedom and property as his basic, fundamental rights. The concept of the *capacidades* was introduced, implying that the public prominence and even intelligence of an individual was foremost determined by the quality and quantity of his properties. As only ownership was supposed to guarantee independence of judgement, only proprietors were considered as full citizens and received political (especially suffrage) rights. The main goal of a citizen when exercising these rights in close collaboration with the state was to guarantee his main civil rights, being his personal freedom and his patrimonial security. Juan Donoso Cortés (1809-1853), one of the most conspicuous representatives of Moderate thought, would call this 'sovereignty of intelligence'. Only those endowed with intelligence and thus striving towards harmony should receive sovereign powers: freedom allows the subject, intelligence enables the sovereign. Man commands because he has intelligence, he obeys because he has freedom. Ultimately, freedom became the faculty to obey. In this direction, Donoso Cortés asserted that the 'sovereignty of intelligence' is simply the Catholic transposition of the search for truth. In other words, only the most intelligent people were considered as capable to seek and find the truth. The truth is undoubtedly what Catholicism offers as a compact moral whole.[18] After his personal crisis in 1848 he would elaborate on this more harshly in his essay on liberalism, socialism and Catholicism: the only way out of the spiritual and material crisis of present-day civilisation, so Donoso Cortés claimed, was a kind of revisited theocracy, a return to the Middle Ages as a moment of spiritual purity enabling to rearm that sick society. Only guided by Catholicism was it possible to find the salvation on earth. This guide was sustained by neo-scholastic thought.[19]

Apart from the idea of legality, with the law as an expression of the general will, also the nation appeared as a key element. There the 'machine' of rule

---

17   Tomás Villarroya, *El sistema político del Estatuto Real*; Id., *El Estatuto Real*; Monerri Molina, *Las Cortes del Estatuto Real*.

18   Donoso Cortés, *Discursos políticos*.

19   Id., *Ensayo sobre el catolicismo, el liberalismo y el socialismo*. Ideas, previously, presented in Id., *Lecciones de Derecho Político*, 121-138.

was located, turning citizens into authentic sovereigns and builders of public power. It was a space where from now on all political power could be constituted, exteriorised in a bicameral parliament representing national reality and especially the social order. Considered as a 'virtuous medium' the nation would be charged with measuring the effectiveness of the rights, eluding both old excesses and new radicalities. The permanent recourse to the idea of order and moderation forged the political and institutional system into a durable self-protecting device, with as its fundamental parts the idea of shared sovereignty, limited suffrage, public life imbued with religion and, finally, a pragmatic and transactional view of political reality, permitting a broad area of political programs as long as they respected the basic pillars of the constitutional regime.

Notwithstanding the *Estatuto Real*'s short lifespan, the text remains highly relevant as it offers a synthesis of that conservative momentum. In the same way the Constitution of 1837 can be seen as a meeting point between Moderantist progressives and the so-called *puritanos*. In turn, the Constitution of 1845 was the perfect expression of the *doctrinarios* ideology, the purest expression of Moderantism.[20] The *Estatuto* remained an important political reference point, as it looked to Spain's past with conservative respect and understanding, but without blind nostalgia and denial. At the same time, it allowed a slow and controlled transit towards a more modern, liberal approach, while still reconciling parliamentarianism and the emerging power of the executive with monarchy.[21]

The constitutional notion was folded into an instrumental rather than an essential concept: it was a framework, a tool to govern the nation. The *Estatuto Real* did not gave birth to power or to a political identity for the (already existing) nation. Formally it could be qualified as a simple law, not superior neither of higher quality then other laws. Finally, it was not engendered by a constituent power, attributed with national or popular sovereignty. On the contrary, it was based on the comfortable idea of a shared sovereignty between the Throne and the national community, between monarchy (Crown) and parliament (Nation). The *Estatuto Real* thus neutralised all revolutionary impulses and secured social stability in a legal way. But as it was born out

20 About the two great liberal families in Spain: Cánovas Sánchez, *El Partido Moderado*; Id., *El Moderantismo*; Colomer Viadel, *Los liberales*; Vilches, *Progreso y Libertad*; Suárez Cortina, ed., *La redención del pueblo*. For a wider framework, see the collective book *El nacimiento de la política en España*. Details of its effective government work in Comellas, *La teoría del régimen liberal español*; Id., *Los moderados en el poder*; Pro Ruíz, *La construcción del Estado en España*.

21 Marcuello Benedicto, *La práctica parlamentaria en el reinado de Isabel II*; Id., "Cortes y proceso político en la monarquía constitucional española"; Id., "La Corona y la desnaturalización del parlamentarismo isabelino"; Id., "Corona y parlamento en la monarquía de Isabel II". As a more general reflection to the nineteenth century, Marcuello Benedicto and Pérez Ledesma, "Parlamento y Poder Ejecutivo"; Garriga, "Gobierno"; Álvarez Alonso, *El Gobierno en el constitucionalismo español*.

of a simple agreement between king and parliament, it could also be easily amended and changed, except for some of its core components, the so-called 'historical constitution' or 'internal constitution'.[22]

The *Estatuto Real* did not offer a complete overview of all 'constitutional matters' because this was not considered necessary. A clear example was the text's silence on religion. The subsequent constitutions of 1837 and 1845 did indeed address the issue but remained ambiguous. The first considered Spaniards as Catholics, but not the Spanish nation. It commissioned the state to take (economic) responsibility for the cult and for its priests. The second text asserted Catholicism as the official religion of the nation, but less radically than the Cadiz Constitution of 1812. The moderates understood that it was possible to officially recognise Catholicism, offering it special protection. But they also advocated a certain tolerance towards other denominations and a healthy separation between Church and State, thus cutting short both the 're-galistic' ambitions of the Progressive Party and the still manifestly theocratic tendencies of the Church.[23]

Catholicism was an essential part of political life. Not only because it provided a doctrine of the origin and practice of power, but also for it established a pedagogy of submission: its teachings dealt with obedience and with how citizens should behave in public and private life. Fermín Gonzalo Morón (1816-1871), a reputed ideologue of Moderantism and a close friend of General R. M. Narváez, clearly placed the moral and political community above the individual. In science and morality, the individual was nothing when he was in opposition to justice and reason. His societal rights disappeared whenever he clashed with the state. In this line of thought and according to the best scholastic tradition, the idea of freedom did not equate autonomy, it was merely a path to justice. Choices were made not freely but in conformity with a given moral. Obedience was defined within Catholic parameters, which meant that an orderly and efficient citizenship was achieved by way of education. Citizens needed to be submissive, not questioning the social order but smoothly integrating in it, speaking rather of duties and obligations then of rights and faculties. The scholastic tradition since the sixteenth century, embodied by Spain's finest scholars of its most outstanding universities had laid the foundations of this Moderate ideology. The School of Salamanca remained its main

---

22   Varela Suanzes-Carpegna, "La doctrina de la Constitución histórica: de Jovellanos a las Cortes de 1845", 45-79; Id., "La doctrina de la Constitución histórica en España", 307-359; Bergareche Gros, *El concepto de constitución interna.*

23   Cuenca Toribio, *Relaciones Iglesia-Estado*; Id., *La Iglesia española ante la revolución liberal*; Revuelta González, "La confesionalidad del Estado en España"; Rodríguez González, "Las relaciones Iglesia-Estado"; *Religión y sociedad en España*; Barrero Ortega, *Modelos de relación entre el Estado y la Iglesia*; Suárez Cortina, *Entre cirios y garrotes*; Alonso, *La nación en capilla*; Núñez Rivero, *La religión católica en la historia política y constitucional española.*

reference, accentuating the social, communitarian dimensions of Thomist thought and insisting on the most basic principles of political philosophy.[24]

The way in which the *Estatuto Real* referred to the idea of *ordo* or social order clearly revealed its Thomist background. This text presupposed a superior, cosmic, eternal and given order, preceding government, parliament, the Crown and all written texts, even the constitution itself. This eternal, perfect and complete order determined the natural sense of power and its limits, capacities and aspirations. All human behaviour needed to accept it without exceptions. Political and social life was to be grounded in this order and needed to reflect the harmony that it embodied. It was clear that the *Estatuto Real* strived towards a moral regeneration of the Spanish nation in which Christian values could offer a barrier against the evils of materialism. A revived Catholicism would help the nation to confront both liberalism and socialism, its main corrupters, as Donoso Cortés had written in 1851. The constitutional reform proposed by Bravo Murillo in 1852 would form the clearest and most explicit attempt to create a perfect symbiosis between the civil and religious world, guaranteeing a harmonious collaboration between Crown and Parliament.[25]

It quickly became clear that the constitutional premises developed by the Moderantists were difficult to operationalise. As we explained earlier, the progressive and conservative factions went separate ways with the latter ending up in neo-Catholicism. Magín Ferrer's work *Las Leyes Fundamentales de la Monarquía española segun fueron antiguamente, y segun conviene que sean en la época actual* (1843) offers a clear illustration of this shift. Ferrer affirmed the fundamental elements of traditional ideology: primacy of natural law, an organic view of society and its intermediate *corpora* (family, municipality, region), existence of a social pluralism, configuration of the juridical order on Christian anthropology, anti-liberalism ... In many cases these arguments led to polarising opinions, positioning the local against uniformity, the *fueros* against the legal codes, the past against the future, history against reason.[26]

Once again, it would be the already mentioned Juan Donoso Cortés (1809-1853) that would offer Moderantist ideology its definitive form by writing in favour of an aristocratic and deeply Catholic dictatorship. Donoso considered that the 'social question' resulted from physical corruption and (above all) spiritual decadence in urban settings, engendered by materialistic liberal thought. He was considered as the most synthetic of Spain's conservative thinkers, along with the romantic and rather pessimistic Jaime Balmes, a good speaker insisting time and again on the close relationship between religion and history. Referring to the example of its medieval monarchs, the Spanish

24 Gonzalo Morón, *Ensayo sobre las sociedades antiguas y modernas y sobre los gobiernos representativos.* Also, for a more general framework, Domingo and Martínez-Torrón, eds., *Great Christian Jurists in Spanish History.*
25 Martínez Martínez, *La vuelta de tuerca moderada.*
26 Ferrer, *Las Leyes Fundamentales de la Monarquía Española.*

state was required to defend the Church and its legitimate rights, properties and organisational autonomy. Donoso was particularly distrustful of liberalism. History was conceived as a fight between good and evil, a continuous struggle to establish the kingdom of God on earth. His Christocentric positions evoked medieval times and gave great value to Providence. Man was considered as fundamentally weak and sinful. Only Catholicism could save humanity and needed to infuse the whole of society, both the public and the private spheres, the national and the international, the written and the oral.[27]

Moderantism moulded into neo-Catholicism would make its definitive appearance in the constituent debate of 1854. In the footsteps of Donoso but using a calmer tone, two new voices come to the fore: Candido Nocedal (1821-1885) and Antonio Aparisi y Guijarro (1815-1872). While resisting the arguments of the Progressists pleading for religious freedom, they both reaffirmed Catholicism as inherent to Spain, its history and its populace. Spain was, is and will forever be a Catholic nation made up by equally Catholic citizens. Nocedal, minister since 1856, was the main promotor of the *Ley Moyano*, the law on public education of 1857 that granted the Church and especially the Jesuit Order growing authority on that field. In the contemporary press we can point to the stances of *El Pensamiento Nacional*, *La Regeneración* and (the somewhat more Carlist) *El Padre Cobos* or *La Esperanza*. Similar arguments were voiced by the academic scholar Juan Manuel Ortí y Lara (1826-1904), the association La Armonía or the traditionalist writings of the already mentioned Vazquez de Mella.[28] They were not deeply antiliberal, like Donoso Cortés, but they understood that liberalism without Catholicism was an empty ideology. Could a solution be found by balancing these two elements under the moral guidance of the latter? Modernity did not imply the disappearance of religion from the public sphere, but limiting its impact. They contemplated on building a new understanding of the nation according to their ideas, less liberal and more religious, although tradition and Catholicism defined their social and political conceptions in a premodern sense, hardly compatible with modernity and its new political and legal concepts.[29]

27   Suárez, *Vida y obra de Juan Donoso Cortés*; Díez González, *La soberanía de los deberes*; *Donoso Cortés. El reto del liberalismo y la revolución*.

28   Urigüen, *Orígenes y evolución de la derecha española*; González Cuevas, *Historia de las derechas españolas*; Seco Serrano, *Historia del conservadurismo español*; Botti, *Cielo y dinero*.

29   Casanova, *Religiones públicas en el mundo moderno*; Haupt and Langewiesche, eds., *Nación y religión en Europa*; Rivera García, *Reacción y revolución en la España liberal*. As a general framework, see Louzao Villar, "La recomposición religiosa en la modernidad"; Id., "Nación y catolicismo en la España contemporánea".

Constitutional and legal ideas of Moderantism, with neo-scholasticism in the background

The question remained, however, how once the Moderantist vision and the great influence that it attributed to religion was anchored down constitutionally, these ideas would be put into practice by acts of government. First of all, the strong role that was attributed to the Crown as a sort of moderating and neutral fourth political power, a 'watchmaker' as Benjamin Constant (1767-1830) called it. For this purpose mainly two instruments were envisioned: the sanction of law and the so-called 'royal prerogative', enabling the monarch to convene, suspend or dissolute parliament. It was based on the idea that the impartial monarchy understood the interests of the given order better than any other political subject and that it was in a better position to defend it. Crown and parliament were supposed to harmoniously collaborate and to avoid confrontation. Meanwhile the Crown also dominated the judiciary and the executive by appointing the prime minister. That powerful monarchy was also considered as the best guarantee to preserve social order. This implied offering more leeway to the traditional ruling classes, especially to the big landowners, all this to the detriment of the nascent and emerging bourgeoisie. At certain moments even the reintroduction of the *mayorazgos* was put on the table.[30] The old social order confirmed its position through the Senado. Its members, nearly all great aristocratic landowners, held important positions within the judicial, administrative, political, scientific and ecclesiastical fields, bringing experience and seniority. The second parliamentary chamber (the Congreso de los Diputados) was composed through elections based on a very limited active and passive suffrage. The Constitution of 1845[31] consolidated the position of the badly married, poorly educated and ill-advised Queen Isabel II. Her support to Moderantism was to the detriment of the other parties aspiring power. Isabel abused her prerogatives and faculties, and dismissed the mediating and consensual role that the constitution had attributed her. Bravo Murillo's conservative, authoritarian and anti-parliamentary project would bring matters to a climax, with a Congreso of only 171 deputies and an ever more aristocratic Senate, further strengthening the Crown and official Catholicism.[32]

The Concordat of 1851 between Isabel II and the Vatican confirmed the Church's dominance in Spain and the protection of all its material interests

---

30 Castilian hereditary practice, unknown in other regions, by which all inherited goods passed to the firstborn who was required to transmit them in full and in the same conditions to his successor. Initially a merely noble custom, the so-called *Leyes de Toro* in 1505 broadened its application to more common inheritances as a symbol of social distinction.

31 Marcuello Benedicto, *La Constitución de 1845*.

32 Id., *Los proyectos de reforma política de Bravo Murillo*; Martínez Martínez, *La vuelta de tuerca moderada*.

by the Crown.[33] Probably, the Concordat of 1851 can be considered as Spain's most important constitutional document without being a constitution in itself. It regulated a highly sensitive and clearly constitutional matter, and defined Spain politically for a particularly long period. The Church accepted its economic losses in exchange for a weapon much more powerful, being its control of the educational system. Apart from regulating several ecclesiastical issues, the Concordat must be remembered for asserting the exclusive position of Roman Catholicism in the country, thus clearly exceeding the clauses of the constitution of 1845. It converted civil authorities into the guardians of morality and good customs, preventing the emergence of new (corrupting) doctrines. The whole educational system, both public and private, the universities included, was placed under ecclesiastical supervision. The Concordat also defined the *contribución de culto y clero*, the contributions that were required for the sustenance of the Church. The matter of the *Desamortización* was finally solved. The Church abandoned its claims on the goods that had already been effectively liquidated but regained ownership of the non-sold ones. Religious institutes were again recognised and obtained a legal form under which they could manage their goods and activities, such as education or charity. The result was an openly Catholic state and a clear victory of the Church. The Concordat restored Spain as a great Catholic nation.[34]

This new situation would be challenged during the two most openly progressive moments in Spain's nineteenth-century history: the *Bienio* (1854-1856) and the *Sexenio* (1868-1874). At both revolutionary instances Moderantism suffered a great defeat. With the Progressive Party, its more refined and profiled ideas would appear; with Krausism a more open and advanced liberalism was introduced. The Constitution of 1869 was an openly liberal manifest, with a clear division of powers and a scenario of rights and freedoms that in a certain way could be considered as natural and humanistic. Religious freedom and liberty of conscience were also consecrated. Krausism, the philosophical movement imported from Germany, overtook most of the academic world with its idealism, defence of universal fraternity, organicism and the broad manner in which it defined individual freedom.[35] One might claim that these two more liberal moments were the result of a retarded application in Spain of Europe's (and particular France's) revolutionary achievements of 1848. In that

---

33 Ibán and González, *Textos de Derecho Eclesiástico*, 96-112. On the additional agreement to the Concordat (1859), Ibid., 113-118.

34 Alsina Roca, *El tradicionalismo filosófico en España*; Fradera, *Jaume Balmes*; Álvarez Alonso, "La legitimación del sistema" (I) and (II).

35 Terrón, *Sociedad e ideología*; Gil Cremades, *El reformismo español*; Id., *Krausistas y liberales*; Id., "El pensamiento jurídico en la España de la Restauración", 55-103 [34-39]; Gómez Molleda, *Los reformadores de la España contemporánea*; Díaz, *La filosofía social del krausismo español*; Lorca Navarrete, "La Filosofía Jurídica Española Contemporánea"; Ureña and Álvarez Lázaro, eds., *La actualidad del krausismo en su contexto europeo*; Capellán de Miguel, *La España armónica*; Suárez Cortina, ed., *Libertad, armonía y tolerancia*.

year General Narváez, then Spain's prime minister, was granted exceptional powers by the parliament to suppress all anti-government movements. Two years later he reformed the Spanish criminal code and plunged it into a 'normal state of exception' which would last until his downfall in January 1851. The crisis of 1848 would also mark the ideas of Donoso Cortés and of other Catholic politicians. Since that year they not only condemned socialism, but now also accused liberalism for having lead Europe to this abysmal situation, according to them mainly a result of not having channelled individual freedom according to religious (Catholic) parameters. Although the effects of the European revolutionary wave of 1848 were neutralised in Spain by political and ideological control, the situation would again explode in September 1868. But, unfortunately, the events did not consolidate a stable and solid political and constitutional regime. They merely engendered a remarkable succession of regimes: regency, a new monarchy, a federal republic, a centralist republic, a unitary republic under General Serrano, and finally the famous proclamation of Sagunto in December 1874. The *Restauración* had begun, re-instating the liberal regime that had been discarded only a few years earlier.

As a result, Moderantism recovered its original meaning and ideological basis, albeit with greater political potential. The above-quoted events allowed it to label and vigorously portray its enemies: socialism, Krausism, extreme or progressive liberalism. Moderantist thought, clearly coloured by neo-scholastic frameworks, reasserted itself, both in politics and in academia.[36] Antonio Cánovas del Castillo (1824-1897) turned out to be the main architect of this restauration process. In essence, Cánovas advocated a pragmatic and consensual Moderantism. Pure rationality, freedom, equality and justice were renounced as unattainable. On the other hand, he also distanced himself of the all too 'apocalyptical' visions of Donoso Cortés and his plea for civil-religious dictatorship. The restoration of the constitutional monarchy was paramount, a new pact between the Crown and the nation needed to be concluded, durably implanting the idea of dual sovereignty.[37] The former renounced its absolute powers, the latter would drop its revolutionary drifts. This allowed to politically and socially stabilise Spain until the end of the century (and even beyond), when the rise of socialism and anarchism with its virulent attacks on private property and its advocacy of equality and worker internationalism would herald a new era.

For the devout Catholic Cánovas del Castillo, politics was born out of the procreative role of religion. A revitalised Catholicism would offer modern society a moral compass. This required its adaptation to the modern (liberal

---

36 *Anales de la Cátedra Francisco Suárez*, 11 (1971) 2; Pérez-Prendes, "Las ciencias jurídicas"; Llano Torres, "Ciencia jurídica y moralismo"; Martín Martín, "Funciones del jurista"; Id., "La utopía krausista".

37 Lario, "La Corona en el Estado Liberal"; Id., *El Rey, piloto sin brújula*.

and constitutional) context, reconciling the defence of the Hispanic Catholic spiritual tradition with scientific, technological and economic progress. Three elements of Canovist thought need to be emphasised: (1) the idea of the nation as a historical community in which race and behaviour were the fruit of tradition and displayed a permanent and transcendental character, (2) the concept of an 'internal' and unalterable constitution derived from history, and (3) the belief that rights and liberties should be considered as normative products of the state, not of nature or reason. The Constitution of 1876 would be the quintessential reflection of this Canovist model. It displayed a Moderantism accepting the experiences of the past and correcting its failures but also incorporating some more progressive ideas derived from dominant moderate ideology. As a result, the famous article 14 of the constitution proclaimed that soon laws would be developed to guarantee the constitutional rights attributed to the Spaniards. This was as much as saying that those rights would only be genuine when they were enacted by law and thus by the state. Moreover, a final clause of the constitution stipulated that this needed to be done without prejudice to the rights of the nation and should not damage the essential attributes of public power.[38]

Faced with the 'social question', the regime reacted quite late and badly, although some initiatives such as the Instituto de Reformas Sociales (1903), a continuation of a previous Comisión de Reformas Sociales, or the Junta para la Ampliación de Estudios (1907) generated relevant results. Safe-guarding property rights was still seen as the main purpose of state and society. At first government opted for repression, not only of the main workers' organisations but also of some republican political factions. Universal suffrage was introduced in 1890. In light of the impotence of Christian charity to answer the growing social needs, state intervention rose and the first social agreements were concluded. When social tensions rose to urgent levels, the defence of public order was entrusted to the regular army and to other armed forces. Cánovas had to operate within oscillating frontiers, reconciling the most moderate voices within Moderantism with the most progressive ones in the Progressive Party.[39] The Constitution of 1876 can be considered as a balanced response to the moderates calling for the restoration of the Constitution of 1845 and the progressist proponents of the text of 1869. The resulting compromise was quite original, incorporating elements of both but without a too manifest resemblance. Meanwhile the text of 1876 once again confirmed the state's role as final protector of the whole political building. Attaining the *in medio virtus* required silencing some more extremist voices.[40]

38   *Constituciones españolas: 1808-1978*, 158-172.
39   *Cánovas, Un hombre para nuestro tiempo*; and Vilches, "Cánovas, padre del liberalismo conservador".
40   Varela Suanzes-Carpegna, *La Constitución de 1876*.

As neo-Catholicism in those decades was not really in the frontline of Conservatism, it somehow lost its political prominence. Nonetheless, it gained considerable influence on the cultural field and in education, particularly at the universities. The neo-Catholics remained an important pressure group in the Conservative Party with huge ideological influence on the populace, not only from the pulpit and in the confessional but also through a whole range of associations and groupings linked to the clerical world. Their disinterest in elections and active politics, however, was manifest. This can probably be linked to their continued striving towards a theocratic societal model, hence their reluctance of representative democracy, parliamentarism, elections, parties and political practice. What they did welcome, was the political rediscovery of older, corporatist forms of representation, asserting social coherence based on older principles linked to religiosity and undermining the modern concept of citizenship as a category referring to personal autonomy, rights and freedoms.[41]

Although the *Restauración* can hardly be considered as a peaceful period, given for instance the harsh public repression of academic teachings that were labelled as 'contrary to the Catholic faith', the 'Canovist building' would last until 1923. It continued to find its main support basis in moderate ideology, although somewhat corrected and optimised. The main elements remained: (1) a historical and axiomatic (and not rational or normative) constitution, (2) a strong Crown attributing some of its powers to government, (3) the omnipresence of Roman Catholicism in public and private life as a result of both the Concordat of 1851 and the Constitution of 1876[42], (4) a parliament subjected to the wishes of the executive which also controlled elections and thus could avoid political surprises even after the introduction of universal suffrage. Furthermore (5) an institutional network perfectly locked and dominated by Madrid, allocating central power through civil governors, *diputaciones provinciales* and local councils (*ayuntamientos*), and (6) an educational system controlled by the Church on all levels, with programs and manuals approved by government. Finally, (7) a stable and healthy political and social order rooted in theology.[43]

As we already argued earlier, the idea of order or *ordo* in nineteenth-century Hispanic constitutional thinking was largely tributary of Thomism. It proved to be a skilful instrument for the protection of the given political and social model, mainly because it offered an encompassing doctrine of obedi-

---

41   Sierra, "La figura del elector en la cultura política del liberalismo español", 131-134.
42   *Constituciones españolas: 1808-1978*, 159-160, Art. 11, Constitution of 1876: "La Religión católica, apostólica, romana, es la del Estado. La Nación se obliga a mantener el culto y sus ministros. Nadie será molestado en territorio español por sus opiniones religiosas, ni por el ejercicio de su respectivo culto, salvo el respeto debido a la moral cristiana. No se permitirán, sin embargo, otras ceremonias ni manifestaciones públicas que las de la Religión del Estado."
43   Comellas, *La Restauración como experiencia histórica*.

ence and respect for authority and, moreover, provided a pedagogy of sub-mission and unconditional acceptance of a whole range of dogmas and prin-ciples. Thomism also entailed wide ranging moral teachings and a broad legal philosophy. Following the call of Leo XIII in his encyclical *Aeterni Patris* (1879) for a revival of Thomist philosophy[44], the study and teaching of Natural Law (or *Elementos de Derecho Natural*) was definitively incorporated in academic legal education, until then inundated by Krausism and the German Histori-cal School.[45] Thomist treatises, particularly targeting university students, de-fended the natural juridical order, the existing institutions and the prevailing codes of law. The idea of order was dominantly present and projected on all the components of the juridical system. The model of the bourgeois state that the *Restauración* embodied reflected this same philosophy. The general plan of the building was executed according to patterns that had been drawn since the mid-nineteenth century.

In passing, we should also mention that the starting point of Krausism was not that different, as it shared a similar kind of spirituality but, of course, strived towards other goals. This doctrine too considered order or *ordo* as uni-tary, harmonious, objective and continuous, encompassing everything and of-fering a logical foundation and objective condition of coexistence, a basis for social behaviour, cooperation, solidarity, sociability and legal relationships. It sought to draw a common ground for the satisfaction of both physical and spiritual needs. The former was defined according liberal terms, particularly on the economic field where competition was supposed to give rise to prog-ress. For the fulfilment of spiritual needs, the Catholic worldview came again into play, providing and guaranteeing social cohesion. The two elements, seemingly opposite, were harmonised to achieve individual but also collective satisfaction.[46]

Neo-scholasticism and law: between philosophy and theology

In neo-scholastic thought, the given social order was already embodied in the existing institutions, legislation had been built on those given principles and responded to them. New codes of law needed to be grounded on the same immutable bases and innate models. Ideology was merely seen as a pattern of behaviour, as a measurer and as a warning against possible future crises. Nat-ural law warned man against possible deviations or incorrectness, thus fulfill-ing almost a constitutional function. There was no opportunity nor a need to fight it. Furthermore, the designs of that natural order were already perfect-

44 Huerga Teruelo, "La recepción de la *Aeterni Patris* en España"; Cárcel Ortí, *León XIII y los católicos españoles*.
45 Llano Torres and Rus Rufino, *Historia del pensamiento filosófico y jurídico*.
46 Martín Martín, "La utopía krausista".

ly fulfilled and materialised in the existing political and juridical structures, by means of wise, fair and often customary laws. As a result of its historical and almost providential premises, this philosophy of law was remarkably undemocratic and rather elitist. It also had a strong anti-voluntaristic effect: the focal point of juridical imputation was not the exercise of rights, but the fulfilment of those duties linked to the given, innate purpose of each member of society. Social order as a whole required that each one carried out those destined duties according to his natural capacities. Individual behaviour should reflect respect and compliance to the general principles. The resulting social model, ensuring harmonious societal coexistence, was grounded in the same God-given goals and their correlated duties. All this resulted in an extremely hierarchical and functionalistic view of society, strict, monolithic, very uncritical and confirming the given order. The Church eagerly defended it because it wanted to preserve its spiritual direction of the nation.[47]

Some important scholars and authors defending this view at the time of the *Restauración* were the followers and disciples of, for instance, Francisco Navarro Villoslada (1818-1895), the most important and brilliant figure of them all.[48] Other important protagonists were Gabino Tejado (1819-1891), Eduardo González Pedroso (1822-1862), and José Selgas (1822-1882), all journalists, playwrights and writers, and also founders of several newspapers and journals, like *El Pensamiento Español*. From a more academic perspective, we should mention Pedro López Sánchez (1831-1882), professor of Legal Philosophy in Oviedo, Salamanca, Sevilla and Madrid, or Juan Manuel Ortí y Lara (1826-1904) who wrote abundant works on Logic, Psychology, Natural Law and Philosophy. Fray Ceferino González (1831-1894) was the author of several treatises on Thomist philosophy.[49] Nicolás María Serrano (1841-1899), lawyer and professor in La Habana, was the author of *Elementos de Filosofía del Derecho* (1872). Antonio José Pous y Ordinas (1834-1900), professor of Roman Law in Zaragoza and Barcelona, was an expert in Thomas Aquinas as evidenced by his numerous collaborations in *El Siglo Futuro* and *La Ciencia Cristiana*.[50] All these scholars forged a Catholic theory of law aligned with the writings of Taparelli, Liberatore, Sanseverino and others connected to the Italian *Civiltà Cattolica*. The politician Alejandro Pidal y Mon (1846-1913) and the Carlist leader Francisco Javier Fernández de Henestrosa (1818-1887) were

47 Aguirre Ossa, *El poder político en la neoescolástica española*; Roldán Álvarez, *Los derechos fundamentales en la cultura jurídica española*; Llano Torres, *Concepto de Derecho y Relación Jurídica en el pensamiento aristotélico-tomista español*.

48 Ballesteros Dorado, "Navarro Villoslada, Francisco".

49 See his *Estudios sobre la Filosofía de Santo Tomás*, 1th ed. 1864, 2nd ed. 1866-1867; *Philosophia elementaria*, with seven editions; *Filosofía elemental*, also with seven editions and his *Historia de la Filosofía*, 1878-1879.

50 Calvo González, "López Sánchez, Pedro"; Garralda Arizcún, "Ortí y Lara, Juan Manuel"; Huerga Teruelo, "González y Díaz-Tuñón, Zeferino"; Martín Martín, "Pou y Ordinas, Antonio José".

the main neo-Catholic political actors that would 'canonise' legal Thomism in Spain during the last third of the nineteenth century. The first one was a prominent leader of the Catholic Party, closely aligned to Leo XIII and Fray Ceferino González, the main architect of the Thomist revival in Spain. The creation of the Unión Católica would be the greatest legacy of Pidal. In 1884, the Jesuit José de Mendive (1836-1906) started a series of Natural Law treatises revitalising the courses of Ethics as part of the philosophical training of priests. The main academic legal scholars teaching philosophy of law at that time, especially Francisco Javier González de Castejón y Elío (1848-1919), Rafael Rodríguez de Cepeda (1850-1918) and Luis Mendizábal y Martín (1859-1931), professed an outspoken scholastic and theocentric approach.[51] Against their dominant position the Krausists could only claim two real academic strongholds: the chair of Gumersindo de Azcárate in the Universidad Central, and the one of the famous naturalist writer Leopoldo García-Alas Ureña, also known as Clarín, in Oviedo.

Spanish neo-scholastic philosophy of law particularly presented itself as 'a science of natural law'. Authors demonstrated how Christianity had impacted both the religious and the historical order. The former was related to its affirmation of the redeeming Truth, leading to salvation. The latter dealt with how Christianity had restored and rehabilitated the rational human nature and had perfected the principles of natural law. Although not using Thomas Aquinas's concept of law directly, these scholars extensively referred to his theory of law. Primarily it provided them an authoritative moral framework for their proper ideas. For example, they did not even follow Thomas' teachings on natural law, nor did they acknowledge the ways in which he had dealt with notions as society and order, or with the juxtaposition of objective law and individual freedom. By always subjugating subjective rights to objective law, they clearly sought to emphasise the primacy of duties on rights, of obedience on autonomy. In short, Thomas was used to brace a doctrine of submission.

It is clear that these authors, often involved in an open struggle with Krausism, above all sought to insert Thomism into the core of modern thought as a response to the both scientific, political, social and religious crises of contemporary society. Except in the case of Mendizábal, these Spanish legal philosophers ignored the new philosophical-juridical and social currents. For that reason, their texts were often marked by an apodictic and auto-referential tone. The doctrinal and abstract messages that they voiced, didn't connect with how dogmatics was taught in other, often highly scientific legal disciplines. As a result, this neo-scholastic legal philosophy remained somewhat

---

51 The respective voices in *Diccionario de Catedráticos Españoles de Derecho (1847-1943)*, written by P. Hernando Serra, E. Cebreiros Álvarez and J. M. Puyol Montero, respectively. For all of them, Rus Rufino, "Notas para una Historia de la Filosofía jurídica universitaria"; and Llano Torres, *Una aproximación a la neoescolástica jurídica española*.

academically isolated. But it, nonetheless, developed into the overall ideology of Spain's *Restauración*, and this without experiencing any serious opposition.[52] Mainly it proved to be an openly moralising current that returned to an ethical concept of law, melting it with morals under the same protective shield, while particularly insisting that a reform of the liberal state required an ethical transformation of man and the recognition of the social function of private property in relation to hereditary law. Hence these writings showed a marked social perspective. Authors as Severino E. Sanz y Escartín (1855-1939), Manuel de Burgos y Mazo (1862-1946), Pedro Sangro Ros de Olano (1878-1959), José María Llovera (1874-1949), Ramón de Torre-Isunza (1855-?) and Severino Aznar y Embid (1870-1959) advocated an organic view of society, often deviating towards the social sciences.[53]

These neo-scholastic philosophers of law displayed an essentially teleological vision of the world, conceived as God's work and imbued with order. In that world God, being the *prima causa*, merely operated indirectly, through second causes: the people, the regularity of law, and the inexorable cycles of nature. In that manner everything had a nature and goal in accordance to natural law. Order, law and justice formed the essential triad disciplining the legal world. The law was thus considered as a juridical-social order, part of a moral order governed by natural law, in turn part of natural moral law. It contained a complete set of rights and duties derived from legal-natural law that man required for the fulfilment of his destination in society and for the conservation of social order in itself. Underneath legal-natural law was the positive order, exclusively composed of positive laws and by the rights and duties that were derived from them. The idea of order presupposed a relationship between several elements according to an eternal hierarchical principle. As its governing moral and legal value it had the will to do good, in as much as is it was necessary for the persistence of the social order, for social harmony or for the coordination of men.[54]

In this intellectual construction, there was indeed a place for subjective right. It was imagined as the faculty or power of every man to act in relation to the goals designated to him and/or to the rules or precepts imposed upon him. The faculties and duties of man needed to comply to the legal order, gov-

---

52 Álvarez de Morales, *La Ilustración y la reforma de la universidad*; Ollero Tassara, *Universidad y Política*; Id., *Filosofía del Derecho como contrasecularización*; Peset Reig and Peset Reig, *La universidad española*; Jara Andreu, *Derecho Natural y conflictos ideológicos*; Escalona Martínez, *Filosofía jurídica e ideología en la universidad española*.

53 Montero García, *El primer catolicismo social y la Rerum Novarum en España*; Id., "Catolicismo social en España: una revisión historiográfica"; Id., "El catolicismo social en España, 1890-1936"; Id. "El catolicismo social en España. Balance historiográfico"; Andrés-Gallego, *Pensamiento y acción social de la Iglesia en España*.

54 Llano Torres, *El concepto de Derecho en la Neoescolástica*, 59-67 and 68-90; Id., *Concepto de Derecho y Relación Jurídica en el pensamiento aristotélico-tomista español*, 38-73 and 74-101.

erned by human law, in turn, derived from natural law. Those authors did not subscribe to an idea of law as the object of justice, but as a relationship of means to purpose and a necessary condition for the legal order to be fulfilled, executed and consolidated. The faculties of man needed always to remain in accordance with the natural order, enabling social life and the existence of man in society. Duties implied the moral and inviolable need to do or refrain from something for the benefit of one's fellow man, allowing him to achieve his goal as required by social justice. In sum, man derived his rights and duties from the preferences recognised or granted to him in respect of the corresponding limitations of his fellow man. Objective law needed preferences and limitations. Legal order was considered as a means of simultaneously preserving harmony and performing individual and social purposes.

Hence the great value attributed to the legal relationship as it integrates, adds and subtracts facts and rules, faculties and duties. Reason was considered by those neo-scholastics as weak and could only help to establish the main criteria of political and social organisation. Free will was very negatively evaluated: it would lead man astray. Every man was supposed to apply himself to a better understanding of the laws of the universe, but he wasn't able to enact or to change the laws of a superior nature. All this helps to explain why the nineteenth-century culture of rights and freedoms, particularly from a constitutional point of view, remained very weak, shy, closed, uncompromised and without humanistic foundations. It primarily focused on civil rights (property and liberty conceived as personal security), but not on political ones (based in autonomy and free will). The latter were contemplated with suspicion, especially when they were not directly restricted by laws.[55] It entailed a very diminished citizenship, passive and well-controlled by religious and civil power.[56]

While neo-scholastic legal philosophy equated the *Lex* with the *Ius*, it did, however, explicitly differentiate between morals (governing all human conduct) and law (regulating society). Similarly, it insisted on the contrasts between natural law and positive law. Justice was contemplated as endowed with a normative conception, its object and main criteria were entangled with the conservation of social order. The interrelation between natural and positive law conditioned the distinction between innate rights, whose juridical character was questionable, and acquired rights. The first ones (dignity, freedom, self-dependence, life, association, property) were primary and somewhat abstract principles grounded in the ethical-legal world (cause, potency, principle). The acquired rights, as their name already suggests, were based on

55   Romero Moreno, *Proceso y derechos fundamentales en la España*; Tomás y Valiente, "Los derechos fundamentales en la historia del constitucionalismo español"; Astarloa Villena, "Los derechos y libertades en las Constituciones históricas españolas"; Puy Muñoz, ed., *Los derechos en el constitucionalismo histórico español*; Álvarez Cora, "Los derechos naturales entre Inquisición y Constitución"; Bilbao Ubillos, *Leyes Políticas Españolas*, vol. 5.
56   Pérez Ledesma, ed., *De súbditos a ciudadanos*.

the innate ones and linked to reality (effect, act, consequence). In this context we must refer to the above-mentioned constitutional dimension.[57] In respect to property, the basis of the whole liberal construction, neo-scholastic legal philosophy affirmed the essential inequality that distinguished this faculty, albeit differentiating between individual and collective property and between innate and acquired property rights. Aligned with Leo XIII's *Rerum novarum*, however, it also highlighted the limitations of property rights, opening the door towards state intervention and social policy. While reflecting on property, these Spanish neo-scholastic scholars also dealt with succession regimes and the connected legislation. They particularly stressed how the goals and purposes of the family limited individual freedom in this area. Some authors also extensively wrote on usury and on contractual issues governed by commutative justice and the principle of equality of benefits. They called upon the responsibility of the higher classes to tackle the growing social tensions in society by displaying moderation and practicing charity. The 'social question' was considered a result of the growing de-Christianisation of society, leading to class antagonism, isolation and moral decay. Additional causes were found in the disappearance of the guilds, the politics of *Desamortización* and the connected liberal propaganda. One should, however, not overlook that Spanish neo-scholastic jurists also urged the state to appease social conflicts and explicitly pleaded for a legal regulation of labour conditions and wages. They advocated an organic conception of society based on respect for individual and social freedom, the notion of subsidiarity and a joint striving towards to the common good. They urged for transcendence against modern immanentism, practiced realism in the face of epistemological problems and professed a theonomic moralism based on a modern reading of divine natural law. This seemingly impossible mixture was nonetheless viable to them. In hindsight, however, it brought them much closer to the Gospel than to the Constitution. In sum, their identity as Spanish citizens and their vision on the political and legal world was clearly overblown by their deep Catholic convictions.

★★★

In Spain neo-scholasticism was omnipresent throughout the nineteenth century, in one form or another. It was a fluid ideology that found accommodation in Traditionalism (Carlism), in Catholicism and in moderate and conservative political life. It was the intellectual substrate of Moderantism, then converted into Conservatism, with 1874 as the main fault line between these two concepts. It gave both of them solid support for building a strong social and political edifice, which would bring order, peace and tranquillity, the basic pur-

---

57   Llano Torres, "La teoría de los derechos naturales en la Neoescolástica española decimonónica".

poses of this construction, and with private property as the foundational basis of society and state. Public power was exercised according to Catholic parameters, the obedience of subjects-citizens followed these same principles. The Concordat of 1851 was the best expression of this symbiosis between nation, state, religion and monarchy, all of them under the rhythm imposed by Catholicism. Hence an explanation of power, sovereignty, subjugation and rights and freedoms was born. Until the middle of the century a fusion of liberalism and Catholicism according to J. Balmes' pragmatic line still seemed possible, but finally it would not become reality. Moderates and conservatives were succeeded in the neo-scholastic creed by the group of neo-Catholics, defrauded by the broad freedom in all senses included in the Constitution of 1869 and by the pragmatism of Cánovas del Castillo in the (not entirely confessional) Constitution of 1876. These *neos*, as they were called contemptuously, did not have a great prominence in political life, with the exception of an isolated minister from time to time. This neo-Catholicism closely approached Carlism, even though the former was separated from the latter by the acceptance of the constitution, parliament and the bill of rights and freedoms. However, these *neos* had a very great cultural impact, through the many newspapers serving their cause and in academia, especially in those disciplines more aligned with the Catholic dogmas such as General Philosophy, Natural Law and Legal Philosophy. They designed an encompassing legal view of the world that derived its main characters and principles, its names and values from Thomas Aquinas. The impact of contemporary trends such as Krausism, known and appreciated by some of these neo-Catholic philosophers, may not be neglected. Their language and concepts, however, were entirely Thomistic. They were no enemies of modernity, but neither were they devoted to it. They understood that, in some aspects, change was possible, but always a meditated and reasoned change, a calm and quiet evolution and never a traumatic revolution. In fact, they accepted modern elements, such as capitalism or industrialisation, thus offering a basis for social Catholicism. All this proofs that they accepted the risks and challenges of modernity and that they were trying to give complete answers within the boundaries of Catholic orthodoxy. Changes and reforms could be eventually integrated into tradition, provided that they contributed to stabilising, consolidating and guaranteeing the *status quo*. Neo-Catholic modernity was defensive, based on the so-called *recta ratio*, the righteous or well-guided reason that fostered prudence, far away from pure and free voluntarism that would only lead to utter chaos. Neo-Catholics, as good neo-scholastics, thus had two constitutions: the first one was the human constitution, created by the politicians of their century, to which they owed obedience and respect. The other one was the divine constitution, the most important and valuable, built around Catholic thought, with the Bible, the Gospel and Thomas Aquinas at the front, to which they all owed devotion and strict subjugation. This second constitution offered them a comprehensive framework for understanding fundamental rights and their subsequent protection. It explained how society and the state should work, how power, sovereignty, its agency and limitations needed to be understood. In case of doubt, it was clear what their choice would be. Between Gospel and Constitution, they would always follow the former, mainly because it answered all questions in every imaginable field of public and private life. These answers provided them an unique form of security, the one that is able to bring the truth.

BIBLIOGRAPHY

Abellán, José Luis. *Historia Crítica del Pensamiento Español*. Vol. 4: *Liberalismo y Romanticismo (1808-1874)*. Madrid: Espasa-Calpe, S. A., 1984.

Aguirre Ossa, José Francisco. *El poder político en la neoescolástica española del siglo XIX*. Pamplona: Ediciones Universidad de Navarra, S. A. (EUNSA), 1986.

Alejandre García, Juan Antonio. *Temas de Historia del Derecho: Derecho del Constitucionalismo y la Codificación I*. Sevilla: Publicaciones de la Universidad de Sevilla, 1978.

Alonso, Gregorio. *La nación en capilla. Ciudadanía católica y cuestión religiosa en España, 1793-1874*. Granada: Editorial Comares, 2014.

Alsina Roca, José María. *El tradicionalismo filosófico en España: su génesis en la generación romántica catalana*. Foreword by Francisco Canals Vidal. Barcelona: PPU, 1985.

Álvarez Alonso, Clara. *Lecciones de Historia del Constitucionalismo*. Madrid-Barcelona: Marcial Pons Ediciones Jurídicas y Sociales, S. A., 1999.

Álvarez Alonso, Clara. "La legitimación del sistema. Legisladores, jueces y juristas en España (1810-1870 c. a.) (I)". *Historia Constitucional*, 4 (2003), 1-43; and (II), *Historia Constitucional*, 5 (2004), 101-139. <www.historiaconstitucional.com>.

Álvarez Alonso, Clara. *El Gobierno en el constitucionalismo español (1808-1978)*. Oviedo: In Itinere. Editorial Digital, 2018.

Álvarez Cora, Enrique. "Los derechos naturales entre Inquisición y Constitución". *Res Pública. Revista de Historia de las Ideas Políticas*, 18 (2015) 1, 11-26.

Álvarez de Morales, Antonio. *La Ilustración y la reforma de la universidad en la España del siglo XVIII*. Madrid: Instituto de Estudios Administrativos, 1971 (2nd edition. Conmemorativa del II Centenario de Carlos III). Madrid: Instituto Nacional de Administración Pública, 1988.

Álvarez Junco, José. *Mater Dolorosa. La idea de España en el siglo XIX*. Madrid: Taurus, 2001.

Álvarez Junco, José and Gregorio de la Fuente Monge. *El relato nacional. Historia de la historia de España*. Barcelona: Taurus, 2017.

Anales de la Cátedra Francisco Suárez, 11 (1971) 2. Thematic issue: *El pensamiento jurídico español del siglo XIX*.

Andrés-Gallego, José. *Pensamiento y acción social de la Iglesia en España*. Madrid: Espasa-Calpe, S. A., 1984.

Andreu Miralles, Xavier. *El descubrimiento de España. Mito romántico e identidad nacional*. Barcelona: Taurus, 2016.

Antón, Joan and Miquel Caminal, eds. *Pensamiento político en la España contemporánea (1800-1950)*. Estudio preliminar de Antonio Elorza. Barcelona: Teide, 1992.

Artola Gallego, Miguel. *El modelo constitucional español del siglo XIX*. Madrid: Fundación Juan March, 1979.

Artola Gallego, Miguel. *Partidos y programas políticos, 1808-1936*. Vol. 1: *Los partidos políticos*. Madrid: Alianza Editorial, 1991.

Artola Gallego, Miguel. *Constitucionalismo en la historia*. Barcelona: Crítica, 2005.

Astarloa Villena, Francisco. "Los derechos y libertades en las Constituciones históricas españolas". *Revista de Estudios Políticos (Nueva Época)*, 92 (1996), 207-250.

Ballesteros Dorado, Ana Isabel. "Navarro Villoslada, Francisco". In *Diccionario Biográfico Electrónico*. Madrid: Real Academia de la Historia, 2018. <http://dbe.rah.es>.

Barrero Ortega, Abraham. *Modelos de relación entre el Estado y la Iglesia en la Historia constitucional española*. Cádiz: Universidad de Cádiz, 2007.

Bergareche Gros, Almudena. *El concepto de constitución interna en el constitucionalismo de la Restauración española*. Madrid: Centro de Estudios Políticos y Constitucionales, 2002.

Bilbao Ubillos, Juan María. *Leyes Políticas Españolas. 1808-1978*. Vol. 5: *Derechos y libertades*. Madrid: Iustel, 2015.

Botti, Alfonso. *Cielo y dinero. El nacionalcatolicismo en España (1881-1975)*. Madrid: Alianza Editorial, 2008 (1st edition 1992).

Bravo Murillo, Juan. "Mi testamento y mis codicilos políticos, o sean los discursos que pronuncié en la Legislatura de 1858". In *Opúsculos de D. Juan Bravo Murillo*, vol. 1. Madrid: Librería de San Martín, 1863, 74-113.

Bravo Murillo, Juan. *Política y Administración en la España Isabelina*. Estudio, notas y comentarios de texto por José Luis Comellas. Madrid: Narcea, S. A. de Ediciones, 1972.

Burdiel, Isabel. *Isabel II. Una biografía (1830-1904)*. Madrid: Taurus, 2010.

Calvo González, José. "López Sánchez, Pedro". In *Diccionario Biográfico Electrónico*. Madrid: Real Academia de la Historia, 2018. <http://dbe.rah.es>.

Cánovas. Un hombre para nuestro tiempo. Study and anthology by José María García Escudero. Foreword by Manuel Fraga Iribarne. Epilogue by Carlos Robles Piquer. 2nd edition. Madrid: Biblioteca de Autores Cristianos. Fundación Cánovas del Castillo, 1998.

Cánovas Sánchez, Francisco. *El Partido Moderado*. Foreword by José Mª. Jover Zamora. Madrid: Centro de Estudios Constitucionales, 1982.

Cánovas Sánchez, Francisco. *El Moderantismo y la Constitución Española de 1845*. Madrid: Fundación Santa María, 1985.

Capellán de Miguel, Gonzalo. *La España armónica. El proyecto del krausismo español para una sociedad en conflicto*. Madrid: Biblioteca Nueva, 2006.

Cárcel Ortí, Vicente. *León XIII y los católicos españoles. Informes vaticanos sobre la Iglesia en España*. Pamplona: Ediciones Universidad de Navarra, S. A. (EUNSA), 1988.

Carpintero Benítez, Francisco. "La modernidad jurídica y los católicos". *Anuario de Filosofía del Derecho*, 5 (1988), 383-410.

Carr, Raymond. *España, 1808-2008*. Revised and updated edition by Juan Pablo Fusi. Barcelona: Ariel, 2009.

Casanova, José. *Religiones públicas en el mundo moderno*. Madrid: PPC, 2000.

Clavero, Bartolomé. *Evolución histórica del constitucionalismo español*. Madrid: Editorial Tecnos, 1984.

Clavero, Bartolomé. *Manual de historia constitucional de España*. Madrid: Alianza Editorial, 1989.

Colomer Viadel, Antonio. *Los liberales y el origen de la Monarquía Parlamentaria en España*. Valencia: Tirant Lo Blanch, 1993.

Comellas, José Luis. *La teoría del régimen liberal español*. Madrid: Instituto de Estudios Políticos, 1962.

Comellas, José Luis. *Los moderados en el poder, 1844-1854*. Madrid: C. S. I. C. Escuela de Historia Moderna, 1970.

Comellas, José Luis. *La Restauración como experiencia histórica*. Foreword by Alberto Carrillo-Linares. 2nd edition. Sevilla: Athenaica Ediciones Universitarias. Editorial Universidad de Sevilla, 2018.

Constituciones españolas: 1808-1978. Edited by Javier Carlos Díaz Rico. Madrid: Universidad Carlos III de Madrid. Editorial Dykinson, 2016.

Craiutu, Aurelian. *Liberalism under Siege. The Political Thought of the French Doctrinaires*. Lanham: Lexington Books, 2003.

Craiutu, Aurelian. *A Virtue for Courageous Minds: Moderation in French Political Thought, 1748-1830*. Princeton-Oxford: Princeton University Press, 2012.

Cuenca Toribio, José Manuel. *Relaciones Iglesia-Estado en la España contemporánea (1833-1985)*. 2nd revised and enlarged edition. Madrid: Alhambra, 1989.

Cuenca Toribio, José Manuel. *La Iglesia española ante la revolución liberal*. Madrid: CEU Ediciones, 2011.

Díaz, Elías. *La filosofía social del krausismo español*. 2nd edition. Valencia: Fernando Torres, Editor, 1983.

Diccionario de Catedráticos Españoles de Derecho (1847-1943). Madrid: Instituto Figuerola de Historia y Ciencias Sociales. Universidad Carlos III de Madrid, 2011. <http://www.uc3m.es/dicionariodecatedraticos>.

Díez del Corral, Luis. *El Liberalismo Doctrinario*. Madrid: Instituto de Estudios Políticos, 1945.

Díez González, Luis Gonzalo. *La soberanía de los deberes. Una interpretación histórica del pensamiento de Donoso Cortés*. Cáceres: Institución Cultural El Brocense. Diputación Provincial de Cáceres, 2003.

Domingo, Rafael and Javier Martínez-Torrón, eds. *Great Christian Jurists in Spanish History*. Cambridge: Cambridge University Press, 2018.

Donoso Cortés, Juan. *Lecciones de Derecho Político*. Preliminary study by José Álvarez Junco. Madrid: Centro de Estudios Constitucionales, 1984.

Donoso Cortés, Juan. *Discursos políticos*. Preliminary study by Agapito Maestre. Madrid: Editorial Tecnos, 2002.

Donoso Cortés, Juan. *Ensayo sobre el catolicismo, el liberalismo y el socialismo*. Editing and preliminary study *Filosofía política de Donoso Cortés: Teología política y crisis del sistema liberal* by José Luis Monereo Pérez, Catedrático de la Universidad de Granada. Granada: Editorial Comares, 2006.

Donoso Cortés. El reto del liberalismo y la revolución. Madrid: Dirección General de Bellas Artes, del Libro y de Archivos. Consejería de Empleo, Turismo y Cultura de la Comunidad de Madrid, 2015.

El nacimiento de la política en España (1808-1869). Madrid: Editorial Pablo Iglesias, 2012.

Escalona Martínez, Gaspar. *Filosofía jurídica e ideología en la universidad española (1770-1936)*. Doctoral dissertation. Madrid: Editorial de la Universidad Complutense, 1982, 2 vols.

Fernández Segado, Francisco. *Las Constituciones históricas españolas (Un análisis histórico-jurídico)*. 4th edition. Madrid: Editorial Civitas, 1986.

Ferrer, Magín. *Las Leyes Fundamentales de la Monarquía Española, segun fueron antiguamente y segun conviene que sean en la época actual, por el R. P. Fr. Magín Ferrer*. Barcelona: Imprenta y Librería de Pablo Riera, 1843.

Fioravanti, Maurizio. *Constitución. De la Antigüedad a nuestros días*. Translation by Manuel Martínez Neira. Madrid: Editorial Trotta, 2001.

Fradera, Josep Mª. *Jaume Balmes: els fonaments racionals d'una política católica*. Vic: Eumo, 1996.

Garralda Arizcún, José Fermín. "Ortí y Lara, Juan Manuel". In *Diccionario Biográfico Electrónico*. Madrid: Real Academia de la Historia, 2018. <http://dbe.rah.es>.

Garriga, Carlos. "Gobierno". In Javier Fernández Sebastián and Juan Francisco Fuentes, eds. *Diccionario político y social del siglo XIX español*. Madrid: Alianza Editorial, 2002, 319-335.

Gil Cremades, Juan José. *El reformismo español. Krausismo, escuela histórica, neotomismo*. Barcelona: Ediciones Ariel, 1969.

Gil Cremades, Juan José. *Krausistas y liberales*. Madrid: Seminarios Ediciones, 1975.

Gil Cremades, Juan José. "El pensamiento jurídico en la España de la Restauración". In *La restauración monárquica de 1875 y la España de la Restauración. Volumen conmemorativo del I Centenario de la Fundación del Real Colegio de Alfonso XII (1875-1975)*. San Lorenzo del Escorial, Madrid: Biblioteca La Ciudad de Dios. Real Monasterio de El Escorial, 1978, 55-103. Also in *Estudios de Filosofía del Derecho y Ciencia Jurídica en Memoria y Homenaje al Catedrático Don Luis Legaz y Lacambra (1906-1980)*. Edition prepared jointly by Professors José Iturmendi Morales and Jesús Lima Torrado. Madrid: Facultad de Derecho de la Universidad Complutense. Centro de Estudios Constitucionales, 1985, vol. 2, 33-67.

Gómez Molleda, María Dolores. *Los reformadores de la España contemporánea*. Foreword by Vicente Palacio Atard. Madrid: C. S. I. C. Escuela de Historia Moderna, 1981. Reprint of the 1st edition of 1966.

Gómez Ochoa, Fidel. "El liberalismo conservador español del siglo XIX". In *Sagasta y el Liberalismo Progresista en España. Catálogo de la Exposición*. Logroño: Cultural Rioja, 2002, 51-68.

González Cuevas, Pedro Carlos. *Historia de las derechas españolas. De la Ilustración a nuestros días*. Foreword by Andrés de Blas. Madrid: Biblioteca Nueva, 2000.

Gonzalo Morón, Fermín. *Ensayo sobre las sociedades antiguas y modernas y sobre los gobiernos representativos, Por Don Fermín Gonzalo Morón, Profesor del Ateneo y Autor de la Historia de la Civilización de España*. Madrid: Imprenta de Don Marcos Bueno, 1844.

Haupt, Heinz-Gerhard and Dieter Langewiesche, eds. *Nación y religión en Europa. Sociedades multiconfesionales en los siglos XIX y XX*. Zaragoza: Institución Fernando El Católico (Excma. Diputación de Zaragoza), 2010.

Historia de España Menéndez Pidal. Dirigida por José María Jover Zamora. 4th edition. Vol. 34: *La era isabelina y el sexenio democrático (1834-1874)*. Foreword by José María Jover Zamora. Madrid: Espasa-Calpe, S. A., 1996.

Historia General de España y América. Vol. 14: *La España liberal y romántica (1833-1868)*. Madrid: Ediciones Rialp, S. A., 1983.

Huerga Teruelo, Álvaro. "La recepción de la *Aterni Patris* en España". *Scripta Theologica. Revista de la Facultad de Teología de la Universidad de Navarra*, 9 (1979) 2, 535-562.

Huerga Teruelo, Álvaro. "González y Díaz-Tuñón, Zeferino". In *Diccionario Biográfico Electrónico*. Madrid: Real Academia de la Historia, 2018. <http://dbe.rah.es>.

Ibán, Iván Carlos and Marcos González. *Textos de Derecho Eclesiástico (Siglos XIX y XX)*. Madrid: Boletín Oficial del Estado. Centro de Estudios Políticos y Constitucionales, 2001.

Jara Andreu, Antonio. *Derecho Natural y conflictos ideológicos en la universidad española (1750-1850)*. Madrid: Instituto de Estudios Administrativos, 1977.

Jover Zamora, José María. *Historia Social de España. Siglo XIX*. Madrid: Guadiana de Publicaciones, S. A., 1972.

Lario, María Ángeles. "La Corona en el Estado Liberal. Monarquía y Constitución en la España del XIX". *Historia Contemporánea*, 17 (1998), 139-157.

Lario, María Ángeles. *El Rey, piloto sin brújula. La Corona y el sistema político de la Restauración (1875-1902)*. Foreword by Javier Tusell. Madrid: Editorial Biblioteca Nueva. Universidad Nacional de Educación a Distancia, 1999.

Llano Torres, Ana. *El concepto de Derecho en la Neoescolástica de finales del siglo XIX (Francisco Javier González Castejón y Elío, Rafael Rodríguez de Cepeda y Marqués, L. Mendizábal Martín)*. Doctoral dissertation. Madrid: Editorial de la Universidad Complutense, 1994.

Llano Torres, Ana. *Concepto de Derecho y Relación Jurídica en el pensamiento aristotélico tomista español de los siglos XIX y XX*. Madrid: Servicio de Publicaciones. Facultad de Derecho Universidad Complutense de Madrid, 1997.

Llano Torres, Ana. "Ciencia jurídica y moralismo en la España del siglo XIX: la neoescolástica". In Francisco Puy and Salvador Rus, eds. *La Historia de la Filosofía Jurídica española*. Santiago de Compostela: Fundación Alfredo Brañas, 1998, 219-274.

Llano Torres, Ana. "La teoría de los derechos naturales en la Neoescolástica española decimonónica". In Salvador Rus Rufino and Javier Zamora Bonilla, eds. *Una Polémica y una Generación. Razón histórica de 1898. Actas del Congreso 1898: Pensamiento político, jurídico y filosófico. Balance de un Centenario. León, 10-13 de noviembre de 1998*. León: Universidad de León. Secretariado de Publicaciones, 1999, 151-183.

Llano Torres, Ana. *Una aproximación a la neoescolástica jurídica española de finales del siglo XIX: Francisco Javier González Castejón Elío, 1848-1919*. Madrid: Servicio de Publicaciones. Facultad de Derecho. Universidad Complutense de Madrid, 2000.

Llano Torres, Ana and Salvador Rus Rufino. *Historia del pensamiento filosófico y jurídico. La enseñanza de las disciplinas iusfilosóficas en la universidad española del siglo XIX y sus protagonistas* [cover title: *El Derecho Natural en la España del siglo XIX*]. León: Universidad de León. Secretariado de Publicaciones, 1997.

Lorca Navarrete, José F. "La Filosofía Jurídica Española Contemporánea" (Appendix). In Guido Fassò. *Historia de la Filosofía del Derecho*. Vol. 3: *Siglos XIX y XX*. Translation and final appendix by José F. Lorca Navarrete, Profesor de la Facultad de Derecho Natural y Filosofía del Derecho en la Universidad de Málaga. 4th edition. Madrid: Ediciones Pirámide, 1985, 289-385.

Louzao Villar, Joseba. "La recomposición religiosa en la modernidad: un marco conceptual para comprender el enfrentamiento entre laicidad y confesionalidad en la España contemporánea". *Hispania Sacra*, 121 (2008), 331-354.

Louzao Villar, Joseba. "Nación y catolicismo en la España contemporánea. Revisitando una interrelación histórica". *Ayer. Revista de Historia Contemporánea*, 90 (2013). Thematic issue: Alejandro Quiroga and Ferrán Archilés, eds. *La nacionalización en España*, 65-89.

Macpherson, C. B. *La teoría política del individualismo posesivo. De Hobbes a Locke*. Translation by Juan-Ramón Capella. Madrid: Editorial Trotta, 2005.

Marcuello Benedicto, Juan Ignacio. *La práctica parlamentaria en el reinado de Isabel II*. Foreword by Miguel Artola. Madrid: Publicaciones del Congreso de los Diputados, 1986.

Marcuello Benedicto, Juan Ignacio. "Cortes y proceso político en la monarquía constitucional española: modelos liberales doceañista y moderado (1810-1868)". *Hispania. Revista Española de Historia*, 189 (1995), 11-36.

Marcuello Benedicto, Juan Ignacio. "La Corona y la desnaturalización del parlamentarismo isabelino". *Ayer. Revista de Historia Contemporánea*, 29 (1998). Thematic issue: Isabel Burdiel, ed. *La política en el reinado de Isabel II*, 15-36.

Marcuello Benedicto, Juan Ignacio. *La Constitución de 1845*. Colección Las Constituciones Españolas. Directed by Miguel Artola. Madrid: Iustel, 2007.

Marcuello Benedicto, Juan Ignacio. "Corona y parlamento en la monarquía de Isabel II". In Xosé Ramón Barreiro Fernández, eds. *O liberalismo nos seus contextos. Un estado da cuestión*. Santiago de Compostela: Universidade de Santiago de Compostela. Servizo de Publicacións e Intercambio Científico, 2008, 123-140.

Marcuello Benedicto, Juan Ignacio. *Los proyectos de reforma política de Bravo Murillo en perspectiva. Conservadurismo autoritario y antiparlamentario en la Monarquía de Isabel II.* Oviedo: In Itinere. Editorial Digital, 2016.

Marcuello Benedicto, Juan Ignacio and Manuel Pérez Ledesma. "Parlamento y Poder Ejecutivo en la España contemporánea (1810-1936)". *Revista de Estudios Políticos (Nueva Época),* 93 (1996), 17-38.

Martín Martín, Sebastián. "Funciones del jurista y transformaciones del pensamiento político-jurídico español (1870-1945) (I)". *Historia Constitucional,* 11 (2010), 89-125. <www.historiaconstitucional.com>.

Martín Martín, Sebastián. "Pou y Ordinas, Antonio José". In *Diccionario de Catedráticos Españoles de Derecho (1847-1943).* Madrid: Instituto Figuerola de Historia y Ciencias Sociales. Universidad Carlos III de Madrid, 2011. <www.uc3m.es/dicionariodecatedraticos>.

Martín Martín, Sebastián. "La utopía krausista: autonomía del sujeto (individual y colectivo) en la polémica jurídica española (1870-1900)". *Quaderni Fiorentini per la Storia del Pensiero Giuridico Moderno,* 43 (2014), 481-539.

Martínez Martínez, Faustino. *La vuelta de tuerca moderada: el Proyecto de Constitución y Leyes Fundamentales de Don Juan Bravo Murillo (Año 1852).* Madrid: Editorial Dykinson, 2019.

Martínez Pérez, Fernando. *Posesión, dominio y Registro. Constitución de la propiedad contemporánea en España (1861-1944).* Madrid: Universidad Carlos III de Madrid. Editorial Dykinson, 2020.

Matteucci, Nicola. *Organización del poder y libertad. Historia del constitucionalismo moderno.* Presentation by Bartolomé Clavero. Translation by Francisco Javier Ansuátegui Roig and Manuel Martínez Neira. Madrid: Editorial Trotta, 1998.

Menéndez Alzamora, Manuel and Antonio Robles Egea, eds. *Pensamiento político en la España contemporánea.* Madrid: Editorial Trotta, 2013.

Monerri Molina, Beatriz. *Las Cortes del Estatuto Real (1834-1836).* Madrid: Editorial Dykinson, 2019.

Montero García, Feliciano. *El primer catolicismo social y la Rerum Novarum en España, 1889-1902.* Madrid: C. S. I. C., 1983.

Montero García, Feliciano. "Catolicismo social en España: una revisión historiográfica". *Historia Social,* 2 (1988), 157-164.

Montero García, Feliciano. "El catolicismo social en España, 1890-1936". *Sociedad y Utopía. Revista de Ciencias Sociales,* 17 (2001): *Doctrina social de la Iglesia y realidades sociales nuevas (En los cincuenta años del Instituto Social León XIII),* 115-134.

Montero García, Feliciano. "El catolicismo social en España. Balance historiográfico". In *L'histoire religieuse en France et en Espagne. Colloque International (Casa de Velázquez, 2-5 avril 2001).* Proceedings collected and presented by Benoit Pellistrandi. Madrid: Casa de Velázquez, 2004, 389-409.

Núñez Rivero, Cayetano. *La religión católica en la historia política y constitucional española (1808-1931).* Madrid: Editorial Dykinson, 2017.

Ollero Tassara, Andrés. *Universidad y Política. Tradición y secularización en el siglo XIX español.* Madrid: Instituto de Estudios Políticos, 1972.

Ollero Tassara, Andrés. *Filosofía del Derecho como contrasecularización. Ortí y Lara y la reflexión jurídica del XIX.* Granada: Departamento de Filosofía del Derecho. Secretariado de Publicaciones de la Universidad de Granada, 1974.

Pérez Ledesma, Manuel, ed. *De súbditos a ciudadanos. Una historia de la ciudadanía en España.* Madrid: Centro de Estudios Políticos y Constitucionales, 2007.

Pérez-Prendes, José Manuel. "Las ciencias jurídicas". In *Historia de España Menéndez Pidal. Dirigida por José María Jover Zamora.* 4th edition. Vol. 39: *La Edad de Plata de la cultura española (1898-1936).* Vol. 2: *Letras. Ciencias. Arte. Sociedad y Culturas.* Madrid: Espasa-Calpe, S. A., 1994, 339-388.

Pérez-Prendes, José Manuel. *Escritos de historia constitucional española.* Edited by Remedios Morán Martín. Madrid: Marcial Pons Ediciones Jurídicas y Sociales, S. A., 2017.

Peset Reig, Mariano and José Luis Peset Reig. *La universidad española (Siglos XVIII y XIX). Despotismo ilustrado y revolución liberal.* Madrid: Taurus, 1974.

Pro Ruíz, Juan. *Bravo Murillo. Política de orden en la España liberal.* Madrid: Editorial Síntesis, 2006.

Pro Ruíz, Juan. *La construcción del Estado en España. Una historia del siglo XIX.* Madrid: Alianza Editorial. Fundación Alfonso Martín Escudero, 2019.

Puy Muñoz, Francisco, ed. *Los derechos en el constitucionalismo histórico español*. Santiago de Compostela: Universidade de Santiago de Compostela. Servicio de Publicacións e Intercambio Científico, 2002.

Religión y sociedad en España (siglos XIX y XX). Seminario celebrado en la Casa de Velázquez (1994-1995). Proceedings assembled and presented by Paul Aubert. Madrid: Casa de Velázquez, 2002.

Revuelta González, Manuel. "La confesionalidad del Estado en España". In Emilio La Parra and Jesús Pradells, eds. *Iglesia, Sociedad y Estado en España, Francia e Italia (Ss. XVIII al XX)*. Alicante: Instituto de Cultura Juan Gil Albert. Diputación Provincial de Alicante, 1991, 373-397.

Rivera García, Antonio. *Reacción y revolución en la España liberal*. Madrid: Biblioteca Nueva, 2006.

Rodríguez González, María del Carmen. "Las relaciones Iglesia-Estado en España durante los siglos XVIII y XIX". *Investigaciones Históricas. Época Moderna y Contemporánea*, 19 (1999), 199-217.

Roldán Álvarez, María del Carmen. *Los derechos fundamentales en la cultura jurídica española: Neotomismo y Krausismo*. Doctoral dissertation. Madrid: Editorial de la Universidad Complutense de Madrid, 1991.

Romeo Mateo, María Cruz and María Sierra, eds. *La España liberal, 1833-1874*. Historia de las Culturas Políticas en España y América Latina, 2. Madrid-Zaragoza: Marcial Pons – Prensas de la Universidad de Zaragoza, 2014.

Romero Moreno, José Manuel. *Proceso y derechos fundamentales en la España del siglo XIX*. Foreword by Gregorio Peces-Barba. Madrid: Centro de Estudios Constitucionales, 1983.

Rosanvallon, Pierre. *El momento Guizot. El liberalismo doctrinario entre la Restauración y la Revolución de 1848*. Translation by Hernán M. Díaz. Buenos Aires: Editorial Biblos, 2015.

Rus Rufino, Salvador. "Notas para una Historia de la Filosofía jurídica española del siglo XIX a través de textos inéditos". In Francisco Puy, Maria Carolina Rovira and Milagros Otero, eds. *XIV Jornadas de Filosofía Jurídica y Social*. Vol. 2: *Problemática actual de la Historia de las Filosofía del Derecho española*. Santiago de Compostela: Universidade de Santiago de Compostela. Servicio de Publicacións e Intercambio Científico, 1994, 73-98.

Sánchez Agesta, Luis. *Historia del Constitucionalismo español (1808-1936)*. 4th revised and expanded edition. Madrid: Centro de Estudios Constitucionales, 1984.

Sánchez-Arcilla Bernal, José. *Historia del Derecho*. Vol. 1: *Instituciones políticas y administrativas*. Madrid: Editorial Dykinson, 1995.

Sánchez García, Raquel. "El liberalismo español en el siglo XIX". In: Pedro Carlos González Cuevas, ed. *Historia del Pensamiento Político Español. Del Renacimiento a nuestros días*. Madrid: Universidad Nacional de Educación a Distancia, 2016, 111-135.

Seco Serrano, Carlos. *Historia del conservadurismo español. Una línea política integradora en el siglo XIX*. Madrid: Temas de Hoy, 2000.

Sevilla Andrés, Diego. "El poder constituyente en España de 1800 a 1868". *Revista del Instituto de Ciencias Sociales*, 4 (1964), 149-169.

Sierra, María. "La figura del elector en la cultura política del liberalismo español (1833-1874)". *Revista de Estudios Políticos (Nueva Época)*, 133 (2006), 117-142.

Sierra, María. "La sociedad es antes que el individuo: el liberalismo español frente a los peligros del individualismo". *Alcores. Revista de Historia Contemporánea*, 7 (2009), 63-84.

Sloterdijk, Peter. "El Antropoceno: ¿una situación procesal al margen de la historia de la Tierra?". In Peter Sloterdijk. *¿Qué sucedió en el siglo XX?* Translation from German by Isidoro Regueira. Madrid: Ediciones Siruela, 2018, 9-31.

Solé Tura, Jordi and Eliseo Aja. *Constituciones y períodos constituyentes en España (1808-1936)*. 15th edition. Madrid: Siglo XXI de España Editores, S. A., 1990.

Starzinger, Vincent E. *The Politics of the Center: The Juste Milieu in Theory and Practice, France and England, 1815-1848*. With a new introduction by the author and a foreword by Russell Kirk. New Brunswick-London: Transaction Publishers, 1991.

Suárez, Federico. *Vida y obra de Juan Donoso Cortés*. Pamplona: Ediciones Eunate, 1997.

Suárez Cortina, Manuel, ed. *Las máscaras de la libertad. El liberalismo español, 1808-1930*. Madrid: Marcial Pons, 2003.

Suárez Cortina, Manuel, ed. *La redención del pueblo. La cultura progresista en la España liberal*. Santander: Editorial Universidad de Cantabria, 2006.

Suárez Cortina, Manuel, ed. *Libertad, armonía y tolerancia. La cultura institucionista en la España contemporánea*. Madrid: Editorial Tecnos, 2011.

Suárez Cortina, Manuel. *Entre cirios y garrotes. Política y religión en la España contemporánea, 1808-1936*. Cuenca: Ediciones de la Universidad de Castilla-La Mancha, 2014.

Terrón, Eloy. *Sociedad e ideología en los orígenes de la España contemporánea*. Barcelona: Ediciones Península, 1969.

Tomás Villarroya, Joaquín. *El sistema político del Estatuto Real (1834-1836)*. Madrid: Instituto de Estudios Políticos, 1968.

Tomás Villarroya, Joaquín. *El Estatuto Real de 1834 y la Constitución de 1837*. Madrid: Fundación Santa María, 1985.

Tomás Villarroya, Joaquín. *Breve historia del constitucionalismo español*. Madrid: Centro de Estudios Políticos y Constitucionales, 2012.

Tomás y Valiente, Francisco. "Los derechos fundamentales en la historia del constitucionalismo español". In *Códigos y Constituciones (1808-1978)*. Madrid: Alianza Editorial, 1989, 153-173.

Tuñón de Lara, Manuel. *La España del siglo XIX*. Barcelona: Editorial Laia, 1973.

Tuñón de Lara, Manuel, ed. *Historia de España dirigida por el profesor Manuel Tuñón de Lara, Catedrático de la Universidad de Pau*. Vol. 8: *Revolución burguesa, oligarquía y constitucionalismo (1834-1923)*. 2nd edition, 2nd reprint. Barcelona: Editorial Labor, S. A., 1981.

Torres del Moral, Antonio. *Constitucionalismo histórico español*. 6th edition. Madrid: Servicio de Publicaciones. Facultad de Derecho. Universidad Complutense, 2009.

Ureña, Enrique M. and Pedro Álvarez Lázaro, eds. *La actualidad del krausismo en su contexto europeo*. Madrid: Parteluz. Fundación Duques de Soria. Universidad Pontificia de Comillas, 1999.

Urigüen, Begoña. *Orígenes y evolución de la derecha española: el neo-catolicismo*. Madrid: Centro de Estudios Históricos. C. S. I. C., 1986.

Vallespín, Fernando, ed. *Historia de la Teoría Política*. Vol. 3: *Ilustración, liberalismo y nacionalismo*. Madrid: Alianza Editorial, 2002.

Varela Suanzes-Carpegna, Joaquín. "La doctrina de la Constitución histórica: de Jovellanos a la Constitución de 1845". *Revista de Derecho Político*, 39 (1995), 45-79.

Varela Suanzes-Carpegna, Joaquín, ed. *Propiedad e Historia del Derecho*. Madrid: Colegio de Registradores de la Propiedad y Mercantiles de España, 2005.

Varela Suanzes-Carpegna, Joaquín. *Política y Constitución en España (1808-1978)*. Foreword by Francisco Rubio Llorente. Madrid: Centro de Estudios Políticos y Constitucionales, 2007.

Varela Suanzes-Carpegna, Joaquín. *La Constitución de 1876*. Colección Las Constituciones Españolas. Directed by Miguel Artola. Madrid: Iustel, 2009.

Varela Suanzes-Carpegna, Joaquín. "La doctrina de la Constitución histórica en España". *Fundamentos. Cuadernos Monográficos de Teoría del Estado, Derecho Público e Historia Constitucional*, 6 (2010): *Conceptos de Constitución en la Historia*, 307-359.

Varela Suanzes-Carpegna, Joaquín. *Historia constitucional de España. Normas, instituciones, doctrinas*. Edited by Ignacio Fernández Sarasola. Madrid: Marcial Pons, 2020.

Vilches, Jorge. *Progreso y Libertad. El Partido Progresista en la Revolución Liberal Española*. Madrid: Alianza Editorial, 2001.

Vilches, Jorge. "Cánovas, padre del liberalismo conservador". *La Ilustración Liberal. Revista Española y Americana*, 52 (2012). <www.lailustracionliberal.com>.

Agostino Gemelli. Photo, c 1920.
[Milan, Archives of the Università Cattolica Sacro Cuore]

THE NOTION OF WAR IN THE *RIVISTA DI FILOSOFIA NEO-SCOLASTICA*, 1914-1918

CINZIA SULAS

A brief summary of the context, history and historiography of Italian neo-Thomism in the nineteenth and twentieth centuries

In 1879, Pope Leo XIII issued the encyclical *Aeterni Patris*, in which he proclaimed the following:

> We exhort you, venerable brethren, in all earnestness to restore the golden wisdom of St. Thomas, and to spread it far and wide for the defence and beauty of the Catholic faith, for the good of society, and for the advancement of all the sciences. "The wisdom of St. Thomas, We say; for if anything is taken up with too great subtlety by the scholastic doctors, or too carelessly stated – if there be anything that ill agrees with the discoveries of a later age, or, in a word, improbable in whatever way – it does not enter Our mind to propose that for imitation to Our age."[1]

The encyclical *Aeterni Patris* proposed a philosophy reconciling theology and the mysteries of faith with most recent scientific findings. Compared to the first paragraph of Pius IX's *Syllabus of Errors*[2], which condemned seven propositions dealing with modern rationalist and naturalist philosophy, Leo XIII

---

1   *Acta Sanctae Sedis* (*ASS*) XII, 114.
2   The most recent critical re-edition of the text, edited by L. Sandoni, with an introduction by D. Menozzi, *Il Sillabo di Pio IX*. For an accurate historical reconstruction of the editorial process, see Martina, *Pio IX (1851-1866)*, 287-356.

decreed the constitution of a Catholic philosophy perfectly compliant with magisterial directives and chose a positive way to confront the dominant contemporary philosophy. This strategy, in continuity with the First Vatican Council, aimed to submit philosophical thought into the process of juridification of faith[3] through a progressive broadening of magisterial power to: "certain truths which were either divinely proposed for belief or were bound by the closest chains to doctrine of faith" ("cum doctrina fidei arctis quibusdam vinculis colligantur").[4]

This renovation of Thomistic philosophy was part of a wider adaptation of the Catholic Church to the modern culture and, therefore, it was interpreted as a turning point for the modern Vatican's policy:

> It was with Pope Leo XIII himself that the Roman papacy, recognising the end of temporal power, fully committed to the defence of Christian civilisation, whose essence should be based on Christian culture. To this Promethean yet failing plan the ecclesiastical hierarchy wanted to focus all its energy and above all the energy of the theologians, called upon to ensure an increasingly demanding institutional solidarity.[5]

Aeterni Patris was then swiftly and widely implemented through the creation of a series of editorial initiatives and institutional bodies on an international scale. First of all, the publication of the *Opera Omnia* by Thomas Aquinas[6], followed by the foundation of various Thomistic academies, such as, for example, the Accademia romana di S. Tommaso d'Aquino in 1880 (of which Monsignor Salvatore Talamo and two Jesuits from the *Civiltà Cattolica*, Father Liberatore and Father Cornoldi were members). But, the most important driving force for neo-Thomistic scholars was the Institut supérieur de Philosophie at the University of Leuven in Belgium, founded in 1889 by the later Cardinal Désiré

---

3   On the history of the origins and meaning of the contemporary Catholic magisterium, see Fuchs, "Origines d'une trilogie ecclésiologique"; Congar, "Pour une histoire sémantique du terme 'magisterium'"; Id., "Bref historique des formes du 'magistère'".

4   Cf. *ASS* XII, 99. The notion of 'truth intimately connected with Revelation' has its prehistory in the Council debates of Vatican I and Vatican II; on its historical development, on the assent required of the faithful in relation to such truths, on the magisterial body from which they emanate and on the international theological debate that has resulted, see Theobald, "Le développement de la notion des 'vérités historiquement et logiquement connexes avec la Révélation'"; Chiron, *L'infaillibilité et son objet*, 407; Theobald and Sesboüé, *Histoire des dogmes*, IV, 612-618.

5   Alberigo, "Dal bastone alla misericordia", 500; on Leo XIII's international political strategy, see Levillain and Ticchi, eds., *Le pontificat de Léon XIII*; Ticchi, *Aux frontières de la paix*. For an examination of the aspects of continuity and discontinuity of the pontificates of Pius IX and Leo XIII on the international political level see the essay of Marotta, "La questione romana".

6   Bataillon, "Le edizioni di Opera Omnia".

Mercier and with the support of Leo XIII.[7] This institute published from 1894 the *Revue néo-scolastique* (now *Revue Philosophique de Louvain*), whose most notable and influential exponents were Désiré Mercier and Maurice De Wulf.

Although the neo-scholastic historiography of the twentieth century tended to trace the origins of Italian neo-scholasticism to as early as the first half of the nineteenth century[8], the terms 'neo-scholasticism' and 'neo-Thomism', unlike what was happening on the German theological scene, began to be used with precise references (in terms of authors and texts that were based on and identified with such categories), only after the issuance of Pope Leo XIII's encyclical.

In Italy, there was great momentum in these new studies, thanks to Salvatore Talamo, who had a huge influence on *Aeterni Patris*.[9] In 1893 Talamo founded and directed the *Rivista internazionale di scienze sociali e discipline ausiliarie* (International journal of social sciences and auxiliary disciplines) together with Giuseppe Toniolo, president of the Catholic Union for Social Studies in Italy. The *Rivista internazionale* was fully in accordance with the focus of the 'theological-political' restoration prescribed by the encyclical, which declared the return to hierarchically ordered power based on divine authority as a remedy to all evil in the world:

> For, when the human race, by the light of the gospel message, came to know the grand mystery of the Incarnation of the Word and the redemption of man, at once the life of Jesus Christ, God and Man, pervaded every race and nation, and interpenetrated them with His faith, His precepts, and His laws. And if human society is to be healed now, in no other way can it be healed save by a return to Christian life and Christian institutions.[10]

The highly articulated programme presented in the first issue of the *Rivista internazionale*, followed in the path of the Pecci papacy and proposed to inform society and its institutions of the moral-religious principles of which only the Church could be the unique and authoritative interpreter. Facing a modern and laic society now legally free from all ecclesiastical restrictions, the *Rivista*

---

7   In 1990 the *Revue Philosophique de Louvain* published a monographic number for the centenary of the foundation of the Institute, where in particular was published the article of Aubert, "Désiré Mercier et les débuts de l'Institut de Philosophie"; on the same topic see also the more recent work of Courtois and Jačov, *Les débuts de l'Institut supérieur de philosophie (Louvain)*, 1-13.

8   For a systematic summary of the international history and historiography of neo-Thomism (included in the broader framework of 'Christian philosophy') see Coreth, ed., *Christliche Philosophie im katholischen Denken*, II, and the most recent Walter, "'Den Weltkreis täglich von Verderben bringenden Irrtümern befreien' (Leo XIII.)", 323-327. For the history of Italian neo-Thomism, see Schmidinger and Marassi, "La disputa sulle origini della neoscolastica italiana"; Schmidinger and Rossi, "La neoscolastica italiana".

9   Piolanti, *La filosofia cristiana in Mons. Salvatore Talamo ispiratore della "Aeterni Patris"*.

10   Leo XIII, *Lett. Enc. Rerum novarum*, *ASS* 23, 1890-1891, 641-670, § 22.

aimed to create the "ultimate empire of the kingdom of Jesus Christ and his Church in society and civilisation".[11]

However, neo-scholasticism in Italy took shape with the pontificate of Pius X, characterised in particular by the fight against modernism (which reached its climax in 1907 with the encyclical *Pascendi dominicis gregis*) and the idealism of Croce and Gentile.

In order to understand the context in which neo-scholasticism developed, closely corresponding to the anti-modernist views of Pius X, we must take a brief look at his ecclesiastical policies, succinctly and clearly summarised by Giuseppe Alberigo as following:

> Pius X – elected in 1903 – faced an extraordinary season of spontaneous thriving of Catholic cultural activities, particularly in the exegetical and historical fields. The papacy felt directly affected by the turmoil of transformation arising as a result of the ambitious attempt to compete with secular culture. Rome saw this modernisation endeavour as a threat to the whole structure of Christianity and was directly involved in the controversy, inevitably assuming the role of the concerned party, often getting carried away and defending the views of the school, rather than the central tenet of the Revelation. In 1907, a decree of the Holy Office was published that condemned more than sixty theological propositions, followed by the encyclical *Pascendi dominici gregis* which viewed several modernist concerns as one doctrinal system which could more easily be rejected as a whole. [...] The anti-modernist battle also introduced another new element: a determination to pursue errors and sinners that echoed the harshest phases of the anti-heretical crusades. An approach based on tip-offs, secret and arbitrary procedures, and coercive means was therefore adopted, with a view to destroying sinners on all levels. [...] With this spirit the ideas of the anti-Protestant *Professio Fidei* were revived, and the Oath Against Modernism was issued in 1910.[12]

During Pius X's pontificate, another important controversy to understand the historical evolution of neo-scholasticism involved two journals: the *Rivista di Filosofia Neo-Scolastica*, founded in 1909 by Franciscan Agostino Gemelli, and *La Critica*, founded by Benedetto Croce, who co-directed it with Giovanni Gentile until 1923. The first conflict between the two, a crucial reference point for future developments, broke out in 1905 in the third issue of *La Critica* with a review by Gentile of the work by Maurice De Wulf, *Introduction à la philo-*

---

11 Talamo, "Programma", 1. The history of this review represents one of the means by which the social function of the Catholic Church was adapted to the new social order and the new semantics that accompany it. On this subject, see Miccoli, "Chiesa e società in Italia", 1504.
12 Alberigo, "Dal bastone alla misericordia", 489.

sophie néo-scolastique.[13] However, it was Gemelli's journal that provided the milieu for the historic self-understanding of Italian neo-scholasticism through an explicit contrast to idealism, starting with the demands and scientific-philosophical issues originally conceived by idealistic philosophers.[14]

It was within this highly tense academic and ecclesiastical climate that the first works by Amato Masnovo[15] were published in the *Rivista di Filosofia Neo-Scolastica,* starting a historiographical discourse, which was somewhat 'apologetic' in nature, yet aimed at providing theoretical and historical explanations.[16] By comparing De Wulf's method with his own, Masnovo positioned himself in a dynamic or genetic analysis of neo-scholastic philosophy.[17] But rather than seeking a sense of continuity with the Belgian historian, Masnovo followed in the footsteps of Gentile, using the critical observations made by him on De Wulf to his advantage and against Gentile. Actually, Masnovo took the thesis of Gentile to the extreme, completely overturning them, up to deny the historic development of philosophy, considered by Masnovo as the immanent and immutable truth of history. In other words, whilst Gentile attributed the historical decline of scholasticism to the disappearance of the contingent needs it had answered until then, i.e. to the redundancy of its function[18], Masnovo provided a counter-attack, transposing the historical-functional analysis conducted by Gentile into unhistorical and substantive levels:

> the function i.e. the reasoning that engenders philosophical thought is immanent to man [...]. Therefore, philosophical thought – true philosophical thought – can never be futile, for as long as time exists. [...] If scholastic philosophy existed, i.e. if scholastic philosophy was (as it certainly was) at a given moment the philosophy, absorbing everything that was vital from the past, it alone will continue to be, though amplified, the philosophy.[19]

13 The same essay was republished by Gentile in *Il modernismo e i rapporti tra religione e filosofia,* 203-221. De Wulf replied to him with the article "La scolastica vecchia e nuova", *La Critica,* 9 (1911), 213-222, to which Gentile answered in the next issue of the review with the article titled "La scolastica e il prof. De Wulf", Ibid., 9 (1911), 306-308. Gemelli took part to in such *querelle* on the pages of the *Rivista di Filosofia Neo-Scolastica* commissioning Bruno Nardi, brilliant student of De Wulf at the University of Leuven, to write an article on the same question: "Scolastica vecchia e nuova", *Rivista di Filosofia Neo-Scolastica,* 3 (1911) 5, 555-562. On the Gentile's medieval philosophy interpretation, see Nardi, "La filosofia del Medio Evo nel pensiero di Giovanni Gentile".

14 Gemelli in the article "Per il programma del nostro lavoro", *Rivista di Filosofia Neo-scolastica,* 11 (1919), 2-3, explained his philosophical strategy with these words: "It is necessary to place ourselves [...] on the same level as idealism, to use idealism, to search in the nucleus of philosophia perennis for the elements that allow us to reconstruct and rethink our philosophy in function of the new demands created by idealism".

15 On the history of Masnovo's work see Vanni Rovighi, "L'opera di Amato Masnovo".

16 Vasoli, "La neoscolastica in Italia", 171.

17 Masnovo, *Il neo-tomismo in Italia,* 14-16.

18 Gentile, "A proposito del libro di M. De Wulf", 132.

19 Masnovo, *Il neo-tomismo in Italia,* 22-23.

Neo-scholasticism was therefore represented as the final and largest ring within in a succession of concentric circles, with 'medieval scholasticism' or rather 'perennial philosophy' at the centre. In 1934, when neo-scholasticism had become established, Agostino Gemelli defined it in this synthetic and clear way:

> The term neo-scholastic philosophy refers to the revival of medieval thought in modern civilisation, considering medieval thought not as a transient expression of a civilisation, but, in its substance, as the final conquest of human reasoning in metaphysics, a conquest matured through Greek philosophy and Christianity, with realism and theism at its core.[20]

From its origin to its crystallisation, neo-scholasticism was defined and legitimated through its continuity with an appropriately selected historical past, i.e., following a process of "the invention of tradition", highlighted by Hobsbawm[21] in other cultural spheres and based on "the use of ancient materials to construct invented traditions of a novel type for quite novel purposes".[22]

Therefore, to what extent has the invention of neo-scholasticism, put to the extreme reality test of the First World War, used materials older than 'Thomism', and to what extent has it extended its ancient symbolic vocabulary beyond its present limits, given the demands that current life places on thought?

War or peace: the aporia of national churches in a world of 'futile slaughter'

In his speech on 22 January 1915, Pope Benedict XV declared the powerlessness of the Church and the failure of his attempts to stop the 'carnage' of the ongoing war. Then, he gave a brief outline of the theological-political structure, justifying and explaining his impartial position[23]:

> To proclaim that no one, for any reason, is allowed to violate justice is without a doubt a duty that belongs first and foremost to the Roman Pontiff, as to the one who is appointed by God to be His supreme interpreter and the vindicator of His eternal law (*summus interpres et vindex legis aeternae*). [...] But to involve the pontifical authority in the quarrels of the belligerents

20 Gemelli, "Neotomismo e neoscolastica", 581.
21 Hobsbawm and Ranger, *The Invention of Tradition*.
22 Ibid., 6.
23 On the political impartiality of Pope della Chiesa, see Morozzo della Rocca, "Guerre mondiale (première)"; Id., "Benedetto XV e il nazionalismo"; Id., "Benedetto XV e la prima guerra mondiale"; Menozzi, *Chiesa, pace e guerra nel Novecento*, 15-46.

would be unbecoming and would serve no useful purpose [...] since the Roman Pontiff (is the) Vicar of Jesus Christ, who died for each and every man.[24]

The image of the sacrifice of Christ, a theological-political image communicating Christ as a universal gift for the salvation of every human being – already represented in itself a clear reason for the unbridgeable distance taken by the Church from every warring parties. The rhetorical mechanism used by Benedict XV put the Church and the pope, as the vicar of Christ, on a different level of logic, superior to the individual interests of the states. This certainly was not an ethical withdrawal of the Church from the conflict, but rather a prudent political-diplomatic positioning.[25] Moreover, this neutrality did not signify a Church's distance from the political arena, but rather a precise political proposal, which did not simply oppose state powers, but that urged states to take a more radical political stance instead of the technical-economic drift that led them to war.

However, the pope found himself somewhat isolated from national churches, which did not comply with the papal directive, creating contradictions and disagreements even among the Christians and also within various religious institutes of different nations.[26]

The Great War highlighted the intrinsic contradictory stance of religious institutions towards modern nationalism. According to Hobsbawm:

> The links between religion and national consciousness can be very close [...] Yet religion is a paradoxical cement for protonationalism, and indeed for modern nationalism, which has usually (at least in its more crusading phases) treated it with considerable reserve as a force which could challenge the nation's monopoly claim to its members' loyalty [...] On the other hand the world religions [...] are universal by definition, and therefore designed to fudge ethnic, linguistic, political and other differences.[27]

At the outbreak of the war in July 1914, two weeks after the meeting in Lourdes, where German and French Catholics gathered to pray together, Jesuit Jules Lebreton wrote in *Études:* "the pilgrims of Lourdes, back in their homeland, in the shadow of their own national flags, attacked each other".[28] Faced with total war, also Catholic universalism succumbed to the particular interests of nations.

---

24   The quotation is taken from the speech given during the consistory convened to assign new bishops to the vacant seats. *Acta apostolicae sedis,* 7 (1915), 33-36.

25   Pollard, *The Unknown Pope Benedict XV,* 112-139.

26   For a differentiated and deepened overview of the relations between the pontifical position and the national churches, see the 28 essays collected in the third section, Reports, of the volume directed by Melloni, Cavagnini and Grossi, *Benedetto XV,* II, 585-931.

27   Hobsbawm, *Nations and Nationalism,* 67-68.

28   Lebreton, "Pensées chrétiennes sur la guerre", 5.

Although it is impossible here to account for all national responses, a very brief summary of the emblematic case of three periodicals by the Society of Jesus, a religious order historically known for its esprit de corps and his attachment to the pope with the fourth vow of obedience will be presented.[29] The German *Stimmen der Zeit*, the French *Études* and the Italian *La Civiltà Cattolica*, the three most reputable Jesuit publications, responded very differently to the war, whilst all utterly condemning extreme nationalism.

As summarised by Klaus Schatz in his well-articulated essay, the opposing positions of the German and French periodicals were formally similar and articulated around two main ideas: the "predictable and uncritical identification with 'the just cause'", and the "effort to be fair against the enemy and the future prospect of a possible reconciliation at the end of the war".[30] The only journal to firmly maintain a clear neutral position was the Italian *La Civiltà Cattolica*, censored by the Italian state, as demonstrated by the dozens of blank pages in the articles written by then director Father Enrico Rosa.

In particular, regarding Italy, the dialectical opposition between national independence and universality represented an unresolved crux in the entire history of the *Risorgimento*. The striving for Italian unification, in the current form of the secular bourgeois state, was limited by a religious unity, realised in Christian-Catholic faith and in church institutions that informed the spiritual history and the social structures of the Italian people.[31]

It was precisely this principle of nationality, despite different views, that formed the main foundation of all war-related discourse. In this respect, still on the subject of Italy, two of the most authoritative and widely heeded voices within the Church were Enrico Rosa (SJ) and Agostino Gemelli. Unlike neutralist Jesuit Rosa, who followed and echoed the universalist and peaceful ideas of Benedict XV, Agostino Gemelli justified Italy's involvement in the war, basing on this principle of nationality.[32]

---

29 Schatz, "La prima guerra mondiale tra nazionalismo e dialogo tra i popoli".
30 Ibid., 224.
31 With regard to the history of nationalism and the relationship between 'nationalism' and religion see Hobsbawm, *Nations and Nationalism*. A historiographic review on the interpretation of the relationship between religion and nation in the Italian *Risorgimento* can be found in Formigoni, *L'Italia dei Cattolici*, 13-32.
32 A special case was the resumption, subject to different interpretations, of an essay, published in 1847 by the Jesuit Luigi Taparelli d'Azeglio (1793-1862), entitled *Della nazionalità*. Taparelli's figure and works have represented a constant reference throughout the twentieth century both for the construction of some ethical and legal cornerstones of the contemporary Catholic magisterium, and for a historical self-representation of neo-scholasticism, being identified as one of the founding fathers of the 'new' philosophy. On the comparison of the opposing positions of the Jesuit Enrico Rosa (1870-1938) and the Franciscan Agostino Gemelli (1878-1959) on the interpretation of the concept of nationality during the war, I would refer to my article "La dissoluzione del concetto taparelliano di nazionalità durante la Grande Guerra".

In the eyes of the Franciscan, in fact, the war represented the chance for Italian Catholics to re-establish a political role, closing that divide between Catholics and Italian citizens that emerged during the *Risorgimento*. On an international level, Gemelli was already in full agreement with the opinions on national resistance initiated and held by his master, the cardinal and archbishop of Mechelen, Désiré Mercier.[33]

More generally, these opinions were shared with all the neo-scholastic authors writing in the *Rivista di Filosofia Neo-Scolastica*, which, unlike its Belgian counterpart *Revue néo-scolastique*, managed to continue publishing into the war period. But the fervent activism of the Franciscan, who personally took part in the war as military chaplain, doctor and director of the Psychophysiological Laboratory of the Supreme Command of the Italian army, was not always approved or endorsed by his superiors at the Vatican under the pontificate of Benedict XV.

The contrasts with the ecclesial hierarchy about the doctrinarian approach to war-related matters were reflected in the change of war-related contributions in the *Rivista di Filosofia Neo-Scolastica*. The war-related articles gradually decreased and were characterised by the progressive abstraction and detachment from the actuality of the ongoing war.[34]

The contribution of the *Rivista di Filosofia Neo-Scolastica* to the significance of war during the First World War

Like all journals of the time, the *Rivista di Filosofia Neo-Scolastica* represented for historians an authentic barometer of the constant strains and worries of a culture called to respond to the challenges of modernity as an irreversible period of change and complete transformation, and of the secularisation of public and private spaces.[35]

Given the theoretical nature of the journal, there are only seven articles on the subject of the war and its imminence, and of these only five are discussed below, as they pertain quite explicitly to the application of neo-Thom-

---

33 About the history of Mercier during the World War, see De Volder, *La résistance d'un cardinal*; Aubert, *Les deux premiers grands conflits du cardinal Mercier avec les autorités allemandes*.

34 Bocci, "Benedetto XV, p. Gemelli e la fondazione dell'Università cattolica", 975.

35 Apruzzese, "Introduzione", 9.

istic philosophy to the historical judgment on the Great War.[36] This subject was only touched upon in a few issues published in 1915 and 1916. From 1917 on, the topic of the war and its implications for the homeland or nationalism were no longer discussed.

The journal *Vita e pensiero*, founded and directed by Gemelli at the dawn of the First World War in December 1914, published a higher number of war-related articles; however, given the journal's more popular and activist slant and its clear warmongering stance, there are no actual reflections on its significance within a historical-philosophical context, nor on the justification or legitimacy of war.[37]

In the *Rivista di Filosofia Neo-Scolastica*, it was obviously the journal's director Agostino Gemelli who initiated the reflection on war and influenced its discussion with his article "Patriottismo e coscienza nazionale" (Patriotism and National Conscience).

As mentioned earlier, this article also revealed the concepts of nationality and homeland as the foundations of the meaning and justification of the ongoing war.

Inspired by the true story of a priest fighting on the front-line, accused of anti-patriotism by his superiors, the article aimed to answer the following question: "What is the actual significance, the foundation of patriotism?". The author provided the following answer: "love for your own country [...] constitutes the foundation of patriotism".[38] But what did Gemelli mean by love? Not love as a feeling or passion, but, as Gemelli specified, love as a duty, as a moral action. The director assimilated the love for one's own homeland to a "strong wish to defend it against the enemy". He then went on to ask, what is the reason for such love or 'attachment'? "Why do I wish it so?" In order to provide an answer to this question, he first clarifies yet another concept: what is the homeland?

---

36   Fraticelli, "La filosofia della guerra in G. De Maistre", *Rivista di Filosofia Neo-Scolastica*, 7 (1915) 2, 167-185; Gemelli, "Patriottismo e Coscienza Nazionale", Ibid., 7 (1915) 6, 573-589; Sturzo, "La Guerra e la pace", Ibid., 7 (1915) 6, 615-619; Queirolo, "Cristianesimo, Patria e Guerra", Ibid., 8 (1916) 1, 73-77; Pepe, "La filosofia cristiana e la guerra", Ibid., 8 (1916) 2, 105-130; Lanna, "La filosofia della guerra secondo i principi di G. B. Vico", Ibid., 8 (1916) 5, 498-519; Cappellazzi, "La guerra europea e la stasi del pensiero", Ibid., 8 (1916) 6, 608-661. The two articles excluded from this brief review are those of Fraticelli and Lanna, who focused on the study of the meaning of the concept of war and its political and moral value in two specific modern authors, Joseph De Maistre and Giambattista Vico. The exclusion of these works from the present analysis depends on their purely historical approach and not directly linked to the history of neo-Thomism and its application to the reading of the contemporary phenomenon of war.
37   Bardelli, "La seconda pietra dell'edificio".
38   Gemelli, "Patriottismo e Coscienza Nazionale", 575.

Let's remember first that the idea of 'homeland' includes the idea of a state, of a nation. A state is an entity made of people ruled by the same government, subject to the same laws, with common interests and the same duties. [...] Nations therefore are neither an arbitrary product of the individual nor a fact of nature. [...] Nations are a product of historical development, the form in which humanity tends to organise itself and settle in its historical existence.[39]

Therefore, according to the author, the idea of homeland incorporates the idea of 'nation state' i.e. a group that organically contains a multitude of individuals:

The representation of a body, unit, nation, of which an individual is part, gradually develops, in each and every one of its members, the awareness of the autonomy of the social group of which they are part.[40]

In turn, autonomy represents the crux of national identity, which:

will become stronger the more conflicts with other social entities during the war and various international hostilities demonstrate to individuals the need to oppose conflicts in order to maintain the unity of the social entity that they are part of.[41]

The relationship with the otherness of each of these autonomous groups is *ipso facto* in reciprocal conflict, and conversely, the love for one's homeland coincides with the desire to defend it from external forces.

As such, aspiring to a territory, a nation, a state being patriotic, means declaring one's belonging to one's own homeland that belongs to a political, moral and religious regime deemed consistent with the historical development and the functions of one's own homeland; it means working hard to ensure that this regime will win and not be replaced by any other.[42]

In this way, firstly Gemelli legitimised war as a logical consequence of a willingness to defend own national identity. Secondly, he moved his reasoning from the moral level to a theological and political one in order to assert the compliance of Italian Catholics, who were still officially banned from voting by the *Non expedit*, to the principle of patriotism, a guarantor of the state's organic cohesion.

39   Ibid., 579-580.
40   Ibid., 582.
41   Ibid., 582.
42   Ibid., 583.

At this point, Gemelli drew on the *Summa Theologica* (II, 2, qu. 101, art. 1), in which the Angelic Doctor placed particular emphasis on Cicero's *De inventione*.

> As St. Thomas says, man is a debtor chiefly to his parents and his country, after God. Wherefore just as it belongs to religion to give worship to God, so it belongs to piety, in the second place, to show reverence to one's parents and one's country. For a Catholic, the source of this love for one's country is God himself, as one's homeland is the tool of power, goodness, Divine Providence, which, after giving us life, preserves it.[43]

On the basis of this theological reinterpretation, one's homeland represented a tool of the providence of God, whose worship, in turn, is preserved through the gift of the homeland.

> The worship of one's homeland is therefore included in the worship of God, like the most in the less and the particular in the general. Loving one's homeland is wanting the common good of the homeland.[44]

As such, taking Gemelli's stringent deductive reasoning to the extreme, if loving and worshipping one's homeland is part of loving and worshipping God, the war as a defence of one's homeland constitutes worshipping and loving one's homeland. Consequently, as the homeland is issued from providence, loving and defending the homeland through the war means loving God himself.

The second article on the topic of war follows just a few pages after Gemelli's. The author of "La Guerra e la pace" (War and Peace) was Mario Sturzo, then bishop of Piazza Armerina and the older brother of the famous Luigi.

Partly continuing along the same lines as Gemelli, the article starts *in medias res* with an almost futuristic rhythm and tone that directly gets to the heart of the matter:

> War is not for death, it's for life; war is not for war, it's for peace. In the eyes of the people, in its simplest form, war is reduced to the concept of homeland: a necessary condition for life.[45]

War is justified as a teleological necessity, the result of which is the exact opposite: peace. Paradoxically, war represents the condition for peace:

---

43 Gemelli, "Patriottismo e Coscienza Nazionale", 585.
44 Ibid., 588.
45 Sturzo, "La Guerra e la pace", 615.

war gives meaning to peace, as it revives a sense of duty in the teleological view of life, under the influence of religion. War teaches us to long for and love peace, it also teaches how to guard peace.[46]

The focus of the second part of the article shifts from an ethical to a theological level:

[War] reduces to its simplest expression even religion, seen as a vision of duty, soul and sense of duty. Hence, in war time, love for one's homeland triggers a rush of love for religion. Homeland is a condition of life, religion is a condition of duty, homeland and religion are the synthesis of all duties.[47]

From the perspective of the war, the religion is reduced to a sense of duty. Consequently, the concepts of war linked the concepts of homeland and religion into a perfect blend: religion, as a base of the sense of duty, constitutes the guarantee of being able to preserve one's homeland, which in turn is the very condition for preserving life.

The first issue of 1916 includes a brief article by Agostino Queirolo, who, compared to previous authors, demonstrated a somewhat eccentric outlook: "Cristianesimo, Patria e Guerra" (Christianity, Homeland and War). One thing that should not be underestimated is the use of the noun 'Christianity' rather than 'religion' or 'Catholicism'. The article begins by discussing two opposite interpretations on the subject of war in the Christian gospel, offered by two contemporary intellectuals:

Around two months ago, Paolo Orano from the University of Rome wrote in the *Giornale d'Italia* that the gospel was the great book of war. In the same publication, around the same time, Gino Valori strongly affirmed that Christianity categorically condemns all war, and that in his love for all men, Jesus establishes the 'international' and denies all notions of 'homeland'.[48]

The author deemed both positions to be incorrect:

Christianity, we say, does not itself deny or affirm homelands, just as it neither denied nor affirmed tribes in past times [...]. Christianity does not deny or affirm homelands, just as it does not deny or affirm different kinds of governments.[49]

---

46   Ibid., 619.
47   Ibid., 616.
48   Queirolo, "Cristianesimo, Patria e Guerra", 73.
49   Ibid., 74.

Queirolo continued by placing a special emphasis on the socialist views of Gino Valori and placed the discussion on an evangelical level, as a message of universal love not just between individuals but also between populations:

> We not only don't deny it, but we happily assert that Christian love, by helping the other forces of human civilisation, may push populations to surpass the notion of homeland and direct them towards the ultimate and final form of grouping, i.e. humanity.[50]

Unlike Gemelli and Sturzo, Queirolo didn't conceive love and religion as duties or defensive fortresses again, but he interpreted love as 'help and respect'.

> This means that the gospel requires us to have a mutual respect for these collective individualities and calls upon mutual help to govern the relationships between human beings. Help and respect which, as a manifestation of love, are intended to unite collective souls of peoples, just as they unite the hearts of individuals.[51]

Without taking away the historic value of homelands, Queirolo finds no place or justification of war within the gospel discourse, as it is rooted in love as a 'communion of hearts'.

> And love, which is stronger than death, knows how to engulf in its flames even those who are beyond the mountain and the sea in a supreme communion of hearts. This is what Christianity aims at. Nothing else. – But if this is what Christianity aims at and nothing else [...], it means that there is no antithesis between the concept of homeland and Christianity, the commandment of universal love [...] Again: Christianity neither affirms nor denies the notion of homeland. It surpasses it, and in so doing, conspiring with the other forces of modern civilisation, it transforms it into a superior form of human co-existence.[52]

Apart from this parenthesis of evangelical recovery, in the second issue of 1916, the discussion on war turned to the framework outlined by Gemelli. In the article "La filosofia cristiana e la guerra" (Christian Philosophy and War), Giovanni Pepe defined war as a 'sacred duty':

> our philosophy drives us to meet pain and death today with the serenity and confidence of those who carry out a sacred duty. We are not pacifists. Pacifism elevated to a school of thought, constitutes a simplistic, anti-historical and antisocial doctrine, which considers peace an absolute good

50   Queirolo, "Cristianesimo, Patria e Guerra", 75.
51   Ibid., 76.
52   Ibid., 77.

> [...] is totally collapsing. We actually oppose to the pacifist ideal the reasons behind war, which are attributable to the nature of man, tendentially evil and to the conditions of his social life: the attachment to material goods, passion, pride, ambition, the thirst for power, tumultuous feline instincts in the hearts of men and even more in the public life of nations.[53]

However, unlike Gemelli and Sturzo, the author focused not on the positive teleological value of war, but on the reasons or negative causes intrinsic to the evil and sinful nature of man. Therefore, war is still an evil in principle, but a necessary evil, which in fact can spill into its opposite, into good:

> War for us is an evil that awakens healthy responses of good: it's a beneficial evil. Though seemingly a paradox, it is actually the reality of life and the history of peoples. War even exercises a pacifying action, not just because it often brings nations closer together more solidly, but also because it almost always emerges in the conscience of people as an effective mean of defending a little known and violated right and as a necessary condition to curb the violence of tyrants and the brashness of unjust oppressors.[54]

Hence Pepe, to justify his own argument, described a genealogy of the Catholic concept of war, leading seamlessly from the Holy Scriptures to the First Vatican Council.

> The peace of Jesus, like that invoked by His representative on earth, is not an end cause of human actions: it's an effect and consequence of love, as demonstrated by St. Thomas, and love is not inertia and acquiescence, but a live flame that devours and consumes the obstacles that hinder its expansion. In order to gradually establish the kingdom of love in the hearts of men, Christianity has always fought and will continue to fight.[55]

By placing peace as the consequence of love and identifying love with the more general concept of fight, the author even went as far as overturning Benedict XV's unequivocal appeal for peace. Going back to the use of the more specific term 'war', rather than the more generic 'fight', Pepe made a clear reference to the doctrine of St. Thomas,

> thereby looking at this painful moment in history from a strictly moral perspective, as a fact of conscience. [...] War stands as the opposite of the Christian law of charity, an inexhaustible source of individual and social peace. Now, if everything opposing virtue and its effects is a sin, then war should be unlawful. Following in the steps of St. Augustine, the sharp philosopher attempted to resolve this contradiction by distinguishing between

---

53 Pepe, "La filosofia cristiana e la guerra".
54 Ibid.
55 Ibid., 122.

just war and unjust war. The question is thus shifted, not resolved: when and how can war be just?[56]

This continues all the way until the First Vatican Council, closing the circle with the following modern views:

> As between the end of the 19th century and the early 20th century up to the outbreak of the ongoing European conflict the study of theology and of scholastic and Thomistic philosophy had made a comeback, the old principles set down by St. Thomas were defended and presented again by F. de Vitoria and F. Suárez in order to argue the legitimacy of war and the rational way of fighting it.[57]

Thus, basing his argument on a long tradition, the author proceeded to make his case by citing examples of war that could be defined as just:

> A legitimate war is a war initiated by public authorities – represented by the sovereign, emperor, prince, head of a republic or confederation and by their ministers, authorised by legislative bodies, etc. in order to defend and preserve the homeland, without which men, created by nature to live in society, could not pursue ordinary life.[58]

Finally, the article concludes on a rather dissonant and unexpected note, with a reference to the position of the current pontiff. But, without mentioning the universalist cornerstone and diplomatic impartiality typical of Benedict XV's policy, the author elevated it to the defence of his own conclusions:

> In the venerable words of peace of the Holy Father Benedict XV, we find a summary of the legal-moral doctrine we are defending: – i.e. that the rational and human way of resolving conflicts between states is that suggested by the precepts of ethics and law, and not by the blind, random force of machine guns and cannons.[59]

The last pages of the journal on the subject in question are part of a short yet penetrating article by Andrea Cappellazzi, "La guerra europea e la stasi del pensiero" (European War and the Stasis of Thought), which features in the sixth issue of 1916 of the *Rivista*:

> Once the European conflict exploded, thought withdrew [...]. History presents documents on ingenious intuitions and discoveries even in unfortu-

---

56 Pepe, "La filosofia cristiana e la guerra", 124.
57 Ibid., 126.
58 Ibid., 127.
59 Ibid., 130.

nate times for intellectual and moral life. However, by distancing ourselves from historical facts, actually starting from historical facts, we can conclude that a general, intense, terrible and distressing upheaval like the one we are witnessing now has never occurred over the centuries.[60]

In this case, the crux of the argument is shifted towards the concept of thought rather than the concept of war, identified at the beginning of the article as a 'stasis of thought'. Thus, the author focused on the reasons behind the coincidence of these two phenomena:

> We must seek the reason for the fact. Today's darkness is not lit by a single thought, as there was no thought before it.[61]

But, following the author, the decline and annihilation of philosophy had preceded and, in some ways, prepared the deadlock of thought, resulting in war, which represents the accidental manifestation thereof. The many forms of human thought and the disappearance of transcendence and religion from modern philosophy together had caused the disintegration of thought itself. So, Andrea Cappellazzi proposed this solution:

> Human thought must be synthetic, eminently one and unifying. Now, without divine thought, human thought is manifold and divisive [...]. In the order of human thought, genius does not invent, but interprets and coordinates. The Saints represent the coordinating genius, and the wise men of Christian philosophy are the interpreters of superior thought. Leo XIII said with a high sense of religion, doctrine and history, that the genius of St. Thomas excelled in divine understanding, inclusive of knowledge, which together form a vision of the future. Discoveries of the genius are unilateral, they touch a side of humanity, they do not pervade the body or include the soul. The more elevated the cause, the wider the effect in its entirety.[62]

Man's creative genius is interpreted as an act of ὕβρις, the power of which is destructive vs. the uniqueness of thought, the only source of which is God. Conversely, the model of unique and synthetic knowledge is the coordinating genius of St. Thomas, that does not invent anything, but that legitimately interprets superior thought.

And yet Cappellazzi did not specifically condemn war and force: "We are speaking for everyone; we make vows for the glory of our homeland". The author's own thoughts end with a fluctuation between contradictory theories: whilst, on one hand, in factual terms, individual patriotism is approved

---

60 Cappellazzi, "La guerra europea e la stasi del pensiero", 608-609.
61 Ibid., 611.
62 Ibid.

and favoured in times of war, on the other hand, theoretically, the opposite is maintained and war (supported by various forms of nationalism) keeps being seen as a brutal force, caused by and consisting of disjointed and disruptive thought.

> Unity of thought produces social unity: multiplicity leads to division, combat and hostilities. Without intellectual thought, material power becomes thought.[63]

Essentially, Cappellazzi didn't condemn war but, accepting it as a matter of fact, condemned modern philosophy as a cause of war. The modern philosophy, with his *Entzauberung der Welt*, has led in his opinion to this reification of thought itself. The return to Thomas and neo-Thomism itself, by ensuring unity of thought, would have therefore allowed for the end of division and conflict, i.e. the return to social unity.

The views of these neo-scholastics, aside from a few fluctuations and various nuances linked to each author's arguments, are fairly uniform and follow three common lines of thought: war as a consequence of secularised philosophy, as a sacred duty and as a necessary condition for restoring peace.

Open questions

The war ended in 1918, yet articles on the war in the *Rivista di Filosofia Neo-Scolastica* ceased to be published in 1916. What was the reason for this silence? Archival research, which I hope to be able to undertake, may provide answers. But for now, I can only assume that this silence was neither a change of course, nor a free choice of the director of the journal. As demonstrated by one of the foremost and most passionate scholars Agostino Gemelli between 1915 and 1916, the Franciscan's public statements on the war, so dissonant with the pope's views, aroused strong criticism and concern, first by the general of the Franciscan Order Serafino Cimino, and later, through him, in the top ranks of the Holy See.[64]

Such criticism may likely explain the many fluctuations and contradictions within the articles, eventually resolved with silence on the matter as a defensive rhetoric strategy juxtaposed to the censorship of the Holy See. However, at this point, the matter remains to be verified and explored in more depth.

---

63   Cappellazzi, "La guerra europea e la stasi del pensiero", 611.
64   Bocci, "Benedetto XV, p. Gemelli e la fondazione dell'Università cattolica", 975-979.

BIBLIOGRAPHY

Alberigo, Giuseppe. "Dal bastone alla misericordia. Il magistero nel cattolicesimo contemporaneo (1830-1980)". *Cristianesimo nella storia*, 2 (1981) 2, 487-521.

Apruzzese, Sergio. "Introduzione". In Sergio Apruzzese, ed. *Repertorio della stampa periodica cattolica italiana dalla crisi di fine Ottocento all'avvento del fascismo. La marcia giovanile del nazionalismo (1898-1925)*. Fscirebook/2. Bologna, 2013, 7-17. <http://collane.fscire.it/it/home/e-book/>.

Aubert, Roger. "Désiré Mercier et les débuts de l'Institut de Philosophie". *Revue Philosophique de Louvain*, 88 (1990) 78, 147-167.

Aubert, Roger. *Les deux premiers grands conflits du cardinal Mercier avec les autorités allemandes d'occupation*. Leuven: Peeters, 1998.

Bardelli, Daniele. "La seconda pietra dell'edificio. Le origini della rivista Vita e Pensiero". *Studium*, 111 (2015) 3, 393-429.

Bataillon, Louis-Jacques. "Le edizioni di Opera Omnia degli scolastici l'edizione Leonina". In Ruedi Imbach and Alfonso Maierù, eds. *Gli studi di filosofia medievale fra Otto e Novecento. Contributo a un bilancio storiografico*. Rome: Edizioni di storia e letteratura, 1991, 141-153.

Bocci, Maria. "Benedetto XV, p. Gemelli e la fondazione dell'Università cattolica". In Alberto Melloni, Giovanni Cavagnini and Giulia Grossi, eds. *Benedetto XV. Papa Giacomo della Chiesa nel mondo dell'"inutile strage"*. Bologna: Il Mulino, 2017, 974-986.

Cappellazzi, Andrea. "La guerra europea e la stasi del pensiero". *Rivista di Filosofia Neo-Scolastica*, 8 (1916) 6, 608-661.

Chiron, Jean-François. *L'infaillibilité et son objet. L'autorité du magistère infaillible de l'Église s'étend-elle aux vérités non révélées?* Paris: Cerf, 1999.

Congar, Yves. "Pour une histoire sémantique du terme 'magisterium'". *Revue de sciences philosophiques et théologique*, 60 (1976), 85-98.

Congar, Yves. "Bref historique des formes du 'magistère' et des relations avec les docteurs". *Revue de sciences philosophiques et théologique*, 60 (1976), 99-112.

Coreth, Emerich, ed. *Christliche Philosophie im katholischen Denken des 19. und 20. Jahrhunderts*. Vol. 2. Graz-Vienna-Cologne: Verlag Styria, 1988.

Courtois, Luc and Milos Jačov. *Les débuts de l'Institut supérieur de philosophie (Louvain) à travers la correspondance de Désiré Mercier avec le Saint-Siège (1887-1904)*. Bibliothèque de la Revue d'histoire ecclésiastique, 96. Turnhout: Brepols, 2013.

De Volder, Jan. *La résistance d'un cardinal. Le cardinal Mercier, l'Église et la Guerre 14-18*. Translation A.-M. Delcourt, C. Janssens and A. Dupont. Namur-Paris: Fidélité, 2016 (original edition: *Kardinaal verzet. Mercier, de Kerk en de oorlog van 14-18*. Tielt, 2014).

De Wulf, Maurice. "La scolastica vecchia e nuova". *La Critica*, 9 (1911), 213-222.

Formigoni, Guido. *L'Italia dei Cattolici. Fede e nazione dal Risorgimento alla Repubblica*. Bologna: Il Mulino, 1998.

Fraticelli, Antonio. "La filosofia della guerra in G. De Maistre". *Rivista di Filosofia Neo-Scolastica*, 7 (1915) 2, 167-185.

Fuchs, Josef. "Origines d'une trilogie ecclésiologique à l'époque rationaliste de la théologie". *Revue de sciences philosophiques et théologiques*, 53 (1969), 185-211.

Gemelli, Agostino. "Patriottismo e Coscienza Nazionale". *Rivista di Filosofia Neo-Scolastica*, 7 (1915) 6, 573-589.

Gemelli, Agostino. "Per il programma del nostro lavoro". *Rivista di Filosofia Neo-Scolastica*, 11 (1919), 2-3.

Gemelli, Agostino. "Neotomismo e neoscolastica". In *Treccani Enciclopedia Italiana*. Vol. 24. Rome: Istituto dell'Enciclopedia Italiana, 1934, 581.

Gentile, Giovanni. *Il modernismo e i rapporti tra religione e filosofia*. Bari: Laterza, 1909.

Gentile, Giovanni. "A proposito del libro di M. De Wulf: *Introduction à la philosophie néo-scolastique*, Louvain, Institut Supérieur de Philosophie, Alcan, Paris 1904". In Giovanni Gentile. *Il modernismo e i rapporti tra religione e filosofia*. Bari: Laterza, 1909, 203-221.

Gentile, Giovanni. "La scolastica e il prof. De Wulf". *La Critica*, 9 (1911), 306-308.

Hobsbawm, Eric J. *Nations and Nationalism since 1780: Programme, Myth, Reality*. Cambridge: Cambridge University Press, 1992 (2nd edition).

Hobsbawm, Eric J. and Terence Ranger. *The Invention of Tradition*. Cambridge: Cambridge University Press, 1983.

Lanna, D. "La filosofia della guerra secondo i principi di G. B. Vico". *Rivista di Filosofia Neo-Scolastica*, 8 (1916) 5, 498-519.

Lebreton, Jules. "Pensée chrétiennes sur la guerre". *Études*, 144 (1915), 5-30.

Levillain, Philippe and Jean-Marc Ticchi, eds. *Le pontificat de Léon XIII: renaissances du Saint-Siège? Actes du colloque de Paris du 2003*. Rome: École française de Rome, 2006.

Marotta, Saretta. "La questione romana". In Alberto Melloni, ed. *Cristiani d'Italia. Politiche, Conciliazioni, Conflitti*. Vol. 4. Rome: Istituto dell' Enciclopedia Italiana Treccani, 2006, 641-654.

Martina, Giacomo. *Pio IX (1851-1866)*. Rome: Editrice Pontificia Università Gregoriana, 1986.

Masnovo, Amato. *Il neo-tomismo in Italia (origini e prime vicende)*. Milan: Vita e pensiero, 1923.

Melloni, Alberto, Giovanni Cavagnini and Giulia Grossi, eds. *Benedetto XV. Papa Giacomo della Chiesa nel mondo dell'"inutile strage"*. Bologna: Il Mulino, 2017.

Menozzi, Daniele. *Chiesa, pace e guerra nel Novecento. Verso una delegittimazione religiosa dei conflitti*. Bologna: Il Mulino, 2008.

Miccoli, Giovanni. "Chiesa e società in Italia dal Concilio Vaticano I al pontificato di Giovanni XXIII". In *Storia d'Italia*. V/2: *I documenti*. Turin, 1973, 1504.

Morozzo della Rocca, Roberto. "Guerre mondiale (première)". In Philippe Levillain, ed. *Dictionnaire historique de la papauté*. Paris: Fayard, 1994, 775-779.

Morozzo della Rocca, Roberto. "Benedetto XV e il nazionalismo". *Cristianesimo nella storia*, 17 (1996), 541-566.

Morozzo della Rocca, Roberto. "Benedetto XV e la prima guerra mondiale". *Annali di scienze religiose*, 8 (2015), 31-44.

Nardi, Bruno. "Scolastica vecchia e nuova". *Rivista di Filosofia Neo-Scolastica*, 3 (1911) 5, 555-562.

Nardi, Bruno. "La filosofia del Medio Evo nel pensiero di Giovanni Gentile". In *Giovanni Gentile. La vita e il pensiero, a cura della fondazione Giovanni Gentile per gli studi filosofici*. Vol. 1. Florence: Sansoni, 1948, 257-284.

Pepe, Giovanni. "La filosofia cristiana e la guerra". *Rivista di Filosofia Neo-Scolastica*, 8 (1916) 2, 105-130.

Piolanti, Antonio. *La filosofia cristiana in Mons. Salvatore Talamo ispiratore della "Aeterni Patris"*. Vatican City: Libreria editrice vaticana, 1986.

Pollard, John F. *The Unknown Pope Benedict XV (1914-1922) and the Pursuit of Peace*. London: Bloomsbury Academic, 1999.

Queirolo, Agostino. "Cristianesimo, Patria e Guerra". *Rivista di Filosofia Neo-Scolastica*, 8 (1916) 1, 73-77.

Sandoni, Luca, ed. *Il Sillabo di Pio IX*. With an introduction by Daniele Menozzi. Bologna-Rome: Clueb-Ceuls, 2012.

Schatz, Klaus. "La prima guerra mondiale tra nazionalismo e dialogo tra i popoli. Il dibattito sulle riviste dei gesuiti". *La Civiltà cattolica*, 4035-4036 (2018), 223-240.

Schmidinger, Heinrich M. and Massimo Marassi. "La disputa sulle origini della neoscolastica italiana: Salvatore Rosselli, Vincenzo Buzzetti e Gaetano Sanseverino". *Rivista di Filosofia Neo-Scolastica*, 82 (1990) 2/3, 353-364.

Schmidinger, Heinrich M. and Giovanni Felice Rossi. "La neoscolastica italiana: dalle sue prime origini all'enciclica 'Aeterni Patris'". In *La filosofia cristiana nei secoli XIX e XX. Vol 2: Ritorno all'eredità scolastica*. Rome: Città Nuova, 1994, 105-117.

Sturzo, Mario. "La Guerra e la pace". *Rivista di Filosofia Neo-Scolastica*, 7 (1915) 6, 615-619.

Sulas, Cinzia. "La dissoluzione del concetto taparelliano di nazionalità durante la Grande Guerra". In Alberto Melloni, Giovanni Cavagnini and Giulia Grossi, eds. *Benedetto XV. Papa Giacomo della Chiesa nel mondo dell'"inutile strage"*. Bologna: Il Mulino, 2017, 644-654.

Talamo, Salvatore. "Programma". *Rivista internazionale di scienze sociali e discipline ausiliari*, 1 (1893) 1, 1.

Theobald, Christoph. "Le développement de la notion des 'vérités historiquement et logiquement connexes avec 'la Révélation' de Vatican I à Vatican II". *Cristianesimo nella storia*, 21 (2000) 1, 37-70.

Theobald, Christoph and Bernard Sesboüé. *Histoire des dogmes*. Vol. 4: *La parole du salut. Doctrine de la Parole de Dieu, Révélation, foi, Écriture, Tradition, Magistère*. Paris: Desclée, 1996.

Ticchi, Jean-Marc. *Aux frontières de la paix. Bons offices, médiations, arbitrages du Saint-Siège (1878-1922)*. Rome: École française de Rome, 2002.

Vanni Rovighi, Sofia. "L'opera di Amato Masnovo". *Rivista di Filosofia Neo-Scolastica*, 58 (1956), 97-109.

Vasoli, Cesare. "La neoscolastica in Italia". In Ruedi Imbach and Alfonso Maierù, eds. *Gli studi di filosofia medievale fra Otto e Novecento. Contributo a un bilancio storiografico*. Rome: Edizioni di storia e letteratura, 1991, 167-189.

Walter, Peter. "'Den Weltkreis täglich von Verderben bringenden Irrtümern befreien'
(Leo XIII.): die Internationalisierung der theo-
logischen Wissenschaftswelt am Beispiel der
Neuscholastik". In Claus Arnold and Johannes Wischmeyer, eds. *Transnationale Dimensi-
onen wissenschaftlicher Theologie*. Göttingen:
Vandenhoeck-Ruprecht, 2013, 319-353.

PROTAGONISTS

Auguste Castelein. Photo by Jean Lemaire, c 1920.
[Leuven, KADOC: Image archive of the Southern Belgian Jesuit Province, 396]

A CONSERVATIVE READING OF *RERUM NOVARUM* THROUGH A NEO-SCHOLASTIC LENS
THE JESUIT AUGUSTE CASTELEIN (1840-1922) AND THE BELGIAN *PATRONS CATHOLIQUES*

PETER HEYRMAN

The extensive historical literature on the encyclical *Rerum novarum* of 15 May 1891 has made it clear that this text not only had a galvanising effect on Western European Catholicism, but also led to profound divisions.[1] Indeed, the papal instructions did not excel in clarity. Particularly in France and Belgium, the disputes on how they were to be read and put into practice were so bitter that some observers compared them to the debates 60 years earlier, following the publication of *Mirari Vos*.[2] Major discussions arose on what the encyclical stated on (1) fair wages, (2) the creation of workers' unions without involvement of their employers and (3) the need for social legislation and thus state intervention. Although the positions evolved and the lines between the different parties were often blurry, nearly all the factions followed the example of the encyclical by calling in the philosophical legacy of Aquinas to substantiate their positions. This once again illustrates that Thomism was far from homogeneous and could provide ammunition for many different causes.[3]

Contemporary analysts of the debates on the interpretation of *Rerum novarum*, soon followed by historians, tried to provide transparency by discerning two opposing *écoles sociales*, labelled according to the dioceses of

1 *Rerum Novarum: écriture, contenu et réception d'une encyclique*; Python, "La genèse de Rerum Novarum"; Boyle, "Rerum novarum (1891)".
2 Brants, *Charles Périn*, XLIV.
3 Chappel, "The Thomist Debate over Inequality and Property Rights in Depression-Era Europe".

which the bishop particularly supported one of the conflicting stances.[4] The 'Liège-Fribourg school' was considered democratic and progressive. The opposing 'Angers school' was characterised as non-interventionist, corporatist and conservative. While the former, especially from 1890 onwards, embraced state-controlled social legislation, the latter considered it an assault on private enterprise and business initiative. 'Angers' only subscribed to minimal regulations, for instance regarding Sunday rest, child and women's labour or excessively long working days. Its protagonists, often connected to the *Revue Catholique des Institutions et du Droit* (°1873), stressed that the encyclical above all exuded a virulent anti-socialism, that the pope remained far from condemning big business culture and that he had clearly stressed the inviolability of property rights and thus endorsed the 'father-like' authority and responsibility of employers.[5] Their patronage, combined with other forms of voluntary charitable assistance, was considered sufficient to guarantee or restore social harmony. For that same reason 'Angers' rejected the idea of separate or independent workers' organisations.

Our understanding of these discourses, however, remains superficial. Prevailing literature has predominantly focused on the stances of 'Liège-Fribourg', for instance demonstrating how they voiced a 'turn of the Church towards the people' and facilitated a rapprochement of ultramontanism with the rising popular movements, especially those of Christian industrial workers.[6] The ways in which conservative Catholics dialogued with the ground-breaking papal encyclical and intellectually underpinned their positions have been studied in far less detail. Belgian historians, for instance, have mainly focused on their opposition to political democratisation, with special attention to the manoeuvres against dissidents, in particular Christian democrat priests such as Adolphe Daens (1839-1907) in Aalst and Antoine Pottier (1849-1923) in Liège.[7] These cases indeed deserve particular attention. But one could also argue that, in light of the plurality and maybe even the fluidity of social-Catholicism, together with its path-dependency in later decades, a thorough un-

4   Gérin, "Les écoles sociales belges"; Mayeur, "Le catholicisme social en France"; Id., "Quelques rencontres entre les catholiques français et les catholiques belges". See also: Gérin, "Catholicisme social et démocratie chrétienne"; Lamberts, "Conclusies"; Art, "De pastorale methodes van de Vlaamse parochiegeestelijkheid".

5   Fillon, "La Revue catholique des institutions et du droit"; see also: Audren and Rolland, "Juristes catholiques"; and Id., "La belle époque des juristes catholiques".

6   Lamberts, *The Struggle with Leviathan*, 304-316; Id., ed., *Een kantelend tijdperk*; De Maeyer, "'Démocratie catholique' et 'démocratie chrétienne'".

7   Gérin, *Les congrès des œuvres sociales tenus à Liège*, 61-87; Id., "Catholicisme social", 101-102; Aubert, "L'encyclique Rerum novarum"; De Maeyer and Van Molle, eds., *Joris Helleputte*, I, 92-108; Id., "Les effets de Rerum Novarum en Belgique"; De Maeyer, *Arthur Verhaegen*; Id., "De Belgische Volksbond"; De Smaele, "Henry Carton de Wiart"; Verdoodt, *Kerk en christen-democratie*. On Pottier, we gladly refer to the contribution of Jean-Pierre Delville in this volume. See also: Jadoulle, "Anthropologie et vision de la société chez Antoine Pottier"; Id., *La pensée de l'abbé Pottier*.

derstanding also requires an insight of its more conservative articulations.[8] This essay focuses on the ideas of a particular actor, notably the Belgian Jesuit scholar Auguste Castelein (1840-1922), the main advisor of the Association des Patrons et Industriels Catholiques (APIC), one of the more prominent pressure groups in Belgian society that advocated a moderate interpretation of *Rerum novarum*. Castelein was a renowned, even notorious figure in pre-war Catholic Belgium. The liberal journalist and later politician Louis Straus (1844-1926) addressed him as "one of the most distinguished men of Belgian clericalism".[9] But when this Jesuit scholar died in January 1922 his legacy was hardly recalled, although we should mention that one of Castelein's studies was quoted in James Joyce's *Ulysses*, a book published that same year.[10]

The rising career of a multitasking Jesuit

To understand Castelein's involvement in the debate on *Rerum novarum*, we first need to look at his curriculum vitae.[11] He started his novitiate in Drongen in 1858 after studying humanities in the Saint Aloysius College of his native town of Menin.[12] His family had a strong juridical background; his grandfather, father and brother were all notaries and thus prominent members of the local Catholic bourgeoisie.[13] In 1868-1869 Castelein finished his philosophical

8   Pelletier, "Le catholicisme social en France". He defines social-Catholicism as a the result of a "succession de sociabilités militantes répondant aux exigences immédiates d'une société en souffrance, au sein desquelles la doctrine sociale de l'Eglise joue un rôle de norme régulatrice" (374). On the societal impact of conservative social-Catholicism during the interwar period, see for instance De Borchgrave, *Zalig de armen van geest*; Art, "De pastorale methodes".

9   *Soixante-Quinzième Anniversaire de la Fondation des Facultés de Philosophie et des Sciences*, 15.

10 Joyce mentions Castelein's study rejecting the theory of rigorism on the number of the elect in "The Wandering Rocks" episode of *Ulysses*, when describing how Father Conmee, looking at the billboards of performer Eugene Stratton, contemplates "on the souls of black and brown and yellow".

11 We were able to reconstruct Castelein's curriculum vitae in detail using the *Catalogus Provinciae Belgicae Societatis Jesu*. Many thanks to Jo Luyten for his assistance. Main biographical notices: Schyrgens, "Le Révérend Père Casteleyn"; Willaert, "Casteleyn, August".

12 Leuven, KADOC-KU Leuven, Archief Jezuïeten – Belgische (1832-1935) en Vlaamse (1935-) Provincie – Provincia Belgica and Provincia Belgica Septentrionalis (hereafter ABSE), 3781.

13 His grandfather Petrus Josephus Castelein (1758-1837) was a notary, alderman and justice of the peace in Menin. His father Charles Auguste Castelein (1805-1867) succeeded him as a notary and became burgomaster of the town. His uncle Felix Henri Castelein (1801-1836) was alderman and also burgomaster of Menin, another uncle, Ludovicus Josephus Castelein (1784-1840) was the local tax-collector in Avelgem. Both his mother [Azemia Maria Anna Gheerbrant (1811-1843)] and stepmother [Marie Eugenie Neuwe (1803-1878)] were born into affluent families. Castelein had one surviving brother, seven sisters and two half-sisters.

training in Leuven and subsequently was sent to Rome to study Theology. The young Jesuit showed high intellectual capacities and enjoyed the protection of both scholastic and later Cardinal Johann Baptist Franzelin (1816-1886) and the eminent theologian Antonio Ballerini (1805-1881). An academic career beckoned. But Castelein's training was interrupted by the capture of the city by Italian troops on 20 September 1870. This disturbing event was to leave him with "an immortal wound to his heart", so wrote his main biographer Joseph Schyrgens (1856-1937).[14] Castelein was forced to return to Belgium, finished his studies in Leuven, was ordained a priest in 1872 and successfully defended his doctorate in Theology on 7 July 1874.[15] A year later he was appointed professor in Dogmatics and Moral Theology at the Collegium Maximum (1839) in Leuven, the main theological training centre of the Belgian Jesuit Province.[16]

Castelein was professed in 1876. Being allowed to take this so-called fourth vow clearly demonstrates that he belonged to the inner circle of the order. His profile perfectly matched the pastoral strategies of the Belgian branch of the Societas Jesu. Scholarly research and teaching went hand in hand with an intense involvement in pastoral care and apologetics. The Belgian Jesuits' apostolate explicitly targeted the country's (aristocratic, entrepreneurial, judiciary, scientific, administrative ...) elites. Their colleges, boarding schools and university colleges in Brussels, Namur and Antwerp proved to be important levers to reach these leading noble, bourgeois and middle-class families. A strong Jesuit presence in the context of the Leuven university, the country's main Catholic intellectual bastion, was of course considered crucial. Closely linked to their educational apostolate the Belgian Jesuits also specialised in offering conferences and leading spiritual retreats, for instance for parish priests, upper-class adolescents, businessmen, engineers and later on, for simple industrial workers as well.[17]

As he later confessed, Castelein above all wanted to study and write.[18] But his eloquence and pedagogical skills did not remain unnoticed. Instead of fulfilling his academic ambitions, his superiors entrusted Castelein with

---

14 Schyrgens, "Le Révérend Père Casteleyn", 340. The Jesuit father Schyrgens was form-master in rhetoric in the episcopal college of Huy and contributed to several newspapers and periodicals, including the *Gazette de Liège*, *La Libre Belgique*, the *Revue Catholique des Idées et des Faits* and *Le XXe siècle*.

15 Castelein, *Theses ex universa theologia*. Several of his theses (e.g. XIV) strongly defended papal infaillability.

16 On the Jesuit infrastructure in Leuven: De Maeyer, Suenens and Luyten, "Louvain".

17 Suenens, "Belgian Jesuits and their Labourer Retreats". The main Belgian Jesuit retreat centers were situated in Drongen (Ghent), Fayt-lez-Manage (Hainaut) and Xhovémont (Liège).

18 "Je n'ai jamais eu que ces trois rêves: étudier, enseigner et écrire". ABSE, 1426: Note "Mon Intervention dans la question sociale en Belgique", s.d. This key document, a draft of a text probably written in May-June 1895 as part of a (lost) dossier in defence of his positions, was extensively annotated by Castelein in later years.

consecutive teaching and pastoral assignments. Even during his Philosophy training in 1860-1868 he had been sent to Antwerp and Tournai as an auxiliary teacher in the lower grades of the local Jesuit colleges. In 1873, when preparing his PhD in Theology, Castelein was dispatched to Liège to act as the form-master in rhetoric of the Saint-Servais College. His pupils later on recalled the invigorating way in which he had prepared them for a school play re-enacting the debates in the French national assembly of 31 March 1849 on a military intervention in Italy in defence of the pope.[19]

In 1877-1878, during a series of vulgarising *Cours de théologie* that the Jesuits organised throughout the country, Castelein offered his first public conferences.[20] He was also charged with leading spiritual retreats for parish priests, an assignment at which he particularly excelled.[21] Castelein, however, was not at all satisfied with these tasks as an *operarius* and *conférencier*. He considered them a waste of his talents and even somewhat as a repudiation. To top it all off, in 1878 Castelein had to abandon his professorship at the Collegium Maximum to take up the directorship of the Jesuit university student association in Leuven. This so-called Sodality was an important pastoral instrument of the order: in 1882 it numbered about 700 members. During fortnightly meetings these students sang hymns, recited the litanies of the Blessed Virgin and the prayer of the Catholic university, and listened to a conference. Castelein's lectures dealt with many different subjects. Spiritual instructions were of course paramount, but political issues were not avoided. In the early 1880s, for instance, he diligently mobilised his pupils against the anticlerical school policy of the liberal government (1879-1884).[22] In 1885, somewhat as a reward for successfully coordinating the festivities celebrating the 300th anniversary of the Leuven Sodality,[23] Castelein was sent to Namur to teach Psychology, Moral Philosophy, Natural Law and Religion at the Faculty of Arts and Philosophy of the local Jesuit university college (1845). There he also acted as a student spiritual guide or *catéchiste des philosophes*. He would remain in

19   Schyrgens, "Le Révérend Père Casteleyn", 340.
20   Under the title *De la prétendue déchéance du clergé dans l'ordre intellectuel depuis le 12ième siècle*, Castelein challenged (liberal) literature stating that the Catholic clergy had degenerated and had made no significant intellectual contribution since the twelfth century. See also: *Le Bien Public*, 5 and 9 November 1877, 11 January 1878. Many years later, in 1912-1913, Castelein would return to this topic, preparing a manuscript on Church history entitled *Progrès ou décadence dans l'Eglise Catholique*, which however remained unpublished. ABSE, 2764 and 1403.
21   In 1891 Castelein stated that he had already preached at 53 priest retreats, and later on he contended that he had been involved in more than a 100 of them.
22   Castelein, *Une loi d'éducation nationale*; Id., *Conferentia de scholis catholicis*.
23   The 'Sodalité des étudiants de l'université catholique sous le titre de la purification de la très sainte vierge Marie' dated back to 1585 and the papal bull *Omnipotentis Dei*. [Steyaert], *Vijftigjarig jubelfeest van het instellen der congregatie van jongelingen*. On the festivities: *Le Bien Public*, 4 and 9 February 1885.

Namur until 1890, when – much to his discontent – he was recalled to Leuven to once more take up the directorship of the Jesuit Sodality.

Thomist revival

His assignment in Namur helps to explain why Castelein began to profile himself explicitly as a philosopher. His comprehensibly structured and fluently written syllabi were of course also aligned with the Thomist revival movement that the new pope Leo XIII (1878-1903) had so strongly endorsed with his encyclical *Aeterni Patris* (4 August 1879).[24] Castelein fully subscribed to Leo's ambition to overcome intellectual fragmentation within Western Catholicism and shared his confidence that the transparent and logical metaphysical matrix offered by Saint Thomas Aquinas (1225-1274) would enable the Catholic elites to enter into a dialogue with secular modernity, in particular with the modern sciences. Applying Aquinas' system of thought would help them to reach a synthesis, while maintaining respect for Church doctrine and tradition.[25]

Neo-scholastic philosophy soon became the intellectual rallying point of a whole generation of Catholic scholars and students. In Belgium the main protagonist was of course the later archbishop and cardinal Désiré-Joseph Mercier (1851-1926), the founder of the university's Higher Institute of Philosophy (1889). Conveniently carrying the motto *Nova et Vetera*, this institution clearly enjoyed papal support and became a crucial node in the European neo-Thomist network.[26] But the training centres of the Jesuits in Namur and Antwerp, and particularly the Leuven Collegium Maximum also played an important role in the Belgian Thomist revival.[27] In his contemporary survey of the landscape of neo-scholasticism, Joseph Louis Perrier (1874-?) states that Castelein, in contrast to Louis de San (1832-1904) and Gustave Lahousse (1846-1928), was more familiar with the spirit of the time and that he somewhat surpassed traditional scholastic logic by studying the inductive process and discussing the value of hypothesis and of experimental methods.[28] Castelein's knowledge

24 Castelein, *Logique*; Id., *Les principes de la philosophie morale*; Id., *Philosophie morale*; Id., *Psychologie. La science de l'âme dans ses rapports avec la physiologie*.
25 Durand, "Léon XIII, Rome et le monde"; De Laubier, "Un idéal historique concret de société"; Hartley, *Thomistic Revival and the Modernist Era*.
26 Steel, "Thomas en de vernieuwing van de filosofie"; Wils, *De omweg van de wetenschap*, 326-341; Van Riet, "Originalité et fécondité de la notion de philosophie élaborée par le Cardinal Mercier"; De Raeymaeker, *Le cardinal Mercier et l'Institut supérieur de philosophie de Louvain*; Id., "Les origines de l'Institut supérieur de Philosophie de Louvain"; Lamberts and Roegiers, *De Universiteit te Leuven*, 220 and 261-262; Aubert, "Désiré Mercier et les débuts de l'Institut de philosophie".
27 De Leeuw, "Neo-Thomism and the Education of a Catholic Elite in Louvain".
28 Perrier, *The Revival of Scholastic Philosophy*, 216-217. Perrier particularly refers to Castelein's teachings on the soul.

theory, however, remained dogmatic. The truth exists and is an undoubted adequacy of thought. Its object can be found in the idea (*materialiter*) and in man's judgment (*formaliter*). Scepticism is an evident contradiction: the objective value of the universal ideas has long since been determined. Materialism, positivism, nominalism, exaggerated realism and the idealism of Plato, Descartes and Leibnitz need to be rejected. Scholasticism has a future rather than a past, as he proudly declared in his *Psychologie*.[29]

In 1885 Castelein and his fellow Jesuit de San were members of the jury evaluating the dissertation of Théodore Fontaine (1858-1898), Mercier's first doctoral pupil.[30] Castelein seems to have been well acquainted with the later cardinal, in any case their correspondence expresses mutual respect.[31] The Jesuit also fully endorsed the pope's and Mercier's appeal to share the revived philosophical insights of Aquinas with the general public, for instance through university extension programmes and other public conferences. Particularly in Brussels, the eloquent Jesuit enjoyed a growing popularity as a *conférencier*, debater and vulgarising author dedicated to the neo-scholastic reconciliation of faith and science. He contributed, for instance, to the *Cours d'apologétique pour hommes* that his fellow Jesuit Jean-Baptiste Paquet (1859-1922)[32] organised at the Cercle Union et Travail.

Starting in 1877 Castelein also regularly preached in the chapel of the Apostolines du Très Saint-Sacrement, a semi-contemplative female religious order founded in 1867 by Fanny Kestre (1824-1882) and Archbishop Victor Dechamps (1810-1883). At that same convent and from 1883 onwards he annually offered a series of winter conferences to the members of the Œuvre des Catéchismes des Dames de Sainte Julienne, a group of noble and bourgeois women that supported the catechetical apostolate of the aforementioned sisters.[33] Castelein explained to them how recent geological and evolutionary insights could be reconciled with the scriptures. Other lectures to the Dames de Sainte Julienne concerned wide-ranging topics as materialism, spiritualism, hypnotism, magnetism and spiritism.[34] Several members of the royal family, including the countess of Flanders Maria van Hohenzollern-Sigmaringen (1845-1912) and possibly even Queen Marie-Henriette (1836-1902), seem to

---

29 Struyker Boudier, *Wijsgerig leven in Nederland, België en Luxemburg*, I, 43-46.
30 Fontaine, *De la sensation et la pensée*. Other members apart from Mercier were the Dominican Emilius Rolin (1860-1949) and the Leuven philosophers Léon Bossu (1837-1916) and Antoine Dupont (1836-1917). *Journal de Bruxelles*, 26 July 1885.
31 ABSE, 1421 and Mechelen, Archives Archdiocese of Mechelen-Brussels (hereafter AAM), Papers Mercier II, 57. See also how Mercier refers to Castelein's *Logique* in his "La théorie des trois vérités primitives", 12.
32 Laurent, "Jean-Baptiste Paquet".
33 Suenens, '*Too robust to be saint*', esp. 354-358.
34 Castelein, *Foi et science*; Id., *La première page de Moïse et l'histoire de la terre*; Id., *Spiritisme, tables tournantes, magnétisme*; Id., *L'hypnotisme et la psychologie*. See also: *Le Bien Public*, 3 December 1884.

have attended his conferences. In February 1891 Castelein offered a much-applauded eulogy at a memorial service in the Brussels Saint Michael's college after the untimely demise of Prince Baudouin (1869-1891).[35] In later years he was also said to be the main philosophy instructor of the future king Albert. All this helps to explain why Castelein was sometimes considered an intimate of the Royal Court.[36]

Discovering the social question

Building on his activities as a lecturer and on the network of former students that he had guided in Leuven and Namur, Castelein obtained quite a scholarly reputation. During the late 1880s his renown in Catholic bourgeois circles was clearly on the rise. All this is crucial to understand his impact in the Belgian debates on the interpretation of *Rerum novarum*. After all, Castelein had little or no experience with social issues. He was not involved in the Archbrotherhood of Saint Francis Xavier (1854), showed no interest in the Catholic initiatives for (young) workers to which the Jesuits devoted so much energy, nor was he active in the national Fédération des Sociétés Ouvrières Catholiques (1867-1891) or its periodical *L'Economiste Catholique* (1879-1891).[37]

    Later on Castelein would recall how he was led to discover the *question sociale* by the inquisitiveness of his students, both in the Leuven sodality and later on in Namur. They questioned him on how Catholic teachings addressed the growing social tensions and the rise of socialism. The year 1886 was a clear turning point: in March, strikes and deadly riots ravaged the regions of Liège and Hainaut, in April the Belgian government installed a national labour commission and in September the Liège bishop Victor-Joseph Doutreloux (1837-1901) presided over a first Belgian Catholic social congress.[38] Later on that year Castelein published his views on the issue under the still-modest title *Un programme social*.[39] Although the Jesuit did not explicitly comment on the aforementioned events, it was clear that his arguments were aligned to the debates at the Liège congress. For Castelein it was obvious that all social issues needed to be addressed in ways that were solidly based on the doctrines of the Catholic Church, "the highest power and greatest benefactor of temporal society".

35 Castelein, *Eloge funèbre de S.A.R. le prince Baudouin adressé aux élèves du collège Saint-Michel*; ABSE, 1424; *Journal de Bruxelles*, 5 February 1891.
36 Wheeler, "Social Works of Ours in Belgium"; Velaers, *Albert I*, 52; Dujardin, "Les jésuites et la Cour de Belgique", cited on p. 498 and 514. See the correspondence in ABSE, 1411-1412.
37 De Maeyer, "De Belgische Volksbond", 19-30.
38 Union Nationale pour le redressement des Griefs, *Congrès des œuvres sociales à Liège. 26-29 septembre 1886*. On Doutreloux: Gérin, "La démocratie chrétienne dans les relations Église-État".
39 Castelein, *Un programme sociale: conférence par A. Castelein SJ, professeur de philosophie*. A second edition followed the next year.

Neither the secular social sciences nor state intervention would provide a durable solution. Restoring social harmony was paramount, and this required a quadruple balance (1) between rights and responsibilities, (2) liberty and authority, (3) social inequalities and human fraternities and (4) between society's needs and resources. Castelein clearly sought to reassure his bourgeois audiences and readers: government had already enacted important measures in favour of the industrial workers, and Catholic congresses and study groups were looking for reasonable instruments and policy answers. But further public intervention in social matters was unnecessary and above all unwanted. Castelein, extensively referring to the Decalogue, particularly stressed the divine roots of authority and the obviousness of social inequality. "It must therefore be agreed", so he stated, "there will always be rich and poor, men who command and men who obey, men who are served and men who serve".[40]

Castelein's *Programme* was widely distributed. In 1887 no less than four editions of the brochure were printed. The Jesuit subsequently conducted a study on socialism that was published in the *Revue Générale*,[41] a leading Catholic periodical managed by Charles Woeste (1837-1922), the unofficial chair of the Belgian Catholic Party.[42] Castelein's conclusions offered no surprises: socialism was "contrary to the natural freedom of the human person; it is contrary to the expansion of human ingenuity and the fertility of productive labour; and it is contrary to the essential conditions for prosperity and public stability".[43] One year later, in a more vulgarising brochure of which no fewer than 35,000 copies were distributed, Castelein was even more explicit.[44] Socialism was "the most criminal enterprise"[45], it would engender war on family, religion and all good citizens. "Under a socialist government, the people, reduced to badly distributed, badly directed and badly executed work, would be condemned, without resources and without remedy, to all misery and despair."[46]

In 1891 Castelein was one of the founders of the Brussels Cercle Léon XIII, a study circle dedicated to the reconciliation of faith and science. When introducing this new structure to the General Catholic Congress in Mechelen

---

40 Ibid., 16.
41 Castelein, "Etude sur le socialisme".
42 On his involvement in the *Revue Générale:* ABSE, 1417 and 1408. The correspondence in this last dossier reflects the amical relationship between Castelein and Woeste. The latter, however, does not mention the former in his memoires and only once referred to him in Parliament (*Parlementaire Handelingen. Kamer van Volksvertegenwoordigers*, 8 March 1899). On the *Revue*: Piepers, *La Revue générale*.
43 Castelein, "Etude sur le socialisme", 274-275.
44 Id., *Qu'est-ce que le socialisme?* On the number of copies: Vermeersch, *Manuel social* (1904), 491.
45 Castelein, *Qu'est-ce que le socialisme?*, 8.
46 Ibid., 11.

that same year, Castelein made no secret of its mission. "No science without faith and no faith without science. [...] This motto, which has always been the motto of the scholastic school, the first scientific school in the world, expresses, alongside their real distinction, the sincere, intimate, fruitful union which must exist, all along their borders, between our Christian beliefs and the sciences."[47] By founding the Cercle Léon XIII Castelein also tried to counterbalance the in his view all-too-radical ideas of a Brussels group of young Catholic intellectuals who had started publishing the periodical *L'Avenir Social* (1891-1895). Its main protagonists Jules Renkin (1862-1934), Léon de Lantsheere (1862-1912) and especially Henry Carton de Wiart (1869-1951), had all been trained at the Jesuit St. Michael's College and continued to gather there in a social study group formerly initiated by their Jesuit teacher François Van Innis (1839-1889).[48] Carton, Renkin and de Lantsheere would take control of the embryonic Catholic social infrastructure in the capital and began to steer it in a more democratic direction. *L'Avenir Social* pleaded for consumer cooperatives and independent labour unions, openly challenged the political monopoly of the conservative electoral associations, appealed for universal male suffrage and for social legislation regulating minimum wages, working hours and conditions. Castelein attended a few meetings of the Saint-Michel study circle, where he debated the "utopies téméraires" of Carton and his friends. He even claimed that he succeeded in reorienting a few moderate members. But he soon concluded that further efforts were in vain.

Castelein's first social studies hardly contained any references; his lengthy footnotes were mainly used to provide additional thoughts and to elaborate on specific concepts. Nonetheless it was clear that his ideas were inspired by Charles Périn (1815-1905), a scholar who Castelein not only applauded as a "consistent Catholic" and an "eminent sociologist", but to whom he also referred as "the first authority of the country".[49] Périn had taught political economy at the Leuven university for decades.[50] His main studies, *De la richesse dans les sociétés chrétiennes* (Paris, 1861) and *Les lois de la société chrétienne* (Paris, 1875) professed a well-elaborated model of a Catholic political economy and argued that this third way – with the principle of renunciation at its core – would soon prove its superiority to both liberalism and Marx-

47 *Journal de Bruxelles*, 11 September 1891; Castelein, *La société Léon XIII*, 5. Some reactions on his lecture in: ABSE, 1421.
48 Hoyois, *Henry Carton de Wiart et le groupe de "La Justice Sociale"*, 11-13; Carton de Wiart, *Souvenirs politiques*, 35. Other members of this circle were the later Cardinal Rafaël Merry del Val (1865-1930), the Liège jurist Edouard Vander Smissen (1865-1926) and the later Belgian minister Pierre de Liedekerke (1869-1943). On Van Innis: ABSE, 6545.
49 ABSE, 1426: Note "Mon Intervention", 2.
50 Louant, "Charles Périn et Pie IX"; Id., "Charles Périn"; Brants, *Charles Périn*; Michotte, "Un économiste belge. Charles Périn".

ism.[51] In the 1860s and 1870s Périn became one of the leading figures of Belgian intransigent Catholicism.[52] His international scientific renown and the clear support that he enjoyed from Pope Pius IX made him *incontournable*. In 1881, however, due to his involvement in a publicly exposed conflict amongst the Belgian episcopacy, Périn was forced to resign from his professorship in Leuven, retired to his castle in Ghlin and found a new intellectual haven at the Catholic University of Lille.[53]

Périn did not attend the social congresses in Liège. Together with the diocesan priest Auguste Onclair (1822-1900) he organised the resistance, for instance by rallying Bishop Charles Freppel (1827-1891) of Angers to the non-interventionist cause.[54] Périn's writings displayed remarkably unwavering ideas on public intervention in social matters. In his book *Le Patron*, finished during the violent social upheavals of March-April 1886, he again argued that only "free and charitable patronage" could provide durable social harmony.[55] Social legislation was an assault on private initiative, an interference of the state in the private sphere, and for that reason should be considered only a step toward socialism. The ills of modern society (individualism, poverty, alcoholism, socialism and so forth) could only be ironed out by charity and religious education enhancing the morality and diligence of the lower classes. Employers possessed the unquestionable power to form and lead their 'workers' family'. Périn, referring to Leo's encyclical *Humanum genus* (1884) and his pastoral message to the French bishops of 8 February 1884, urged them to place their entire life "in conformity with their faith" and to Christianise their factories by creating apologetic and devotional initiatives, different social provisions and deliberative structures where they could dialogue with their workers.

Throughout the 1870s and 1880s this model of the *bon patron catholique* had been actively propagated in the cross-border industrial area of Northern France and Belgian Wallonia. It was clearly inspired by the Leplaysian ideas on patronage but even more explicitly referred to the writings and exemplary initiatives of Léon Harmel (1829-1915), the owner of a medium-sized wool spin-

51   Teixeira and Almodovar, "Economics and Theology in Europe"; Id., "Catholic in its faith, Catholic in its manner of conceiving science".
52   De Maeyer, "Belgium from 1831".
53   A biography of Périn by Fred Stevens will shortly be published in the volume *Great Christian Jurists of the Low Countries*, edited by Wim Decock and Janwillem Oosterhuis in the series Cambridge Studies in Law and Christianity. Alina Potempa (Ruhr Universität Bochum) is studying Périn as part of her PhD- project "Wie Katholiken die moderne Ökonomie entdeckten".
54   Gérin, "Les écoles sociales belges", 271-273; Naudet, "Monseigneur Freppel". Freppel hosted the 15th Congrès des jurisconsultes catholiques in Angers, 7 to 9 October 1890. There it was decided to create a Société catholique d'économie politique with the bishop as its president. Freppel's opening speech offers a good summary of the viewpoints of Angers: *Revue Catholique des Institutions et du Droit*, (1890) 2, 414-426.
55   Périn, *Le patron, sa fonction, ses devoirs, ses responsabilités*.

ning mill near Reims.[56] Périn's book *Le Patron* was particularly applauded by the Association Catholique des Patrons du Nord (1884), a structure supported by the Jesuits and grounded in the longstanding Catholic and legitimist entrepreneurial networks of this region.[57] Belgian Catholic industrialists soon followed their example and also reinforced their collaboration. The Union des Patrons en Faveur des Ouvriers, for instance, was the result of an explicit plea of local bishop Doutreloux at the first Catholic social congress in Liège of September 1886.[58] Other regional associations followed, for instance the Association des Patrons Chrétiens de Charleroi (1890)[59] or the Liège Ligue pour la Défense de l'Industrie et de la Propriété (1894), preparing the ground for the Belgian Association des Patrons et Industriels Catholiques (APIC, 1894). It was in these circles that Castelein's writings were particularly appreciated.[60]

Rerum novarum

The publication of *Rerum novarum* in mid-May 1891, so Castelein confessed, "was for me a powerful stimulus and, I dare say, a luminous direction in the pursuit of my studies and efforts to spread what I believed more and more to be the true social doctrine".[61] As we know, the Belgian bishops strategically waited until February 1892 to inform their flock of the contents of the encyclical.[62] Although the main Belgian Catholic journals had already reported on

56   Heyrman, "Imagining the *bon patron catholique*"; Le Play, *L'organisation du travail selon la coutume des ateliers et la loi du Décalogue*; Harmel, *Manuel d'une corporation chrétienne*; Id., *Catéchisme du Patron*. See also: Id., *Le Val des Bois et ses institutions ouvrières*; Trimouille, *Léon Harmel et l'usine chrétienne du Val des Bois*.

57   Talmy, *Une forme hybride de catholicisme social*. To accommodate its legal recognition under the law of 1884, the ACPN renamed itself in 1890 to Association Professionnelle Catholique des Patrons du Nord. Following objections of the local *Préfet* in April 1891 the adjective 'Catholique' was dropped.

58   Union Nationale pour le redressement des Griefs, *Congrès des Œuvres sociales à Liège*, 1886, I, 152-153 and II, 157-173. The name referred to the German Arbeiterswohl circle founded by industrialists following the Katholikentage in Cologne in 1881. Dohat, "Utilité des unions de patrons et moyens de les propager"; *Bulletin de l'Union des patrons en faveur des ouvriers. La Paix sociale*, 1888-[1909]. See also: *Les devoirs des classes dirigeantes. Discours d'ouverture par S.G. Monseigneur Doutreloux* (1886); *Les devoirs des patrons envers les ouvriers. Discours de S.G. Monseigneur Doutreloux* (1887); *Léon et les questions ouvrières. Discours d'ouverture par Mgr. l'évêque de Liège* (1890).

59   Leuven, KADOC-KU Leuven, Archives of the Verbond van Kristelijke Werkgevers (VKW), 250; Isaac, *Conseils pratiques sur les rapports qui doivent exister entre patrons et ouvriers*.

60   Gérin, "Catholicisme social", 101-102; Id., *Les origines de la démocratie chrétienne à Liège*, 113. Other priests linked to this structure were the canon and later bishop of Tournai Charles Walravens (1841-1915) and the archpriest and later canon Jean Noël Joseph Fisse (1848-1896) of Namur.

61   ABSE, 1426: Note "Mon Intervention", 1.

62   De Maeyer, *Arthur Verhaegen*, 278-279.

Rerum novarum in earlier months, Castelein would be the first to write a more in-depth analysis.[63] This essay in the August 1891 issue of the *Revue Générale* was well structured and eloquently written. Castelein displayed much enthusiasm but, nonetheless, offered a rather one-sided and even biased summary. He above all applauded the strong rhetoric of the pope on socialism. Leo only envisaged a limited role for the state, so Castelein contended while referring to his previous encyclical *Immortale Dei* (1885). Public authorities merely needed to punish abuses and assure safe working conditions. Moreover, "in this protection due to the working class, they must not take the place of the free associations created for this purpose".[64] Castelein stressed how the encyclical prioritised the religious, moral and reconciliatory vocation of workers' organisations. He contended that the pope had urged for the creation or revival of mixed corporations and did not mention that the encyclical also endorsed independent workers' unions.

When pleading against state intervention and social legislation, Castelein of course highlighted how *Rerum novarum*, in line with the writings of Thomas Aquinas, advocated the perpetuity (RN § 6), inviolability (§ 9) and even sacredness (§ 46) of property rights as "the first and most fundamental principle" (§ 15). Leo had called ownership "the natural right of man" (§ 22). Today we know that this papal interpretation, probably based on the writings of the Jesuit Luigi Taparelli d'Azeglio (1793-1862), did not fully correspond with the teachings of the *doctor angelicus*. Thomas had only devoted a few ambiguous paragraphs of his *Summa Theologica* (II, 2, q. 66, 1-2) to private property rights, asserting that they, although aligned with natural law, resulted from the 'law of nations' (*ius gentium*) and thus remained subordinate to mankind's God-given collective dominion over creation.[65] Castelein, of course, did not highlight this divergence. Leo's assertion of the right to private property offered him one of his strongest arguments. He also eagerly stressed that the encyclical had advocated only an "effusion of charity" as a durable solution to the social question. "The prime virtue recommended to workers is patience, based on the acceptance of the law that trials and sufferings are inherent to our earthly condition."[66] Social inequalities were considered legitimate and even beneficial. They should not be the cause of social conflict, "for there can be no capital without labour and no labour without capital: the poor are as useful

63   Castelein, "Le problème social et l'encyclique 'Rerum novarum'".
64   Ibid., 179.
65   On Catholic teachings regarding property rights: Habiger, *Papal Teaching on Private Property*; Fortin, "'Sacred and Inviolable': Rerum Novarum and Natural Rights"; Boyle, "Natural Law, Ownership and the World's Natural Resources"; Chappel, "The Thomist Debate over Inequality and Property Rights in Depression-Era Europe"; Finnis, "Aquinas as a Primary Source of Catholic Social Teaching".
66   Castelein, "Le problème social et l'encyclique 'Rerum novarum'", 182.

to the rich as the rich are to the poor".[67] Castelein also repeatedly highlighted how Leo had again called upon the charitable commitment of the Catholic employers. But he also stressed, again extensively referring to Thomas, that their duties towards their indigent workers were not a matter of justice, but merely of charity, except in cases of extreme necessity.[68]

It is of course not easy to evaluate the impact of Castelein's article. But unquestionably it helped to set a tone and clearly coloured the way in which the content of the encyclical was at first perceived by the Belgian clergy and Catholic bourgeoisie. The summary offered by Guillaume Verspeyen (1837-1912) at the general assembly of the Belgian Catholics in Mechelen in September 1891 displayed remarkable similarities.[69] The same, but less surprisingly, can be said of the comments by Charles Périn.[70] Meanwhile the Belgian bishops remained divided and therefore hesitant to intervene in the debates on how to read and implement *Rerum novarum*. Some of them, in particular Doutreloux in Liège and Antonius Stillemans (1832-1916) in Ghent, supported or at least tolerated the involvement of some of their priests and ultramontanist *hommes d'œuvres* in Christian workers' organisations and their struggle for social and political rights. The other members of the Belgian episcopacy remained hesitant or outright negative towards emerging Christian democracy, pointing to its vast political consequences. More and more voices demanded that the candidates of Christian workers' unions and other popular associations be included on the unitary Catholic electoral lists, thus breaking the time-honoured monopoly of Woeste's Fédération des Cercles Catholiques et des Associations Conservatrices. Other Christian democrats considered creating a separate party.[71] In September 1892 the Ligue Démocratique Belge organised its first congress, urging for, among other things, social legislation, a more just tax system and even co-shareholdership for workers.[72]

67   Castelein, "Le problème social et l'encyclique 'Rerum novarum'", 174.
68   Ibid., 177.
69   *Assemblé générale des catholiques de Belgique. Session de 1891*, I, 68-89.
70   Périn, *L'économie politique d'après l'encyclique sur la condition des ouvriers*; Id., *Note sur le juste salaire d'après l'encyclique Rerum novarum*. See also the intervention of Claudio Jannet "L'organisation chrétienne de l'usine et la question sociale" during the regional congress of the Œuvres sociales in Mons on 3 July 1892.
71   De Maeyer, "De Belgische Volksbond", 46-47.
72   Id., *Arthur Verhaegen*, 273-274.

Into the debate with Christian democracy

This last event clearly triggered the conservative Catholic networks under the leadership of Woeste to organise the resistance.[73] Castelein eagerly joined those efforts. In the spring of 1892 he had published a slightly amended version of his essay in the *Revue Générale* as a separate brochure. By adding several footnotes he now, for instance, elaborated on how to understand the encyclical's plea for a *cura providentiaque singulari*, a special care for and protection of wage-earners by the state. This did not necessarily imply extensive social legislation, so contended Castelein.[74] A few months later he finally succeeded in convincing his superiors to dismiss him from the directorship of the Leuven Sodality and subsequently moved to the Jesuit college of Mons. On his arrival he was invited to present his analysis of the encyclical at the yearly Assemblée des Catholiques du Nord in Lille in late November 1892.[75] His contribution there left quite an impression. Castelein's controversial paper was not incorporated in the congress report. However, the diligent Jesuit himself had it published later that year in Brussels.[76]

A close comparison of this third version of Castelein's *Le problème social et l'encyclique 'Rerum novarum'* with the two earlier ones enabled us to clarify how in Lille he not only kept on demonstrating a remarkably one-sided reading of the encyclical, but now even willingly deviated from the text. The controversy that was sparked by his intervention is therefore perfectly understandable. Castelein would again and even more ardently demonstrate that *Rerum novarum* had not pleaded for social legislation. To substantiate this argument he once more invoked *Immortale Dei* and now even called it the "sister encyclical" of *Rerum novarum*.[77] Castelein also added some extra paragraphs on the inviolability of property rights and eagerly stressed that the

---

73 Woeste, *Mémoire pour servir à l'histoire contemporaine de la Belgique*, II, esp. 10-19 and 28-45.

74 Castelein, *Le problème social et l'encyclique 'Rerum novarum'*. Other additions: 1. a footnote (p. 6) on the different forms of socialism, 2. a few paragraphs (p. 14) on how the pope had demonstrated how socialism was against the genuine interests of the workers, 3. some extra paragraphs (p. 15-17) on the importance of the family, 4. a footnote on the pre-eminence of the paternal authority (p. 16), 5. a few lines on Sunday rest (p. 20-21) and divine providence (p. 22), and 6. a few sentences (27-28) stressing the allusive nature of the papal instructions regarding the structure of workers' organisations and emphasising the encyclical's plea for class reconciliation.

75 *Assemblée générale des Catholiques du Nord et du Pas-de-Calais tenue à Lille du 22 au 27 Novembre 1892.* Amongst the participants: Bishop Doutreloux of Liège, Désiré Mercier and Léon Harmel. On these congresses (from 1873 onwards), see Jovenaux, "Les congrès catholiques du Nord et du Pas-de-Calais"; Michel, "Les catholiques sociaux du Nord et les modèles belge et allemand".

76 Castelein, *Le problème social et l'encyclique 'Rerum novarum' avec un appendice sur la théorie du salaire et de la participation aux bénéfices.*

77 Ibid., 24 fn 1.

pope, "more incisive and decisive than Saint Thomas", had made it clear how they were grounded in natural law.[78]

The "undeserved misery" of workers, on which the pope had elaborated, needed to be interpreted in a general way, as both an economic and political but above all religious problem. Castelein also contented that Leo, when writing on the "misery and wretchedness pressing so unjustly on the majority of the working class" (RN §3) and the "great inhumanity" with which they were treated by their "grasping employers" (§61), had above all referred to the situation in Italy and in some parts of France and Germany. The conditions in Belgium and England were totally different. "One cannot arm oneself with such general terms of the encyclical", so Castelein wrote, "to affirm as a matter of priority that in such and such determined [industrial] centre, the leaders of great industry fail to do justice to their workers or that the misery of the latter comes from the inadequacy of their wages. We do not believe it for Belgium".[79] In later comments it was also claimed that Castelein had openly questioned the doctrinal nature of *Rerum novarum* and/or had (rightfully) stated that it was no *ex cathedra* decree, declared under papal infallibility.[80] These rumours are hard to substantiate, the published version of his lecture in any case does not contain such a statement. Nonetheless it is remarkable to read how Castelein eloquently downplayed the nature of the papal text, for instance by referring to it as a "declaration of principles" or as a "magnificent page of social philosophy".[81]

Furthermore, Castelein devoted a lengthy footnote to the much-debated issue of fair wages, stating that the encyclical had not really decided the issue, but contained "the principles and considerations that enable us to resolve it".[82] At that same congress the Belgian Jesuit would further elaborate on that topic while offering a public rebuttal to a lecture by priest Paul-Antoine Naudet (1859-1929), a known supporter of Pottier. His intervention – Castelein called it "a very small lesson in philosophical and theological science" – was

78   Castelein, *Le problème social et l'encyclique 'Rerum novarum' avec un appendice sur la théorie du salaire et de la participation aux bénéfices.*, 14 fn 1.

79   "On ne peut s'armer des termes si généraux de l'encyclique pour affirmer à priorité que dans tel ou tel centre déterminé, les chefs de la grande industrie manquent à la justice vis à vis de leurs ouvriers ou que la misère de ceux-ci provident de l'insuffisance des salaires. Nous ne le croyons pas pour la Belgique". Ibid., 32-33 fn 1.

80   *L'Univers*, 13 October 1894, 2; Verspeyen made reference to the debate on the dogmatic nature of *Rerum novarum* in his comment on the encyclical of September 1891, however, without mentioning Castelein. The Jesuit would come back on the issue 23 years later, in his *Leo XIII et la question sociale*, 7-8.

81   Castelein, *Le problème social et l'encyclique 'Rerum novarum' avec un appendice*, 12. Paul Gérin ("Les écoles sociales belges", 278), referring to Castelein's first commentary in the *Revue Générale*, claims that Castelein wrote that it was merely "un simple exposé philosophique, dénué de toute portée pragmatique". The text, however, does not contain this quoted statement.

82   Castelein, *Le problème social et l'encyclique 'Rerum novarum' avec un appendice*, 19 fn 1.

publicly applauded, in particular by Charles Périn. The Jesuit published it both as an annex to his own paper on *Rerum novarum* and as an article in *La Réforme sociale*. He strongly refuted the idea that workers were entitled to a share of their company's profits, as an extra to the salary that they had "freely and equitably" negotiated with their employer. Castelein also took a position on the then much disputed issues of minimum and family wages, particularly rejecting the last notion. According to him the pope had clearly stated that industrial salaries should only be sufficient to guarantee the livelihood of the "sober and honest worker" himself.[83]

Castelein's intervention during the Lille congress of November 1892 clearly made his reputation as a protagonist of Angers and secured him with strong allies, both amongst the Catholic industrial elites of Northern France and Wallonia, and in the Brussels conservative salons. He became an active member of the Belgian Société d'Economie Sociale, founded by Victor Brants (1856-1917), a pupil of Frédéric Le Play (1806-1882) and the successor of Périn in the Leuven chair of Political Economy. In December 1892 Castelein eagerly entered into a verbal dispute with the Liège priest Antoine Pottier, who had been invited by some of his fellow Jesuits to offer a conference at the Brussels Cercle Union et Travail. Just a few weeks later, as a sort of retaliation, Castelein would set out his own points of view during a lecture at the Liège Cercle Saint-Joseph. Although he stressed that his speech was "ten times more moderate than the one of Pottier in Brussels", their dispute clearly caused uneasiness within the Belgian episcopacy. Indeed, the bishops were being increasingly asked by both opposing camps to substantiate their positions. In February 1893 they urged both the Ligue Démocratique Belge and Woeste's network to be more cautious.

Although Castelein already in late 1892 had been questioned on his views by Nuncio Francica-Nava di Bontife (1846-1928), he did not moderate his tone.[84] During the next year he would eagerly join Woeste's efforts to broaden the ecclesiastical support for the non-interventionist cause. Castelein corresponded and discussed with Bishop Joannes Faict (1813-1894) of Bruges and his colleague Isidore du Roussaux (1826-1897) of Tournai. During spiritual retreats for the parish clergy of these dioceses Castelein could set out his views in detail. In February 1893 Roussaux even joined Castelein at a meeting of the Société Belge d'Economie Sociale where he seems to have endorsed his

---

83 Ibid., 38-47; Id., "La participation aux bénéfices et la théorie du salaire". A response by Naudet and the consecutive comments of Castelein in *La Réforme sociale*, 16 March 1893, 466-469 and 469-471. Other voices on the issue: Cooreman, *L'encyclique Rerum novarum et les industriels*; Verhaegen, *Le minimum de salaire*; Lagasse de Locht, "Le minimum de salaire"; Nicotra, *Le minimum de salaire et l'encyclique Rerum Novarum*.
84 ABSE, 1426: Note "Mon Intervention", 2.

stances.[85] In September 1893 Castelein was invited to offer a conference on the social issue during a spiritual retreat of about 180 parish priests of the archdiocese of Mechelen. Afterwards he claimed that not only his audience but also Cardinal Goossens (1827-1906) had applauded his intervention.[86] In November Castelein was again at the yearly Assemblée des Catholiques du Nord. He avoided the plenary meetings but intervened ardently in the committee discussions, and once more raised controversy by offering a devastating response to the intervention of another socially progressive priest, Hippolyte Gayraud (1856-1911) of Toulouse.[87]

Counsellor of the *Patrons Catholiques*

The growing disputes amongst Belgian Catholics on the way the papal encyclical should be read and implemented had placed the Belgian episcopacy in a difficult situation. But until January 1894 the divisions could somewhat be confined. In the middle of that month, however, Bishop Doutreloux of Liège published a pastoral letter clearly endorsing the ideas of Pottier on for instance separate workers' organisations, social legislation and state intervention.[88] Doutreloux choosing that particular moment to break the stalemate in the Belgian episcopacy was far from coincidental. On 22 January the Belgian proponents of 'Angers', of whom approximately 34 were industrial entrepreneurs, would meet in the Brussels café Globe, where they decided to found an Assemblée Générale or Association des Patrons (et Industriels) Catholiques de Belgique.[89]

Castelein not only attended that meeting but would, four days later, deliver yet another lecture on *Rerum novarum*, this time at the bi-monthly meeting of the Catholic industrialists of Northern France at the Jesuit centre for spir-

85   During this session Victor Brants presented a paper on workers' councils. De Baets, *Monseigneur I.J. du Roussaux*, 177-178; *Le Courrier de Bruxelles*, 28 February 1893; Levie, *Michel Levie (1851-1939) et le mouvement chrétien social de son temps*, 160.
86   On Goossens: De Maeyer, "De wending van de kerk naar het volk, 1884-1926".
87   On the dispute with Gayraud: Montuclard, "Aux origines de la démocratie chrétienne", 63. An account in "Congrès des 23, 24 et 25 Novembre 1893 tenu à Lille. Section des œuvres sociales".
88   De Maeyer, *Arthur Verhaegen*, 280; Gérin, *Les origines de la démocratie chrétienne à Liège*, 108-112; Id., "Les écoles sociales belges", 283. The letter was dated 14 January and published on 21 January.
89   The invitation (15 January) was sent by the Gougnies mining and marble industrialist Henri Pirmez, the renowned Liège entrepreneur Jules Dallemagne and the Tournai industrialist Henri Desclée (1830-1917), a former Zouave and prominent Vincentian and ultramontanist. The Desclées were involved in different industries (gas production, copper and bronze foundries) but particularly in printing and publishing companies. Desclée owned or controlled several Catholic newspapers such as the *Courrier de l'Escaut* (Tournai) and *Le Courrier de Bruxelles*.

itual retreats of Notre-Dame du Haut-Mont in Mouvaux.[90] "Finally", so wrote the superior of Haut-Mont Leo Bastien (1842-1906), "we know where we stand and will be able to distinguish between so many different interpretations of the pope's statements".[91] Although the Patrons du Nord ardently pleaded to have Castelein's lecture published, the Jesuit provincial superior Jozef Janssens (1826-1900) hesitated. Castelein subsequently decided to repeat this lecture on 10 February 1894 at the Société d'Economie Sociale in Brussels. This intervention caused quite a media storm. Its content was of course briefed to Doutreloux, who alerted the Jesuit superior and urged for a re-evaluation. Castelein's "L'Encyclique Rerum novarum et ses rapports avec l'économie politique" would never be published.[92]

Castelein of course contested the way in which the '*forces pottiéristes*' had silenced him. But for him and his friends this was only a minor setback. They even increased their efforts to convince the other bishops of their arguments. Castelein again approached Bishop du Roussaux of Tournai. His eminence at first remained quite favourable to his ideas but then forbade the Jesuit to offer further conferences on the subject to his priests. Later on the two would reconcile over dinner. Castelein was even invited to dine with Cardinal Goossens, amicably discussing his speech at the Société d'Economie Sociale. "When I left the cardinal", so he wrote, "I was convinced that he wanted me to continue to fight the good fight, as long as he didn't have to interfere".[93]

Meanwhile the young Association des Patrons Catholiques de Belgique, chaired by the Gougnies industrialist Henri Pirmez (1839-1902), prepared its memorandum. The prominent Liège mining entrepreneur Jules Dallemagne (1840-1922) seems to have been mandated to author the piece. But the industrialists of course consulted Castelein, wanted to involve him more explicitly and urged his superior Janssens to officially appoint him as a counsellor of APIC. Meanwhile Bishop Doutreloux and the nuncio kept on pressuring the

---

90 *Conférences d'Etudes Sociales de Notre-Dame du Haut-Mont*, 4 (1894), 43. This brief account of Castelein's lecture does not elaborate on its content. In January 1894 Castelein also wrote a memo on the debates at the request of the nuncio in Brussels: De Baets, *Monseigneur I.J. du Roussaux*, 213.

91 ABSE, 1434: Bastien to Provincial Janssens, 28 January 1894.

92 Brants, "Rapport sommaire sur les travaux de la Société belge d'économie sociale", 777. An account of the lecture with reference to this title in: *Le Journal de Bruxelles*, 16 February 1894, 2. It seems to have been the plan to publish Castelein's updated analysis in the *Revue Générale*. We were unable to retrieve the manuscript. From his own account we know that his intervention was based on two older and already quoted papers, the one for the archdiocesan clergy (September 1893) and the other for the Patrons du Nord (26 January 1894). Castelein referred to this last lecture in Mouvaux as "L'Encyclique Rerum novarum et l'économie sociale". De Baets, *Monseigneur I.J. du Roussaux*, 214-215.

93 ABSE, 1426: Note "Mon Intervention", 3; De Baets, *Monseigneur I.J. du Roussaux*, 213-214.

Jesuits to relinquish their support of the industrialists' association.[94] After long deliberations Janssens finally yielded to APIC, albeit under the condition that Castelein – who in those years increasingly called himself a sociologist[95] – would limit his role to that of a '*théologien consulté*'. When the Patrons Catholiques gathered again in Brussels on 5 July 1894, they could proudly list 57 members on the second page of their *Mémoire sur la situation de l'industrie en Belgique et sur la question ouvrière*. Castelein called them "the finest men of the Catholic Party" and summarised their mission as "to defend their rights, to fight against utopian fantasies and to achieve all reforms and progress in accordance with the true spirit of the encyclical 'Rerum novarum'".[96]

The *Mémoire* of APIC counted 96 pages, accompanied by nearly 50 pages of (statistical) annexes, documenting the (supposedly) high average wages and low cost of living in Belgium. The Catholic entrepreneurs presumptuously contended that they "fully and wholeheartedly adhered to the teachings of the Holy See and of the bishops, in particular those of the encyclical *Rerum Novarum*".[97] They merely wanted to protest "the exaggerated interpretations and unrealistic applications of some ideologues, who have decorated themselves with the title of Christian democrats".[98] The APIC judged it false and outright insulting that just like the socialists, these "neo-democrats" were invoking the encyclical to state that the present social situation in Belgium was unjust. On the contrary, to them it was clear that the country's population enjoyed ever-increasing wealth and manifestly improving living conditions. The Belgian Catholic industrialists argued that respect for private property was "the economic base of the encyclical" and that they had already given sufficient proof of their social commitment by investing in different kinds of social and devotional initiatives within and outside their factory walls.[99]

The APIC memorandum was not officially authored and Castelein was not even mentioned. The Jesuit contended that he had only been involved once Dallemagne had already finished the first draft. He had forwarded this text to his superiors and after receiving some vague instructions had "correct-

---

94   Castelein suggested possible alternatives such as the already quoted Namur canon Fisse and the Leuven professor De Becker and contended that Goossens had agreed on them. Goossens indeed had a meeting with APIC in January 1894 but claimed to have made no promises. AAM, Papers Goossens, 125. Many thanks to Gerrit Vanden Bosch for his aid in consulting this dossier.

95   Castelein, *La méthode des sciences sociales. Compte-rendu du troisième congrès scientifique international des catholiques, tenu à Bruxelles du 3 au 8 septembre 1894*. See also *Journal de Bruxelles*, 5 and 9 September 1894. An updated version: Castelein, *La méthode des sciences sociales* (1901).

96   ABSE, 1426: Note "Mon intervention", 3.

97   *Mémoire sur la situation de l'industrie en Belgique et sur la question ouvrière*, 5.

98   Ibid., 10.

99   Ibid.

ed and softened" some 50 passages.[100] Nevertheless it is clear that Castelein left a strong mark on APIC's manifesto, particularly on its 15 conclusions and on its annexes.[101] APIC claimed that the demands of the workers were all too radical and that they infringed on the property rights and paternal authority of the employers. It rejected the idea that commutative justice obliged all industrialists to offer their workers minimum wages, family wages or steady employment. The support of several bourgeois *hommes d'œuvres* for Christian democracy clearly annoyed the authors. For them it proved that this "tranformist democratic movement" was not rooted in the populace but emanated from "the mass of degraded people that our schools and universities throw yearly on the pavement of our cities: teachers without students, clerks without jobs, engineers without a position, lawyers without causes, doctors without patients".[102] The Catholic industrialists were gladly willing to continue supporting the clergy in founding workers' associations and social provisions, but merely if these did not voice dualism and egalitarianism, respected their paternal authority and fostered a "return to the Catholic faith and the practice of its precepts". They were not opposed to consumer co-operatives but warned that these could harm the interests of small shopkeepers. A durable social policy needed to focus on the "reconstitution of the working-class family aligned with the principle of employers' authority". APIC only supported social legislation that aimed at "safeguarding the legitimate rights of the worker (incl. his wife and children) as a citizen and as an individual factor of production".

The manifesto of APIC would bring the conflict to its climax. The bishops only received the text late in July 1894. Goossens, Doutreloux, Stillemans and now also Roussaux reacted furiously. They tried to limit its circulation, afraid as they were that the *Mémoire* would harm the efforts of the Christian democrats to win the popular vote in the upcoming October elections, the first ones to be held under universal male suffrage moderated by a plural voting system. The industrialists, however, did not abide by the episcopal instructions. The tone of their discourse became increasingly bitter.[103] On 24 September 1894

---

100 ABSE, 1426: Note "Mon Intervention", 4.
101 See his documentary notes on wages, prices and family budgets in: Leuven, KADOC-KU Leuven, Archives des Jésuites – Province Belge Méridionale et du Luxembourg (ABML), 2792 (2).
102 *Mémoire sur la situation de l'industrie en Belgique et sur la question ouvrière*, 14-15.
103 See for instance the harsh letter of Chairman Pirmez to Goossens, 10 August 1894: "Finally, we would like to ask [the bishops] to tell us, once and for all, what theories should be generally accepted by Christian employers and which the Encyclical R.N. would require them to renounce. If these misunderstandings are not soon cleared, we believe that the Episcopate would have to answer before God and before the country of the deep turmoil into which the democrats, who believe themselves to be supported by certain bishops, are throwing Belgium" (Transcript in: ABSE, 1426). On the report of the audience granted by the archbishop to the industrialists on 18 August 1894: De Baets, *Monseigneur I.J. du Roussaux*, 233-234.

Cardinal Goossens, after a lengthy conference with his fellow bishops, wrote a nine-page response to the memorandum of the Catholic industrialists, strongly disapproving their attacks on the Christian democrats and indicating the points where their interpretations were in conflict with *Rerum novarum*. The bishops also questioned their claim that the conditions of the Belgian workers had improved significantly. The statement that *Rerum novarum* only allowed mixed workers' associations was labelled false.[104] Although the bishops' arguments were clearly endorsed by Rome, Castelein made no secret of how he evaluated their analysis: "*Il est mal fait, très mal fait*".[105] The Belgian *patrons catholiques* refused to comply with Goossens' instructions and sought (and found) foreign ecclesiastical support for their arguments by sending their text to Bishop Michael-Felix Korum of Trier (1840-1921), who gladly offered a laudatory comment.[106]

Goossens was of course not pleased with this last manoeuvre. But the results of the parliamentary elections of October 1894 made the Belgian bishops once again more indulgent of the industrialists' arguments. Although the Catholic Party retained its parliamentary majority, the political breakthrough of the socialists, especially in Wallonia, was a painful political uppercut. Castelein described the results as disastrous, blamed them on the divisive actions of the Christian democrats and mocked their naive belief that they could win back the workers' vote with their "demagogic propaganda". In early November 1894 Castelein made a final attempt at convincing Goossens to endorse the APIC memorandum, suggesting several changes but also arguing that the Christian democrats and Pottier in particular had not always attuned their ideas with the episcopacy. He asked to grant the *patrons catholiques* an audience and even cunningly suggested using the occasion to launch a public subscription in favour of the Catholic *œuvres ouvrières*, so that the industrialists could immediately demonstrate their financial generosity, but to no avail.[107] The archbishop considered the suggested changes insufficient and refused. On 11 December, over dinner, he ordered the Jesuit to refrain from any further involvement in the matter, a demand to which Castelein groaningly agreed.[108]

The APIC nonetheless continued distributing its memorandum and urging the bishops to consider their arguments. On 3 April 1895 the association even published a second brochure, elaborately answering the criticism that

104 Lannoye, *De houding van Kardinaal Goossens*, 119-121; Verdoodt, *Kerk en christen-democratie*, 23 and 43-46; AAM, Papers Goossens, 125: Castelein to Goossens, 6 September 1894 and Belgian bishops to APIC, 24 September 1894.
105 ABSE, 1426: Note "Mon Intervention", 4.
106 De Maeyer, *Arthur Verhaegen*, 281; ABSE, 1426: Note "Mon Intervention", 4; AAM, Papers Goossens, 125: Korum to Dallemagne, 10 November 1894.
107 AAM, Papers Goossens, 125: Castelein to Goossens, 6 November 1894.
108 Ibid.: Castelein to Joseph Jacops (1830-1906), forwarded to Goossens on 4 December 1894; De Baets, *Monseigneur I.J. du Roussaux*, 251-257.

the bishops had formulated in September.[109] The *patrons catholiques* reasserted their positions on Christian democracy and now even blamed the bishops for silencing their association and thereby fostering the creation of a neutral employer federation, the Comité Central du (Travail) Industriel (CCI).[110] Although the arguments of author Jules Dallemagne were again clearly inspired by Castelein, the Jesuit now declined all responsibility. In spite of this second APIC manifesto, in that same period the whole conflict would nevertheless be somewhat appeased. Two major French Catholic industrialists who were considered as the protagonists of the similarly conflicting French socio-Catholic factions, the previously mentioned Léon Harmel and his more conservative colleague Camille Féron-Vrau (1831-1908) of Lille, brought the question of how Christian workers needed to be organised (in mixed corporations or in independent unions) directly before the pope. Leo endorsed their compromise: both forms could co-exist without exclusivism and should strive towards co-operation.[111] In *Permoti nos*, a letter to the Belgian bishops dated on 10 July, the pope urged also the Belgian Catholics to cease their discussions and to restore unity, a message that the episcopacy eagerly communicated to the clergy and to all the faithful. In the enclosed secret instructions to the Belgian episcopacy Leo acknowledged that he hadn't targeted Belgium when writing on the "undeserved misery" of the workers. He preferred mixed workers' associations but in particular circumstances also independent ones could be admitted.[112]

After the conflict

Castelein clearly saw himself as the '*bête noire*', the scapegoat of the whole affair. He even considered leaving his order and greatly regretted that the Jesuits had not taken a stronger stance on the issue. Pointing to the way in which they had dealt with Protestantism, Jansenism, Gallicanism and liberalism, he warned that socialism and the "perils created by our 'ultra-democrats' consti-

109 Dallemagne, *Défense du mémoire sur la situation de l'industrie en Belgique en réponse à une lettre des évêques belges du 24 septembre 1894*.

110 Brion, *100 ans pour l'entreprise*; De Leener, *L'organisation syndicale des chefs d'industrie*.

111 The text that was approved during their audience on 1 April 1895 in: *Conférences d'Etudes Sociales de Notre-Dame du Haut-Mont*, 8 (September 1896), 656-657; Talmy, *Une forme hybride de catholicisme social*, 180-186.

112 The pope stressed that "workers should in no way abandon their respect for and trust in their employers, and the employers should treat their workers with just kindness and prudent care" (*Permoti nos* § 6). Pastoral letters of the bishops to the clergy on 30 July and to their flock on 8 September 1895; AAM, Papers Goossens, 125; Lannoye, *De houding van Kardinaal Goossens*, 142-149.

tuted an equal danger".[113] Nonetheless, Castelein abided by the archiepiscopal instructions and reduced his public commitments. In January 1896 he was allowed to return to Leuven as a professor of Philosophy and of Moral and Social Theology at the Jesuit Collegium Maximum.[114] He left the university city four years later to take up his courses again in Namur, where he would reside until his death in January 1922.[115]

Now that his dream of an academic assignment had finally come true, Castelein of course needed to devote a lot of time to his lectures and (re)writing his syllabi.[116] However, the fiery Jesuit did not disappear completely from the public scene. Castelein kept on offering conferences and publishing vulgarising studies. He remained involved in the *Revue Générale* and also was an active member, later on even a chair (1898-1899) of the Société Belge d'Economie Sociale.[117] Time and again, Castelein asserted himself as a literate antisocialist. In 1895 he for instance wrote a public response to the for Catholics particularly disturbing speech on the roots of public morals by the socialist deputy and Brussels professor Hector Denis (1842-1913).[118] And a year later he published an intricate study of the way in which socialism dealt with ownership rights.[119] In this last book Castelein again eagerly invoked Thomas Aquinas (as well as De Soto, Lessius and Suárez) to substantiate his view on property as an innate and absolute right of man, intricately linked to authority. He now also pointed to the divergences between *Rerum novarum* and Thomas on that issue.[120]

In 1897-1898 the Jesuit was involved in a university extension programme for women in Antwerp, where he delivered a lecture on the "philosophy of truth, beauty and goodness".[121] Most of his conferences were indeed based on the courses that he had taught in Leuven and Namur and thus remained somewhat abstract. His bourgeois audience and readers nonetheless appreciated

---

113 ABSE, 1426: Note "Mon Intervention", 4; Ibid., 1402: Correspondence of Superior Joseph Janssens with the Jesuit general Luis Martín Garcia (1846-1906), July-August 1895.
114 In succession of Jean Van der Aa (1843-1926).
115 In 1900 Castelein succeeded in the chair of Father Alphonse Capart (1840-1900). An overview of the courses and professors of the Namur University College in 1896-1921 (*Soixante-quinzième anniversaire*, 89-93) suggests that Castelein only retired from teaching in 1918-1919.
116 Castelein, *Institutiones philosophiae moralis et socialis*; Id., *Logique, logique formelle, critériologie, méthodologie*; Id., *Cours de philosophie: morale*; Id., *Psychologie. La Science de l'Ame dans ses rapports avec l'Anatomie, la Physiologie et l'Hypnotisme, Cours de philosophie* (1904); Id., *Psychologie. La Science de l'Ame dans ses rapports avec l'Anatomie, la Physiologie et l'Hypnotisme* (1916).
117 *La Réforme sociale*, July-December 1898, 932.
118 Castelein, *La morale rationaliste et la morale chrétienne*.
119 Id., *Le Socialisme et le Droit de Propriété*. This book was quoted in the bibliography of Cathrein, "Property", 472.
120 Castelein, *Le Socialisme et le Droit de Propriété*, 510-525.
121 *XXième Siecle*, 4 January 1897; Vermeersch, *Manuel social* (1904), 478, n. 2.

these vulgarising summaries. Castelein's introduction to the historical method, based on a chapter of his Logics syllabus, offers another fine example. This
brochure was broadly read and discussed, and the renowned historian God-
froid Kurth (1847-1916) assigned it to his students as required reading.[122] But
we should also point out Castelein's concise introduction to Islam[123] and to his
essay on Judaism, where he clearly catered to the traditional antisemitism of
his Catholic readers.[124] In the late 1890s the Jesuit again raised controversy by
strongly refuting the salvation doctrine of some so-called rigorist theologians.
He ardently argued that the number of saved souls at the Final Judgement
would be far greater than they claimed. When refuting their arguments he, of
course, also needed to by-pass Aquinas' famous *"pauciores sunt qui salvan-
tur"* (*Summa* 1a, 23, 7).[125]

These writings and interventions confirmed the public renown of the Jesuit, but the topics also illustrate how in those years Castelein indeed kept his
distance from the controversial issues that had caused him to clash with the
Belgian episcopacy in 1894. The Jesuit nonetheless remained in contact with
his APIC friends. His conference on "charity and justice" for the members of
the Society of Saint-Vincent de Paul of the diocese of Tournai at the end of
June 1895 explicitly referred to the debate that had led to Cardinal Goossens'
'coup de crosse'. Talking to that particular audience, he of course elaborated
on man's God-given charitable duties, repeatedly referring to Leo's statement
that only an "effusion of charity" could lead to social salvation.[126]

Castelein was also a known supporter of the Belgian Ligue du Coin de
Terre et du Foyer Insaisissables (1895). In dialogue with likeminded promoters
of 'terrianism' in Northern France, this somewhat patchy union pleaded for a

122 Castelein, *La méthode des sciences historiques*. See also *Revue d'Histoire Ecclésiastique*, 2
(January 1901), 899-900. Kaat Wils (*De omweg*, 289) quotes Castelein's positive evaluation
of Tain's *Les orgines de la France contemporaine*.
123 Castelein, "L'Islamisme".
124 Id., "Le Judaïsme". "Without advising the violent expulsion of the Jews, we must monitor
and try to limit their invasion. If they treat us like strangers and agree to exploit us, as
Israel's petty loan sharks and big financiers frequently do, let us treat them like strangers
and agree to keep them away. In some localities, an anti-Semitic league, with a pledge
never to buy or borrow from Israel, may be of public use to Christians" (545). Castelein was
clearly inspired by Claudio Jannet (1844-1894), in particular his *Le Capital: la spéculation
et la finance au XIXe siècle*. See also his position on the Dreyfus affair, when responding
to a contribution of Edouard Trogan in *Revue Générale*, March 1898, 410-419. Mayeur, "Les
Catholiques Dreyfusards".
125 Castelein, "Le Rigorisme et la question du nombre des élus"; Id., *Le rigorisme, le nombre
des élus et la doctrine du salut*; ABSE, 1404, 1435-1436 and 1440. Castelein's views were
particularly questioned by the Redemptorists. See for instance Godts, *De paucitate salvandorum quid docuerunt sancti*; Coppin, *La question de l'évangile*. On the controversy within
the Jesuit order, see ABSE, 1402. See also: Schultenover, "Luis Martín García, the Jesuit
General of the Modernist Crisis", 450 fn. 56. Castelein, however, did not leave his order.
126 Castelein, *Charité et Justice*, 6.

'*retour à la terre*' of the urban industrial proletariat and strived towards legally securing the inviolability of small rural property. The local chapters of the Ligue, often supported by Catholic noblemen and industrialists, leased small parcels of land to well-chosen workers' families. Growing their own vegetables in an allotment or *jardin populaire*, so contented the promoters while often referring to *Rerum novarum* (esp. its § 46-47), did not only foster the health, family stability and happiness of workers' families, it would eventually also allow them to save up enough money to buy their own home, preferably one in the countryside. "And if, in the future, there are still some remnants of that dangerous utopia that was socialism, in fact there will be no more socialists: the worker will have become an owner", read the founding manifesto of the Ligue.[127] Castelein got involved in the Belgian allotment movement through Joseph Goemaere (1866-1943), a distant relative and one of his favourite Brussels publishers.[128] The Jesuit considered the Belgian working-class population too large and questioned the future employment potential of the country's rapidly mechanising industry. In order to avoid rising unemployment and the accompanying social tensions, the relocation of urban workers' families to the countryside seemed to be a viable strategy. For Castelein this was yet another reason for extensively arguing the innate inviolability of (rural) property rights, now mostly invoking Mosaic law, in particular Leviticus and Deuteronomy. By cleverly adjusting the Belgian inheritance and fiscal laws a further rural exodus should in any case be avoided.[129]

Another intervention proving that he had far from abandoned his former allies was his speech on the recently voted Belgian law on professional unions during the annual congress of the French Société d'Economie Sociale on 10 June 1898. The Jesuit commented quite positively on the new legal framework, but he was also glad to see that it did not offer workers "a sword of attack", but merely "a defence and protective shield".[130] He clearly regretted that the law had not explicitly favoured the creation of mixed corporations, which for him remained the only viable model for workers' organisations.[131] Castelein would also elaborate on this topic during an international congress on labour regulations and contracts in Antwerp in September 1898. While discussing with for instance the French economist Yves Guyot (1843-1928) and

---

127 Gruel and Goemaere, *Plus de socialistes!*, 16.
128 Heyrman, "Het Werk van den Akker".
129 Castelein, "Quelques vérités sur l'agriculture et les classes rurales à vulgariser"; Id., "La crise agricole et son remède par les ligues agricoles". In 1893 Castelein was involved in founding a diocesan farmers' league in the region of Mons-Soignies, a structure that afterwards – and much to his discontent – would be entrusted to the care of his more progressive *confrère* Jules Lechien (1844-1914). On 'terrianism', see: Heyrman, "*Het Werk van den Akker* ", 49-53; Cabedoce and Pierson, *Cent ans d'histoire des jardins ouvriers*.
130 Castelein, *La loi belge sur les unions professionnelles*, 309.
131 *La réforme sociale*, 16 August 1898, 293-314; Castelein, *La loi belge sur les unions professionnelles*.

the Ghent social-liberal lawyer Louis Varlez (1863-1930), the Jesuit again re-jected further public intervention in social matters and strongly argued that labour contracts, like prices, were merely subject to commutative justice.[132]

Rehabilitation and apologia

The public resonance of his interventions during this last congress, including grumbling in government circles, probably triggered Castelein to re-engage more explicitly with Christian democracy. In late 1898, in an article for the *Revue Générale*, he elaborated on some recent papal pronouncements regard-ing the social question: (1) the already cited letter from Leo XIII to the Belgian bishops of 10 July 1895 urging for unity and "friendly co-operation" amongst the country's Catholics; (2) the pope's cautions to Albert De Mun (1841-1914) of the French Œuvre des Cercles Catholiques d'Ouvriers in April 1897 that Cath-olic social activism should strive for unity and avoid "democratic excesses"; and (3) the similar papal admonishments to the pilgrimage of '*la France du travail*' led by Léon Harmel on 8 October 1898.[133] According to Castelein, all these papal reproaches made it clear that Rome was far from content with so-called Christian democracy. Some of the *hommes d'œuvres* who had adorned themselves with that label had yielded too easily to social egalitarianism and political interventionism. They should bear in mind that Christian charity re-mained "the queen", the core characteristic of Christian society. Castelein also suggested that the way in which the pope had explicitly greeted the employers accompanying Harmel to Rome once again illustrated that he did not question their social commitment at all. The allegations against Christian industrialists needed to cease, both in Belgium and in France.

---

132 *Congrès international de la législation douanière et de la réglementation du travail, tenu à Anvers, du 12 au 17 septembre 1898*, I, 3-6 and II, 325-331; *Journal de Bruxelles*, 15, 16 and 17 September 1898. On 5 January 1897 Castelein had already delivered a conference on property rights for the Antwerp Syndicat de l'Industrie et du Commerce. In September of that same year he attended the international congress on labour legislation in Brussels. Probably invited by Brants, he even joined its organising committee and made several interventions. *Congrès international de Législation du Travail tenu à Bruxelles du 27 au 30 Septembre 1897*, 653-655 and 696-697; Castelein, "Le contrat de travail. Discours prononcé au congrès international d'Anvers".

133 Castelein, "Les dernières déclarations de Rome sur la question sociale". See the polemics with the Liège Christian democrat periodical *Le Bien du Peuple*. Some of his fellow-Jesuits questioned the need to revive the old arguments and accused Castelein of deliberately distorting the papal message. See e.g. the evaluation of the manuscript by Eduard Génicot (1856-1900) in ABSE, 2764: "The condition of the workers is presented with an optimism that stands in stark contrast to the way the encyclical depicts it. In dealing with the just wage, nowhere does the speaker explicitly propose the teachings which the Holy Father offers so insistently."

Castelein's reappearance in the debate on social legislation is significant for the general atmosphere in the Belgian Catholic community in those years. The conservatives were clearly on the rise again. The more radical Christian democrats, Daens and Pottier in particular, had been silenced or were politically marginalised. The moderate ones in the Ligue Démocratique were forced into a defensive position, experiencing fierce opposition from both Woeste and his entrepreneurial allies, the Royal Court and the Belgian bishops. The episcopacy still pleaded for unity, but now refused any further infringement of the leadership of Woeste's conservative federation, afraid as it was for the political fall-out.[134] After the nominations of Martin Rutten (1841-1927) in Liège and Walravens in Tournai the balances in the Belgian episcopacy had clearly shifted.

This growing suspicion in the Catholic community towards democracy was of course not merely a Belgian phenomenon. In January 1901 the elderly Pope Leo XIII published a second encyclical on the social question. *Graves de communi re* again confined social-Catholic activism to its traditional moral and religious dimensions and (esp. §7) explicitly rejected its political application under the flag of Christian democracy. The papal instructions were again eagerly debated. Castelein would only interfere quite late, with an essay in the September issue of the *Revue Générale*.[135] In this "plaidoyer contradictoire", as one of his fellow Jesuits called it,[136] he of course highlighted *Graves de communi re* as the "coronation and authentic commentary" of *Rerum novarum*. Somewhat self-righteously, he underlined how the encyclical was in line with the papal instructions to Harmel and De Mun that he had commented on two years earlier. Catholic social action towards the popular classes could take on many forms, with Christian democracy only one of its many manifestations. One could not at all claim that Christian democrats implemented the pontifical social doctrines in *Rerum novarum* in a superior way. On the contrary, so Castelein concluded, the pope had clearly asserted that the social crisis was above all a moral and religious one. "Let us put an end to these dangerous statements about the black misery of the workers, as if it were the effect of the capitalist regime and the injustice of the Christian employers. The encyclical *Graves de Communi* does not contain a word that encourages such exaggerated comments of the encyclical *Rerum Novarum*."

---

134 De Maeyer, *Arthur Verhaegen*, 321-334.
135 Castelein, "L'Encyclique 'Graves de Communi'"; Id., *L'Encyclique 'Graves de Communi'*.
136 ABSE, 2764: Letter of Désiré Mélot (1838-1901).

In short, *Graves de communi re* offered Castelein the ultimate confirmation that his opinions and arguments had always been correct. This sense of rehabilitation also permeated his *magnum opus*, an extensive (965 pages!) study on natural law and its contemporary significance, published in 1903. Particularly in its chapter on social justice, with for instance theses regarding 'the nature of justice', 'socialism' (98 pages!), 'property rights', 'fair prices' and 'just wages', Castelein eagerly returned to his older arguments, extensively referring to Thomas Aquinas, but also to Ballerini and even the Bruges bishop Gustave Waffelaert (1847-1931). He elaborated on the 'obligations of charity'[137], demonstrating its pre-eminence but also underlining that Thomas (*Summa* 2, 2, q 32, 5) had limited the charitable involvement of a Catholic to "le superflu de son rang", the surplus on what he needed to live according to his status. He also expanded on the distinctions between the extreme, serious and ordinary needs of the indigent: only these first two categories called for charitable support. In his extensive footnotes Castelein also criticised the ideas of his fellow Jesuit Arthur Vermeersch (1858-1936) on family wages and usury.[138] Castelein's *Droit naturel*, although in part a compilation of older course materials and writings, was very positively reviewed, both in Belgian and French academic circles.[139] And apparently the book was also widely distributed. In 1912 the Jesuit would publish a second, slightly updated edition.[140]

Other studies and publications of Castelein in the decade before the First World War dealt with very different issues. In 1905-1907 Castelein made some strong statements in the ongoing discussions on the significance of studying classical languages in secondary schools.[141] He also elaborated on the importance of technical education.[142] The Jesuit interfered in the debate on Belgium's declining birth rate, an issue which he skilfully linked to the spiritual meaning of love and marriage.[143] Castelein even rediscovered his initial love for theology, with a thorough and well-received study on the writings of Saint

---

137 Castelein, *Droit naturel*, 146-151.
138 Ibid., 319, 334-335 and 339, particularly focusing on Vermeersch, *Questiones acerca de la Justitia* (1904). On Vermeersch, see the contribution of Vincent Genin to this volume. Vermeersch taught canon law and moral theology at the Leuven Collegium Maximum. His *Manuel Social. La Législation et les Œuvres en Belgique* (first of several editions in 1900) offered a concise overview of social legislation in Belgium and the quickly expanding landscape of Catholic and other œuvres sociales.
139 On its reception, see ABSE, 1434. Particularly laudatory reviews in the *Revue Catholique des Institutions et du Droit*, July 1904, 89-91 and in the *Revue sociale catholique*, January 1904, 93-94.
140 Positive comments by Victor Brants (1856-1917) in the *Revue des sciences philosophiques et théologiques*, 7 (1913), 498.
141 Castelein, "Les humanités gréco-latines et les exigences de notre prospérité économique".
142 Id., *L'Enseignement professionnel*.
143 Id., "La passion de l'amour".

Paul.[144] And in 1911 he published two bestsellers, one dealing with the societal and moral dangers of hypnotism and a second on how to interpret the Marian apparitions in Lourdes.[145] He also intervened in the politically extremely sensitive Congo issue, where he obstinately defended the achievements of Leopold II.[146] Once the take-over by the Belgian state was prepared, Castelein pleaded for gratitude and a worthy compensation for the king. That position was of course applauded by the Royal Court.[147] But it again provoked a controversy between Castelein and Vermeersch, not only confirming but now also publicly exposing the intergenerational fissures within the Belgian Jesuit province.[148]

Castelein's stances on Congo must of course also be considered an appendix to his long-lasting feud with the Christian democrats. The memories of the debate on *Rerum novarum* clearly kept on haunting him. In 1914 Castelein would write his final apologia on the issue, a book prefaced by no less than two ministers of State: Jules Van den Heuvel (1854-1926) and Charles Woeste.[149] This *Mise au point* clearly shows how the protagonist of 'Angers' looked back on the past two decades. A censor of the book compared it to a "critique d'un chef d'état-major après la manœuvre".[150] Castelein, of course, recalled that his reading of the papal instructions had at first been discarded and ridiculed, but that the viability of the theological truths that he had invoked had been clearly confirmed afterwards by the magisterium, not only in *Graves de communi re* but also in the paragraphs on Christian democracy in Pius X's *motu proprio 'Fin dalla prima'* (1904) and by his condemnation of Le Sillon (1910). Invoking several linguistic arguments, Castelein reasserted that the "*misera et calamitosa*" that Leo had attributed to the "*pars maxima*" of the workers due to their "*cupidos dominos*", was not at all referring to Belgium of the early 1890s, with its relatively high industrial wages, low cost of living and so-

---

144 Id., *Saint Paul. Valeur de son témoignage*, with a second edition the same year.
145 Id., *Les Phénomènes de l'Hypnotisme et le Surnaturel; Id., Le Surnaturel dans les apparitions et dans les guérisons de Lourdes*. On their success see: *Journal de Bruxelles*, 1 December 1911 and the letters of Goemaere in ABSE, 1140.
146 Castelein, "L'État du Congo. Ses origines, ses droits, ses devoirs" (in: *Revue Générale*); Id., *L'État du Congo. Ses origines, ses droits, ses devoirs; Id., L'État du Congo. Ses origines, ses droits, ses devoirs, le réquisitoire de ses accusateurs*. A report of Castelein's conference in the Société d'Economie Sociale, 12 March 1906: *Revue sociale catholique*, April 1906, 184-186.
147 ABSE, 1410-1411: Letters of Ferdinand Goffart (1874-1916).
148 Castelein's article and books contradicted several passages of Vermeersch' *La question Congolaise* (1906). The controversy especially focused on the property rights of the indigenous. ABSE, 21231; De Maeyer, *Arthur Verhaegen*, 472; Gijs, "Entre ombres et lumières, profits et conflits"; Deneef, "Promoteurs et auxiliaires", 362.
149 Castelein, *Léon XIII et la Question sociale*.
150 ABSE, 2764: Note by Théophile Thisquen (1848-1936).

cially committed industrialists. The Jesuit again offered a broad overview of the many provisions that Belgian entrepreneurs had set up for their workers. He particularly stressed the support they offered to pension and mutual-aid funds, child allowances and social housing, which, he cleverly remarked, should all be considered a kind of profit-sharing.[151] Leo had not labelled the Christian employers in general as unjust, the encyclical had condemned neither liberal capitalism nor free competition, it had merely pointed to some abuses, which were due to the absence of religion in social relations. Castelein still asserted that *Rerum novarum* had urged for minimal state intervention in social matters and had never mentioned family or minimum wages. Nor had it pleaded for public regulation of production, prices or competition, whether domestic or international. "Those who want to transform, by means of laws or ultra-democratic institutions, the workers into associates and the proletarians into co-owners, should not refer to the encyclical."[152]

When looking back on the remedies that the encyclical had suggested, especially regarding the disputed issues of fair wages, social legislation and independent workers' organisations, Castelein could of course only acknowledge that things had clearly evolved since 1891. Some of the Christian democrat leaders, especially the 'utopists' of the Jesuit Saint Michael's College who he vainly had tried to convert in the late 1880s, had since then become esteemed members of government. Although Woeste and his political friends had put up firm resistance and clearly managed to limit their scope and impact, Belgium had indeed enacted several pieces of social legislation, for instance on workers' salaries (1887/1896/1901), industrial employment of women and adolescents (1889), workplace regulations (1896), professional unions (1898), the labour contract (1900), working hours (1901), industrial accidents (1903) and Sunday rest (1905). Government needed to continue on this "voie sagement démocratique", so Castelein contended.[153] The Jesuit also acknowledged that the corporatist formula of mixed workers' associations had failed. He applauded the French *syndicats jaunes* as an efficient bulwark against socialism[154] and praised the conciliatory nature of the Belgian Christian trade unions, as they were organised by the Dominican Georges Rutten (1875-1951), a pupil of Brants. But by pointing out the many other and often new charitable initiatives in Belgian society, in particular those financed by Catholic industrialists, Castelein also noted with pleasure that Christian de-

---

151 See also the extensive overview of social provisions (sponsored) by industrialists in France and Belgium in his *Droit Naturel*, especially the second edition of 1912.

152 Castelein, *Léon XIII et la Question sociale*, 65.

153 Ibid., 111.

154 At a conference of the Patrons du Nord on 7 October 1910. Castelein, "Syndicats ouvriers et contrat collectif".

mocracy had far from taken over the multifaceted field of social Catholicism. Now calling *Rerum novarum* a "charter of democracy and conservative wisdom", Castelein expressed the hope that it would keep on inspiring both "conservateurs-démocrates" and "démocrates-conservateurs" in their social activism.[155]

Some concluding remarks

The reception of *Rerum novarum* and the debates that it engendered within Western-European Catholicism have been studied intensely by historians and from many different angles. Our contribution aimed at shedding more light on the ways in which the more conservative factions of the Belgian Catholic bourgeoisie responded to and dialogued with the papal encyclical. As the discussions on how to read and implement the encyclical were intricately interwoven with those on political democratisation the conflict was particularly deep and bitter, cutting straight through the heart of the Catholic bourgeois community. To substantiate their viewpoints both parties eagerly invoked the teachings of the *doctor angelicus*.

We focused our analysis on the writings and polemic activism of the Jesuit father Auguste Castelein. Although merely one particular actor, his life path and networks allowed us to sketch a broader panorama, with particular attention paid to the Jesuit order and the cross-border Catholic industrial elite of Belgium and Northern France. Castelein was an ecclesiastical scholar, called upon by these entrepreneurial networks to articulate their arguments and to substantiate them within Catholic doctrine and Church tradition. The somewhat complacent and professionally frustrated Jesuit jumped at the opportunity, enjoyed a brief period of public prominence, but soon overestimated his leeway, made some crucial mistakes and was publicly reprimanded. During the rest of his life he kept on seeking retribution for this scolding, obstinately holding on to his original positions and arguments, only reluctantly accepting the diverging paths of Catholic social activism and evidently applauding the rebound of the Church under Pius X.

Castelein's writings reflect the discourses of Belgian right-wing bourgeois Catholicism in those years. The Catholic upper class and the traditional (often older) clergy did not understand the necessity of the emancipatory turn in social teachings initiated by *Rerum novarum*. They of course recognised the threat of socialism, but were sincerely convinced that their charitable efforts, following earlier papal instructions, would be sufficient to face this challenge.

---

155 Castelein, *Léon XIII et la Question sociale*, 116.

Particularly amongst the resisting Catholic industrial entrepreneurs, many of whom had an ultramontanist background, it was quite unclear why the pope, who only a few years earlier had applauded and encouraged their paternalist social commitment, was now reprimanding them, apparently opening the door to state intervention and social conflict. They were horrified by the popular socio-political commitment of a growing number of (mostly young) clergymen, tolerated and even supported by their superiors. In short, they refused to understand and accept that the Church's more explicit involvement with modern industrialised society and the rapidly secularising working class required an adjustment of its teachings on the balance between justice and charity in social relations, let alone a cautious endorsement of democracy.

To a large extent their response to *Rerum novarum* was that of an ostrich facing imminent danger. They sought self-reassurance by ignoring and even denying the disputed passages in the encyclical or by downplaying its importance. Castelein assuaged their fears by putting the document into perspective, by pointing out its wide-ranging and often contradictory content and by interconnecting the encyclical to other sources of ecclesiastical authority. He particularly highlighted the arguments of the pope that were aligned with entrepreneurial positions, in particular those on the inviolability of property rights and their link to paternal authority. *Rerum novarum* had not condemned industrial capitalism! Raising public suspicion of Christian democracy was another popular tactic. By pointing to its most radical stances and actions and by warning how they resembled the socialist ones, Castelein and his friends illustrated the dangers connected to an incorrect or all-too-superficial reading of the papal instructions. Meanwhile they waited for the winds in Rome to turn.

When applying this strategy the Jesuit's scholarly reputation and his dedication to the neo-scholastic conciliation of faith and science came in quite handy. Given the papal plea for a Thomist revival, it was particularly beneficial to quote Aquinas when one wanted to substantiate a more moderate and even deviant reading of his encyclical. Castelein eagerly did so. But although his bibliography – even by Jesuit standards – was extremely long and diverse, he never published an article or a book explicitly dealing with the *doctor angelicus*. For him Aquinas above all was a fashionable source of authority who he cited to validate his own, highly traditionalist arguments and statements, not only when writing on the social question, but also on many other subjects. Invoking natural law and quoting Thomas on the nature of public authority, the content and limits of commutative and distributive justice, the pre-eminence of charity and its conditions, but also on luxury, usury, the malice of lying and so forth allowed Castelein to make authoritative arguments and to demonstrate his erudition. But his Thomist lens often remained hazy. The teachings of the *doctor angelicus* that did not fit into his agenda, for instance on the origin of property rights or the number of the elect, were carefully circumvented and/or re-interpreted.

How can we evaluate the societal impact of Castelein's highly instrumental involvement in neo-scholasticism? Besides being a teacher of many generations of students, the Jesuit also was a popular apologist reaching many, albeit mainly bourgeois and clerical audiences. His numerous vulgarising books and brochures were well sold, widely read and often quoted by the conservative Catholic press. The effect of his conferences and writings on these readers and listeners can of course not be accurately measured. However, one can only assume that he, and the many other members of the Catholic intellectual elites voicing similar messages, indeed influenced public opinion. The more traditionalist and paternalist view of social activism that they propagated would remain a durable component of multi-layered social Catholicism throughout the twentieth century. Substantiating the roots of these different layers within the many networks connected to the Thomist Revival movement before and after the First World War clearly offers a relevant perspective for further research.

BIBLIOGRAPHY

Art, Jan. "De pastorale methodes van de Vlaamse parochiegeestelijkheid: verandering of continuïteit". In Emiel Lamberts, ed. *Een kantelend tijdperk / Une époque en mutation / Ein Zeitalter im Umbruch (1890-1910). De wending van de Kerk naar het volk in Noord-West-Europa / Le Catholicisme social dans le Nord-Ouest de l'Europe / Die Wende der Kirche zum Volk im nordwestlichen Europa*. Leuven: Leuven University Press, 1992, 227-243.

Assemblé générale des catholiques de Belgique. Session de 1891. Vol. 1. Mechelen: Ryckmans, 1891.

Assemblée générale des Catholiques du Nord et du Pas-de-Calais tenue à Lille du 22 au 27 Novembre 1892. Lille: Ducolombier, 1893.

Aubert, Roger. "Désiré Mercier et les débuts de l'Institut de philosophie". *Revue Philosophique de Louvain*, 88 (1990) 2, 147-167.

Aubert, Roger. "L'encyclique Rerum novarum, une charte des travailleurs". In Françoise Rosart and Guy Zelis, eds. *Le monde catholique et la question sociale*. Brussels: Editions Vie Ouvrière, 1992, 13-28.

Audren, Frédéric and Patrice Rolland. "Juristes catholiques". *Revue Française d'Histoire des Idées Politiques*, (2008) 2, 227-231.

Audren, Frédéric and Patrice Rolland. "La belle époque des juristes catholiques(1880-1914)". *Revue Française d'Histoire des Idées Politiques*, (2008) 2, 233-271.

Boyle, Joseph. "Natural Law, Ownership and the World's Natural Resources". *The Journal of Value Inquiry*, 23 (1989), 191-207.

Boyle, Joseph. "Rerum novarum (1891)". In Gerard Bradley and E. Christian Brugger, eds. *Catholic Social Teaching: A Volume of Scholarly Essays*. Cambridge: Cambridge University Press, 2019, 69-89.

Brants, Victor. "Rapport sommaire sur les travaux de la Société belge d'économie sociale pendant sa 13e session". *La Réforme sociale*, 16 November 1894, 775-780.

Brants, Victor. *Charles Périn. Notice sur sa vie et ses travaux*. Annuaire de l'Université Catholique de Louvain, 1906. Leuven: Van Linthout, 1906.

Brion, René. *100 ans pour l'entreprise. Fédération des Entreprises de Belgique, 1895-1995*. Tielt: Lannoo, 1995.

Cabedoce, Béatrice and Philippe Pierson. *Cent ans d'histoire des jardins ouvriers 1896-1996: la Ligue française du coin de terre et du foyer.* Grâne: Créaphis, 1996.

Carton de Wiart, Henry. *Souvenirs politiques. 1878-1918.* Bruges: Desclée De Brouwer, 1948.

Castelein, Auguste. *Theses ex universa theologia quas praeside R.P. Van den Acker Societatis Jesu studiorum praefecto et collegii Soc. Jesu Lovaniensis rectore defendet P. Augustus Castelein ejusdem societatis Lovanii in collegio societatis Jesu die 7 julii 1874.* Leuven: Peeters, 1874.

Castelein, Auguste. *Conferentia de scholis catholicis. Instructio circa modum concionandi de "quaestione scolari".* S.l., s.d.

Castelein, Auguste. *Une loi d'éducation nationale. Trois conférences sur la loi de 1879.* Leuven: Peeters, 1882 (5th edition).

Castelein, Auguste. *Foi et science. 4 conférences: conflits apparents entre la foi et la science. – Accord entre la foi et la science. – Le matérialisme. – Le spiritualisme.* Leuven: Fonteyn, 1883.

Castelein, Auguste. *La première page de Moïse et l'histoire de la terre.* Paris-Leuven: Lecoffre-Fonteyn, 1884.

Castelein, Auguste. *Spiritisme, tables tournantes, magnétisme.* Leuven: Peeters, 1885.

Castelein, Auguste. *Logique.* Namur: Douxfils, 1887.

Castelein, Auguste. *Un programme sociale: conférence par A. Castelein SJ, professeur de philosophie.* Namur: Wesmael-Charlier, 1887.

Castelein, Auguste. "Etude sur le socialisme". *Revue Générale,* 26 (September 1890), 257-278.

Castelein, Auguste. *L'hypnotisme et la psychologie.* Namur: Douxfils, 1890.

Castelein, Auguste. *Les principes de la philosophie morale.* Namur-Leuven-Liège-Paris-Brussels-Ghent: Douxfils-Delvaux-Peeters-Demarteau-Retaux-Bray-Librairie Générale-Van der Schelden, 1890.

Castelein, Auguste. *Philosophie morale.* Namur: Douxfils, 1890.

Castelein, Auguste. *Psychologie. La science de l'âme dans ses rapports avec la physiologie.* Namur: Douxfils, 1890.

Castelein, Auguste. *Éloge funèbre de S.A.R. le prince Baudouin adressé aux élèves du collège Saint-Michel le 4 février 1891.* Brussels: Polleunis et Ceuterick, 1891.

Castelein, Auguste. *La société Léon XIII pour le progrès des sciences philosophiques, historiques et sociales. Rapport au Congrès de Malines le 10 Septembre 1891.* Leuven: Istas, 1891.

Castelein, Auguste. "Le problème social et l'encyclique 'Rerum novarum'". *Revue Générale,* 27 (August 1891), 165-187.

Castelein, Auguste. *Qu'est-ce que le socialisme? Question actuelle.* Brussels: Goemaere, 1891.

Castelein, Auguste. *Le problème social et l'encyclique 'Rerum novarum'.* Brussels: Société belge de Librairie, 1892.

Castelein, Auguste. *Le problème social et l'encyclique 'Rerum novarum' avec un appendice sur la théorie du salaire et de la participation aux bénéfices. Rapport du Congrès des catholiques du Nord, à Lille.* Brussels-Leuven: Schepens-Istas, 1892.

Castelein, Auguste. "La participation aux bénéfices et la théorie du salaire". *La Réforme sociale,* 16 February 1893, 290-296.

Castelein, Auguste. *Charité et Justice. Allocution prononcée par le R.P. Castelein, S.J. à l'assemblée diocésaine des conférences de Saint-Vincent-de-Paul tenue à Boussu le 30 juin 1895.* Tournai: Casterman, 1895.

Castelein, Auguste. "La crise agricole et son remède par les ligues agricoles". *Revue Générale,* 29 (November 1895), 695-713.

Castelein, Auguste. *La méthode des sciences sociales. Compte-rendu du troisième congrès scientifique international des catholiques, tenu à Bruxelles du 3 au 8 septembre 1894.* Brussels: Polleunis et Ceuterick, 1895.

Castelein, Auguste. *La morale rationaliste et la morale chrétienne (question actuelle). Réponse au système moral de M. Denis.* Brussels: Sté belge de librairie, 1895.

Castelein, Auguste. *Le Socialisme et le Droit de Propriété.* Brussels: Goemaere, 1896.

Castelein, Auguste. "Quelques vérités sur l'agriculture et les classes rurales à vulgariser". In *3e Congrès International d'Agriculture tenu à Bruxelles du 8 au 16 Septembre 1895.* Vol. 2: *Règlement et programme. Rapports préliminaires.* Brussels: Weissenbruch, 1896, 597-617.

Castelein, Auguste. "L'Islamisme". *Revue Générale,* 33 (July 1897), 5-33.

Castelein, Auguste. "Le Judaïsme". *Revue Générale,* 33 (September 1897), 329-358 and (October 1897), 526-545.

Castelein, Auguste. *La loi belge sur les unions professionnelles.* Paris: Secrétariat de la Société d'Economie Sociale, 1898.

Castelein, Auguste. "Le contrat de travail. Discours prononcé au congrès international d'Anvers". *Bulletin du Comité central du travail industriel*, 1898, 897-898.

Castelein, Auguste. "Le Rigorisme et la question du nombre des élus". *Revue Générale*, 34 (January 1898), 40-67; (February 1898), 211-236; (March 1898), 337-364; (May 1898), 630-651 and (July 1898), 47-73.

Castelein, Auguste. *Le rigorisme, le nombre des élus et la doctrine du salut*. Paris: Ch. Poussielgue, 1898.

Castelein, Auguste. "Les dernières déclarations de Rome sur la question sociale". *Revue Générale*, 34 (December 1898), 743-760.

Castelein, Auguste. *Institutiones philosophiae moralis et socialis quas in Collegio Maximo Lovaniensi Societatis Jesu tradebat A. Castelein SJ*. Brussels: Schepens, 1899.

Castelein, Auguste. *Le rigorisme, le nombre des élus et la doctrine du salut. Seconde édition, revue et augmentée*. Brussels: Schepens, 1899.

Castelein, Auguste. *La méthode des sciences historiques*. Namur: Douxfils, 1901.

Castelein, Auguste. *La méthode des sciences sociales*. Namur-Brussels: Douxfils-Schepens, 1901.

Castelein, Auguste. "L'Encyclique 'Graves de Communi'". *Revue Générale*, 37 (September 1901), 371-381.

Castelein, Auguste. *L'Encyclique 'Graves de Communi'*. Brussels: Société belge de Librairie, 1901.

Castelein, Auguste. *Logique, logique formelle, critériologie, méthodologie*. Brussels: Schepens, 1901.

Castelein, Auguste. *Droit naturel: devoir religieux, droit individuel, droit social, droit domestique, droit civil et politique, droit international*. Paris: Lethielleux, 1903.

Castelein, Auguste. *L'Enseignement professionnel. Son utilité sociale et économique*. Schaarbeek, 1903.

Castelein, Auguste. *Cours de philosophie: morale*. Brussels: Albert Dewit, 1904.

Castelein, Auguste. *Psychologie. La Science de l'Ame dans ses rapports avec l'Anatomie, la Physiologie et l'Hypnotisme, Cours de philosophie*. Brussels: Albert Dewit, 1904.

Castelein, Auguste. "Les humanités gréco-latines et les exigences de notre prospérité économique". *Revue Générale*, 42 (February 1906), 81-112.

Castelein, Auguste. "L'État du Congo. Ses origines, ses droits, ses devoirs". *Revue Générale*, 42 (April 1906), 515-536 and (May 1906), 703-728.

Castelein, Auguste. *L'État du Congo. Ses origines, ses droits, ses devoirs*. Brussels: Dewit, 1906.

Castelein, Auguste. *L'État du Congo. Ses origines, ses droits, ses devoirs, le réquisitoire de ses accusateurs*. Brussels: Goemaere, 1907.

Castelein, Auguste. "La passion de l'amour. Le mariage. La natalité". *Revue générale*, 45 (August 1909), 161-184 and (September 1909), 353-374.

Castelein, Auguste. *Saint Paul. Valeur de son témoignage sur le Christ, l'Eglise et la doctrine du salut*. Paris-Brussels: Lethielleux-Goemaere, 1909.

Castelein, Auguste. "Syndicats ouvriers et contrat collectif". In *Conférences d'Etudes Sociales de Notre-Dame du Haut-Mont*. Lille: Ducoulombier, 1910, 216-223.

Castelein, Auguste. *Les Phénomènes de l'Hypnotisme et le Surnaturel*. Brussels: Librairie Albert Dewit, 1911.

Castelein, Auguste. *Le Surnaturel dans les apparitions et dans les guérisons de Lourdes*. Brussels: Goemaere, 1911.

Castelein, Auguste. *Droit naturel: devoir religieux, droit individuel, droit social, droit domestique, droit civil et politique, droit international. Nouvelle édition revue et complétée*. Brussels: Dewit, 1912.

Castelein, Auguste. *Léon XIII et la Question sociale. Mise au point*. Brussels: Dewit, 1914.

Castelein, Auguste. *Psychologie. La Science de l'Ame dans ses rapports avec l'Anatomie, la Physiologie et l'Hypnotisme*. Brussels: Albert Dewit, 1916.

Catalogus Provinciae Belgicae Societatis Jesu. Brussels: Greuse, 1858-1922.

Cathrein, Victor. "Property". In *The Catholic Encyclopedia*, 12. New York: Robert Appleton Company, 1911.

Chappel, James. "The Thomist Debate over Inequality and Property Rights in Depression-Era Europe". In: Rajesh Heynickx and Stéphane Symans, eds. *So What's New About Scholasticism? How Neo-Thomism Helped Shape the Twentieth Century*. Berlin-Boston: De Gruyter, 2018, 21-38.

Conférences d'Etudes Sociales de Notre-Dame du Haut-Mont, 4. Lille: Ducoulombier, 1894.

Conférences d'Etudes Sociales de Notre-Dame du Haut-Mont, 8, September 1896. Lille: Ducoulombier, 1896.

"Congrès des 23, 24 et 25 Novembre 1893 tenu à Lille. Section des œuvres sociales". *Conférences d'Etudes Sociales de Notre-Dame du Haut-Mont*. Lille: Ducoulombier, 1894, 68-72.

Congrès international de la législation douanière et de la réglementation du travail, tenu à Anvers, du 12 au 17 septembre 1898. Rapports et discussions du congrès. Antwerp: Theunis, 1898.

Congrès international de Législation du Travail tenu à Bruxelles du 27 au 30 Septembre 1897. Rapports et compte rendu analytique des séances. Brussels: Weissenbruch, 1898.

Cooreman, Gustave. *L'encyclique Rerum novarum et les industriels*. Ghent: Siffer, 1891.

Coppin, Joseph. *La question de l'évangile, Seigneur, y en aura-t-il peu de sauvés? ou Considérations sur l'écrit du R. P. Castelein, S. J. intitulé "Le rigorisme et la question du nombre des élus"*. Brussels: Société Saint-Charles Borromée, 1899.

Dallemagne, Jules. *Défense du mémoire sur la situation de l'industrie en Belgique en réponse à une lettre des évêques belges du 24 septembre 1894*. Liège: Demarteau, 1895.

De Baets, Armand. *Monseigneur I.J. du Roussaux, bisschop van Doornik (1880-1897). Een onderzoek naar zijn houding tegenover sociaal-politiek-religieuze problemen van zijn tijd*. Master thesis, KU Leuven, 1977.

De Borchgrave, Christian. *Zalig de armen van geest. Vlaanderen 1918-1940: een kerk in strijd met het moderne materialisme*. Antwerp: Vrijdag, 2019.

De Laubier, Patrick. "Un idéal historique concret de société. Le projet de Léon XIII". *Revue thomiste*, 1978, 385-412.

De Leener, Georges. *L'organisation syndicale des chefs d'industrie*. Brussels: Misch et Thron, 1909.

De Leeuw, Thijs. "Neo-Thomism and the Education of a Catholic Elite in Louvain, 1880-1914". *Trajecta*, 21 (2012), 345-372.

De Maeyer, Jan. "De Belgische Volksbond en zijn historische antecedenten". In Emmanuel Gerard, ed. *De christelijke arbeidersbeweging in België 1891-1991*. Vol. 2. Leuven: Leuven University Press, 1991, 19-65.

De Maeyer, Jan. *Arthur Verhaegen 1847-1917. De rode baron*. Leuven: Leuven University Press, 1994.

De Maeyer, Jan. "De wending van de kerk naar het volk, 1884-1926". In: Jan De Maeyer, Eddy Put, Jan Roegiers and Gerrit Vanden Bosch, eds. *Het aartsbisdom Mechelen-Brussel: 450 jaar geschiedenis*. Antwerp: Halewyn, 2010, 100-171.

De Maeyer, Jan. "'Démocratie catholique' et 'démocratie chrétienne'. Toile de fond d'une controverse idéologique à la fin du XIXe siècle". In Jan De Maeyer and Vincent Viaene, eds. *Worldviews and Worldly Wisdom: Religion, Ideology and Politics 1750-2000*. Leuven: Leuven University Press, 2016, 75-88.

De Maeyer, Jan. "Belgium from 1831: a model for the ultramontane movement in Europe or a model student of the Black International?" In Olaf Blaschke and Francisco Javier Ramon Solans, eds. *Weltreligion im Umbruch. Transnationale Perspektiven auf das Christentum in der Globalisierung*. Frankfurt-New York: Campus Verlag, 2019, 273-291.

De Maeyer, Jan, Kristien Suenens and Jo Luyten. "Louvain: le réveil religieux après la Révolution française (c. 1800-c. 1870)", in: *Dictionnaire d'histoire et de géographie ecclésiastiques*. Turnhout: Brepols Publishers, 2020, 33, col. 131-135.

De Maeyer, Jan and Leen Van Molle, eds. *Joris Helleputte (1852-1925), architect en politicus*. Vol. 1: *Biografie*. Leuven: Leuven University Press, 1998.

De Maeyer, Jan and Leen Van Molle. "Les effets de Rerum Novarum en Belgique". In: Gabrielle De Rosa, ed. *I tempi della Rerum Novarum*. Rome: Istituto Luigi Sturzo - Soveria Mannelli: Rubbettino, 2003, 133-141.

Deneef, Alain. "Promoteurs et auxiliaires". In Alain Deneef, Xavier Rousseaux et al., eds. *Les Jésuites au Congo-Zaïre. Cent ans d'épopée. De la mission du Kwango à la province d'Afrique centrale*. Brussels: AESM, 1995, 362-367.

De Raeymaeker, Louis. "Les origines de l'Institut supérieur de Philosophie de Louvain". *Revue Philosophique de Louvain*, 49 (1951) 24, 505-633.

De Raeymaeker, Louis. *Le cardinal Mercier et l'Institut supérieur de philosophie de Louvain*. Leuven: Publications universitaires de Louvain, 1952.

De Smaele, Henk. "Henry Carton de Wiart (1869-1905). Christen-democratisch politicus en literator". *Trajecta*, 4 (1995) 1, 22-41.

Dohat, Henri. "Utilité des unions de patrons et moyens de les propager". *Congrès des Œuvres sociales à Liège. Troisième session – 7-10 septembre 1890.* Vol. 3. Liège: Demarteau, 1890, 1-4.

Dujardin, Vincent. "Les jésuites et la Cour de Belgique: de Léopold Ier au Albert II". In: Alain Deneef and Xavier Rousseaux, eds. *Quatre siècles de présence jésuite à Bruxelles / Vier eeuwen jezuïeten te Brussel.* Brussels: Propopon - Leuven: KADOC, 2012, 495-517.

Durand, Jean-Dominique. "Léon XIII, Rome et le monde". In Vincent Viaene, ed. *The Papacy and the New World Order: Vatican Diplomacy, Catholic Opinion and International Politics at the Time of Leo XIII, 1878-1903.* Leuven: Leuven University Press, 2005, 55-67.

Fillon, Catherine. "La Revue catholique des institutions et du droit, le combat contre-ré-volutionnaire d'une société de gens de robe (1873-1906)". In Hervé Leuwers, Jean-Paul Barrière and Bernard Lefebvre, eds. *Élites et sociabilité au XIXe siècle: Héritages, identités.* Villeneuve d'Ascq: Publications de l'Institut de recherches historiques du Septentrion, 2001, 199-218.

Finnis, John. "Aquinas as a Primary Source of Catholic Social Teaching". In Gerard V. Bradley and E. Christian Brugger, eds. *Catholic Social Teaching: A Volume of Scholarly Essays.* Law and Christianity. Cambridge: Cambridge University Press, 2019, 11-33.

Fontaine, Théodore. *De la sensation et la pensée.* Leuven: Peeters, 1885.

Fortin, Ernest. "'Sacred and Inviolable': Rerum Novarum and Natural Rights". *Theological Studies,* 53 (June 1992), 203-233.

Gérin, Paul. *Les origines de la démocratie chrétienne à Liège.* Études sociales, 14-17. Brussels: La Pensée catholique - Paris: Office général du livre, 1958.

Gérin, Paul. "La démocratie chrétienne dans les relations Église-État à la fin du XIXe siècle. L'action de Mgr. Doutreloux". In *L'Église et l'État à l'époque contemporaine (Mélanges dédiés à la mémoire de Mgr. Aloïs Simon).* Brussels: Presses de l'Université Saint-Louis, 1975, 225-287.

Gérin, Paul. "Catholicisme social et démocratie chrétienne (1884-1904)". In: Emmanuel Gerard and Paul Wynants, eds. *Histoire du mouvement ouvrier chrétien en Belgique.* Vol. 1. Leuven: Leuven University Press, 1991, 59-113.

Gérin, Paul. "Les écoles sociales belges et la lecture de Rerum Novarum". In: *Rerum Novarum: écriture, contenu et réception d'une encyclique.* Rome: École française de Rome, 1997, 267-289.

Gérin, Paul. *Les congrès des œuvres sociales tenus à Liège en 1886, 1887 et 1890.* Liège: Commission communale de l'histoire de l'ancien pays de Liège, 2002.

Gijs, Anne-Sophie. "Entre ombres et lumières, profits et conflits. Les relations entre les Jésuites et l'État indépendant du Congo (1879-1908)". *Revue belge de philologie et d'histoire,* 88 (2010) 2, 255-298.

Godts, François-Xavier. *De paucitate salvandorum quid docuerunt sancti.* Roeselare: De Meester, 1899.

Gruel, Léon and Joseph Goemaere. *Plus de socialistes! Ligue du coin de terre et du foyer pour la reconstitution de la famille ouvrière.* Brussels: La Presse Catholique, 1896.

Habiger, Matthew H. *Papal Teaching on Private Property 1891-1981.* Lanham Md.: University Press of America, 1990.

Harmel, Léon. *Manuel d'une corporation chrétienne.* Tours: Alfred Mame et fils, 1877.

Harmel, Léon. *Catéchisme du Patron, élaboré avec le concours d'un grand nombre de théologiens.* Paris: Bureau de la Corporation, 1889.

Harmel, Léon. *Le Val des Bois et ses institutions ouvrières.* Paris: Œuvre des Cercles Catholiques d'Ouvriers, 1890.

Hartley, Thomas. *Thomistic Revival and the Modernist Era.* Toronto: Institute of Christian Thought, University of St. Michael's College, 1971.

Heyrman, Peter. "Het Werk van den Akker. Georganiseerd tuinieren met een sociale missie". In Yves Segers and Leen Van Molle, eds. *Volkstuinen. Een geschiedenis.* Leuven: Davidsfonds-KADOC – Ghent: Provincie Bestuur Oost-Vlaanderen, 2007, 37-81.

Heyrman, Peter. "Imagining the *bon patron* catholique. Industrial entrepreneurs in Belgium and Northern France, and their apostolate of the factory (1870-1914)". *Schweizerische Zeitschrift für Religions- und Kulturgeschichte,* 113 (2019), 109-134.

Hoyois, Giovanni. *Henry Carton de Wiart et le groupe de "La Justice Sociale".* Paris-Courtrai-Brussels: Vermaut, 1931.

Isaac, Isaac (sic). *Conseils pratiques sur les rapports qui doivent exister entre patrons et ouvriers: causerie faite à l'association des patrons chrétiens de Charleroi le 4 avril 1892.* Charleroi: Delacre, 1892.

Jadoulle, Jean-Louis. "Anthropologie et vision de la société chez Antoine Pottier (1849-1923)". *Revue d'histoire ecclésiastique*, 84 (1989), 30-47.

Jadoulle, Jean-Louis. *La pensée de l'abbé Pottier (1849-1923). Contribution à l'histoire de la démocratie chrétienne en Belgique*. Louvain-la-Neuve: Collège Erasme, 1991.

Jannet, Claudio. *Le Capital: la spéculation et la finance au XIXe siècle*. Paris: Plon, 1892.

Jovenaux, Jean-René. "Les congrès catholiques du Nord et du Pas-de-Calais". *Revue du Nord*, 53 (1971) 208, 155-157.

Lagasse de Locht, Charles. "Le minimum de salaire: communication faite le 26 mars à la Société d'Economie Sociale". *La Réforme Sociale*, 16 April 1892, 565-576.

Lamberts, Emiel, ed. *Een kantelend tijdperk / Une époque en mutation / Ein Zeitalter im Umbruch (1890-1910). De wending van de Kerk naar het volk in Noord-West-Europa / Le Catholicisme social dans le Nord-Ouest de l'Europe / Die Wende der Kirche zum Volk im nordwestlichen Europa*. Leuven: Leuven University Press, 1992.

Lamberts, Emiel. "Conclusies". In Emiel Lamberts, ed. *Een kantelend tijdperk / Une époque en mutation / Ein Zeitalter im Umbruch (1890-1910). De wending van de Kerk naar het volk in Noord-West-Europa / Le Catholicisme social dans le Nord-Ouest de l'Europe / Die Wende der Kirche zum Volk im nordwestlichen Europa*. Leuven: Leuven University Press, 1992, 245-251.

Lamberts, Emiel. *The Struggle with Leviathan: Social Responses to the Omnipotence of the State, 1815-1965*. Leuven: Leuven University Press, 2016.

Lamberts, Emiel and Jan Roegiers. *De Universiteit te Leuven 1425-1985*. Leuven: Universitaire Pers Leuven, 1986.

Lannoye, Maurice. *De houding van Kardinaal Goossens tegenover het arbeidersvraagstuk en de christen-democratie (1884-1906)*. Master thesis, KU Leuven, 1973.

Laurent, Theo. "Jean-Baptiste Paquet". In: *ODIS*. Record last modified date: 28 April 2015. <www.odis.be/lnk/PS_92667>.

Léon et les questions ouvrières. Discours d'ouverture par Mgr. l'évêque de Liège. Liège: Dumarteau, 1890.

Le Play, Frédéric. *L'organisation du travail selon la coutume des ateliers et la loi du Décalogue*. Tours: Alfred Mame et fils, 1870.

Les devoirs des classes dirigeantes. Discours d'ouverture par S.G. Monseigneur Doutreloux, Evêque de Liège. Liège: Demarteau, 1886.

Les devoirs des patrons envers les ouvriers. Discours de S.G. Monseigneur Doutreloux, Evêque de Liège. Liège: Demarteau, 1887.

Levie, Jean. *Michel Levie (1851-1939) et le mouvement chrétien social de son temps*. Leuven: Nauwelaerts, 1962.

Louant, Armand. "Charles Périn et Pie IX". *Bulletin de l'Institut historique belge de Rome*, 27 (1952), 181-220.

Louant, Armand. "Charles Périn". *Biographie nationale de Belgique*, 2 (1959), 666-670.

Mayeur, Jean-Marie. "Les Catholiques Dreyfusards". *Revue Historique*, 261 (1979) 2, 337-360.

Mayeur, Jean-Marie. "Le catholicisme social en France: orientations idéologiques". In Emiel Lamberts, ed. *Een kantelend tijdperk / Une époque en mutation / Ein Zeitalter im Umbruch (1890-1910). De wending van de Kerk naar het volk in Noord-West-Europa / Le Catholicisme social dans le Nord-Ouest de l'Europe / Die Wende der Kirche zum Volk im nordwestlichen Europa*. Leuven: Leuven University Press, 1992, 43-47.

Mayeur, Jean-Marie. "Quelques rencontres entre les catholiques français et les catholiques belges". *Le Mouvement social*, 178 (January-March 1997), 27-35.

Mémoire sur la situation de l'industrie en Belgique et sur la question ouvrière adopté par l'Assemblée générale des patrons catholiques. Brussels: Société belge de librairie, 1894.

Mercier, Désiré. "La théorie des trois vérités primitives". *Revue néo-scolastique*, 2 (1895) 5, 7-26.

Michel, Alain-René. "Les catholiques sociaux du Nord et les modèles belge et allemand". *Revue du Nord*, 73 (1991) 290-291, 321-328.

Michotte, Paul. "Un économiste belge. Charles Périn". *Revue Sociale Catholique*, June-July 1905, 267-293.

Montuclard, Maurice. "Aux origines de la démocratie chrétienne. L'influence du contexte socio-culturel sur les 'croyances' religieuses de divers groupes catholiques entre 1893 et 1898". *Archives de sociologie des religions*, 6 (1958), 47-90.

Naudet, Jean-Yves. "Monseigneur Freppel, un évêque engagé dans la bataille économique et sociale". In Jean-Yves Naudet. *La Doctrine sociale de l'Église*. Vol. 3: *Une réponse pertinente aux désordres du monde*. Aix-en-Provence: Presses Universitaires d'Aix-Marseille, 2018, 37-53.

Nicotra, Sébastien. *Le minimum de salaire et l'encyclique Rerum Novarum*. Brussels: Société belge de Librairie, 1893.

Pelletier, Denis. "Le catholicisme social en France (XIXe-XXe siècles). Une modernité paradoxale". In Benoît Pellistrandi, ed. *L'Histoire religieuse en France et en Espagne. Colloque international*. Madrid: Collection de la Casa de Velazquez 87, 2004, 371-387.

Périn, Charles. *Le patron, sa fonction, ses devoirs, ses responsabilités*. Lille: Desclée-de Brouwer, 1886.

Périn, Charles. *L'économie politique d'après l'encyclique sur la condition des ouvriers*. Paris: Librairie Lecoffre, 1891.

Périn, Charles. *Note sur le juste salaire d'après l'encyclique Rerum novarum*. Mons: Desguin, 1892.

Perrier, Joseph-Louis. *The Revival of Scholastic Philosophy in the Nineteenth Century*. New York: Columbia University Press, 1909.

Piepers, Norbert. *La Revue générale de 1865 à 1940. Essai d'analyse du contenu*. Paris-Leuven: Nauwelaerts, 1968.

Python, Francis. "La genèse de Rerum Novarum". *Sources*, 37 (May-June 2011) 3, 149-153.

Rerum Novarum: écriture, contenu et réception d'une encyclique. Rome: École française de Rome, 1997.

Schultenover, David G. "Luis Martín García, the Jesuit General of the Modernist Crisis (1892-1906): On Historical Criticism." *The Catholic Historical Review*, 89 (2003) 3, 434-463.

Schyrgens, Joseph. "Le Révérend Père Casteleyn". *Revue Générale*, 1922, 339-348.

Soixante-Quinzième Anniversaire de la Fondation des Facultés de Philosophie et des Sciences, 1845-1921. Namur: Wesmael-Charlier, 1921.

Steel, Carlos. "Thomas en de vernieuwing van de filosofie. Beschouwingen bij het thomisme van Mercier". *Tijdschrift voor filosofie*, 53 (1991), 44-89.

[Steyaert, Auguste.] *Vijftigjarig jubelfeest van het instellen der congregatie van jongelingen*. Leuven: Peeters-Ruelens, 1885.

Struyker Boudier, Cees. *Wijsgerig leven in Nederland, België en Luxemburg 1880-1980*. Vol. 1: *De Jezuïeten*. Nijmegen: Katholiek Studiecentrum, 1985.

Suenens, Kristien. "Belgian Jesuits and their Labourer Retreats (c. 1890-1914)". In Urs Altermatt, Jan De Maeyer and Franziska Metzger, eds. *Religious Institutes and Catholic Culture in 19th and 20th-Century Europe*. Leuven: Leuven University Press, 2014, 161-176.

Suenens, Kristien. *'Too robust to be saint'. Female Congregation Founders in 19th-century Belgium: Double-Voiced Agency, Religious Entrepreneurship and Gender Tension*. Doctoral dissertation, KU Leuven, 2018.

Talmy, Robert. *Une forme hybride de catholicisme social: L'Association Catholique des Patrons du Nord (1884-1895)*. Lille: Lille Facultés Catholiques, 1962.

Teixeira, Pedro and Almodovar, António. "Catholic in its faith, Catholic in its manner of conceiving science: French Catholic Political Economy in the 1830's". *The European Journal of the History of Economic Thought*, 19 (2012) 2, 197-225.

Teixeira, Pedro and Almodovar, António. "Economics and Theology in Europe from the 19th Century: From Early 19th Century's Christian Political Economy to Modern Catholic Social Doctrine". In Paul Oslington, ed. *The Oxford Handbook of Christianity and Economics*. Oxford: Oxford University Press, 2014, 113-134.

Trimouille, Pierre. *Léon Harmel et l'usine chrétienne du Val des Bois (1840-1914): fécondité d'une expérience sociale*. Lyon: Centre d'histoire du catholicisme, 1974.

Union Nationale pour le redressement des Griefs. *Congrès des œuvres sociales à Liège, 26-29 septembre 1886*. Liège: Demarteau, 1886.

Van Riet, Georges. "Originalité et fécondité de la notion de philosophie élaborée par le Cardinal Mercier". *Revue Philosophique de Louvain*, 79 (1981) 44, 532-565.

Velaers, Jan. *Albert I. Koning in tijden van oorlog en crisis, 1909-1934*. Tielt: Lannoo, 2009.

Verdoodt, Jos. *Kerk en christen-democratie. De Katholieke Kerk tegenover de christen-democratie in België, inzonderheid tegenover de door haar als dissident beschouwde priester Adolf Daens en diens medestanders (1890-1907)*. PhD dissertation, Ghent University, 1988.

Verhaegen, Arthur. *Le minimum de salaire*. Ghent: Siffer, 1892.

Vermeersch, Arthur. *Manuel social. La législation et les œuvres en Belgique*. Leuven: Uystpruyst – Paris: Giard & Brière, 1904.

Wheeler, Ferdinand C. "Social Works of Ours in Belgium". *Woodstock Letters*, 39 (October 1910), 364-365.

Willaert, Leopold. "Casteleyn, August". In *Biographie nationale*, 30. Brussels: Bruylant, 1959, 269-270.

Wils, Kaat. *De omweg van de wetenschap. Het positivisme en de Belgische en Nederlandse intellectuele cultuur 1845-1914*. Amsterdam: Amsterdam University Press, 2005, 326-341.

Woeste, Charles. *Mémoire pour servir à l'histoire contemporaine de la Belgique*. Vol. 2: *1894-1914*. Brussels: Dewit, 1927.

Arthur Vermeersch. Photo by Emile Morren, c 1910.
[Leuven, KADOC: Image archive of the Southern Belgian Jesuit Province, 1535]

ARTHUR VERMEERSCH ON COLONIAL AND CONJUGAL MORALITY
A PRESENTIST APPROACH TO SAINT THOMAS*

VINCENT GENIN

An intellectual renewal

The Thomist revival of the last third of the nineteenth century had a particular, if not unparalleled, resonance at the University of Leuven. Bishop Gioacchino Pecci, who would become Pope Leo XIII, had been interested in the thought of St. Thomas Aquinas (1225-1274) since his early years in the diocese of Perugia. Since the 1850s – notably with Fr. Liberatore, Fr. Gratry and Canon Dupont – Thomas' social philosophy had been a source of inspiration for a growing number of Catholic intellectuals, offering a way out of Cartesian spiritualism or scholasticism as it had been modified by eighteenth-century rationalism. The author of *Summa* seemed more adapted to the end of the nineteenth century and its spiritual and social crises than Suárez, who was more aligned with the absolutist atmosphere of the sixteenth and seventeenth centuries.[1] From the early weeks of his pontificate Leo XIII engendered a strong wind of renewal in the Catholic Church. The harmonisation of the theses of Christian anthropology with new medical and psychological knowledge and the need to make the Church enter into dialogue with social, political and intellectual modernity, but also with positivism and scientism,

* I want to thank Peter Heyrman (KADOC-KU Leuven) and Wim Decock (KU Leuven) for their suggestions.
1 Aubert, "Die Enzyklika 'Aeterni Patris'"; Viaene, "Introduction. Réalité et image sous le pontificat de Léon XIII", 30 and sqq. On neo-Thomism: Heynickx and Symons, eds., *So What's New About Scholasticism?* (and the article of Chappel, "The Thomist Debate over Inequality and Property Rights in Depression-Era Europe"). See also Chappel, *Catholic Modern*.

were at the heart of his project. For this reason he published the encyclical *Aeterni Patris* on 4 August 1879. This text can be considered as the founding act of neo-Thomism, wishing to return to the doctrine of St. Thomas, because "reason, carried on the wings of St. Thomas to the summit of human intelligence, can hardly rise higher, and faith can hardly hope for more or more powerful help from reason than that which St. Thomas provides".[2]

In Rome, especially at the Gregorian University, the pope renews the ecclesiastical body, although Suárez's teaching remains very present there. He entrusted the Dominicans with the task of making a critical edition of the works of St. Thomas.[3] In the face of Roman resistance, Leo XIII quickly thought of making Leuven the intellectual and vital seat of the Thomistic revival. He intended to create a special chair of Thomist philosophy there despite the reluctance of the Belgian bishops who, at the time, were in the middle of the school war and feared both the financial cost of this intellectual project and the fact that it could feed the anticlerical opposition. This teaching was entrusted in 1882 to a young professor of the seminary of Mechelen, Désiré Mercier. Influenced by Canon Dupont's Thomism, he was made aware of the fact that in Italy, Thomas was studied without taking into account modern philosophy. Dupont communicated to him the idea that to be too faithful to Thomas' doctrine is to be unfaithful to his spirit. He introduced him to an "open Thomism".[4]

On 27 October 1882, Mercier gave the first course of "haute philosophie de Saint-Thomas".[5] He responded to the spirit of the encyclical of 1879, insofar as, for him, philosophical speculation must be anchored in the real, in a world where positivism dominates; he was moreover open to intellectuals embodying this movement: he thus attended Professor Charcot's psychiatry classes in Paris in 1887 and gave his students, outraged by Descartes or Kant, the philosopher Joseph Delboeuf to read. A Belgian student of Charcot, the latter was a specialist in hypnosis whose work was analysed by Freud.[6] Mercier attracted many students and the Higher Institute of Philosophy of Leuven was founded in 1889. In-depth courses were added to the cursus to deal with special cases of application of the doctrine of St. Thomas to situations specific to modernity. The *Revue néo-scolastique* was founded in 1894, the *Revue catholique de droit* in 1898 and the *Revue sociale catholique* a year earlier.[7] As Peter Heyrman points out, this intellectual atmosphere contributes to creating a fashion effect: it is good to quote Thomas, even if it means instrumentalising him, interpreting him excessively with regard to his time, and making him an

---

2   Quoted in Aubert, "Désiré Mercier et les débuts de l'Institut de Philosophie", 148.
3   Jaccard, "La renaissance thomiste dans l'Église", 139.
4   Aubert, "Le Cardinal Mercier, un prélat d'avant-garde", 268.
5   Id., "Désiré Mercier et les débuts de l'Institut de Philosophie", 151; Tambuyser, "L'érection de la chaire de philosophie thomiste à Louvain".
6   Rizzo, "Les chemins de Delboeuf".
7   Heyrman, "Belgian Catholic Entrepreneurs' organisations", 167.

author who can serve a progressive as well as a conservative discourse (we will see this with Arthur Vermeersch, an author oscillating, depending on the question, between conservatism and progressivism).[8]

The reception of *Aeterni Patris* in Belgium experienced a decisive revival in 1884, with the beginning of a thirty-year period of Catholic governments and the structuring of social Catholicism around the Congresses of Liège (1886, 1887 and 1890).[9] It deals with the workers' question and its solutions: neo-Thomism finds a field of development there, with personalities such as Victor Brants and, more broadly, Theodore Fontaine, Léon de Lantsheere, Simon Deploige and Maurice Defourny.[10]

This dynamic was not met with unanimous approval either in Leuven or in Rome. In 1896, the Congregation for Studies, headed by Cardinal Mazzella, opposed the ratification of the Institute. It demanded that the courses be given in Latin, not in French. The situation calmed down in 1898. Some people were worried about the liberties taken by Mercier with regard to Thomism, at a time when the expression 'neo-Thomism' was becoming more and more widespread. Critics felt that Thomas' thought should not be too much mixed up with the natural and modern sciences. To this, those close to Mercier replied that the true Thomist is one who does not interpret Thomas' thought in a narrow way, but rather one who adapts it to his time, preserving the spirit of the Saint. This perspective has often been synthesised as follows: "For us, St. Thomas is a beacon, not a landmark". The Dominicans will play an important role in the promotion of neo-Thomism, but it was the seculars and the Jesuits who were among the first intellectuals to defend this dynamic, which is more a matter of philosophy than of Thomistic theology.[11] Among these Jesuits, Arthur Vermeersch occupies a central position. In this contribution, I will not deal with his work as a canonist or as a sociologist in depth, but rather with his moralist reflection, in particular in the field of conjugal morality.

Jesuit Father Arthur Vermeersch (1858-1936)[12] was a theologian, a moralist, a canonist, but also a sociologist – insofar as this notion had not yet been stabilised. This Christian intellectual enjoyed significant international influence in the renewal of moral theology around 1900. He was open to psychology and sociology, which was still considered a heterodox position by many theologians. He developed a more empirical methodology than his predecessors, attached to the real. The renewal embodied in neo-Thomism cannot be

---

8   See Peter Heyrman's contribution in this book.
9   Gérin, "Les congrès sociaux de Liège".
10 Wils, "België in de negentiende eeuw", 35 and sqq.; see the contribution of Joeri De Smet in this book.
11 Mayeur, Review of Rossini, ed., *Aspetti della cultura cattolica nell'éta di Leone XIII*.
12 Creusen, "In Memoriam"; Id., "Le vœu d'abnégation du R.P. A. Vermeersch"; Id., *Le Père A. Vermeersch, S.J., l'homme et l'œuvre*; Ceriani, "P. Arturo Vermeersch, theologo moralista", 402; *The Catholic Encyclopedia and its makers*, 178; Bergh, "Vermeersch, Arthur".

conceived without considering the renewal that Vermeersch wished to apply to moral theology. Moral theology broke free from dogmatism as early as the sixteenth century and, according to the moralists who have traced the history of this discipline, it declined into three periods: the Patristic Age, the Scholastic Age and the post-Tridentine era.[13]

Vermeersch is in favour of the neo-scholastic method, to the detriment of positive and moral theology. Neo-Thomistic moral theology is conceived by him as the science which, starting from the articles of faith, gives the rules to human acts. This theology (which is advantageous to a philosophy) does not concern only duties and sin, but proposes a more global scope. Through this approach, Vermeersch reappropriates this field of thought, formerly treated by ascetic and mystical theologians. Faithful to St. Thomas, he does not separate dogmatics from morality. In short, he gives theology a scientific framework.[14]

Arthur Vermeersch was sometimes confronted with opposition. His conception of a broader and deeper moral theology marked one of his Gregorian students, Charles Robert:

> From the top of his pulpit, in the filthy semi-darkness of the ancient Gregorian, in Rome, Fr. Vermeersch never ceased to demand the right of citizenship for a professor of morals who consented to be just that. For, at the time, around 1925, in order to impose himself, this man still had to take something else, preferably canon law, since his subject did not seem to provide him with a sufficient title in the world of theologians.[15]

In an article he wrote in 1929, Vermeersch makes it clear that the sources of morality have been misused. Coming from Scripture and the Apostolic Tradition, moral theology is conceived by the Jesuit, as a good neo-Thomist, as "born from Heaven to come down to Earth". Consequently, the moralist must be a protagonist of the century and deal with the social and economic questions before his eyes.[16]

Vermeersch asked that old arguments of moral theology be the object of an aggiornamento. In doing so, he did not fail to show his attachment to some basic principles: according to him, the field had to remain supernatural. Moral theology is revealed from God and then turns to him. The personal love of Christ made possible the double love of God and men. Vermeersch was an innovative author, to the extent that he wished to break with a morality that would boil down to an inventory of the sins of humanity, as described in the old penitential books, the *Summae confessorum* or *Modi Confitendi*. He

---

13 Mahoney, *The Making of Moral Theology*; Gallagher, *Time Past, Time Future*; Keenan, *History of Catholic Moral*.
14 De Franceschi, "La théologie morale catholique", 120.
15 Robert, "Chronique de théologie morale fondamentale", quoted in De Franceschi, "La théologie morale catholique", 120.
16 Vermeersch, "Soixante ans de théologie morale".

criticised the traditional rhetoric of injunction, prohibition and fear, in which sin, whether venial or mortal, dominated thinking.[17] Vermeersch clearly preferred more rational, moral teachings, based on duties and advice. Their formulation was linked to an experimental knowledge of society, keeping in mind the order of virtues, in the spirit of St. Thomas. It favoured the promotion of the virtue of chastity over the condemnation of sin. Doctrine (*principia*), cases (*responsa*) and the search for perfection (*consilia*) were the main milestones of this intellectual renewal. A theology in which obligation was central gave way to mysticism and evangelical counsel. In an account which it devoted in 1924 to its *Epitome iuris Canonici* (published with the Jesuit J. Creusen), the *Revue thomiste* underlines the "celebrity of R.P. Vermeersch in canonical science" and illustrates his way of thinking and his return to the thought of St. Thomas. The review returns to the commentaries of canon 1366 which prescribes that teachers follow the teaching of Thomas. Vermeersch's commentary reduces the scope of what the Code says: he uses the word *principia* to limit the meaning of the word *doctrinam*. For him, it is enough to stick to the scholastic method and the fundamental theses of St. Thomas to be faithful to the prescriptions of the Church. One must stick to the "principles of solution" (*principia*) to a question dealt with by Thomas, to his doctrine (*doctrinam*) if he has dealt with the question, or to his method (*rationem*) if no principle or doctrine is at his disposal.[18]

This openness to the world, to other disciplines and to an expertise that took it out of the circle of church people manifested in its various interests. His reflections on marital morality were largely nourished by the literature produced by the medical profession. Concerned about the rise of individualism in Western society at the end of the nineteenth century, he drew the attention of his fellow men to the importance of social justice, charity and social duties. Geographical openness and concern for the moral and social conditions of human beings were clearly felt in his texts on Congo.

The man

Turning towards the man himself, this part of the article outlines Vermeersch's biography.[19] Arthur Vermeersch was born in Ertvelde, in the region of Ghent. After four years of humanities at the Episcopal College of Dendermonde and two others at the Jesuit College of Saint-Servais in Liège, where he particularly distinguished himself, he continued his studies at the University Faculties of Namur and then at the Catholic University of Leuven. As a Doctor of Civil Law and Political and Administrative Sciences, in 1881 he began a decade of study

17 de Ghellinck and Gilleman, "Arthur Vermeersch".
18 *Revue thomiste*, 1924, nouvelle série, VII, 526.
19 de Ghellinck and Gilleman, "Arthur Vermeersch".

in which his literary, philosophical and theological training were particularly advanced. After entering the novitiate of the Society of Jesus in Drongen in 1879, he studied for several years at the Gregorian University in Rome. Ordained as a priest in 1889, a Doctor of Theology and Canon Law, and armed with a significant weight of intellectual baggage, he began to teach canon law and then morals at the scholasticate of his order in Leuven in 1893. For twenty-five years he did not leave his home base. In 1918, he succeeded Father Buccheroni to the chair of Moral Theology at the Gregorian University. There, at the apex of his discipline and at the heart of the teaching of his favourite subject, he held this position until 1934. Consequently, as his interests and publications grew, he was entrusted with sociology and philosophy of law courses.

He began his career as a canonist, publishing in 1897 a commentary on Leo XIII's constitution *Officiorum ac munerum* on the censorship and prohibition of books. He continued in 1902 with *De Religiosis institutis et personis tractatus canonico-moralis*. These are the first steps of a work that would count forty-four books, the crowning achievement of which is undoubtedly his *Theologiae moralis principia*. Consultant to the Belgian episcopate, adviser to the Roman courts, consultor to the Congregations of the Council, the Sacraments and the Religious, Vermeersch was also a man of great influence, whose ideas were often adopted by Cardinal Mercier and then by the pope. A first climax was his contribution to the codification of canon law in 1904.

As a 'sociologist', at a time when this terminology was less popular in Belgium than in France[20], Vermeersch benefited from a fertile ground, both geographically and circumstantially. In Leuven, he was in an environment and context where critical sociology was in the process of being integrated into theological thinking. This 'strategic opening', as Kaat Wils labelled it, rested on the capacity of the Leuven Institute of Philosophy, directed by Désiré Mercier, to include new social sciences in its curriculum. The School of Political and Social Sciences, founded in 1892 by the lawyer Jules Van den Heuvel, a conservative Catholic who as Minister of Justice would be tempted to censor a whole body of literature advocating contraception, was reluctant to accept these new perspectives. In 1896 he asked the rector of Leuven not to introduce a course in sociology, arguing that "Sociology today is more often than not a poor philosophy hidden behind long quotations of more or less picturesque customs and morals".[21] Mercier's intellectual, but also political, strategy can be summed up as follows: that the sociology developed by Émile Durkheim – whose adherence to French secularism was poorly measured at the time – should act as a bulwark against Marxism.[22]

20   Mosbah-Natanson, *Une "mode" de la sociologie*.
21   Gerard, *Sociale Wetenschappen aan de Katholieke Universiteit te Leuven*, 30.
22   Baubérot, "Durkheim et la laïcité"; Wils, "Les intellectuels catholiques et la sociologie en Belgique".

As an academic discipline, sociology was still in its infancy in Belgium. It aroused mistrust. The one who was most likely to teach it was the jurist Victor Brants, who was very much influenced by the school of Frédéric Le Play. He believed however, like his teacher, that sociology was nothing but a manifestation of positivism and socialism.[23] When he founded the Société d'Economie Sociale in 1881, together with his colleague from Liège Charles De Jace, he did so without any sociological or proto-sociological perspective. In Leuven in 1893, Mercier entrusted a new course in the history of economic and political doctrines to the jurist Simon Deploige and a chair in the history of social theories to the philosopher Maurice Defourny.[24] The latter had followed the teachings of Gabriel Tarde and Émile Durkheim and was influenced by the German historical school of Gustav von Schmoller, with whom many young Belgian intellectuals were perfecting their skills, including the jurist Ernest Mahaim or the historian Henri Pirenne.

And it is to Deploige that Mercier entrusted the 'sociology' province of this intellectual field. He did not wish to position it in opposition with morality but, on the contrary, he wanted to make it a means of highlighting this morality, which he had renovated and rethought in the light of the new mores of the time. One of his strategies was a harsh polemic with Durkheim (notably in the *Revue Néo-Scolastique*, in 1909), reproaching him for developing a positivism that was opposed to morality, even if it meant forgetting too quickly the importance that the French sociologist gave to the category of the sacred in morality. Arthur Vermeersch fully integrates this movement of re-appropriation of sociology by moral theology, so that this new science did not reduce religion to a simple 'social fact' or epiphenomenon. Saint Thomas is considered a 'sociologist' in his own way, long before Comte or Durkheim, and allows, through his doctrine, to build a moral science whose *ancilla* would be sociology (re-founded by this new configuration).[25] The function of neo-Thomism is to emancipate the social sciences in a context where the social question, which has been clearly posed since the 1840s in Western Europe, must be resolved by cooperation between employers and workers, by a new corporatist social order and not by a socialist solution. Showing signs of fraternity with regard to religious sociology, Vermeersch believed, however, that it could only be practised from the inside, that is to say, from a reflection proposed by a Catholic author. The Catholicity of the author was a determining factor. Vermeersch, sometimes in collaboration with his fellow Jesuit Albert Müller, was the author of a *Manuel social* in 1900 and a *Guide social de Belgique* in 1911, presenting a kind of critical repertory of social legislation and works.

23   Brants, "La part de la méthode de Le Play dans les études sociales en Belgique"; De Bie, *Naissance et premiers développements de la sociologie en Belgique*; Deferme and De Maeyer, "Entre sciences sociales et politiques"; Dejace, "Frédéric Le Play"; Gerard, *Sociale Wetenschappen*; Wils and Rasmussen, "La sociologie en perspective transnationale".

24   See Joeri De Smet's article in this book.

25   Ibid.

Colonial morality

Canonist and sociologist, Vermeersch was also and above all a moralist. In addition to his positions on conjugal morality, to which I will devote the rest of this reflection, he made himself known by means of his positions on the Belgian Congo. And, more precisely, on the takeover (i.e. annexation) of the Belgian Congo, the personal property of Leopold II, by the Belgian state, the debate on which was in full swing in 1906-1908. Leo XIII had been one of the most faithful allies of the Congolese project of Leopold II, with whom he maintained regular correspondence, particularly since the Berlin conference of 1885.[26] The king took the stance of the 'Christian prince' relying upon the role played by the missionaries. This mutual understanding lasted until the years 1903-1905, at a time when Pius X was increasingly sensitive to international investigations into atrocities committed in the Congo and where the role of the missions was sometimes questioned. It was in this climate of cooling between the Holy See and Brussels that in 1906 the Vatican supported Vermeersch's critical book *La Question congolaise*.[27]

This book was, among other issues, an opportunity for Vermeersch to criticise a too narrow reading of St. Thomas. In a chapter entitled "La ligne d'Alexandre VI: une digression", he draws a parallel between Pope Alexander VI's *Inter Caetera* bull (1493), providing for a division of the lands of the New World between Spain and Portugal, and the 1885 Berlin Conference on Central Africa. Vermeersch opposes the interpretation of canonists, economists and historians that the 1493 text is an application of medieval principles on universal property "which Christ bequeathed to his Vicar".[28] This universal sharing couldn't please Vermeersch, especially on a political level, since he saw its doctrine within socialism. Faithful to Vitoria but also to the tradition of Jesuit thought, he did not think that the pope's jurisdiction gave him private property. As for the bull, he criticised the commentators of St. Thomas who interpreted it, Cardinal Cajetan[29] and Cardinal Bellarmin[30]. They saw it as a privilege granted to Madrid and Lisbon to bring Catholicism to these lands

---

26   Viaene, "La religion du Prince", 173-179.
27   Ibid., 188.
28   Vermeersch, *La question congolaise*, 41.
29   Alias Thomas de Vio (1469-1534), Italian theologian and philosopher. Apostolic Legate to the Diet of Augsburg (1518), trying to convince Martin Luther to stop his schismatic project, he is one of the inspirers of the bull *Exsurge domine* of 1519. He was one of the first commentators on St. Thomas (his *Summa Theologica*) to draw a logical and systematic interpretation from it (Laurent, "Cajétan (Thomas de Vio)").
30   Roberto Francesco Romolo Bellarmino (1542-1621), Italian Jesuit, theologian and apologist. He completed his studies in Leuven and taught the thought of St. Thomas at the Jesuit theologate. Close to Pope Paul V, he contributed to the condemnation of Giordano Bruno. He was canonised in 1930 and proclaimed Doctor of the Church the following year. See Brodrick, *Robert Bellarmine*.

and to protect the converted. For Vermeersch, considering himself faithful to the spirit of Thomas and to an attachment to empires and the social effects of religious decisions, he sees in this text a much wider implication. Indirectly, Vermeersch questions the Congo, which is contemporary to him. One can no longer limit oneself to the image of a land conquered by philanthropy (he points out that no "philanthropist" was interested in the opinion "of the main interested parties: the Congolese") and in a moral concern for evangelisation.[31]

The question of the civilisation and morality of the 'natives' is at the heart of Vermeersch's concerns. These concerns were mainly directed towards the fate of the Jesuit missionaries, whom Vermeersch found particularly neglected by the Leopoldian administration of the Independent State of the Congo. He did not hesitate to enter the public arena. In the context of the agitated parliamentary debates of the spring of 1906, he published *La question congolaise* and, faithful to his methodology, both empirical and drawing on the most diverse sources, he based his work on the report of the British Commission of Inquiry denouncing the abuses perpetrated by Congo Free State officials in the territory. Although he refrained from attacking the king – who, as we now know, was quite irritated by the Jesuit – Vermeersch emphasised the incoherent nature of a project that wished to combine two irreconcilable objectives, namely material enrichment and civilisation. It is reasonable to think that Vermeersch's attack was intended to be defused by his hierarchy within the Society of Jesus. Indeed, a document written by the Jesuit censor of his book clearly reports that: "The whole Belgian Society is supposed to speak through Vermeersch" and "if the interest of the black man excuses the author's audacity, does not the same interest defend him from exposing the missions to the malevolence of the almighty sovereign".[32] The Belgian Society of Jesus, as always avoiding being linked exclusively to one of the conflicting factions in the Catholic Party, asked one of its other members Auguste Castelein (1840-1922) to write a more moderate piece on the issue.[33] His analysis, somewhat an intellectual antidote, openly applauded the achievements of the king. Castelein had strong ties with the royal court and the conservative faction of the party, led by Charles Woeste.[34] They vehemently criticised Vermeersch' authority on the issue, for never having visited Africa. Vermeersch finally went in 1913, Castelein never did.

---

31 Vermeersch, *La question congolaise*, 46.
32 Leuven, KADOC-KU Leuven, Archief Jezuïeten – Belgische (1832-1935) en Vlaamse (1935-) Provincie – Provincia Belgica and Provincia Belgica Septentrionalis (hereafter ABSE), 21229.
33 Gijs, "Entre ombres et lumières, profits et conflits".
34 See Peter Heyrman's contribution in this book.

Conjugal morality

It is as a moralist that Vermeersch leaves his most enduring work. Placing scholastic theses at the heart of his moral theology, he published in 1901 *Quaestiones de justitia ad usum hodiernum scholastice disputatae* and later *Quaestiones de virtutibus religionis et pietatis*. If this Christian intellectual presented a remarkable eclecticism between different categories of thought, this richness can be found within his work as a moralist. He was interested in questions such as lying, probabilism and tolerance (in the sense of the relationship of the state with the different confessions it contains), to which he devoted a book in 1912.[35] A few years after the separation of Church and State in France and after having welcomed many Jesuits expelled from France, where they could no longer practice their teaching, Vermeersch did not write in the abstract but in an intellectual context of an empirical nature.

But his main field of reflection as a moralist focuses on marital morality. In that field, he is among the harshest opponents of the influence of late-nineteenth-century neo-Malthusianism. Campaigning for the limitation of births with regard to limited terrestrial resources, the neo-Malthusians revived the thought of Robert Malthus at the end of the nineteenth century in France. Coming from socialist, pacifist and libertarian circles (Paul Robin or the writer Octave Mirbeau), they add several aspects to Malthus' theory. According to them, limiting births was a way of giving fewer soldiers, fewer miserable workers and fewer prostitutes to the industrial upper bourgeoisie who wanted a "revanche" against Germany and to produce "chair à canon".[36]

In 1909, Vermeersch published a programmatic article in the *Nouvelle Revue Théologique*, which he entitled "Un grave péril moral". In his mind, it is clear that neo-Malthusianism, carrying with it the defence of contraceptive practices which the Church condemns, is a phenomenon intrinsically linked to socialism. The latter was then in full expansion in Belgium, where it had had parliamentary seats for about ten years: "Spread by announcements, conferences, books, this vice invades us, threatens to overwhelm us. People join together to propagate it; a whole party, the Socialist Party, declares itself to be its advocate"[37], writes Vermeersch. Myth or reality? The Jesuit does not speak from nothing. We know that socialist newspapers, such as *La Bataille de Liège*, declared themselves neo-Malthusians (the limitation of births being considered as a means against worker precariousness) in a series of articles published in 1908, a few months before Vermeersch's reflection.[38] We also know that the thing is not new and that the Catholic power was very attentive to this

35   Vermeersch, *La tolérance*.
36   Drouard, "Aux origines de l'eugénisme en France".
37   Vermeersch, "Un grave péril moral", 65.
38   Stengers, "Les pratiques anticonceptionnelles", 1157.

phenomenon.[39] Auguste Castelein also condemned socialism ("contrary to the natural freedom of the person"; "criminal enterprise") and at the same time dealt with questions of birth rate.[40] A man we have already met, Jules Van den Heuvel, Minister of Justice from 1899 to 1907, would go on to suggest censoring in the context of a press offence and article 383 of the Penal Code on insult to morals. In the brochure published by Greuell, *Plus de grossesse*, Van den Heuvel writes to the Public Prosecutor's Office:

> Under the guise of a more or less scientific work, the author of the brochure directly favours, in my opinion, with the shameful aim of making a profit, the debauchery of his readers. If his text sounds decent, it is pure tactic. While appearing to be interested only in the well-being of married people, he is in fact addressing everyone: the popularisation of the condom ring he advocates is for the benefit of all those, men or women, married or not, who are tempted by debauchery. One cannot be fooled by the pseudo-scientific tone chosen by the author. To close one's eyes would be to give a real bonus to the skill of public corrupters.[41]

In the interests of equality before the law, and for the sake of consistency, another pamphlet entitled *Plus d'avortements* also had to be censored.

The nervousness of the Belgian Catholic elite regarding the issue of contraception, both in the political and religious fields, is largely due to the rapid, if not sudden, evolution of morals in their country. In contrast, France experienced a liberalisation of bourgeois marital relations during the nineteenth century, so much so that the Church, in order not to lose a large mass of believers, had to come to terms with such a situation. It was a real trench warfare over moral issues. In February 1908, Cardinal Mercier wanted to take a stand on this issue and opened it up to the Belgian episcopate. He quickly took advice from Vermeersch, whose influence would continue to grow, both in Mercier's network and in the Vatican. The Jesuit spoke clearly to the Primate of Belgium about the "action of the enemy".[42] The ideology to be defeated was neo-Malthusianism. He was aware that it could only be attacked by a moralisation of couples who use contraception. This led him to write his 1909 text on the 'peril'. This was an important moment in the evolution of moral theology at the beginning of the twentieth century. Vermeersch imposed a new style of writing and a new tone, rather rigorous and belonging to a moral theology 'à la belge' as Jean Stengers would say, compared to a more permissive French conception. This had a certain influence in Belgium,

39 Belgium was ruled by Catholic governments from 1884 to 1914.
40 Castelein, "Etude sur le socialisme", and Id., "La passion de l'amour". Simon Deploige's positions against socialism are also significant (see the article by Joeri De Smet in this book).
41 Jules Van den Heuvel to the Public Prosecutor, 12 October 1899 (Parquet C.A., n°191).
42 Mechelen, Archives Archdiocese Mechelen-Brussels (hereafter AAM), Fonds Mercier, dossier 'Réunion des évêques belges, 1906-1910': Arthur Vermeersch to Cardinal Mercier, 8 February 1907.

in line with the moral and theological heritage of Father Jean-Baptiste Bouvier (1783-1854), but Vermeersch seems to have been little affected by this movement.[43]

Vermeersch, along with demographer Camille Jacquart, helped to forge Mercier's personal opinion on the question of the birth rate. He submitted to him a note entitled "General Instruction to the Believers" about Christian marriage and the "absolute prohibition of practices contrary to the first purpose of marriage". The procreative end goal of the sexual act goes back to St. Thomas and St. Augustine, if we follow Vermeersch's reasoning.[44] However, it is very likely that the case of marital morality represents an example of a posteriori instrumentalisation of the thought of St. Thomas. As already mentioned, following Peter Heyrman, the legitimacy that the neo-Thomistic authors seek in this great reference has sometimes justified their positions on socio-economic issues that had not been envisaged or known to St. Thomas, but which some nineteenth-century Catholic intellectuals thought they would resolve in the spirit of Thomas' doctrine. According Vermeersch, the sexual act was legitimate if: 1) penetration took place in the 'due vessel' (*penetratio vasis debiti*); 2) there was ejaculation; 3) the woman withheld semen. This last point refers to the 'Crime of Onan' in *Genesis* chapter 38, describing the loss of semen which inspired great divine anger. It is, in other words, the condemnation of *coitus interruptus*. This 'onanism', which is not yet synonymous with masturbation, is a mortal sin, an "intrinsic and gravitating evil", Vermeersch wrote in 1919.[45] If the main target of his note are couples, another group that this small informal think tank around Mercier wants to reach are priests and confessors. We know how important the director of conscience was in nineteenth- and early twentieth-century societies, especially among female believers.[46] Vermeersch wants to address women. He wants "precise instructions" to be sent to the confessors on "the firm conduct to be taken to prevent the invasion of Malthusian practices in the cities that are still free".[47] He asks the confessor to harden his positions, breaking with what the existing moral theology foresaw. The confessor is not entitled to treat in the same way a woman who speaks in confession of a husband using a condom or practicing *coitus interruptus*. In 1908, he called for a structured response from the Church, which in his eyes was acting in a way that was too dispersed. In his note "Against the progress of immorality", he confided to the cardinal, in a very worried tone, the need to act quickly: "It is important to know this; in the city and among the well-off, the most ordinary 'condom' method is the use of a condom. What right do confessors have, therefore, without inquiring about the pro-

43   Pelletier, *Les catholiques en France*, 82 and sqq. See Langlois, *Le 'Crime d'Onan'*.
44   Wils and Di Spurio, "Sexualité"; Christens, "De orthodoxie van het zaad". See also Burggraeve, "Historical Building Blocks for a Consistent Relational and Sexual Ethics".
45   Vermeersch, *De Castitate et de vitiis contrariis*, 266.
46   Müller, *Une histoire intime des catholiques*.
47   AAM, Fonds Mercier, dossier 'Réunion des évêques belges, 1906-1910': Arthur Vermeersch to Cardinal Mercier, 7 February 1907, annexes.

cedure, to assume that the husband simply withdraws, and allow the wife to be approached by the onanist husband?"[48] He wants a "firmness of the confessional". He no longer wants this place of confidence to be a place of connivance and laxity which would be the consequence of several years of frequenting the same penitent: "The silences (of the confessors) let the abuse take hold; they often go through connivance. After some time, abusive practices become commonplace; opinion itself becomes vitiated. It becomes morally impossible to react. And on the outside the Church has the effect of being without serious power over morals. She does not obtain from her faithful that superior honesty which would form one of her most persuasive apologies."[49] In 1909, Mercier published a pastoral letter on the duties of married life.

Vermeersch's influence was clear in this hardening of moral theology 'à la belge' about marital morality. It was a question of cutting short not only neo-Malthusianism but also the growing tolerance which had come from France and to which the space was becoming more and more sensitive. The confessor could no longer be satisfied with advising but rather had to interrogate, or *interrogare*. He also had to get as much information as possible from the woman who confessed. The latter had to give him the reasons for the practice of *coitus interruptus* by her husband. If the reasons were not *ob gravem causam*, the wife had to convince her husband to turn away from this "awful sin, by all possible means, *omni quo posit modo*, mainly by his prayers and caresses!" There was a break in the term 'severity'. Vermeersch encouraged the confessor to show 'severity' rather than 'indulgence'. That was a real turning point. Finally, he asked the wife to be clear and precise about the circumstances of her husband's practice of onanism. If the reason for it was not serious, imperious (a medical recommendation for example), it could not be accepted by the Church: "May we be listened to and followed", Mercier confided to Vermeersch, giving the impression that this is a common struggle in which he owed much to his subordinate.[50]

The desire to present to the Christian people a clear position on conjugal morality was already apparent in the correspondence between Vermeersch and Mercier of 1906 to 1907. But it would only find its culmination in 1930, with the publication of Pius XI's encyclical *Casti Connubii*. A symbolic book of that time was *L'honnêteté du lit conjugal* (1910).[51] The profound influence of Vermeersch,

48 Ibid.
49 Ibid.
50 ABSE, 21127: "Malthusianisme et natalité", 15 February 1909.
51 This is an obvious reference to chapter 39 of the third part, dedicated to marriage, of the *Introduction à la vie dévote* of St. François de Sales. This chapter was entitled: "L'honnêteté du lit nuptial". The 1910 book is the compilation by the publisher of Leuven René Fonteyn of several texts by Vermeersch and Mercier. The reference to François de Sales is common: the Sorbonne sociologist Edouard Jordan was, at that time, the founder of the Ligue pour la Vie. This association wanted to tackle the disturbance of morals and the often clumsy anti-Malthusianism of the Church. Before a legislative reform, the Ligue wanted a moral reform. See Sevegrand, *Les Enfants du bon Dieu*, 41, 396.

who was appointed to the Gregorian in 1918, was exerted at the highest level
of the pontifical hierarchy. This period corresponds to a clarification of the
Church on these questions of morals.[52] It also brings to an end a period of relative tolerance with regard to the limitation of births, which extended, to use
Claude Langlois' chronology, from 1816 to 1930.[53] Henceforth, this issue was
no longer just part of the textbooks, alongside the condemnation of actors. It
was no longer just an old precept, held in high esteem by the majority. On the
contrary, Vermeersch has helped to define the Church's position in condemning contraception, with the exception, and this will be my last point, of the
Ogino method. Father Vermeersch was not the first Leuven scholar to question
birth control and natural means of contraception. The Leuven theologian Au-
guste-Joseph Lecomte was already interested in chastity from a moral point of
view in 1873. Lecomte suggested that couples who did not wish to have children could have intercourse during the wife's period of sterility. That being so,
is this not a sin?[54]

   This practice of periodic continence was the subject of increasing debate
in the Church at the end of the nineteenth and beginning of the twentieth century. In the eyes of Catholic moral theology, this method respected the natural
sexual act whose physical goal would be procreation. The Japanese gynaecol-
ogist Ogino and the German Knaus devoted a great deal of research to these
questions. While it is doubtful that Pius XI was aware of these medical works,
it is certain that Vermeersch had heard or read them. His use of scientific texts
is well known.[55] These porosities between the religious and medical fields
became apparent in 1929 when the work of the Belgian physician Raoul de
Guchteneere entitled *La limitation des naissances* was prefaced by the abbot
Jacques Leclercq. 'Partial continence' was favoured. As for Vermeersch, he expressed a certain reservation about the Ogino-Knaus method, but never went
as far as to condemn it. His position would remain that of 'indifference'. The
1930 encyclical would just be as cautious as its inspirer and not pronounce itself on the morality of periodic continence. It is, however, permissible to interpret the silences and prudence of Vermeersch or the Vatican in this regard. For
the Redemptorist Dorsaz, the encyclical implicitly authorises the method and
Vermeersch is "an unofficial interpreter of the papal word".[56] What I would
call an 'indifferent tolerance' of the Ogino-Knaus method must also be seen
as a response of the Vatican to neo-Malthusianism. If it had maintained intransigent positions, the Church would only have accentuated this movement

52   ABSE, 6716; Stengers, "Les pratiques anticonceptionnelles", 1173; Charles, 'Vermeersch
     (Arthur-Marie-Théodore)".
53   Langlois, *Le 'Crime d'Onan'*.
54   Sevegrand, "La méthode Ogino et la morale catholique", 78; Id., "Limiter les naissances";
     Id., "L'affaire Chanson".
55   See Creusen's book on Vermeersch: *Le Père Arthur Vermeersch*, 137.
56   Dorsaz, *Le contrôle des naissances*, 179.

which it had opposed for decades. By not condemning periodic continence, it competed with its ideological opponent. Vermeersch was the intellectual linchpin of this strategic positioning of the Church in the face of the birth rate problem which, beyond being moral or religious, is also political, inasmuch as it is assimilated to the socialist enemy.

One last word. In terms of conjugal morality, Vermeersch appears to be more rigorous than on other issues. He shows, it is at least a hypothesis, that the mobilisation of the thought, or even, simply, of the aura of St. Thomas, by his belonging to the neo-Thomist current, represents a projection of the stakes of the nineteenth century on the thirteenth century. Conversely, he proposes a very free interpretation of what could have been the doctrine of St. Thomas in such a situation, limiting himself to fidelity to his method (which dominates in Vermeersch). Taking up again the conceptual analysis grid of Marcel Detienne, Gérard Lenclud and François Hartog, one could speak of a *presentist* interpretation (looking at the past through the prism of the paradigms of an omnipotent present) of the thought of Saint Thomas, which lends itself very well to it.[57] Like an oracle, his words are both a source of projection and interpretation, sometimes very subjective. This presentism that dominates the reception of St. Thomas, justified by *Aeterni Patris*, contributes to what Claude Langlois rightly called "théologie pratique" or "théologie d'urgence".[58] With Vermeersch, it seems that a limit of respect for the spirit of St. Thomas is reached and that conjugal morality, integrated into the field of medicine (concerned since 1879 by *Aeterni Patris* in the adaptation to modern science), is one of the areas where St. Thomas became more of an argument than a doctrinal source.

BIBLIOGRAPHY

Aubert, Roger. "Die Enzyklika 'Aeterni Patris' und die weiteren päpstlichen Stellungnahmen zur christlichen Philosophie". In Emerich Coreth, Walter M. Neidl and Georg Pfligersdorffer, eds. *Christlichen Philosophie im katholischen Denken des 19. und 20. Jahrhunderts*. Vol. 2. Graz-Vienna-Cologne: Styria, 1988, 310-332.

Aubert, Roger. "Désiré Mercier et les débuts de l'Institut de Philosophie". *Revue philosophique de Louvain*, 88 (1990), 147-167.

Aubert, Roger. "Le Cardinal Mercier, un prélat d'avant-garde". *Bulletin de l'Académie royale de Belgique. Classe des Lettres, Sciences Morales et Politiques*, 5-7-12 (1994), 267-289.

Baubérot, Jean. "Durkheim et la laïcité". *Archives de sciences sociales des religions*, 69 (1990), 151-156.

Bergh, Émile. "Vermeersch, Arthur". In *Biographie nationale de Belgique*. Vol. 38. Brussels: Palais des Académies, 1973, 803-807.

Brants, Victor. "La part de la méthode de Le Play dans les études sociales en Belgique". *La Réforme sociale*, 6 (1906) 2, 636-652.

Brodrick, James. *Robert Bellarmine, Saint and Scholar*. Westminster: Newman Press, 1961.

Burggraeve, Roger. "Historical Building Blocks for a Consistent Relational and Sexual Ethics". In James Keenan, ed. *Catholic Theological Ethic Past, Present, and Future: The Trento Conference*. New York: Orbis Books, 2011, 86-95.

57 They forged the concept of 'Régime d'historicité'. See Detienne, *Comparer l'incomparable* and Hartog, *Régimes d'historicité*.
58 Langlois, "Conférence".

Castelein, Auguste. "Etude sur le socialisme". *Revue générale*, 26 (September 1890), 257-278.

Castelein, Auguste. "La passion de l'amour. Le mariage. La natalité". *Revue générale*, 45 (August 1909), 161-184 and (September 1909), 353-374.

Ceriani, D.G. "P. Arturo Vermeersch, theologo moralista". *Scuola Cattolica*, 64 (1936) 4, 402-408.

Chappel, James. *Catholic Modern: The Challenge of Totalitarianism and the Remaking of the Church*. Cambridge-London: Harvard University Press, 2018.

Chappel, James. "The Thomist Debate over Inequality and Property Rights in Depression-Era Europe". In Rajesh Heynickx and Stéphane Symons, eds. *So What's New About Scholasticism? How Neo-Thomism Helped Shaped the Twentieth Century*. Berlin-Boston: De Gruyter, 2018, 21-38.

Charles, V. "Vermeersch (Arthur-Marie-Théodore)". In *Biographie coloniale belge*, vol. 4. Brussels, 1955, 913-917.

Christens, Ria. "De orthodoxie van het zaad. Seksualiteit en sekse-identiteit in de Rooms-katholieke traditie". In Kaat Wils, ed. *Het Lichaam (m/v)*. Alfred Cauchie Reeks 3. Leuven: Leuven University Press, 2001, 231-249.

Creusen, Joseph, S.J. "In Memoriam". *Nouvelle revue théologique*, 1936, 817-838.

Creusen, Joseph. "Le vœu d'abnégation du R.P. A. Vermeersch". *Gregorianum*, 1940, 607-627.

Creusen, Joseph. *Le Père A. Vermeersch, S.J., l'homme et l'œuvre*. Museum Lessianum 45. Brussels: Édition universelle – Paris: Desclée de Brouwer, 1947.

De Bie, Pierre. *Naissance et premiers développements de la sociologie en Belgique*. Louvain-la-Neuve: Ciaco, 1988.

Deferme, Jo and Jan De Maeyer. "Entre sciences sociales et politiques. La pensée leplaysienne et les milieux catholiques belges". *Études sociales*, (2009) 149-150, 147-166.

de Franceschi, Sylvio Hermann. "La théologie morale catholique et ses critiques dans l'entre-deux-guerres. Situation au temps de la formation du dominicain Jean Tonneau (1903-1991), moraliste du Saulchoir". *Revue d'éthique et de théologie morale*, 290 (2016) 3, 113-128.

de Ghellinck, J. and G. Gilleman. "Arthur Vermeersch". In *Dictionnaire de théologie catholique*, vol. 15/2. Paris: Letouzey et Ané, 1950, 2690.

Dejace, Charles. "Frédéric Le Play, sa vie et ses œuvres". *Revue générale*, 18 (1882) 1, 812-830.

Detienne, Marcel. *Comparer l'incomparable*. Paris: Seuil, 2000.

Dorsaz, Armand. *Le contrôle des naissances*. Paris: Mignard, 1935.

Drouard, Alain. "Aux origines de l'eugénisme en France: le néo-malthusianisme (1896-1914)". *Population*, 47 (1992) 2, 435-459.

Gallagher, John A. *Time Past, Time Future: An Historical Study of Catholic Moral Theology*. Mahwah: Paulist Press, 1990.

Gerard, Emmanuel. *Sociale Wetenschappen aan de Katholieke Universiteit te Leuven 1892-1992*. Politica Cahier 3. Leuven: Politica-oudstudentenvereniging, 1992.

Gérin, Paul. "Les congrès sociaux de Liège (1886, 1887 et 1890), carrefours du catholicisme social international". *Bolletino dell'Archivio per la storia del Movimento sociale cattolico in Italia*, 38 (2003), 304-339.

Gijs, Anne-Sophie. "Entre ombres et lumières, profits et conflits. Les relations entre les Jésuites et l'État indépendant du Congo (1879-1908)". *Revue belge de philologie et d'histoire*, 88 (2010) 2, 255-298.

Hartog, François. *Régimes d'historicité. Présentisme et expériences du temps*. Paris: Seuil, 2003.

Heynickx, Rajesh and Stéphane Symons, eds. *So What's New About Scholasticism? How Neo-Thomism Helped Shaped the Twentieth Century*. Berlin-Boston: De Gruyter, 2018.

Heyrman, Peter. "Belgian Catholic Entrepreneur's organisations, 1880-1914. A dialogue on social responsability". *Zeitschrift für Unternehmensgeschichte*, 56 (2011) 2, 163-186.

Jaccard, Pierre. "La renaissance thomiste dans l'Église: du Cardinal Mercier à M. Jacques Maritain". *Revue de Théologie et de Philosophie*, 15 (1927) 63, 134-161.

Keenan, James F. *History of Catholic Moral in the Twentieth Century: From Confessing Sins to Liberating Consciences*. London-New York: Continuum, 2010.

Langlois, Claude. "Conférence de M. C. Langlois: Histoire et sociologie du catholicisme contemporain". *Annuaire de l'École pratique des hautes études*, 103 (1994-1995), 407-416.

Langlois, Claude. *Le 'Crime d'Onan'. Le Discours catholique sur la limitation des naissances (1816-1930)*. Paris: Les Belles Lettres, 2005.

Laurent, M.-H. "Cajétan (Thomas de Vio)". In *Dictionnaire d'histoire et de géographie ecclésiastique*, vol. 11. Paris: Letouzey et Ané, 1949, 248-252.

Mahoney, John. *The Making of Moral Theology: A Study of the Roman Catholic Tradition*. The Martin d'Arcy Memorial Lectures, 1981-2. Oxford: Clarendon Press, 1987.

Mayeur, Jean-Marie. Review of Rossini, ed., *Aspetti della cultura cattolica nell'éta di Leone XIII. Atti del convegno di Bologna il 27-28-29 dicembre 1960*, Rome: Cinque Lune, 1961. *Archives de sociologie des religions*, 13 (1962), 189-190.

Mosbah-Natanson, Sébastien. *Une "mode" de la sociologie. Publications et vocations sociologiques en France en 1900*. Paris: Classiques Garnier, 2017.

Müller, Caroline. *Une histoire intime des catholiques au XIXe siècle*. Paris: PUF, 2019.

Pelletier, Dennis. *Les catholiques en France de 1789 à nos jours*. Paris: Albin Michel, 2019.

Rizzo, Rémy. "Les chemins de Delboeuf". In Vincent Genin, ed. *Une Fabrique des Sciences humaines. L'Université de Liège dans la mêlée (1817-2017)*. Coll. Studia 163. Brussels: Archives Générales du Royaume, 2019, 87-102.

Robert, Charles. "Chronique de théologie morale fondamentale". *Revue des Sciences religieuses*, 29 (1955) 3, 267-283.

Sevegrand, Martine. "Limiter les naissances. Le cas de conscience des catholiques français (1880-1939)". *Vingtième siècle. Revue d'histoire*, 30 (1991) 1, 40-54.

Sevegrand, Martine. "La méthode Ogino et la morale catholique: une controverse théologique autour de la limitation des naissances (1930-1951)". *Revue d'histoire de l'Église de France*, 78 (1992) 200, 77-99.

Sevegrand, Martine. "L'affaire Chanson (1950-1952): continence conjugale ou érotisme catholique?" *Revue d'Histoire ecclésiastique*, (1993) 2, 439-483.

Sevegrand, Martine. *Les Enfants du bon Dieu. Les catholiques français et la procréation au XXe siècle*. Paris: Albin Michel, 1995.

Stengers, Jean. "Les pratiques anticonceptionnelles dans le mariage au XIXe et au XXe siècle: problèmes humains et attitudes religieuses (2e partie)". *Revue belge de philologie et d'histoire*, 49 (1971) 4, 1119-1174.

Tambuyser, Raphaël. "L'érection de la chaire de philosophie thomiste à Louvain (1880-1882)". *Revue philosophique de Louvain*, 51 (1958), 479-509.

The Catholic Encyclopedia and its makers. New York: Encyclopedia Press, 1917.

Vermeersch, Arthur. *La question congolaise*. Brussels: Imprimerie scientifique C. Bulens, 1906.

Vermeersch, Arthur. "Un grave péril moral". *Nouvelle Revue Théologique*, 41 (1909), 65-72.

Vermeersch, Arthur. *La tolérance*. Paris: Beauchesne – Leuven: Uystpruyst-Dieudonné, 1912.

Vermeersch, Arthur. *De Castitate et de vitiis contrariis. Tractatus doctrinalis et moralis*. Rome: Università Gregoriana – Bruges: Beyaert, 1919.

Vermeersch, Arthur. "Soixante ans de théologie morale". *Nouvelle revue théologique*, 56 (1929) 10, 863-884.

Viaene, Vincent. "Introduction. Réalité et image sous le pontificat de Léon XIII". In Vincent Viaene, ed. *The Papacy and the New World Order: Vatican Diplomacy, Catholic Opinion and International Politics at the Time of Leo XIII (1878-1903)*. Leuven: Leuven University Press, 2005, 30-52.

Viaene, Vincent. "La religion du Prince: Léopold, le Vatican, la Belgique et le Congo (1855-1909)". In Vincent Dujardin, Valérie Rosoux and Tanguy de Wilde, eds. *Léopold II. Entre génie et gêne. Politique étrangère et colonisation*. Brussels: Racine, 2009, 173-179.

Wils, Kaat. "Les intellectuels catholiques et la sociologie en Belgique, 1880-1914". *Archives de sciences sociales des religions*, 179 (2017) 3, 71-88.

Wils, Kaat and Laura Di Spurio. "Sexualité". In Éliane Gubin and Catherine Jacques, eds. *Encyclopédie d'histoire des femmes en Belgique, XIXe-XXe siècles*. Brussels: Racine, 2018, 528-536.

Wils, Kaat and Anne Rasmussen. "La sociologie en perspective transnationale: Bruxelles 1890-1914". In Jean Ferrette, ed. *Anamnèse*. Vol. 10: *Généalogie des sociologues et anthropologues belges disparus*. Paris: L'Harmattan, 2015, 13-29.

Wils, Lode. "België in de negentiende eeuw: religieus, politiek en sociaal". In Emmanuel Gerard, ed. *De Christelijke Arbeidsbeweging in België*. KADOC Studies 11. Leuven: Leuven University Press, 1991, 18-55.

Joannes Aengenent as professor at Warmond Seminary. Photo by J. Otto.
[Nijmegen, Katholiek Documentatie Centrum: AFBK-7b1014]

JOANNES AENGENENT (1873-1935) A THOMISTIC SOCIOLOGIST'S CALL FOR A MORE HUMANE ECONOMY[*]

ERIK SENGERS

Christianity and the problems of the economy

In traditional Christian theology, man has to work for his living. After he was chased out of paradise, the fruits of the earth no longer came to him automatically. He had to work with his hands, to labour, to eke out a living from the earth. Outside paradise, his efforts are always at risk of failure, and of more suffering. By performing acts of charity, the more fortunate in society can and must help the less fortunate. In the nineteenth century, however, technical, political and social developments and their consequences challenged this traditional vision. The division between the rich and the poor became wider, the traditional associations that had taken care of the poor were abolished, the state was unwilling to intervene in the social sphere, and the principles of the free market economy ruled the relationships between employers and employees. These changes could no longer be dealt with by the framework of charity; the social problems that resulted were too vast to ignore. A new perspective had to be developed, and the Catholic Church found this in the neo-scholastic, or more specifically neo-Thomistic, view of society introduced by Pope Leo XIII.

*   Many thanks to my colleague Dr. Harm Goris who provided valuable additions by pointing at medieval discussions on the economy.

Although industrialisation came late to the Netherlands compared to other European countries, the social problems that accompanied this modernisation of the economy and society were not absent.[1] Around the turn of the century, it became clear that the liberal view on the state and society that had dominated Dutch politics since 1848 was no longer viable. The conservative-liberal elite was challenged by three groups: the socialists, Abraham Kuyper's orthodox (neo-Calvinist) Protestants, and the Roman Catholics all formulated their own alternative discourse on modern society and tried to implement their ideas through political action.[2] One of the more prominent and productive authors of the Catholic discourse was Joannes Aengenent. This priest of the diocese of Haarlem was a professor of philosophy and sociology at Warmond Seminary, and was active in many organisations of the Catholic social movement, as secretary, spiritual advisor, or moderator. When he became a bishop in 1928, he had even more opportunities to promote his vision on society and the economy. Although he published on many themes, ranging from war and peace to women and youth, most of his contributions focused on economic questions.[3]

This article will concentrate on the neo-Thomistic influence in Joannes Aengenent's works on the economy. The first part offers a biographical portrait of Aengenent, focusing specifically on his philosophical education. Born into a lower-middle-class family in 1873, he was educated at a time when neo-scholastic views were first being introduced and were being made obligatory for all types of Catholic theological education. These views influenced him in his scholarly life, as a leader of the social movement and in his policy as a bishop. The second part describes the typical situation of Dutch Catholics as they faced the social question. From the Reformation on, until well into the first half of the nineteenth century, Dutch Catholics were a discriminated minority, and to a large extent therefore the social question in the Netherlands was a Catholic problem. The historical perspective that neo-Thomism offered helped Dutch Catholics to formulate a social identity and a political program for the reconstruction of society. The third part will discuss Aengenent's ideas on the economy. I will analyse a selection of his writings according to three themes, deduced from the principles of neo-scholasticism: rights and duties, the corporatist society, and the just price.[4] The fourth part will sketch the efforts Aengenent undertook as a bishop to make medieval society and culture, idealised by neo-scholastic scholars of that time, available for Catholics and

1   Van der Woud, *Koninkrijk vol sloppen*.
2   Hellemans, *Strijd om de moderniteit*.
3   For an overview of his life and work see: Sengers, *Roomsch socioloog – sociale bisschop*.
4   This includes some recently rediscovered publications.

especially those Catholics bearing responsibility in social organisations. He did this by reorganising and stimulating neo-scholastic philosophical studies at his seminaries, and by restoring medieval devotional practices in his diocese. The last section will summarise the conclusions of the findings presented in this chapter.

From the slums to sociology

Joannes Aengenent was born in Rotterdam on 14 March 1873. His father was a blacksmith in what was one of the slums of the city. In 1875, the family moved to Delft, where the social situation was not substantially better. At this time, the cities of Holland were experiencing huge population growth, but were still confined within the medieval city walls with their old housing stock. His father registered as a domestic servant in Delft and only later took up his former profession again. There were two Roman Catholic parishes in Delft at the time: Saint Joseph's parish, run by Franciscan priests, and Saint Hippolytus' parish, run by the diocesan clergy. Dioceses had only been re-established 25 years previously for the first time since the Reformation – the last bishop of Haarlem had fled in 1578 and the diocese was dissolved in 1592. In 1853, the newly-appointed bishop of Haarlem, Van Vree, organised his territory and asserted his authority against the opposition of local lay people and the regular clergy, who, during the period of the underground church, had continued Catholic life and were unwilling to give up their position in schools and charity. The Aengenent family lived in Saint Hippolytus' parish; as a consequence their son Jan was influenced by what was at the time the modern appearance of Catholicism: diocesan, ultramontane, and Rome-oriented. Neo-classical churches were being replaced by neo-Gothic edifices that were supposed to better represent Catholic ideas.[5]

In 1886, Jan Aengenent went to the diocesan minor seminary of Hageveld in Voorhout. He was one of the best students there and concluded his studies *summa cum laude*. In 1893, he went to the major seminary of Warmond to continue his studies for the priesthood. At the time Warmond was becoming one of the most prominent seminaries in the Netherlands.[6] This was one of the reasons that it attracted students in great numbers, and it became necessary to rebuild and refurbish the seminary's buildings, and to reform the curricu-

---

5   Saint Hippolytus' church was demolished, but the magnificent Saint Joseph's church (now dedicated to Mary of Jesse) still exists. For the development of Catholics in Delft see Warffemius, *Kerken in de Papenhoek* and Van der Laarse, "'Verzwolgen door den Ultramontaansen vloed'".

6   Winkeler, "Het onderwijs op Warmond", 145-150.

lum and the spiritual life. Again, Aengenent was the best of his class almost in every year. As he continued his studies he received the minor orders according to the normal pattern, and he was ordained a deacon in August 1896. As his father had died during his studies, the fees were being paid by the parish priest of Saint Hippolytus's. He was ordained a priest at the seminary on 3 April 1897 and was appointed an associate pastor in the rural village of Roelofarendsveen. He did not work in parish ministry for long, as he was appointed to the teaching staff at Hageveld seminary after a year, and in 1904 he became professor of philosophy and sociology at Warmond seminary.

Following Pope Leo XIII's decision in his encyclical *Aeterni Patris* (1879) to give greater prominence to philosophy in clerical training, the philosophy course was transferred from Hageveld to Warmond and extended to a full year. While studying at Warmond, Aengenent's professor of philosophy was Josephus Th. Beysens, who is regarded as one of the founders of neo-scholastic philosophy in the Netherlands. This philosophy was first introduced to the Netherlands from the Catholic University of Leuven, where Professor Mercier taught that scholastic thinkers should be interpreted in the light of contemporary problems. He tried to incorporate the nascent science of sociology into neo-Thomistic philosophy by focusing not only on empirical facts, as the new science did, but also on God as the ultimate truth and source of knowledge, to highlight the importance in human life of the soul and of morality, and to develop a solidaristic and corporatist view on society as *Rerum novarum* promoted it. As there were close contacts between the newly-founded seminaries in the Netherlands and Leuven University, his ideas were incorporated into the Dutch curriculum, with the Dutch primarily emphasising scholastic teachings about state and society. Beysens was a typical example of this neo-scholastic philosophy. He considered that which common sense could accept as true and certain as containing objective truth. In his moral philosophy, he tried to establish fixed standards that reflected the purpose and meaning of human beings. Beysens regarded ethics as a practical philosophy, with concrete guidelines for a moral life that could be found in God as the standard of all morality.[7]

---

7   Aengenent defended this position of his teacher's in "Een universiteitsprofessor over de scholastieke wijsbegeerte". For an overview of neo-scholastic philosophy in the Netherlands see Sassen, *Wijsgeerig leven in Nederland*, 108-111, 113-117.

Thomism and the social question in the Netherlands

To obtain a good perspective on the importance of neo-scholastic philosophy for Dutch Catholics' ideas on the reconstruction of society, it is important to look at their own social position in society. After the Reformation, which affected most parts of the Northern Netherlands, Catholics were forced into a second-class position politically and economically. Like most other non-Calvinistic faiths, their religion could not be exercised in public, and the church's infrastructure disintegrated and went underground. It was only when the French invaded the country in 1795 that the Catholic religion was emancipated, and full freedom of religion was granted in the liberal constitution of 1848. At the time industrialisation came to the Kingdom of the Netherlands, the Catholics were among the poorest and least educated groups in society. Their fate in the political and economic sphere was in the hands of liberal Protestant elites who owned the land and the factories, and who controlled the banking sector. It is not surprising, therefore, that *Rerum novarum* was positively received by Dutch farmers and workers. They were among the groups that suffered most from the emerging social question and they longed for change in the ruling free-market capitalist economy.[8]

As the Catholic University in Nijmegen was only founded in 1924, there was no other intellectual elite that could realise this program in the Netherlands except seminary-trained clergy. They fell back on the neo-scholastic teachings promoted in *Aeterni Patris* and *Rerum novarum*. The centre of this philosophy was that God, in creating the world, had given it a certain natural order, which placed human beings in a particular relationship with each other, with corresponding duties and rights. These rights and duties were moral norms with a power and jurisdiction that went beyond positive law; and they had an ethical component from which specific norms for social life could be deduced. It was the aim of Catholic neo-scholastic sociology to order society according to the will of God, so that both the individual and society as a whole could reach their supernatural goals. Since man was perceived as comprising a body and a soul, his earthly needs also had to be respected in order for him to achieve his supernatural goals. For this reason the Church afforded itself the right to intervene in the temporal order and to become politically active. Two leading principles of neo-scholastic philosophy in particular became important for the organisation of society: first the organic ordering of society into different socio-economic groups to which individuals belonged by birth, second the idea of a just price, an idea which implies that economic relation-

---

8   Although the bishops were not very positive about the papal letter: Jacobs, "Een kentering in de katholieke sociale actie", 14-19.

ships must be arranged according to certain reasonable norms, which must, if necessary, be guaranteed by the public authorities.[9]

Aengenent was not the only Dutch priest-intellectual at the beginning of the twentieth century to write about the social question from a neo-Thomistic perspective. In fact, there was a dense but loosely connected network, working from more or less the same principles laid down in *Aeterni Patris* and *Rerum novarum*, later also in other papal letters. Here, some of the most important players are mentioned. Especially the Franciscans, who began to teach sociology in their seminary in 1911[10], had important scholars. G. Vrijmoed proposed the guilds as model for economic reconstruction to bring back social justice and solidarity. D. de Kok criticised inequality in the capitalist system which disturbed peace between the members of society. C. Hentzen promoted social justice as a virtue to restore just and harmonious relations in society, that he grounded in the order of creation.[11] Of course the Dominicans were very important in promoting neo-Thomistic ideas about society. A. Rijken is remembered as the great organiser of the Catholic social network. He was advisor of many of its leaders and as professor in moral theology of his seminary he was creative in applying Thomistic principles to contemporary problems. A. Weve promoted thinking about the *bonum commune*, which he defined as the common goal that binds everyone and enables human flourishing, therefore the state had to order the different interest groups in society.[12] Also the Jesuits were very productive neo-scholastic scholars on the social field. P. Bruin was the first to write a study in which he treated sociology as a part of ethics and deduced rules for the organisation of society according to the nature of man from the general moral order. He described man as part of the moral, God-given order and by studying this order one could learn how society should be ordered and what are the rights and duties of citizens and the state.[13]

Also many secular clerics engaged in the neo-scholastic study of the social question. The influential politician Nolens started a course in sociology at Rolduc seminary in Limburg already in 1893.[14] Then of course the two most prominent leaders of the Catholic social movement – A. Ariëns in the diocese of Utrecht and H. Poels in the Roermond diocese – strongly engaged in the workers movement using medieval notions of class and guilds. And Aengenent, whose papers soon caught the attention of readers, notably of the

---

9   See Schuster, *Die Soziallehre*, 15-57; Van Diepenbeek, *Coöperatieve organisatie*, 20-22. For a
     discussion on 'just price' see De Gelder, *Just price*, 20-31.
10   Winkeler, "Sociografie en pastoraal beleid", 178-180.
11   Struyker Boudier, *Wijsgerig leven*, III, 154-165.
12   Ibid., II, 149-163.
13   Ibid., I, 179-204.
14   Hamans et al., *Bisdom langs de Maas*, 436.

prominent priest and politician Schaepman. In 1902, the newspaper *Katholiek Sociaal Weekblad* started to write about social questions and Schaepman mentioned to its editor, Piet Aalberse, that the talented author Aengenent was not a member of the editorial board. Aalberse appointed Aengenent to the board and when the Katholieke Sociale Actie was founded 1904, Aengenent was made its spiritual advisor. This was the beginning of an impressive public career for Aengenent. Within the KSA, he participated in the social weeks it organised and in its social study club. He was the secretary of the Dutch *Katholiekendagen* (Catholics Days), mass meetings of the whole Catholic social movement following the example of the German *Katholikentage*. He was strongly involved in the Catholic press as a means of propaganda for the Catholic cause, although his efforts to create a national newspaper for the workers did not bear fruit during his lifetime. He was proposed as a candidate for the Upper House of parliament in 1920, but his bishop probably forbade him to accept it. Instead, his friend Aalberse had him appointed to the High Council of Labour, a government advisory institution, in 1926.

'Labour, not capital, is the central value'

Already as a teacher at Hageveld minor seminary, Aengenent started to publish about social questions. In several profound analyses he attacked socialism and liberalism. He attacked Marx's theory that all value is derived from labour and that modern capitalism tries to extract value by exploiting the workers. Aengenent broadened this vision by arguing that value could also be created by other means, and that it had a social and cultural component as well. Philosophically, he attacked historical materialism, which he considered too absurd to be discussed. For him this theory meant that everything was always in transition, a point of view which denies the existence of eternal truths, but it also meant that the social and economic sphere were ruled by class struggles, a theory which denies the influence of spiritual forces.[15] Aengenent also attacked liberalism on the basis of its materialism, for example when discussing the relationship between Darwinism and democracy. These suppose that social life is ruled by the laws of nature, which are basically the rule of the strongest and the fittest. This would also imply that morals are dependent on power or subjectivity. For Aengenent, who accepted the rule of God over society, natural laws could not explain the development of society. Christian charity or governmental control of the economy would in that case hinder the development of society. But in his view these things were essential to reform

15   Aengenent, "Wetenschappelijk socialisme van Karl Marx".

capitalism so as to make it a more humane system that benefited the workers and would prevent class struggle.[16]

Aengenent wrote about many subjects. For two decades, he wrote sociological reviews of recent publications for *De Katholiek*, Warmond seminary's academic journal, reviewing works by Catholic, Protestant, socialist and liberal authors from the Netherlands and abroad. He published handbooks of psychology, philosophy, and sociology that were used not only in his own courses at the seminary, but elsewhere too. His handbook on sociology followed the views of the German sociologist Heinrich Pesch on the social question. In other articles, Aengenent discussed the Catholic attitude towards the liberal state. He wrote several articles about what was called the question of women and the family: early feminists, who were well-educated and demanded the right to vote, also had supporters among Dutch Catholics. Moreover, given that men were able to support a family on one income, what should women's role in society then be? After the First World War, Aengenent reflected on many themes that had caused this catastrophe for European culture, and he came to the conclusion that only a profound renewal of society through Christian values and Christian culture, and through the Catholic Church, could prevent a future disaster. But most of his publications dealt with economic questions: the right order of the economy, the organisation of workers, and labour conditions. These publications will be discussed using the three lines of neo-scholastic principle that were identified in the previous section: rights and duties, organic society, and the just price.[17]

Rights and duties

One of the central propositions of *Rerum novarum*, and therefore of modern Catholic social theory, is that private property is not evil in itself, but that it should be oriented to the common good. Total liberty is unacceptable, as are complete socialisation or collective property. Aengenent defended this position in a debate with a Catholic lawyer, who accused him of socialist tendencies. Aengenent described private property as the norm in human societies and he legitimised this on the basis of natural law (and not, like his opponent,

---

16   Id., "Darwinisme en democratie". For this last point see also Id., "De kapitalistische maatschappij".

17   For the influence of Pesch's solidaristic vision on Dutch intellectuals, including Aengenent, see Van den Eerenbeemt, "Ideeën rond 1900 van katholieken in Nederland".

on the basis of positive law).[18] The principle of private property therefore could not be touched. In addition to these arguments on principles, Aengenent also mentioned a number of practical points, for example that there would be no stimulus to self-improvement, or collective improvement, in societies without private property, because there would be no way of enjoying the fruits of one's work. He also regarded private property as a guarantee for social order and freedom. Without private property, the state would decide what happens with that and who can enjoy it, and this would result in corruption. At the same time Aengenent recognised the state's right to limit the use of property, and in extreme cases, for example famine, to nationalise it. Taxes were allowed too, as long as the revenues were used for the whole of the community.[19]

But these general norms demanded practical implementation in concrete questions. One of these questions was the discussion about retired workers' pensions, or, in the terminology of the social question: the pensions of workers who were too old to earn a living through work. How could this group be guaranteed a decent living? Early European welfare societies experimented with three forms: state pensions funded through taxation, compulsory financial savings, or insurance (either voluntary or compulsory). Aengenent dismissed the solution of state pensions as it meant the government would have to intrude into the individual well-being of people who are responsible themselves for their own fate and happiness. Moreover, under this kind of system, people who do not work in industry must nonetheless pay for those who do, so that the burden is not well-balanced. Aengenent also dismissed compulsory savings. First because many people do not earn enough to be able to save money for after their retirement. More importantly, forcing people to save affects private property and the right to use it in whatever way suits the owner best. The government would be taking over responsibility, and the citizen would no longer be free to dispose of it as he wants. Voluntary insurance was not a good option either, as many workers did not have sufficient responsibility when it came to spending their wages. The only remaining solution was a system of compulsory insurance: this meant that the state would intervene in the labour contract to oblige both parties to pay a part of the income into an insurance fund for workers' pensions.[20]

18 The question whether private property was only introduced after the Fall, and was consequently reflected in human legislation, or whether it was an absolute right based on natural law, is a classical debate in scholastic theory. Church fathers and medieval scholastics espoused the former view (Pierson, *Just property*, 63-124), whereas the latter became dominant in the late Middle Ages (Pels, *Property and Power*, 53-55).
19 Aengenent, "Eigendom en natuurrecht".
20 Id., "Waarom verplichte verzekering?", 231-232.

Organic society

Rerum novarum promoted the cooperation of workers as a natural way of building associations, and it stimulated labour unions. But the question was whether the workers should be organised separately as a class, or per profession. This difference caused a fierce debate in the Dutch context in the first two decades of the twentieth century. Aengenent and Aalberse represented one camp that was opposed to the view espoused by leaders like Alfons Ariëns and Henri Poels, who promoted vocational organisations of workers. Vocational organisations implied national (instead of diocesan) and even ecumenical organisations, and minimised the influence that the Church could exercise through spiritual advisors, something which the archbishop of Utrecht did not favour. Aengenent viewed this discussion about the organisation of the workers from the perspective of the reorganisation of capitalist society. In his view, modern capitalism had destroyed the geographical, cultural, and legal bonds that were capable of taming this new economic order. This unboundedness was the cause of the great injustices that Aengenent observed: poverty, low wages, moral disorientation, absence of charity. He sought the reorganisation of society into classes and guilds along medieval lines. In his view, these were a way of organising all aspects of people's lives, of giving due attention both to the material, and to the spiritual interests of the members of a profession. The government should make membership of these classes obligatory, so that they could operate as public corporations for the general good. In fact, this idea of classes was not very different from Ariëns's and Poels's view: the point is that Aengenent's and Aalberse's classes integrated vocational organisations, whereas Ariëns and Poels proposed a dual structure.[21]

The idea of organising the workers along class or vocational lines culminated in the vision of a corporatist organisation of the economy – a vision broadly shared among Catholic intellectuals in Europe at that time. In one paper, Aengenent sketched the organisation of this economic order. At the grass roots, there would be councils of companies in certain branches of the economy. These councils offered opportunities for workers to discuss the social, technical, and (eventually also) commercial aspects of the firms involved. This council would be entitled to draw up collective agreements and to resolve conflicts about these agreements. At a higher level, there would be three general councils: one for large companies, one for the middle classes, and one for agricultural firms. These councils' task was to promote social peace by stimulat-

---

21 The conflict ended in 1916 when the episcopate decided that there would be a dual structure of class-based and vocational Catholic workers' organisations, with a preference for the class organisations. See also: Aengenent, "Reorganisatie der kapitalistische maatschappij".

ing collective agreements and to make price agreements that could guarantee a just wage for the sector as a whole. At the highest level there was the Roman Catholic Central Council of Companies (established 1919). This Council aimed to promote social peace between the classes through collective agreements and price policies, but it also strove for public (governmental) recognition of the councils, and recognition from non-Catholics. Aengenent provided specific advice on how the power balance between workers and employers could be maintained. At its first conference, the Central Council took far-reaching decisions about dismissals, minimum wages, and work circumstances.[22]

In another paper, Aengenent elaborated on the philosophical background of this corporatist system. For him, it was the beginning of an organisation of firms to be established under public law. He believed that binding, collective agreements in different branches of the economy were signs of how this system might contribute to combating individualism. According to Aengenent, the social bonds between workers had been broken in modern capitalism, and collective agreements could assure that workers and employers would come together again. He pointed to two central ideas of Catholic sociology that are realised in this system. First the idea of the organic state. In the Catholic view, man is a social being and the state is founded on natural social bonds. This view put some distance between him and socialism. The second concept is the idea of solidarity, both individually and collectively, to distinguish his view from that of liberalism, which denies these fundamental social bonds. Aengenent did not doubt that the councils would realise their ultimate goal – social peace – as long as one condition was fulfilled: that workers and employers would internalise the spirit of solidarism, which he called subjective socialisation. In clear terms he complained about egocentric thinking in society, which placed individual (or class) interests at the forefront and forgot about the common good. Only if both employers and workers focused on what they had in common would it be possible to build a new social order in which the interests of human labour, rather than those of capital, would be at the heart of the economy.[23]

In this corporatist system, the representation and co-determination of workers was a central point of discussion. This was a controversial point, because socialists regarded this as the beginning of the overthrow of the capitalist production system. Aengenent regarded participation of the workers in companies' decision making processes as a normal, natural demand. First,

22   Id., "Het bedrijfsradenstelsel". It must be remarked that corporatism for Dutch social scientists had nothing to do with the experiments in Portugal and Spain, because there, the economy was integrated into the state, whereas the Dutch defended the independence of the economic system.

23   Aengenent, *Het bedrijfsradenstelsel verwezenlijkt*.

workers' and employers' interests ran parallel to each other: without employers, workers cannot earn their living, and employers need workers, so both have an interest in the optimal functioning of the company. Second, agreements on labour conditions and on pay should be made by the people who are party to them. Thus participation can be a defence against state intervention in the economy. Third, worker participation shows that workers are not a 'means of production', but are active and reasonable participants in the production process: participation expresses the worker's humanity. Aengenent trusted that Christian employers would introduce participation in their firms as they supported social justice and charity and recognised that worker participation furthered the common good. He underlined that worker participation did not jeopardise the employers' right of property.[24]

Just price

The principle of the just price was relevant to the social question in the discussion about wages. Aengenent was not the only Catholic sociologist to discuss this subject. The prominent Norbertine Professor L. van Aken had previously addressed it in his eighth lecture for employers, and Aengenent followed Van Aken's arguments. In the wage question, he distinguished between strict justice, social justice, and charity; these three conditions must be satisfied in establishing the just wage. According to strict justice, the wage is equivalent to the value of the performance achieved. But, Aengenent added, the wage should at least be enough for an ordinary family to live a normal life. People must work for their living, but this must be enough to live a decent life. This principle of strict justice must also be applied to workers who are not (yet) married. People have a natural right to marry and establish a family. Whether a worker uses this right or not is not relevant for Aengenent: the wage should be sufficient to maintain a family. In extraordinary cases where such a wage does not in fact suffice, the principles of social justice and charity should be applied. This might be the case for example if a worker needs extra income to support many children. Finally, a just minimum wage must be enough to permit the worker to live a decent life even if he is no longer able to work, in case of illness, old age, or disability. The level of income should also take future situations into account, and should guarantee a dignified life to every worker.

---

24   Id., *Bedrijfsorganisatie en medezeggenschap.*

Therefore, Aengenent argued in another article, insurance should be a part of this just wage.[25]

One of the discussions to which Aengenent applied these principles of Catholic sociology was the debate about the income of civil servants. The question was whether their salary should be an absolute wage (equal pay for equal work, as the socialists proposed) or a relative wage (which took into account the employee's married state and number of children, as the Christian parties proposed). Aengenent started his argument with the absolute wage principle. Salaries express and recompense the worth of the work delivered. He underlined that many Catholic sociologists supported this vision; the relative wage principle can also have adverse effects, as it could stimulate employers to give preference when hiring staff to the unmarried, the childless, and to women, who are all cheaper. The absolute wage must be sufficient to support a normal family. At the same time, Aengenent argued, this strict justice cannot be the only principle that guides the setting of wages. It might be necessary to pay a bonus for the rent of a house or for the support of a large family. Social justice and solidarity should also play a role in wage policies. A public fund raised by taxes could be set up to provide for this support; given that families with children contribute to the general good there would be justification for this. Charity could also play a role: as human beings, employers had a responsibility to take care of their employees. If an employer were willing to give support, he would set a good example for other employers. But Aengenent was not very consistent in his argument: he argued elsewhere that workers who married should receive extra support for housing and children.[26]

Aengenent also drew on neo-scholastic principles in his defence of the eight-hour working day, introduced in the Netherlands in 1920. This law was heavily attacked by liberals and employers, who contended that it was responsible for the social and moral degeneration of society that they claimed to observe. Aengenent replied that the law should not be evaluated too hastily, and that judgment should be suspended until the law had been fully implemented. Second, he provided financial statistics to show that it was not the law but the international monetary situation that was responsible for the economic malaise of his time. Using other statistics, including from other countries, he demonstrated that earlier restrictions on the length of the work-

---

25   Aengenent, "De theorie van mr. Pelster", 355-356; Id., "Verplichte verzekering", 255.
      Van Aken's contribution is published in his *Tien sociale studiën*. It must be noted that
      St. Thomas discussed the question of the just price in the context of trade, not of wages,
      but drawing the same conclusion that earnings should be enough to support 'oneself and
      his own', a standard phrase in medieval canon law. As the neo-scholastics saw the labour
      contract as a trade agreement, they could use this argument in this context. Langholm,
      The Legacy of Scholasticism, 118-136, esp. 124-125.
26   Aengenent, *Salarisregeling*; Id., "Gezinsloon", 445-446.

ing day had stimulated worker productivity, had resulted in a more efficient production process, and an increase in collective wealth. Opponents had also claimed that an eight-hour working day would lead to an increase in alcohol abuse, but Aengenent cast doubt on the connection. What was needed was for workers to learn how to use their extra leisure time properly. But the main argument he used in defence of the limited working day was of a philosophical nature. Following *Rerum novarum*, and the idea that man is made up of body and soul, Aengenent stated that the working day should be limited as soon as the workers' health and well-being were in danger. It is the state that must defend its citizens physically, but also morally. Man not only has economic duties, but to be a full human being he must also have the time to exercise his social, family, and religious duties. Even if a limited working day were in fact to have economic consequences, Aengenent still defended it because the immaterial benefits were much higher: "material well-being alone cannot make people happy".[27]

Reconstruction medieval harmony

On 29 June 1928 – the feast of Saints Peter and Paul – Aengenent received the message that he had been appointed bishop of the diocese Haarlem, the previous bishop, August Callier, having died two months before. He was ordained on 25 July in Saint Bavo's Cathedral, which was just in the process of being finished. Aengenent laid the first stone for the two spires in the same year of 1928. His nomination put a stop to his scientific work. He relinquished all his positions (Catholic Social Action, *Katholiekendagen*, and the Council of Labour) and he discontinued his sociological reviews. But this did not mean that he abandoned his philosophical orientation: we can say that as a bishop he turned his activity into the implementation of his philosophical views. This was already recognisable in his episcopal motto: *Justitia et Pax*. At his death it was said that Aengenent had been inspired by Saint Thomas in choosing this motto, as he was convinced that true peace between the classes could only materialise when true justice would rule the world, that social justice and social peace between the classes would bring about the divine order, and that it was his task as a bishop to further this peace and justice. In his first pastoral letter, he concentrated on charity as the solution to the problems of his time: justice was important, but love of one's neighbour led to peaceful social relationships and moderated strict (legal) justice. This included non-Catholics, who were children of the same Father and who also strove for the common good. His other pastoral letters, for example at Lent, were 'co-productions'

---

27   Id., *De beteekenis van den achturendag*. Quotation p. 18.

with other bishops, or were explanations of papal encyclicals such as *Quadra-gesimo anno*.

Though his neo-scholastic inspiration is difficult to identify in his publications as a bishop, it is evident in his deeds. First, he invested in the philosophical foundations of social action for priests and laity alike. As early as 1929 he reorganised the Warmond seminary's philosophy course. After the anti-modernist campaign of the beginning of the century, which led to the dismissal of some of the best professors, the intellectual level of the courses had declined. Aengenent wanted to bring back the old days, in which he had been able to profit much from his studies, and he started with the philosophical foundations by extending the philosophy course from two to three years. He also laid the foundation for a new philosophical institute adjacent to the major seminary, which was inaugurated in the academic year of 1930-1931. In three ornaments on the wall of this institute, he honoured Pope Leo XIII, *Aeterni Patris*, and the restauration of Thomistic philosophy. In 1928 Aengenent published his handbook for the lay apostolate. He wrote in the introduction that he was inspired by the social conferences organised by Cardinal Mercier, which had been published together in a volume called *Code social, esquisse d'une synthèse social catholique*. But the handbook can also be seen as a summary of his textbook sociology, to be used by laypersons so that they would have a sound foundation for their social action and for their discussions with non-Catholics.[28]

Second, Aengenent's neo-scholastic inspiration is evident in his efforts to reconstruct the medieval history of his diocese. Neo-scholastic authors regarded medieval society as the ideal society, in which the religious ideas espoused by a united Catholic Church had ordered society justly and harmoniously. They used medieval examples to construct their own society without the complicated social problems that had, according to these authors, been caused by the Reformation, the Enlightenment, the French Revolution, secularisation, and the loss of religious principles in general. A specifically Dutch aspect was that medieval history was used to provide Dutch Catholics with a social identity in their country, an identity that had been lost since their suppression after 1648. Aengenent was involved in an attempt to make this medieval history a living experience for the Catholics of his time, so that they would be inspired and nourished by it in their social action. He rebuilt the sanctuary of the Martyrs of Gorkum, a group of priests killed by Protestant rebels in 1572 that was sanctified 1867. A great celebration was held in April 1933, in the presence of the entire Dutch episcopate, of the 500th anniversary of the death

---

28   Winkeler, "Het onderwijs op Warmond", 154-158; for a description of this first year see Van der Poel, "Het eerste jaar philosophicum". Aengenent, "Katholieke beginselen op sociaal gebied".

of Lidwina of Schiedam, a young woman who had lived a life of faithfully en-
dured suffering after injuring herself in a fall on the ice. Aengenent renovated
the medieval Marian places of pilgrimage of Heiloo and Middelburg. He stimulated settlement of several religious orders in his diocese, both active and
contemplative. The best example of his reconstruction efforts is the settlement
of Benedictine monks on the grounds occupied by the famous Egmond Abbey
before its complete destruction in 1573. Aengenent also made efforts to turn
the burial place of Saint Adalbert (the Anglo-Saxon missionary who accompanied Saint Willibrord) into a place of pilgrimage, the place where his body had
rested before it was transferred to the medieval abbey.[29]

Conclusion

The consecration of Egmond Abbey was Bishop Aengenent's last public act.
Shortly afterwards, he went to hospital for treatment of a stomach complaint,
from which he died on 3 September 1935. He was buried in the episcopal crypt
at Overveen's Roman Catholic cemetery on 7 September. Aengenent was a
unique bishop in the history of the diocese of Haarlem and of pre-Vatican II
Dutch Catholicism. Other bishops focused much more on the Church's internal organisation and left social action to others, although this did not stop
them from intervening in Catholic social organisations whenever they considered this necessary for the salvation of souls. Aengenent had built a vast
social and political network as a professor already, and was active in a variety
of social and political organisations. As a bishop, he continued to intervene in
political and social questions (notably the discussion about fascism and National Socialism) and directed the reorganisation of the youth organisations
himself. His perspective was broader than the Catholic Church, and included
the whole of society, which he considered a means and not a goal in itself. He
was succeeded by Mgr. Huibers, the Dean of Amsterdam, who was an opponent of the reorganisation of youth work in the diocese.[30]

In his work as a bishop and as a professor, Aengenent was clearly influenced by neo-scholastic philosophy. He received his training right after this
philosophy was made the standard norm in the universal Church. Interestingly however, he almost never referred explicitly to Saint Thomas or to other

---

29 For a more detailed overview of Aengenent's activities see Sengers, *Roomsch socioloog –
    sociale bisschop*, 222-230. See also Raedts, *De ontdekking van de middeleeuwen* and Sen-
    gers, *"Al zijn we katholiek"*.
30 Compare for other bishops the biography of Cardinal De Jong, who was trained as a church
    historian, was strongly opposed to the German occupation, and enforced Catholic unity
    after World War II: Van Osch, *Kardinaal de Jong*.

scholastic thinkers. But in his first works already he used elements of this phi-losophy to attack Marxism and liberalism on the fundamental level of prin-ciple. In his writings about the economy, which constituted the greater part of his publications, he clearly used elements of neo-scholastic philosophy to sketch the lines of a Christian economy. He focused on natural rights and duties to discuss property rights, and the best way to insure workers. Many publications dealt with the organisation of the workers into classes or profes-sions, so that they would create bonds of solidarity among themselves and with other classes. And he used the theory of a just price to claim a just income for workers as well as a restricted working day. As a bishop, too, his debt to neo-scholastic influences is clear. His episcopal motto must be interpreted as a reference to his views on how society should be reconstructed according to the divine social order. He stimulated philosophical studies at the seminary, and the ornaments on the seminary building make clear which philosophy he meant. He also made a great effort to reconstruct medieval history to make Catholics experience what this society could be like in their own time.

Aengenent certainly was not an original philosopher, nor was he en-gaged in scientific and scholarly philosophical networks. He was an autodi-dact and seminary professor with a focus on the practical usage of neo-scho-lastic thinking for the Catholic social movement, collaborating with lay people or instructing them. He referred to papal documents and other, mostly German thinkers, and it is difficult to identify any place where he developed a philosophical position of his own. This can be explained by the fact that neo-Thomistic social philosophy was relatively new during his active life, and only received its final shape with *Quadragesimo anno* in 1931 – shortly before Aengenent died. It was relatively safe to refer to papal documents, so as to avoid being suspected of modernist opinions. His originality lay in the adap-tation of this philosophy to the social field, where he confronted it with con-temporary social questions, and in his social and political action, in which he tried to put the principles and background of this philosophy into practice. At the same time, this also shows the great continuity of Catholic social thought up to the present day. Many of the principles that Aengenent and his fellow activists in the economic field used, and many positions that they took are still in force and have been incorporated in the *Compendium of the Social Doctrine of the Church*. The neo-scholastic vision on the human person, as a being with a body and a soul, living in the world and oriented to his final destination, sol-idaristic and working for the common good, thus still guides the social action of the Catholic social movement.[31]

---

31   Te Velde, "Neothomisme als cultuurkritiek voor politiek, economie en samenleving".

BIBLIOGRAPHY

Primary sources

Aengenent, J.D.J. "Het wetenschappelijk socialisme van Karl Marx". *De Katholiek*, 118 (1900), 34-59, 163-184 and 119 (1901), 105-134, 399-422.

Aengenent, J.D.J. "Eigendom en natuurrecht". *De Katholiek*, 120 (1901), 158-243.

Aengenent, J.D.J. "Darwinisme en democratie". *De Katholiek*, 122 (1902), 331-354.

Aengenent, J.D.J. "De kapitalistische maatschappij". *De Katholiek*, 124 (1903), 351-365.

Aengenent, J.D.J. "Reorganisatie der kapitalistische maatschappij". *De Katholiek*, 125 (1904), 361-396.

Aengenent, J.D.J. "Een universiteitsprofessor over de scholastieke wijsbegeerte". *De Katholiek*, 128 (1905), 79-81.

Aengenent, J.D.J. "Verplichte verzekering, vrijwillige verzekering of staatspensioneering?" *Katholiek Sociaal Weekblad*, 8 (1909), 253-257.

Aengenent, J.D.J. "Waarom verplichte verzekering?". *Katholiek Sociaal Weekblad*, 11 (1912), 230-237.

Aengenent, J.D.J. *Salarisregeling en katholieke sociologie*. Leiden: Futura, 1917.

Aengenent, J.D.J. "Het bedrijfsradenstelsel". *De Katholiek*, 158 (1920), 149-165.

Aengenent, J.D.J. *Het bedrijfsradenstelsel verwezenlijkt*. 's-Hertogenbosch: Teulings, 1920.

Aengenent, J.D.J. *De beteekenis van den achturendag en de taak der vrouw*. Leiden: Futura, 1921.

Aengenent, J.D.J. "De theorie van mr. Pelster omtrent het arbeidsloon". *Katholiek Sociaal Weekblad*, 21 (1922), 355-357, 365-367, 369-371, 377-379.

Aengenent, J.D.J. *Bedrijfsorganisatie en medezeggenschap*. [Zwolle]: Nederlandse R.K. Metaalbewerkersbond, 1924.

Aengenent, J.D.J. "Gezinsloon". *Katholiek Sociaal Weekblad*, 24 (1925), 445-447.

Aengenent, J.D.J. "Katholieke beginselen op sociaal gebied". In J.D.J. Aengenent and J.H. Visser. *Handboek voor den leekenapostel*. Utrecht: Futura, 1929², 11-146.

Secondary sources

Aken O. Praem., L. van. *Tien sociale studiën voor werkgevers*. 's-Hertogenbosch: Teulings, 1915.

Diepenbeek, Wilhelmus J.J. van. *De coöperatieve organisatie. Coöperatie als maatschappelijk en economisch verschijnsel*. Delft: Eburon, 1990.

Eerenbeemt, H.F.J.M van den. "Ideeën rond 1900 van katholieken in Nederland over een reconstructie der maatschappij". *Sociale Wetenschappen*, 13 (1970) 4, 257-284.

Gelder, Eefje de. *Just price within Thomas Aquinas' theology*. MA thesis, Tilburg University.

Hamans, Paul et al. *Bisdom langs de Maas. Geschiedenis van de kerk in Limburg*. Maastricht: TIC, 2010.

Hellemans, Staf. *Strijd om de moderniteit. Sociale bewegingen en verzuiling in Europa sinds 1800*. Leuven: Universitaire Pers Leuven, 1990.

Jacobs, J.Y.H.A. "Een kentering in de katholieke sociale actie. Een terugblik op de encycliek *Rerum novarum* honderd jaar na dato vanuit een Nederlands perspectief". *Documentatieblad voor de Nederlandse kerkgeschiedenis na 1800*, 14 (1991) 35, 1-22.

Laarse, R. van der. "'Verzwolgen door den ultramontaansen vloed'. Leken en clerus in katholiek Delft in de negentiende eeuw". In J.C.H. Blom and C.J. Misset, eds. *'Broeders sluit u aan'. Aspecten van verzuiling in zeven Hollandse gemeenten*. [Amsterdam]: De Bataafsche Leeuw, 1985, 68-109.

Langholm, Odd. *The Legacy of Scholasticism in Economic Thought: Antecedents of Choice and Power*. Cambridge: Cambridge University Press, 1998.

Osch, Henk van. *Kardinaal de Jong. Heldhaftig en behoudend*. Amsterdam: Boom, 2016.

Pels, Dick. *Property and Power in Social Theory: A Study in Intellectual Rivalry*. London-New York: Routledge, 1998.

Pierson, Christopher. *Just Property: A History in the Latin West*. Vol. 1: *Wealth, Virtue and the Law*. Oxford: Oxford University Press, 2013.

Poel, G. van der. "Het eerste jaar philosophicum". In *Waar eens een Franse kostschool stond. Opstellen over Warmonds studentenleven*. Warmond: Cassiciacum, 1949, 115-123.

Raedts, Peter. *De ontdekking van de middeleeuwen. Geschiedenis van een illusie*. Amsterdam: Wereldbibliotheek, 2012.

Sassen, Ferd. *Wijsgeerig leven in Nederland in de twintigste eeuw*. Amsterdam: N.V. Noord-Hollandsche Uitgevers Mij., 1947.

Schuster S.J., Johann Baptist. *Die Soziallehre nach Leo XIII. und Pius XI. unter besonderer Berücksichtigung der Beziehungen zwischen Einzelmensch und Gemeinschaft*. Freiburg im Breisgau: Herder & Co, 1935.

Sengers, Erik. "*Al zijn we katholiek, we zijn Nederlanders". Opkomst en verval van de katholieke kerk in Nederland sinds 1795 vanuit rational choice perspectief*. Delft: Eburon, 2003.

Sengers, Erik. *Roomsch socioloog – sociale bisschop. Joannes Aengenent als ideoloog en bestuurder van de katholieke sociale beweging 1873-1935*. Hilversum: Verloren, 2016.

Struyker Boudier, C.E.M. *Wijsgerig leven in Nederland, België en Luxemburg 1880-1980*. Vol. 1: *De Jezuïeten*. Nijmegen: Katholiek Studiecentrum – Baarn: Ambo, 1985.

Struyker Boudier, C.E.M. *Wijsgerig leven in Nederland en België*. Vol. 2: *De Dominicanen*. Nijmegen: Katholiek Studiecentrum – Baarn: Ambo, 1986.

Struyker Boudier, C.E.M. *Wijsgerig leven in Nederland en België 1880-1980*. Vol. 3: *In Godsnaam, de Augustijnen, Carmelieten en Minderbroeders*. Nijmegen: Katholiek Studiecentrum – Baarn: Ambo, 1987.

Velde, Rudi te. "Neothomisme als cultuurkritiek voor politiek, economie en samenleving." In Erik Sengers, ed. *Sociaal saamhorig solidair. Rerum novarum en de actuele sociale kwesties*. Vogelenzang: Centrum voor de Sociale Leer van de Kerk, 2017, 49-58.

Warffemius, A. *400 jaar kerken in 'De Papenhoek'. De Maria van Jessekerk en haar voorgangers*. Zeist: Rijksdienst voor de monumentenzorg – Delft: Sint Hippolytusparochie, 2005.

Winkeler, Lodewijk. "Het onderwijs op Warmond, 1799-1967". *Trajecta*, 9 (2000) 2, 134-167.

Winkeler, Lodewijk. "Sociografie en pastoraal beleid 1946-1957. Franciscanen en de opkomst van de godsdienstsociologie in Nederland". In: J. van Gennip et al., eds. *Het geloof dat inzicht zoekt. Religieuzen en de wetenschap*. Hilversum: Verloren, 2010, 178-192.

Woud, Auke van der. *Koninkrijk vol sloppen. Achterbuurten en vuil in de negentiende eeuw*. Amsterdam: Bert Bakker, 2010.

Antoine Pottier. Photo, 1923.
[Leuven, KADOC: KB7537 (*Monseigneur Pottier. Hommage de ses amis Liégeois*, 1924)]

ANTOINE POTTIER AND THE NEO-THOMISTIC ROOTS OF SOCIAL JUSTICE

JEAN-PIERRE DELVILLE

This essay aims to illustrate how neo-Thomism offered a philosophical grounding to the concept of social justice and gave it a universal dimension. An outstanding proponent of this line of thought was the Christian democrat priest of the diocese of Liège Antoine Pottier, who was born in Spa in 1849 and died in Rome in 1923.[1] Pottier was given the title of 'Doctor of Christian Democracy', in line with the great doctors of the Church, such as the 'Angelic Doctor' (Thomas Aquinas), the 'Universal Doctor' (Albert the Great), or the 'Seraphic Doctor' (Bonaventure of Bagnoregio).[2] Pottier was a professor of moral theology at the Seminary of Liège. During the widespread workers' strikes in Belgium of March 1886, he experienced a social conversion that led him to search for an answer to the social injustice in the industrial region of Liège. He pleaded for structural solutions to social misery: Catholics should not only show a personal (charitable) involvement in social matters but also needed to embrace trade unionism and political action. Pottier was supported by his bishop Victor-Joseph Doutreloux (1837-1901),[3] who also showed a high

---

1   Pelzer, ed., *Monseigneur Pottier*; Gerin, *Les origines de la Démocratie chrétienne à Liège*;
     Id., *Catholiques liégeois et question sociale*; Id., "Pottier"; Id., "L'abbé Antoine Pottier";
     Jadoulle, *La pensée de l'abbé Pottier*; Id., "Anthropologie et vision de la société chez
     Antoine Pottier"; Id., "La question sociale, une question religieuse avant tout", 47 and 66;
     Delville, "Antoine Pottier"; Id., "Réseaux démocrates chrétiens et appuis pontificaux".
2   Cardolle, *Un précurseur, un docteur, un pionnier social, Mgr Pottier*.
3   On Doutreloux, see Gérin, "La démocratie chrétienne dans les relations Église-État";
     Simon, "Doutreloux, Victor-Joseph"; Id., *Évêques de la Belgique indépendante*.

personal involvement in social matters and in 1886 convened the first Social Congress of Belgian Catholics in Liège.[4]

Pottier began his social agency in 1888 by founding a workers' association (Cercle St. Joseph) in Spa and a consumer cooperative in Liège, the Society of St. Alphonse.[5] A year later he wrote *La coopération et les sociétés ouvrières*, a study mainly approaching the social issue from a sociological and economical perspective and thus not primarily philosophical or theological in nature. In 1890 Pottier was a keynote speaker at the third Social Congress of the Belgian Catholics in Liège. There he was introduced to a broad range of Western European social-Catholics: the French Catholic entrepreneur Léon Harmel (1829-1915)[6]; Carl Bachem (1858-1945), a member of the German Reichstag for the Zentrumspartei[7]; Gaspar Decurtins (1855-1916) from Switzerland[8]; Paul Naudet (1859-1929), a Christian democrat priest from Bordeaux and founder of the journal *La Justice Sociale* (1893-1908)[9]; Henri Lorin (1857-1915), president of the Union d'Etude des Catholiques Sociaux[10] and vice-president of the Fribourg Union (1884-1891)[11], an international think tank that clearly influenced Pope Leo XIII (1810-1903) and his social encyclical *Rerum novarum* (1891).[12] Pottier also met other members of the Fribourg Union, including René de la Tour du Pin (1834-1924), Franz von Kuefstein (1841-1918)[13], Baron Karl von Vogelsang and Stanislao Medolago Albani (1851-1921), from 1892 onwards president of the second section of the Italian Opera dei Congressi.[14] In his lecture to the Liège social congress of 1890, entitled "Ce qu'il y a de légitime dans les revendications ouvrières", Pottier argued that workers' wages should not only depend on the contractual negotiations between individual workers and their employers, but that also the state needed to intervene, for instance by establishing minimum standards and providing a legal framework enabling wages to be collectively negotiated between trade unions and employers' associations. Wages needed to be adequate to support the worker's family. Pottier's position in favour of state intervention in social matters would become a main characteristic of the so-called Liège school. The socially committed

---

4   Gerin, "Les Congrès sociaux de Liège (1886, 1887 et 1890)".
5   About the Société St-Alphonse, see Gerin, *Catholiques liégeois et question sociale*, 350-351.
6   Guitton, *Léon Harmel*; Trimouille, *Léon Harmel et l'usine chrétienne du Val-des-Bois*.
7   Kiefer, *Karl Bachem*.
8   Fry, *Kaspar Decurtins*; Flury, *Decurtins Kampf um die Kirche*.
9   Sorrel, "Réformisme ou anticléricalisme croyant?"; Poulat, "Naudet (Paul)".
10 Voog, "Lorin (Henri)".
11 Hoyois, "Aux origines de 'Rerum Novarum'"; Chenaux, "Les origines de l'Union de Fribourg".
12 T'Serclaes, *Le pape Léon XIII*; Spahn, *Leo XIII*; Viaene, ed., *The Papacy and the New World Order*; Ledure, *"Rerum Novarum" en France*.
13 Bayot, "Kuefstein (comte Franz)". Secretary of the Union of Fribourg, he presented to the congress of Liège in 1890 the Union's ideas about the minimum wage and about the intervention of the state, ideas similar to those of Pottier.
14 Brezzi, *Cristiano-sociali e intransigenti*; Id., "Medolago Albani, Stanislas".

priest had based his arguments on the ideas of the Jesuit Taparelli d'Azeglio (1793-1862)[15], who insisted on the equivalence of exchanged goods, labour and wages in particular. Similar arguments had been made by theologians of the sixteenth and seventeenth century, such as Juan de Lugo (1583-1660)[16], Juan Azorius (1536-1603)[17], Martin Bonacina (1585-1631)[18], Luis de Molina (1535-1600)[19], Leonardus Lessius (1554-1623)[20], Gabriel Vasquez (1549/1551-1604)[21], and Paul Laymann (1574-1635)[22]. Pottier also extensively referred to Thomas Aquinas[23], the Bible[24], Anaclet Reiffenstuel (1642-1703)[25] and Henri Lacordaire (1802-1861)[26]. He also highlighted the views of liberal economists. Adam Smith (1726-1790)[27] for instance, had clearly argued in favour of family wages, while Paul Leroy-Beaulieu (1843-1916)[28] had even equated minimum wages to natural wages.

Pottier also gladly underlined how several contemporary moral theologians defended similar positions of minimum and fair wages: known neo-Thomists such as Matteo Liberatore[29] or August Lehmkuhl[30], Edward De Gryse (1843-1916)[31], professor at the seminary of Bruges; P.H. Marres[32], profes-

---

15   Teisseyre, "Taparelli d'Azeglio (Luigi)". Jesuit, a proponent of natural law, specialist in moral philosophy, Taparelli was one of the principal editors of *La Civiltà cattolica* and a pioneer in the area of international rights. Quoted by Pottier, "Ce qu'il y a de légitime dans les revendications ouvrières", 22, 26, 27, 28, 31.

16   Juan de Lugo (Spanish Jesuit), *Disputationes de iustitia et iure*, Lyon, 1642 (quoted p. 23, 24, 32, 35). Cf. C. I., in *Catholicisme hier, aujourd'hui, demain*, vol. 7, Paris, 1969, 1279.

17   Juan Azorius, Spanish Jesuit, author of the *Institutiones morales*, Rome, 1600-1611. See Brouillard, "Azor (Juan)" (quoted p. 24).

18   Martin Bonacina (priest in Milan), *De contractibus* (quoted p. 25, 36).

19   Luis de Molina, *De justitia et iure* (quoted p. 45, 52, 131-132, 235, 238, 239).

20   Léonard Lessius, *De iure et iustitia* (quoted p. 23, 82, 85, 96).

21   Gabriel Vazquez, *Dubia* (quoted p. 23); *De restitutione* (quoted p. 237).

22   Paul Laymann, *Theologia moralis*, Munich, 1625 (quoted p. 23-24). See Bailly, "Laymann (Paul)".

23   Thomas of Aquinas, *Summa theologica* (quoted p. 22, 24, 44); *In caput II Gen* (quoted p. 31)

24   Gn 3,19 (quoted p. 30); Jac 5,4 (quoted p. 22).

25   Anaclet Reiffenstuel, *Ius canonicum universum*, Munich, 1700-1714 (quoted p. 23-24, 33-34). See Schmitt, "Reiffenstuel, Anaclet".

26   Baron, "Lacordaire (Henri-Dominique)". Lacordaire is quoted for his phrase: "Le commencement de la charité, c'est la justice" (quoted p. 29).

27   Adam Smith, *Recherches sur la cause et la nature des richesses des nations*, 1776 (quoted p. 32 and 40). Cf. Luterbacher-Maineri, *Adam Smith*.

28   Leroy-Beaulieu (Catholic liberal economist), *Essai sur la répartition de la richesse et sur la tendance à une moindre inégalité des conditions*; Id., *De l'état moral et intellectuel des populations ouvrières et de son influence sur le taux des salaires*; Id., *La question ouvrière*. Cf. Warshaw, *Paul Leroy-Beaulieu and Established Liberalism in France*; on his brother, see Mayeur, "Anatole Leroy-Beaulieu", 79.

29   Liberatore, *Principii di economia politica* (quoted p. 37).

30   Lehmkuhl, *Le contrat entre patrons et ouvriers et les grèves* (quoted p. 37).

31   De Gryse, *Notre droit national et la révolution* (quoted p. 37); Id., *Katholieke kerk en christene volksschool*. Cf. Decoene, *Doctor Edward De Gryse*.

32   Marres, *De iustitia secundum doctrinam theologicam* (quoted p. 37).

sor at the seminary of Roermond; Francis Patrick Kenrick, bishop of Baltimore (1797-1863)[33], and Rafael de Cepeda (1850-1918)[34], professor at Valencia. But he also stressed that his positions were in firm contradiction with those of Thomas Robert Malthus (1766-1834)[35]. Pottier also eagerly distanced himself from the ideas of the socialist Louis Blanc (1811-1882), who had argued that work was an individual right and that the state had to provide labour for everyone.[36] Labour, according to Pottier, is a means that is characterised by its utility; the worker has the right to profit from his work.[37] He has the right to subsist and the right to receive the fruits of his work, also when he is not the proprietor of his job.[38]

The publication of *Rerum novarum* gave further impetus to Pottier's social action. Decurtins had sent Pottier a Latin text of the encyclical even before its publication.[39] Antoine Pottier now founded the Saint Joseph Cooperative and different trade unions, for example one for stonecutters. In 1891 he participated in the foundation of the Ligue Démocratique Belge with Arthur Verhaegen, Michel Levie and Godefroid Kurth.[40] On 1 April 1892, Pottier and Arthur Verhaegen[41] launched their political Christian Democratic programme at the national level.[42] On 9 October, Pottier started the journal *Le Bien du Peuple: Journal démocrate chrétien*. The concept 'Christian democracy' seems to have originated in Liège with Pottier; he actually wrote about this later: "After this designation was launched in Liège, it was greeted with enthusiasm by our friends in the north of France, then by our friends in other countries, mainly in Italy". In 1894 the *Osservatore Romano* published a laudatory essay on Pottier. In 1895, he participated in founding the journal *La Justice Sociale* in Brussels.[43] Another journal with the same title had been launched in 1893 in France under the direction of Naudet. In 1895 this French priest would publish a biography of Pottier in *Le Monde*. Pottier and Bishop Doutreloux journeyed to Rome in May where they briefed the pope on the conflict that had arisen be-

33   Francis Patrick Kenrick, bishop of Philadelphia, afterwards archbishop of Baltimore, biblical scholar and theologian (quoted p. 38); cf. Nolan, *The Most Reverend Francis Patrick Kenrick*; Brokhage, *Francis Patrick Kenrick's Opinion on Slavery*.
34   Rafael Rodríguez de Cepeda, Professor of Philosophy of Right in Valence, author of *Elementos de derecho natural*.
35   Thomas Robert Malthus, English economist, author of *Essai sur le principe de population*, and of *Definitions in Political Economy*. Cf. Laurent, "Malthus et les malthusianismes".
36   Cf. Humilière, *Louis Blanc* (quoted p. 41).
37   Pottier, "Ce qu'il y a de légitime dans les revendications ouvrières", 42.
38   Ibid., 30.
39   Riche, *Une page d'histoire sociale*, 7.
40   Deneckere, *Les turbulences de la Belle Époque*, 148; Hensmans, *Les origines de la démocratie chrétienne en Belgique*; Rezsohazy, *Origines et formation du catholicisme social en Belgique*.
41   De Maeyer, *Arthur Verhaegen*.
42   Gérin, *Catholiques liégeois et question sociale*, 127-128.
43   *La justice sociale*, 1895-1902.

tween the Belgian Christian democrats and the more conservative social Catholics, Pottier and Léon Collinet (1842-1908)[44] in particular. Pottier returned to Rome in August where he was instructed to tone down his social commitment.

In that same period, probably in early 1896, he welcomed to Liège his friend Giacomo Radini-Tedeschi (1857-1914), who was then vice-president of the Opera dei Congressi, a structure coordinating the Catholic social organisations in Italy.[45] In 1898, he wrote to the great Italian Catholic sociologist Giuseppe Toniolo[46]: "When Monsignor Radini came to see me in Liège, I was inclined to offer an essay on the requirements of natural right and divine right in the matter of labour contracts". This seems to indicate that Pottier was planning to write a study for the *Rivista internazionale di scienze sociali*, founded by Toniolo in 1893, and that he aimed to focus it on the scholastic categories of natural right and divine right. Another letter to Toniolo, also written in 1898, seems to confirm this. "All the professors of theology in this seminary were delighted by your two essays in the *Rivista* on Christian democracy [...]", so Pottier wrote. "All those who assert that democracy rests on scientific bases will be encouraged by the deeply wise, historical as well as philosophical, analysis that you magnificently develop in your essays in the *Rivista*".

In 1899 Pottier would write his treatise *De jure et justitia. Dissertationes de notione generali juris et justitiae et de justitia legali.*[47] In his foreword Pottier notes that the *Dissertationes* were based on the courses that he had offered to his seminarians over the past eleven years and that they were firmly anchored in scholastic philosophy. In his footnotes he actually cites Thomas 102 times, especially the *Summa theologica, Contra gentiles, De regimine principum, De obligationibus justitiae, In Politicam*, and the *Quolibet*.

---

44 President of the Union Nationale pour le Redressement des Griefs and member of the Fribourg Union.
45 Tedeschi later became bishop of Bergamo, where he was assisted by his secretary Fr. Angelo Roncalli (1881-1963), the future Pope John XXIII. Later on, at Roncalli's request, Pottier would write an eulogy for Radini-Tedeschi. Roncalli, ed., *In memoriam di Mons. Giacomo Maria Radini Tedeschi*; Id., *Mons. Giacomo Maria Radini Tedeschi*; Battelli, *Un pastore tra fede e ideologia. G.M. Radini-Tedeschi*.
46 About Giuseppe Toniolo: Sorrentino, *L'economista di Dio*; Id., *Giuseppe Toniolo: una biografia*; Id., *Giuseppe Toniolo: una chiesa nella storia*; Aubert, "Toniolo après la traversée du désert"; Andreazza, *Alle origini del movimento cattolico pisano*; Pecorari, *Toniolo: un economista per la democrazia*; Id., *Ketteler e Toniolo*; Burgalassi, *Alle origini della sociologia*; Trucco and Molesti, eds., *Il pensiero economico-sociale di Giuseppe Toniolo*; Spicciani, *Giuseppe Toniolo tra economia e storia*; Id., *Agli inizi della storiografia economica medioevistica in Italia*; Da Persico, *La vita di Giuseppe Toniolo*. The Apostolic Library of the Vatican holds the letters of Toniolo in Carteggi Giuseppe Toniolo, 25.2.1885 - 7.9.1917. The letters he wrote are published: Toniolo, *Lettere (1871-1918)*. His works are published: Id., *Opera Omnia*.
47 On right and justice. Dissertations on the general notion of right and justice and on legal justice.

Pottier's sources further include the Bible[48] (36 quotations); some classical authors, such as Aristotle[49], Augustine[50], Clement of Rome[51] and Justinianus[52]; the authors of treatises about justice which he had already used in his lecture of 1890[53], including Juan de Lugo[54], Luis de Molina[55], Francis Leonard Lessius[56], Gabriel Vasquez[57], and Martin Bonacina[58], but also adding Suárez[59] and Fernand Rebellus[60]. Pottier additionally referred to commentators on Thomas such as Francis Sylvius[61], Gregorius of Valencia[62], Cajetanus[63] and Roderichus of Arriaga[64]. His most recent references are to three documents of the Roman Magisterium: a letter from Mgr. Domenico Jacobini, prefect of the Congregation of the Propaganda Fide, to Decurtins[65], a letter from Pope Leo XIII to Willem II[66] and a letter from Cardinal Zigliara to Cardinal Goossens[67]. His favourite authors were Antonio Burri[68], Giuseppe Toniolo[69],

48   Gn 1,28 (quoted p. 103, 168 and 212); Gn 2,2 (213); Gn 3,19 (24-25, 224); Gn 13,1-19 (43-44); Ex 20,8 (213); Sag 10,10 (67); Ps 31,5 (88); Ps 36,7 (88); Ps 118,13 (88); Pr 14,34 (155); Pr 30,8.9 (156); Is 32,17 (155); Mt 1,19 (66); Mt 5,6 (66); Mt 5,20 (66); Mt 5,39 (95); Mt 6,1 (66); Mt 6,33 (67); Mt 16,4 (168); Lc 2,41 (28); Lc 12,50 (94); Lc 6,20 (95); Jn 17,21 (70); Rm 10,12 (212); 1 Co 9,14 (241); 1 Co 6,7 (95); 2 Thess 3,10 (234); 2 Thess 3,12 (25); 2 Tim 2,6 (257); He 10,34 (95); James 5,4 (255).
49   Aristotle (384-322 BC), *Politique* (quoted p. 32, 103, 106, 133).
50   Augustine (354-430), *Liber de haeresibus* (quoted p. 42); *De civitate Dei* (quoted p. 82).
51   Clement of Rome († 97) (quoted p. 46).
52   Justinian (482-565) (quoted p. 41).
53   See above, notes 15-28.
54   Card. Juan de Lugo, *De iustitia et iure* (quoted p. 8, 44, 45, 52, 94, 96, 187, 191).
55   Luis de Molina, *De justitia et iure* (quoted p. 45, 52, 131-132, 235, 238, 239).
56   Leonard Lessius, *De iure et iustitia* (quoted p. 23, 82 85, 96).
57   Gabriel Vazquez, *Dubia* (quoted p. 23); *De restitutione* (quoted p. 237).
58   Martin Bonacina (quoted p. 235, 237).
59   Francisco de Suárez (Spanish Jesuit, 1548-1617), *De Deo effectore* (quoted p. 47); *De legibus* (quoted p. 129-131, 155); *In tertiam partem S. Thomae* (quoted p. 241).
60   Fernandus Rebellus (1546-1608, professor in Ebora in Portugal), *De obligationibus justitiae* (quoted p. 132, 156).
61   Francis Sylvius (1581-1649, professor in Douai), *Commentarium in 2am 2ae S. Thomae*, Douai, 1628 (quoted p. 93, 111).
62   Gregory of Valencia (Spanish Jesuit, 1549-1603), *Commentarii in 1am 2ae* (quoted p. 111, 138).
63   Cajetan (Thomas de Vio, Italian Dominican, 1469-1534), *In summam theologicam commentarium* (quoted p. 136, 149).
64   Roderich de Arriaga (Spanish Jesuit, 1592-1667), *Disputationes théologicae in Iam 2ae S. Thomae* (quoted p. 56).
65   Jacobini to Decurtins, 1 May 1889, "pour une législation européenne contre le travail des enfants" (quoted p. 122).
66   Leo XIII to Willem II, 14 March 1890, on the same object.
67   Letter from Cardinal Zigliara to Cardinal Goossens, 1891, following T'Serclaes, *Le pape Léon XIII* (quoted p. 250).
68   Burri, *Le teorie politiche di San Tommaso e il moderno diritto pubblico* (quoted p. 148). See Agocs, "Christian Democracy and Social Modernism in Italy".
69   Toniolo, "Il concetto cristiano della democrazia"; translated into French: *Le concept chrétien de démocratie* (quoted p. 75, 190).

Auguste Lehmkuhl[70], Georges Vaes[71], Edouard Vandersmissen[72], and the journals *La Civiltà Cattolica*[73] and *Le Bien Public*[74].

By extensively referring to Thomas, Pottier asserted that his *Dissertationes* were firmly based on natural right[75] and the right of the people[76]. Besides offering an analysis of property rights and their limits[77], Pottier particularly explained the subdivisions of justice[78] and defined the notions of legal justice and social justice (*De justitia legali seu sociali*).[79] According to the Liège scholar the concept 'social justice' derives from the Thomist definition of 'general justice' and 'legal justice': "Justice, which is divided into two integral parts comprises general justice, either social or legal, and individual justice, or at least commutative justice".[80] He emphasised that justice not only encompasses commutative justice, based on a contract between two persons: "In itself, legal justice directly considers a sort of finality, the common good, while commutative justice concerns the good of the individual as such".[81]

Social justice is considered by Pottier as part of general justice, as it is based on the common good of a whole society and on the right of everybody to a decent life: "Legal or social justice is a special moral virtue through which the actions of members of society are regulated for the common good".[82] "It is also called social, especially today, because it considers the common or social good as a formal objective."[83] Social injustice can be defined following Aquinas: "therefore, and in this sense, Saint Thomas said: 'as regards intention, injustice against the law is a general vice, because contempt of the common good may lead a person to all kinds of sin'".[84] In accordance with general justice, people have the right to live, which implies that everybody should have

70 Lehmkuhl, *Le contrat entre patrons et ouvriers et les grèves* (quoted p. 207).
71 Vaes, *Les conditions du travail dans les marchés publics* (quoted p. 266).
72 Vandersmissen, "Le contrat de travail" (quoted p. 267).
73 "La ricchezza secondo l'idea cattolica", *Civiltà Cattolica*, 3 (189) 8, 25 (quoted p. 225 in Italian).
74 *Le Bien Public*, Ghent, 7 March 1900, article about mortality in Brussels (quoted p. 231).
75 Pottier, *De jure et justitia*, 9.
76 Ibid., 14-18.
77 Ibid., 18-54.
78 Ibid., 60-87.
79 Ibid., 97-164.
80 Ibid., 81, § 35: "Justitia quae sic dividitur in duas partes integrales est justitia generalis seu socialis seu legalis et justitia particularis saltem commutativa".
81 Ibid., 72, § 20: "Justitia legalis per se respicit directe quasi finem, bonum commune: justitia commutativa bonum privatorum, in quantum tales".
82 Ibid., 97, § 1: "Justitia legalis seu socialis est virtus moralis specialis qua actus membrorum societatis ad bonum commune ordinantur".
83 Ibid., 144, § 80: "Vocatur quoque socialis, praesertim in usu loquendi hodierno, quia respicit quasi objectum formale bonum commune seu sociale".
84 Ibid., 90, § 66: "Propterea et in hoc sensu dixit S. Thomas: 'quantum ad intentionem, injustitia illegalis est vitium generale, quia per contemptum boni communis potest homo ad omnia peccata deduci'" (*Summa theologica*, 2a 2ae, q. LIX, Arti. 1).

enough material goods to live in happiness: "The natural order ought to provide man with a sufficient quality of life [...]. Thus, happiness is the ultimate end of man".[85] Pottier adds: "Now human beings need society to obtain a sufficient quality of life".[86] Thus "by nature, a worker who is engaged by an employer for a job has the right – notwithstanding any official agreement to the contrary – to receive a wage that can maintain a worker who is honest and of good character".[87] In order to apply those principles[88], the intervention of the state is particularly necessary[89] in regulating the total amount of the wage.[90] As a consequence, workers also have the right to strike: "Where the contract is unjust, or not entered into freely, or has been changed by the employer against the will of the workers, it is permitted by agreement to desist from work that is not yet finished or has not been finished on time".[91] He adds[92]: "It will be permitted to workers who are united in a trade union to commit themselves to strike unanimously, in those cases in which (as has been here explained) it is permitted to strike, and not otherwise".[93]

Pottier clearly analysed the writings of Thomas Aquinas and his sixteenth- and seventeenth-century commentators to highlight the necessity of social justice and the duty of the state to regulate wages. He combined his concrete commitment to trade unions and cooperatives with his intellectual thought based on Thomism.

After the publication of his treatise *De jure et Justitia* (1900) and the death of Bishop Doutreloux (1901), Pottier somewhat became persona non-grata in Belgium and subsequently moved to Rome. He became a professor at the Leonianum, a school founded by Leo XIII and was granted the title of Monsignor, which gave him moral authority. He had an influence on Christian democracy in Italy, Spain and Latin America. This is, however, another history![94]

---

85 Pottier, *De jure et justitia*, 98, § 3: "Ordinatio naturalis debet procurare homini vitae sufficientiam perfectam [...]. Ergo beatitudo est finis ultimus hominis" (cf. S. Thomas, *Ethic. Libr.* 1. *Lect.* 2).

86 Ibid., 103, § 13: "Hominem indigere societate ad obtinendam vitae sufficientiam".

87 Ibid., 144, § 80: "a natura habet jus operarius cujus opus a hero conducitur ut non obstante quacumque contraria conventione positiva, quotam salarii consequatur haud imparem ad alendum opificem frugem et bene moratum".

88 Ibid., 165-201.

89 Ibid., 202-219.

90 Ibid., 220-265.

91 Ibid., 206, § 177: "Ubi contractus est injustus, aut non libere initus, aut a hero, obstantibus operariis, mutatus, licet ex condicto recedere ab opere nondum absoluto aut debito tempore non elapso".

92 Ibid., 207, § 178: "Propterea licebit operariis collegio adunatis se obligare ad unanimiter recedendum in casibus in quibus secundum exposita recedere licet et non ultra".

93 Ibid., 220-265.

94 Delville, "Un intellectuel au cœur de la question sociale"; Id., "Monseigneur Pottier dans la tourmente espagnole".

BIBLIOGRAPHY

Agocs, Sandor. "Christian Democracy and So-cial Modernism in Italy during the Papacy of Pius X". *Church History*, 42 (1973) 1, 73-88.

Andreazza, Mario. *Alle origini del movimento cattolico pisano: il card. Piertro Maffi e il prof. Giuseppe Toniolo*. Pisa: Giardini, 1991.

Aubert, Roger. "Toniolo après la traversée du désert". *Revue d'histoire ecclésiastique*, 91 (1996), 488-503.

Bailly, Paul. "Laymann (Paul)". In *Catholicisme, hier, aujourd'hui, demain*. Vol. 7. Paris: Letouzey et Ané, 1969, 102-103.

Baron, P. "Lacordaire (Henri-Dominique)". In *Catholicisme, hier, aujourd'hui, demain*. Vol. 6. Paris: Letouzey et Ané, 1963, 1568-1572.

Battelli, Giuseppe. *Un pastore tra fede e ideologia. G.M. Radini-Tedeschi, 1857-1914*. Bologna, 1990.

Bayot, Jean. "Kuefstein (comte Franz)". In *Catholicisme, hier, aujourd'hui, demain*. Vol. 6. Paris: Letouzey et Ané, 1963, 1490-1491.

Brezzi, Camillo. *Cristiano-sociali e intransigenti. L'opera di Medolago Albani fino alla "Rerum Novarum"*. Rome, 1971.

Brezzi, Camillo. "Medolago Albani, Stanislas". In *Dizionario storico del movimento cattolico in Italia, 1860-1980*. Vol. 2. Turin, 1984, 366-370.

Brokhage, Joseph D. *Francis Patrick Kenrick's Opinion on Slavery*. Washington: Catholic University of America Press, 1955.

Brouillard, R. "Azor (Juan)". In *Catholicisme, hier, aujourd'hui, demain*. Vol. 1. Paris: Letouzey et Ané, 1948, 1146.

Burgalassi, Silvano. *Alle origini della sociologia: G. Toniolo, e la scuola pisana (1878-1915)*. Pisa: ETS,1984.

Burri, Antonio. *Le teorie politiche di San Tommaso e il moderno diritto pubblico*. Rome: Società Cattolica Istruttiva, 1884.

Cardolle, J. *Un précurseur, un docteur, un pionnier social, Mgr Pottier (1849-1923)*. Brussels: Éd. du Mouvement ouvrier chrétien, 1951.

de Cepeda, Rafael Rodríguez. *Elementos de derecho natural*. Valencia: Domenech, 1888.

Chenaux, Philippe. "Les origines de l'Union de Fribourg". In *"Rerum Novarum". Ecriture, contenu et réception d'une encyclique*. Rome, 1997, 255-266.

Da Persico, Elena. *La vita di Giuseppe Toniolo*. Verona: Attivita' sociali Elena Da Persico, 1959.

Decoene, Alberic. *Doctor Edward De Gryse, deken van Kortrijk: zijn leven, zijn werk*. Bruges: Groenys, 1944.

De Gryse, Edward. *Notre droit national et la révolution*. Roeselare: De Meester, 1885.

De Gryse, Edward. *Katholieke kerk en christene volksschool: schets eener geschiedenis van het volksonderwijs*. Roeselare: De Meester, 1890.

Delville, Jean-Pierre. "Monseigneur Pottier dans la tourmente espagnole (1920-1922)". In *Le Semeur sortit pour semer. Grand Séminaire de Liège 1592-1992*. Liège: Dricot, 1992, 271-293.

Delville, Jean-Pierre. "Antoine Pottier (1849-1923), le 'Docteur de la démocratie chrétienne'. Ses relations internationales jusqu'à son exil à Rome en 1902". In Guy Zélis, Luc Courtois, Jean-Pierre Delville and Françoise Rosart, eds. *Les intellectuels catholiques en Belgique francophone (19ᵉ-20ᵉ siècles). Mélanges offerts à Jean Pirotte*. Louvain-la-Neuve: Presses universitaires de Louvain - Arca, 2009, 209-260.

Delville, Jean-Pierre. "Réseaux démocrates chrétiens et appuis pontificaux. L'action de Mgr Antoine Pottier (1849-1923) à Rome, de 1900 à 1908". In Jean-Pierre Delville and Marko Jacov, eds. *La papauté contemporaine: hommage au chanoine Roger Aubert, professeur émérite à l'Université catholique de Louvain, pour ses 95 ans. Il papato contemporaneo (secoli XIX-XX): omaggio al canonico Roger Aubert, professore emerito all'Università cattolica di Lovanio, per i 95 anni*. Louvain-la-Neuve: Collège Erasme, 2009, 195-228.

Delville, Jean-Pierre. "Un intellectuel au cœur de la question sociale: Mgr Antoine Pottier à Rome de 1905 à 1908". In Dries Vanysacker, Pierre Delsaerdt, Hedwig Schwall and Jean-Pierre Delville, eds. *The Quintessence of Lives: Intellectual Biographies in the Low Countries Presented to Jan Roegiers*. Bibliothèque de la RHE, 91. Turnhout: Brepols, 2010, 445-468.

De Maeyer, Jan. *Arthur Verhaegen 1847-1917, de rode baron*. Leuven: Universitaire Pers Leuven, 1994.

Deneckere, Gita. *Les turbulences de la Belle Époque. 1878-1905*. Nouvelle histoire de Belgique, 1878-1905, vol. 1. Brussels: Le Cri, 2010.

Flury, Johannes. *Decurtins Kampf um die Kirche: Antimodernismus in Schweizer Katholizismus*. Chur: Verlag Bündner Monatsblatt, 1997.

Fry, Karl. *Kaspar Decurtins: der Löwe von Truns: 1855-1916*. Zürich: Thomas Verlag, 1949-1952, 2 vols.

Gérin, Paul. *Les origines de la Démocratie chrétienne à Liège*. Brussels: La pensée catholique, 1958.

Gérin, Paul. *Catholiques liégeois et question sociale (1833-1914)*. Brussels: Études sociales, 1959.

Gérin, Paul. "Pottier". In *Biographie nationale*, vol. 30, Supplément. Brussels: Bruylant, 1959, 726-730.

Gérin, Paul. "La démocratie chrétienne dans les relations Église-État à la fin du XIXe siècle. L'action de Mgr Doutreloux". In *L'Église et l'État à l'époque contemporaine. Mélanges dédiés à la mémoire de Mgr Aloïs Simon*. Brussels: Facultés universitaires Saint-Louis, 1975, 255-287.

Gérin, Paul. "L'abbé Antoine Pottier: un maître à penser et à suivre". In *Le Grand Séminaire de Liège 1592-1992. Ouvrage historique*. Liège: Dricot, 1992, 149-168.

Gérin, Paul. "Les Congrès sociaux de Liège (1886, 1887 et 1890), carrefours du catholicisme social international". *Bollettino dell'Archivio per la storia del Movimento cattolico in Italia*, 38 (2003), 304-339.

Guitton, Georges. *Léon Harmel, 1829-1915*. Paris: Spes, 1927, 2 vols.

Hensmans, Martine. *Les origines de la démocratie chrétienne en Belgique*. Brussels: Éd. du Mouvement ouvrier chrétien, 1953.

Hoyois, Giovanni. "Aux origines de 'Rerum Novarum'. L'Union de Fribourg". *Dossiers de l'Action sociale*, 5 (1951).

Humilière, Jean-Michel. *Louis Blanc (1811-1882)*. Paris: Éditions ouvrières, 1982.

Jadoulle, Jean-Louis. "Anthropologie et vision de la société chez Antoine Pottier (1849-1923)". *Revue d'Histoire ecclésiastique*, 84 (1989), 30-47.

Jadoulle, Jean-Louis. *La pensée de l'abbé Pottier (1849-1923)*. Louvain-la-Neuve: Collège Erasme, 1991.

Jadoulle, Jean-Louis. "La question sociale, une question religieuse avant tout. Réponse d'un démocrate chrétien: Antoine Pottier (1849-1950)". In Françoise Rosart and Guy Zélis, eds. *Le monde catholique et la question sociale (1891-1950)*. Brussels: Editions Vie Ouvrière, 1991, 47-66.

Kiefer, Rolf. *Karl Bachem, 1858-1945. Politiker und Historiker des Zentrums*. Mainz: Grünewald, 1989.

Laurent, A. "Malthus et les malthusianismes". In *Catholicisme, hier, aujourd'hui, demain*. Vol. 8. Paris: Letouzey et Ané, 1976, 278-283.

Ledure, Yves. *"Rerum Novarum" en France. Le Père Dehon et l'engagement social de l'Église*. Paris: Éditions universitaires, 1991.

Lehmkuhl, Auguste. *Le contrat entre patrons et ouvriers et les grèves*. Leuven: A. Uystpruyst-Dieudonné, 1893.

Leroy-Beaulieu, Paul. *De l'état moral et intellectuel des populations ouvrières et de son influence sur le taux des salaires*. Paris: Guillaumin et cie, 1868.

Leroy-Beaulieu, Paul. *La question ouvrière au 19e siècle*. Paris: Charpentier et Cie, 1872.

Leroy-Beaulieu, Paul. *Essai sur la répartition de la richesse et sur la tendance à une moindre inégalité des conditions*. Paris: Guillaumin & cie., 1883.

Liberatore, Matteo. *Principii di economia politica*. Rome: A. Befani, 1889.

Luterbacher-Maineri, Claudius. *Adam Smith theologische Grundannahmen: Eine textkritische Studie*. Freiburg im Breisgau, 2008.

Malthus, Thomas Robert. *Essai sur le principe de population*. Paris, 1798.

Malthus, Thomas Robert. *Definitions in Political Economy*. London: Murray, 1827 [New York, 1963].

Marres, P.H. *De iustitia secundum doctrinam theologicam et principia iuris recentioris, speciatim vero neerlandici*. Roermond: Romen, 1879.

Mayeur, Jean-Marie, ed. *Histoire du christianisme*. Vol. 12: *Guerres mondiales et totalitarismes (1914-1958)*. Paris: Desclée, 1990, 154-186.

Mayeur, Jean-Marie, ed. *Histoire du christianisme des origines à nos jours*. Vol 11: *Libéralisme, industrialisation, expansion européenne (1830-1914)*. Paris: Desclée, 1995.

Mayeur, Jean-Marie. "Anatole Leroy-Beaulieu: un catholique libéral devant l'orthodoxie". In Miroslav Filipowicz, ed. *Churches, States, Nations in the Enlightenment and in the Nineteenth Century*. Lublin: Instytut Europy Šodkowo-Wschodniej, 2000, 79-107.

Nolan, Hugh Joseph. *The Most Reverend Francis Patrick Kenrick, third Bishop of Philadelphia, 1830-1851*. Washington: Catholic University of America, 1948.

Pecorari, Paolo. *Ketteler e Toniolo. Tipologie sociali del movimento cattolico in Europa*. Rome: Città Nuova, 1977.

Pecorari, Paolo. *Toniolo: un economista per la democrazia*. Rome: Studium, 1991.

Pelzer, Auguste, ed. *Monseigneur Pottier. Hommage de ses amis liégeois à l'occasion de l'anniversaire de son décès à Rome le 24 novembre 1923*. Brussels: Dewit, 1924.

Pottier, Antoine. *La coopération et les sociétés ouvrières*. Liège: Demarteau, 1889.

Pottier, Antoine. "Ce qu'il y a de légitime dans les revendications ouvrières". In *Congrès des œuvres sociales. 3e session. 7-10 septembre 1890*. Liège: Demarteau, 1890, 2nd section, 20-48.

Pottier, Antoine. *De jure et justitia. Dissertationes de notione generali juris et justitiae et de justitia legali*. Liège: Ancion, 1900.

Poulat, Emile. "Naudet (Paul)". In *Catholicisme, hier, aujourd'hui, demain*. Vol. 9. Paris: Letouzey et Ané, 1982, 1116-1117.

Rezsohazy, Rudolf. *Origines et formation du catholicisme social en Belgique, 1842-1909*. Leuven: Publications universitaires de Louvain, 1958.

Riche, Richard. *Une page d'histoire sociale: Léon Mabille et le mouvement ouvrier chrétien dans le Centre*. Gembloux: Duculot, 1933.

Roncalli, Angelo, ed. *In memoriam di Mons. Giacomo Maria Radini Tedeschi, vescovo di Bergamo*. Bergamo: S Alessandro, 1916.

Roncalli, Angelo. *Mons. Giacomo Maria Radini Tedeschi vescovo di Bergamo*. Rome: Storia e letteratura, 1963.

Schmitt, Cl. "Reiffenstuel, Anaclet". In *Catholicisme, hier, aujourd'hui, demain*. Vol. 12. Paris: Letouzey et Ané, 1988, 742-743.

Simon, Aloïs. "Doutreloux, Victor-Joseph". In *Biographie nationale*, vol. 30. Brussels, 1959, 346-348.

Simon, Aloïs. *Évêques de la Belgique indépendante 1830-1940: sources d'archives*. Leuven: Nauwelaerts, 1961.

Sorrel, Christian. "Réformisme ou anticléricalisme croyant? Réflexions sur l'itinéraire de deux abbés démocrates, Paul Naudet et Pierre Dabry". In *L'anticléricalisme croyant (1860-1914). Jalons pour une histoire. Actes du Colloque de Chambéry, 2003*. Chambéry: Université de Savoie, 2004, 147-160.

Sorrentino, Domenico. *Giuseppe Toniolo: una chiesa nella storia*. Milan: Paoline, 1987.

Sorrentino, Domenico. *Giuseppe Toniolo: una biografia*. Milan: Paoline, 1988.

Sorrentino, Domenico. *L'economista di Dio: Giuseppe Toniolo*. Rome: AVE, 2001.

Spahn, Martin. *Leo XIII*. Munich: Kirchheim, 1905.

Spicciani, Amleto. *Agli inizi della storiografia economica medioevistica in Italia: la corrispondenza di Giuseppe Toniolo con Victor Brants e Godefroid Kurth*. Rome: Jouvence Ed., 1984.

Spicciani, Amleto. *Giuseppe Toniolo tra economia e storia*. Naples: Guida Ed., 1990.

Teisseyre, Charles. "Taparelli d'Azeglio (Luigi)". In *Catholicisme, hier, aujourd'hui, demain*. Vol. 14. Paris: Letouzey et Ané, 1996, 765-768.

Toniolo, Giuseppe. "Il concetto cristiano della democrazia". *Rivista internazionale* (1897); translated into French: *Le concept chrétien de démocratie*. Lille: Ducoulombier, 1898.

Toniolo, Giuseppe. *Lettere (1871-1918)*. Raccolte da G. Anchini ordinate e annotate da N. Vian. Vatican City, 1952-1953, 3 vols.

Toniolo, Giuseppe. *Opera Omnia*. Vatican City, 1947-1953, 20 vols.

Trimouille, Pierre. *Léon Harmel et l'usine chrétienne du Val-des-Bois (1840-1914). Fécondité d'une expérience sociale*. Lyon: Centre d'histoire du catholicisme, 1974.

Trucco, Silvio and Romano Molesti, eds. *Il pensiero economico-sociale di Giuseppe Toniolo*. Pisa: IPEM, 1990.

T'Serclaes, Charles de. *Le pape Léon XIII: sa vie, son action religieuse, politique et sociale*. Paris: Desclée de Brouwer, 1894-1906.

Vaes, Georges. *Les conditions du travail dans les marchés publics*. Leuven: Peeters, 1900.

Vandersmissen, Edouard. "Le contrat de travail". *La revue des deux mondes*, 1891.

Viaene, Vincent, ed. *The Papacy and the New World Order: Vatican Diplomacy, Catholic Opinion and International Politics at the Time of Leo XIII, 1878-1903*. Leuven: Leuven University Press – Rome: Institut historique belge de Rome, 2005.

Voog, R. "Lorin (Henri)". In *Catholicisme, hier, aujourd'hui, demain*. Vol. 7. Paris: Letouzey et Ané, 1975, 1082-1083.

Warshaw, Dan. *Paul Leroy-Beaulieu and Established Liberalism in France*. DeKalb: Northern Illinois University Press, 1991.

Léon de Lantsheere. Photo, c 1910.
[Leuven, KADOC: KFA5949]

NEO-THOMISM AND THE DEBATES ON THE JUST WAGE IN BELGIUM (1879-1914)[*]

KWINTEN DEWAELE

A t the end of the nineteenth century, a clamour for societal reform rocked Europe at its core. Industrialisation and the political revolutions of the late eighteenth and the nineteenth century had severely transformed society, paving the way for the rise of both a wealthy bourgeoisie and an impoverished proletariat. The subsequent 'social question' was at the heart of a political debate between two competing ideologies, each promoting a different solution to these societal issues: liberalism and socialism.[1] Faced with competition from both these ideologies, the Roman Catholic Church (hereafter: the Church) developed its own social teachings.[2] At the core of this Catholic social doctrine stood the ideal of a corporatist organisation of the economy, heavily

---

[*] This essay is a reworked and shortened translation of an earlier article in Dutch: Dewaele, "Het neothomisme in België en het rechtvaardig loon (1879-1914)". I am very grateful for the support and supervision of Professor Wim Decock and the useful advise of Professor Andrea Robiglio. Special thanks go to Dr. Vincent Genin for his support in identifying some of the lesser known contributors to the Third Congress of Liège discussed below. Of course, any and all omissions or defaults were made despite of their advice and are to be contributed entirely to myself.

1 Castelein, *Le problème social*, 4-7. Please note the use of 'liberalism' in this context. In accordance with the traditional continental approach 'liberalism' refers to an economic-political theory in favour of the free market and *laissez faire* economic policy as opposed to socialism which favours strict(er) regulation and government intervention. I will use this meaning of 'liberalism' throughout this work. In this context, 'liberalism' should not be confused with its contemporary (Anglo-American) namesake, which is more closely linked to a progressive social (justice) theory and is often considered to be 'left-wing'.

2 Deferme, *Uit de ketens van de vrijheid*, 29-37.

influenced by the (nineteenth-century interpretation of the) Thomistic idea of justice. Within Catholic social doctrine however, the question on what constituted a 'just wage' proved to be one of the most contentious issues of the day.

This essay aims to provide a concise but solid overview of the developments on this issue at the end of the nineteenth century amongst the Belgian Catholic movement.[3] Central to this overview is the question whether nineteenth-century neo-Thomism should be considered to be Thomistic at all. Despite all the claims of drawing inspiration from the teachings of Thomas Aquinas, neo-Thomistic scholars differed widely in their views on the problem of the just wage.[4] Moreover, they often defended completely opposite standpoints on the same textual basis. This contributes to the general feeling that neo-Thomism is not really a philosophical movement in its own right with connections to the Thomistic ideals of the thirteenth century, but rather a disperse amalgam of political views that are all somehow rooted in Catholic tradition. Focusing on the Belgian case between 1879 and 1914, the essay further investigates this hypothesis.

The research only concerns the timeframe between 1879 and 1914.[5] 1879 serves as a useful point of departure, since it is the year in which Leo XIII issued his encyclical *Aeterni Patris*. This encyclical not only revived the interest in the work of Thomas Aquinas, thus making it one of the 'engines' of nineteenth-century neo-Thomism, but is also exemplary of the social concerns that would echo throughout the remainder of Leo's pontificate.[6] The research ends in 1914, the year in which the First World War not only made an end to

---

3   The nineteenth century should be understood as the 'long' nineteenth century and consequently includes the first decade of the twentieth century up to the outbreak of the First World War in 1914.

4   These discussions not only include major authors, but also lesser known figures who wrote about the just wage and referred to the teachings of Thomas Aquinas, e.g. Gustavus Waffelaert, bishop of Bruges. However several notable figures within the neo-Thomist movement, such as Simon Deploige or Maurice Defourny, are not discussed here, since they did not express their opinion on the topic or because their writings do not correspond to the timeframe of this research. It is self-explanatory that not all publications could be researched. This essay is limited to those publications selected on the basis of the authority of the author (e.g. Périn or Brants), the importance of a corresponding event (e.g. the Congress of Liège in 1890) or their link with any of the above (e.g. De Gryse, Waffelaert). With regard to journals, the research is mainly limited to the *Revue Sociale Catholique* because of its prominent neo-Thomistic influence without being particularly progressive (unlike, for example, *L'avenir social* and *La justice sociale*).

5   For a similar delineation in time, see the contribution of Joeri De Smet in this book.

6   Other encyclicals issued by Leo XIII conveyed a similar message and are equally derived from neo-Thomistic teachings [e.g. *Arcanum Divinae Sapientiae* (1880), *Diuturnum Illud* (1881), *Humanum Genus* (1884), *Immortale Dei* (1885), *Spientiae Christianae* (1890) and *Graves de Communi* (1901)]. Together they form the basis of Catholic social teachings with regard to family, marriage, political philosophy and democracy.

thirty years of Belgian governments dominated by the Catholic Party, but also brought down the curtain on a European era as a whole.[7]

This essay is built up in the following way. First, the (self-proclaimed) roots of the neo-Thomistic movement(s) are briefly discussed, by looking at the views of Thomas Aquinas. These serve as a framework to contextualise the claims of neo-Thomistic authors throughout the rest of the research. Second, the socio-economic and political context of Belgium in the late nineteenth century is touched upon and linked to discussions within the Catholic movement. Several competing views within this movement are then discussed in the subsequent parts. Part three concerns the period before *Rerum novarum* and pays specific attention to the Third Congress of Liège (1890). Then, *Rerum novarum* itself is discussed in part four. Subsequently, the period after *Rerum novarum* and the different interpretations of the encyclical are dealt with in part five. Afterwards, some final remarks are made concerning neo-Thomism in general, providing a provisory answer to the guiding research question.

Thomas Aquinas and the just wage

Thomas Aquinas (ca. 1225-1274) needs no introduction. As one of the most influential scholars within the Church, his work constitutes the basis of Catholic social doctrine developed under the pontificates of Leo XIII and his successors. Although a thorough study of Aquinas' teachings is not warranted here, it is necessary to briefly emphasise his views on the just wage. The *Doctor Angelicus* never fully developed an economic theory in his own right, nor did he address the issue of the 'just wage' in a consistent theory.[8] Nevertheless, traditionally, Aquinas' views on the just wage are derived from his teachings on labour, value and exchange.[9] Indeed, Aquinas himself seems to suggest a parallel between his views on a just price and wages in the *Summa Theologiae* (hereafter: the *Summa*).[10] Furthermore, the Thomistic views on private prop-

---

7   Gaddis, *On Grand Strategy*, 258.

8   Langholm, *Economics in the Medieval Schools*, 206-207. Elsewhere, Langholm goes as far as stating that Aquinas' teachings "do not even form the embryo of a doctrine of the just wage" (Langholm, "The Medieval Schoolmen (1200-1400)", 476). Indeed, the views explained below should be seen as an evaluation of the source material on which neo-Thomists based themselves, rather than an explanation of a Thomistic theory on the subject (See also: Wilson, "The Economics of the Just Price", 73-74).

9   Langholm, *Economics in the Medieval Schools*, 226-227; Chafuen, *Faith and Liberty*, 105; Langholm, "Thomas Aquinas", 10; Frémeaux and Noël, "Qu'est-ce qu'une juste rémunération?", 84-85. However, it is often difficult to decide were Thomas' views stop and the interpretation of the reader begins.

10   Aquinas, *Summa* II-II Q114(1), resp (*quasi quoddam pretium ipsius*). See in support of this interpretation: Bigo, *La doctrine sociale de l'Église*, 314; Chafuen, *Faith and Liberty*, 105 and Caracausi, "The Just Wage in Early Modern Italy", 120.

erty should be discussed as well, as nineteenth-century neo-Thomists often invoked these views in justification of their own position (cf. *infra*).

It is however expedient to note the impossibility to provide a 'true' overview of the views of Aquinas, without relying on *ex post* interpretation.[11] Moreover, Aquinas himself is but one shackle in a long chain of interpretation of Aristotelian, Roman and Patristic sources.[12] Therefore, the following paragraphs are necessarily 'tainted' by centuries of Thomistic and pre-Thomistic reception. Insofar this is possible, the interpretative elements are made explicit throughout the text and in the footnotes. As a preliminary remark, the current interpretations of Aquinas discussed in this paragraph foreshadow (or rather, reflect) the interpretation battle of the nineteenth century discussed further below.

Thomas Aquinas on labour and wages

Aquinas mentions labour on several occasions throughout his work.[13] Most relevant to the topic of this essay however, are his remarks in the *Summa*. For Aquinas, the necessity of labour can only be derived from its purpose, which is fourfold.[14] Labour is mainly (*principaliter*) directed towards sustenance of the labourer, but also constrains sloth and the sinful human nature.[15] In addition, labour facilitates charity as well.[16]

Can it be inferred that if labour is only useful insofar it is needed for human sustenance[17], it follows *a contrario* that labour that does not provide enough income to realise this purpose, is useless, perhaps even unnatural? Does it then follow that a just wage must necessarily be sufficient to provide in the sustenance of the labourer? Some would argue it does.[18] Indeed, Frémeaux and Noël conclude that wages must be sufficient to enable in the sustenance

---

11   Wilson, "The Economics of the Just Price", 73-74. My previous contribution "Het neo-
     thomisme in België en het rechtvaardig loon" did not address this issue expressly and was
     perhaps too brief on Aquinas.
12   Noell, "In Pursuit of the Just Wage", 467 and Langholm, "Thomas Aquinas", 8.
13   Langholm, *Economics in the Medieval Schools*, 92. Please note that 'labour' and 'labourer'
     do not only refer to manual, but also to intellectual labour in this context (see Aquinas,
     Summa II-II Q187(3)).
14   Aquinas, *Summa* II-II Q187(3), resp.
15   Ibid.
16   Ibid.
17   Ibid. (*Unde si quis absque manducatione posset vitam transigere, non teneretur manibus
     operari*).
18   Although they may prefer a less 'fierce' expression of this idea.

of the labourer and his family.[19] Similarly Langholm infers from Aquinas' *"Liber contra impugnantes"* a duty to pay at least a subsistence wage.[20] A similar position is defended – albeit only indirectly – by Hirschfeld.[21] Moreover, in my view, this may also be inferred from the duty to pay labourers promptly.[22] Indeed, according to Aquinas, labourers "toil for their daily bread" and thus should be paid at once "lest they lack food".[23] Would this precept[24] not be self-defeating if it allowed to pay labourers promptly, but insufficiently? Indeed, in both instances, they would lack food; it follows labourers should also be paid sufficiently to provide in their sustenance.[25]

The duty to pay *at least* a subsistence wage is however only the *minimum minimorum*. Indeed, a subsistence wage does not (necessarily) equate a just wage.[26] Aquinas deals with the concept of a just wage in two separate questions of the *Summa*: II-II Q71(4) on the fees of counsel and (indirectly) II-II Q77(1) and (4) on just pricing and commerce.[27] With regard to the fees of counsels (and similar professions), Aquinas maintains that they may take "a moderate fee, with due consideration for persons, for the matter in hand, for the labour entailed, and for the custom of the country".[28] Aquinas refers to the

19   Frémeaux and Noël, "Qu'est-ce qu'une juste rémunération?", 84-85. The link to the family of the labourer is an addition which in my view goes beyond what can be inferred from the text of the *Summa* and is reminiscent of what in neo-Thomistic terms would be dubbed a 'salaire familial'. See for example for a similar (progressive) neo-Thomistic interpretation: Pottier, "Ce qu'il y a de légitime", 45. Some support for this interpretation may however be found in *Summa* II-II Q77(4), resp. with regard to merchants and trade (*ad domus suae sustentationem*).

20   Langholm, *Economics in the Medieval Schools*, 228 and Id., "Thomas Aquinas", 10.

21   Hirschfeld, *Aquinas and the Market*, 166-167.

22   Of course, this is but an interpretation *ex post*; it is not necessarily what Aquinas had in mind when writing.

23   Aquinas, *Summa*, I-II Q105(2), reply to objection 6.

24   Contained in Lev. 19:13 and discussed by Aquinas.

25   This is also in line with the views of Francisco de Vitoria (ca. 1483-1546), but contrary to the teachings of later scholastics like Luis de Molina (1535-1600) and Leonard Lessius (1554-1623). See: Chafuen, *Faith and Liberty*, 106-109 and Langholm, "Voluntary Exchange and Coercion in Scholastic Economics", 8.

26   Insofar as 'sustenance' is considered in its most original meaning, i.e. a wage that allows survival. Of course it is possible to envisage 'sustenance' as including all necessities of a decent life, taking into account all elements discussed below. An elaborate view on this subject is provided by Hirschfeld, who argues Aquinas' teachings on what is necessary for the sustenance of a person is also determined by his 'standard of living', a view reminiscent of the dominant feeling that social status is a relevant factor to determine the just price, see fn. 29. (Hirschfeld, *Aquinas and the Market*, 170-180).

27   As stated above (cf. fn. 10), Aquinas' views on just pricing should be applied *mutatis mutandis* to the question on a just wage. In II-II Q114(1) resp. Aquinas considers a wage to be like (*quasi*) a price. Moreover, in II-II Q77(4) resp. he makes a similar (but reverse) comparison, stating that a merchant's price is like a compensation for his labour, i.e. a wage (*quasi stipendium laboris*).

28   Aquinas, *Summa* II-II Q71(4) resp.

condition of the parties; one might think of the bargaining power of parties, but also on their needs taking into account their societal position.[29]

Furthermore, Aquinas also mentions the (quality of the) labour and the regional customs, possibly referring to the customary price/fee in a certain region.[30] With regard to Aquinas' views on just pricing (and thus the just wage), attention must be paid to *Summa* II-II Q77(1) and (4). These rules mainly feature in a broader theory on the sin of greed and how to avoid it.[31]

After having defended the conditional permissibility of commerce in *Summa* II-II Q77(4)[32], Aquinas touches on the crucial question what constitutes a just price(/wage). In *Summa* II-II Q77(1) he proposes the yardstick to determine the *iustum pretium*: all contracts should observe "equality of thing and thing" (*aequalitatem rei inter eos*); therefore it is illicit to sell or buy a thing for more or less (respectively) than it is worth (*vendere aut vilius emere rem quam valeat est secundum se iniustum et illicitum*).[33] This corresponds to the first principle of what Langholm describes as Aquinas' "double pricing rule": it is forbidden to sell or buy a good above or below its value.[34] This value should then be estimated – because it will always be a rough estimation[35] – on the basis of the costs and needs of the seller and the needs of the buyer.[36] A comparison with the "consideration for persons" in Q71 (cf. *supra*) comes to mind, but both expressions need not necessarily mean the same.

Moreover, a *caveat* is warranted: the just price(/wage) must be reached in the absence of (economic) coercion or fraud.[37] Consequently, a pressing need

29 Langholm, *Economics in the Medieval Schools*, 227. The idea that societal status is a relevant factor to determine the just wage is contested by – amongst others – Langholm, but was still a widely accepted interpretation in the previous century. For a concise overview on this matter, see: Noell, "In Pursuit of the Just Wage", 471.

30 Langholm, *Economics in the Medieval Schools*, 227-228. (The reference to the customary price is an addition of my own, but support can be found in Noell, "Bargaining, Consent and the Just Wage in the Sources of Scholastic economic thought", 476. Noell refers to Baldwin and Langholm).

31 Nureev and Petrakov, "Doctrine of Fair Price by Thomas Aquinas", 20.

32 Koehler, "The Thirteenth Century Economics of Thomas Aquinas", 60-61.

33 Aquinas, *Summa* II-II Q77(1) resp.

34 Langholm, *Economics in the Medieval Schools*, 232 and subsequent pages.

35 Aquinas, *Summa* II-II Q77(1), reply to the first objection (*iustum pretium [...] non est punctualiter determinatum*).

36 Langholm, *Economics in the Medieval Schools*, 232 and subsequent pages and Lapidus, "Norm, Virtue and Information", 438-442. This is however one of the most contentious elements about the *iustum pretium*-theory of Aquinas. Indeed, the same text has given rise to interpretations that support a cost-production theory of value as well as interpretations that equate value with the market value (Decock, *Theologians and Contract Law*, 420; Nureev and Petrakov, "Doctrine of Fair Price by Thomas Aquinas", 20).

37 Langholm, *Economic in the Medieval Schools*, 234-236; Noell, "Bargaining, Consent and the Just Wage in the Sources of Scholastic Economic Thought", 476; Langholm, "Voluntary Exchange and Coercion in Scholastic Economics", 8; Decock, *Theologians and Contract Law*, 421.

for one of the parties cannot be exploited to extort a higher or lower price. This emphasises the importance of freedom to contract and the conditions of free bargaining which are contained in the second principle of the so-called "double pricing rule".[38]

Summarised, the (currently) predominant interpretation of the Thomistic (and/or scholastic) notion of *iustum pretium* holds that the just price is to be determined on the basis of the normal value in exchange, estimated by the parties involved, provided these are normal, reasonably intelligent people unaffected by coercion.[39] Some authors (including later scholastics and many neo-Thomists) have equated this interpretation with the market price, yet this seems a bridge too far.[40] Indeed, a market price could not be considered a just price where it fails to protect the weaker party against exploitation of their necessities. Moreover, with regard to the specific application of wages, at least a subsistence wage should be paid (cf. *supra*). Frémeaux and Noël argue this means wages should be excluded entirely from market fluctuations.[41] Implicitly this would also exclude most factors that determine a just price (and thus wage) in general, which seems equally hard to reconcile with Thomism as pure undiluted market fundamentalism.

Thomas Aquinas on private property

Aquinas' views on the just wage – insofar they exist – cannot be separated from his views on private property. Indeed, the question on how to exchange private property (cf. *supra*) can only be meaningful when there is an answer to the question whether and how private property can be established.[42] Moreover, many neo-Thomists made explicit reference to the Thomistic concept of private property in support of their views.[43] Nevertheless, the question on private property is only ancillary to the debate on the just wage; therefore it suffices to discuss this only briefly.

38 Langholm, *Economics in the Medieval Schools*, 234. One must be careful though not to overestimate the importance of the freedom to contract either. Aquinas clearly condemns contracts that are valid under Roman law and based on free will. He reasserts that human law is not only made for the virtuous and allows things that are contrary to virtue (unlike the Divine law), see Aquinas, *Summa* II-II Q77(1) reply to the first objection.

39 See (merely exemplary): De Roover, "The Concept of the Just Price", 422-423; Noell, "Bargaining, Consent and the Just Wage in the Sources of Scholastic Economic Thought", 476; *contra* Hollander, "On the Interpretation of the Just Price", 616-632 (Hollander however takes a nuanced position equating the just price with the market price in some circumstances); Frémeaux and Noël, "Qu'est-ce qu'une juste rémunération?", 84-85 (on wages in particular).

40 Langholm, "Thomas Aquinas", 11 and Decock, *Theologians and Contract Law*, 423.

41 Frémeaux and Noël, "Qu'est-ce qu'une juste rémunération?", 84-85.

42 Langholm, *Economics in the Medieval Schools*, 223-224.

43 See for example the contributions of De Gryse, Pottier, Castelein and de Lantsheere discussed further below.

The topic of ownership and private property is mainly dealt with in *Summa* II-II Q66(1), (2) and (7) and in Aquinas' *Commentary on Aristotle's Politics* (hereafter *Politics*) II, chapter 4. Aquinas first confirms the natural dominion of men with regard to the use (only) of "external things".[44] This however, only concerns "ownership"[45] in the abstract sense and leaves the question on private property unanswered. In *Summa* II-II Q66(2) however, Aquinas explicitly recognises the existence and legitimacy of private property as a creation of positive man-made law, an addendum to the natural law in which common ownership of mankind is prescribed.[46]

Two consequences may be derived from the positive law-status of private property. First, private property, being only positive law, is in need of justification.[47] Second, and most relevant to the topic of this essay, private property is only conditional. Indeed, for Aquinas, "whatever certain people have in superabundance is due, by natural law, to the purpose of succouring the poor".[48] In theory, it was up to those who had a superabundance to distribute and share their property with the needy out of their own motion.[49]

Yet, in times of dire need, the needy could serve themselves and "succour their own needs".[50] This seems logical: insofar private property is created as an institution to better fulfil human needs, it can and must be overruled when it obstructs those needs, e.g. when the poor starve.[51] Interestingly, Aquinas' views may give rise to the theory that private property is conditional on the payment of a just wage or at least a subsistence wage. Although this idea can certainly not be attributed to Aquinas himself, it was supported by some of the more progressive neo-Thomists, such as de Lantsheere, and firmly linked both the Thomistic notion of just pricing and private property together (cf. *infra*).

---

44   Aquinas, *Summa* II-II Q66(1) resp. and reply to the first objection.
45   One might argue it is more a kind of 'usufruct' (in the modern sense of the word), since only God has the ultimate ownership over the nature of things; see: Aquinas, *Summa* II-II Q66(1) resp.
46   Aquinas, *Summa* II-II Q66(2), resp. and reply to the first objection; Langholm, *Economics in the Medieval Schools*, 210-211 and Höpfl, *Jesuit Political Thought*, 296.
47   Aquinas provides three such justifications in both the *Summa* and the *Politics*: an argument based on efficiency, one based on order and, finally, one based on peace (see Aquinas, *Summa* II-II Q66(2) resp. and Aquinas, *Politics* II, chapter 4; in the latter, Aquinas also deals with Aristotle's pleasure-based arguments in favour of private property). See for an elaborate explanation: Langholm, *Economics in the Medieval Schools*, 212-215 and Hirschfeld, *Aquinas and the Market*, 165 and subsequent pages. Remarkably, Hirschfeld seems to argue private property is part of natural law ("a picture of private property as an institution in accordance with natural law"; Ibid., 167). This contradicts the *Summa* (cf. *supra* and *infra*).
48   Aquinas, *Summa* II-II Q66(7) resp.
49   Ibid.
50   Ibid.
51   Langholm, *Economics in the Medieval Schools*, 218.

Catholic social thinking in the late nineteenth century

The historical context in which Catholic social thinking was developed is well-known.[52] Yet it remains necessary to briefly point out three distinctive elements that have shaped the discussions within the Belgian Catholic movement: the traditional concept of the 'liberty of labour', the year 1886 as a turning point and the political and ideological conflict between conservative and progressive Catholics from 1890 onwards.

First, the debates in the late nineteenth century on what constituted a just wage cannot be understood without mentioning the so-called 'liberty of labour'. This liberty entailed the absolute and unrestricted freedom of both employer and employee to freely negotiate the terms and conditions of the employment contract (duration, performance, wage etc.), without any intervention from the government.[53] The liberty of labour had been enshrined in law by the Decree d'Allarde and the Le Chapelier-law during the French Revolution as a reaction against a corporatist organisation of the economy and became a dominant economic theorem of the nineteenth century.[54]

At its proclamation, it really was a liberation from a system in which professions were generally determined by birth and often closed off by (medieval) guilds.[55] Famous economist Charles Dunoyer hailed this liberty as "the freedom of men to use his forces and liberate himself of the obstacles that bound him in the past". Yet in the course of the nineteenth century, the liberty of labour became a means for both liberals and conservative Catholics to fight off any and all government intervention regulation on labourers' rights or labour agreements.[56]

Deferme argues this is exemplary of wider trend in the nineteenth century when the universal ideals of the French Revolution were transformed into conservative values, aimed at maintaining social order and the entrenchment of the powers of the bourgeoisie.[57] Moreover, this strict interpretation of the liberty of labour gave rise to many issues that constituted the social question and created the need for a Catholic social doctrine.[58]

Second, the year 1886 proved to be pivotal for the developments in the Belgian Catholic movement. The Belgian economy had been hit hard by the

---

52   See also the introduction to this essay.
53   Deferme, *Uit de ketens van de vrijheid*, 27 and Blanpain, *Hebben de vakbonden nog een toekomst?*, 82-84.
54   Blanpain, *Hebben de vakbonden nog een toekomst?*, 82-84. See for a discussion on the developments in the Netherlands: Van Ommen Kloeke, *De vrijheid van beroep en bedrijf*, 126-129.
55   Dunoyer, *De la liberté du travail*, 278-279; Van Ommen Kloeke, *De vrijheid van beroep en bedrijf*, 52 and subsequent.
56   Deferme, *Uit de ketens van de vrijheid*, 72.
57   Ibid., 36. This seems perhaps too strong as a generalisation.
58   Gérin, *Les origines de la démocratie chrétienne à Liège*, 63-71.

so-called 'Long Depression' since 1873, leading to the total collapse of wages and famine amongst the working class.[59] As cities impoverished rapidly, clamour for reform became increasingly hard to ignore.[60] Attempts had already been made in the past to improve the conditions of the poor, but hunger uprisings and failed revolts in 1848 fuelled the fear for a proletarian revolution.[61]

Government intervention to limit the liberty of labour was seen as possible the first 'flake' in a snowball effect that could ignite such a revolution and was consequently out of the question. Paternalistic charity was seen as a much safer way to solve societal issues.[62] Yet reality would catch up with these theories in 1886 because of three (largely) independent events that occurred that year.

1886 saw the Catholic Party taking control over the government.[63] They would maintain their majority for thirty years until the outbreak of World War I. Moreover, 1886 also marks the beginning of the (Catholic) 'Social Congresses of Liège'.[64] Both the rule of a Catholic government and the Social Congresses amplified the importance of neo-Thomism in Catholic social thought. Finally, 1886 is also considered the year of the social *reveil* in Belgium.[65] Low wages, the rise of an organised socialist movement (the Belgian Labourers Party) and embitterment amongst the working class, lead to several strikes and riots in the second half of March 1886.[66] Factories and machines were destroyed, property was pillaged and factory owners were threatened.[67] The government answered with harsh military repression, but the developments of 1886 nevertheless paved the way for social reforms and a (hesitant) regulatory

---

59   Gérin, "Sociaal-katholicisme en christen-democratie", 58-59.
60   Wils, "België in de negentiende eeuw", 29-30.
61   Gérin, "Sociaal-katholicisme en christen-democratie", 59-62; Wils, "België in de negentiende eeuw", 29-30 and Witte et al., *Nieuwe geschiedenis van België*, I, 382-386.
62   Witte et al., *Nieuwe geschiedenis van België*, I, 385-386.
63   In reality, the Catholic Party had already gained a parliamentary majority in 1884, leading to the formation of the Malou government. Fierce opposition and street protests from the liberals however in the so-called (First) 'Schoolstrijd' and severe electoral losses in the communal elections of 19 October 1884 forced the cabinet to resign. Malou would be succeeded by the more prudent and moderate Catholic Auguste Beernaert. The (partial) elections of 1886 strengthened Catholic control and made their position less precarious (see: Wils, "België in de negentiende eeuw", 52; Gérin, "Sociaal-katholicisme en christen-democratie", 57 and Witte et al., *Nieuwe geschiedenis van België*, I, 486-497).
64   Gérin, "Sociaal-katholicisme en christen-democratie", 62. The third of these Congresses is discussed below.
65   Verdoodt, "Roma locuta, causa nondum finita", 248.
66   Gérin, *Les origines de la démocratie chrétienne à Liège*, 71-75; Scholl, "Werkstakingen", 208-210; Gérin, "Sociaal-katholicisme en christen-democratie", 59-60 and Witte et al., *Nieuwe geschiedenis van België*, I, 503-507.
67   The destruction of the Baudoux factory and castle is perhaps the most infamous and extreme example of the rage of the strikers (see: Scholl, "Werkstakingen", 210 and Witte et al., *Nieuwe geschiedenis van België*, I, 505-506).

framework with regard to the payment of wages.[68] Moreover, it put the social question at the centre of the political debate.[69]

Finally, the rivalry between two competing factions within the Catholic movement also heavily influenced the development of Catholic social doctrine in Belgium. Indeed, this rivalry would explicitly manifest itself in the debates on the just wage (cf. *infra*) and the related neo-Thomistic interpretation battle.

On the one hand, the self-proclaimed 'Catholics' upheld a paternalistic and conservative view on the matter. Charles Périn (1815-1905) and Auguste Castelein (1840-1922) were among the driving forces of this movement, which was led on a political level by Charles Woeste (1837-1922).[70] On the other hand, the so-called 'Christians' were more progressive. Major names include Adolf Daens (1837-1907) and Antoine Pottier (1849-1923), but also Léon de Lantsheere (1862-1912), who would eventually become minister of Justice.[71] This struggle within the Catholic Party would eventually catch the attention of the Holy See, which would intervene with – amongst others things – its encyclical *Rerum novarum*.[72] To avoid any confusion, I will refer to the conservative and progressive faction within the Catholic movement. 'Catholic' thus refers to both factions (i.e. Catholics *sensu stricto* and the Christians/early Christian democrats) and must be distinguished from the liberal and socialist positions on the social question.

Neo-Thomism and the just wage before *Rerum novarum* (1879-1890)

Before the issuing or *Rerum novarum*, the rivalry between progressive and conservative Catholics largely remained indoors. However, renewed attention for Aquinas' work had already found its way to representatives of both factions. Two main authors are discussed below: Edward De Gryse[73] and Victor Brants. Furthermore, particular attention is paid to the third Congress of Liège in 1890. The debates not only illustrate the tensions between two lines of thought within the Catholic movement, but also show how both factions relied on the same source of inspiration.

---

68   Deferme, *Uit de ketens van de vrijheid*, 91-94; Witte et al., *Nieuwe geschiedenis van België*, I, 507-510 and Heirbaut, *Een beknopte geschiedenis van het sociaal, het economisch en het fiscaal recht in België*, 41.

69   Verdoodt, "Roma locuta, causa nondum finita", 248.

70   See the contribution of Joeri De Smet in this book.

71   Verdoodt, "Roma locuta, causa nondum finita", 243.

72   A first struggle within the Catholic Party between ultramontanists and liberal-Catholics had been decided in favour of the latter in 1874. The first 'Schoolstrijd' had somewhat restored the Catholic front as one, yet the social question would disrupt the peace once more.

73   Alternatively, his name is also spelled 'De Grijse'.

Edward De Gryse: Notre Droit National et la Révolution (1885)

Edward De Gryse (1848-1909) was professor at the seminary of Bruges and would later become dean of the Saint Martin's church in Courtrai.[74] His work is mostly remembered today for its contribution to the resurged interest in the Middle Ages at the end of the nineteenth century[75], but he also wrote on the social question.[76] Most relevant in that regard is his work *Notre Droit National et la Révolution*[77] (hereafter: *Notre Droit National*), in which he discusses a great variety of topics, including inheritance law, education, freemasonry and of course also the social struggles of his time. Although *Notre Droit National* cannot be considered to be neo-Thomistic – De Gryse does not explicitly refer to Aquinas – it often served as a source of inspiration for later neo-Thomists and was picked up at the Congress of Liège (cf. *infra*).

In *Notre Droit National*, De Gryse states that labour is the labourer's private property and is sold as a commodity.[78] Consequently, he holds that market principles of supply and demand should determine how much a labourer was paid, referring to Adam Smith.[79] In doing so, De Gryse explicitly refutes those that seek to exclude wages from the functioning of the free market, such as the German economist-socialist Johann Karl Rodbertus (1805-1875).[80] Al-

---

74   For an elaborate overview on De Gryse, see: Decoene, *Doctor Edward De Gryse*.
75   Gérin, "Sociaal-katholicisme en christen-democratie", 67.
76   De Gryse's oeuvre on the social question deserves to be discussed in a publication in its own right (Decoene, *Doctor Edward De Gryse*). This essay merely deals with *Notre Droit National*, because it was widespread and highly influential (many of the other authors discussed here referred to it). Other publications on the topic that must be mentioned but cannot be dealt with in detail in this essay are *De contractu conductionis* (in Latin); *Les socialistes et les citations des Pères de l'Eglise sur le droit de propriété* and *Zijn de H. Vaders voorloopers der socialisten?* (In the latter, De Gryse explicitly rejects the suggestion that patristic teachings were opposed to private property.)
77   The preceding Dutch publication, *Vaderlandsch recht en revolutie: verhandelingen over de sociale questiën van heden*, was already available in 1881. It seems to have been less influential however, probably because of language issues. Moreover, *Vaderlandsch recht* did not deal with the just wage, unlike the French publication.
78   De Gryse, *Notre Droit National*, 230-235. *Prima facie* this is close to the Thomistic notion that the wage of a labourer is like a price for the labour he 'sells' (cf. *supra*). It should be pointed out however, that Aquinas – unlike others like Saint Antoninus of Florence – maintained that a price was only like (*quasi*) a wage; this position is slightly more nuanced (see: Chafuen, *Faith and Liberty*, 105). Also, Aquinas does not (explicitly) consider labour to be the 'property' of the labourer.
79   De Gryse, *Notre Droit National*, 230-235.
80   Ibid., 240-241.

though De Gryse is no neo-Thomist himself, these views are particularly in line with those of the late scholastics, yet not Aquinas himself.[81]

Although linking the wage level with fundamental market principles may not exactly be Thomistic, De Gryse was not insensitive to the negative consequences of unbridled competition.[82] To remedy these issues, De Gryse relied on morality: for him, morality demanded that wages be sufficient to cover the costs of production of labour. Thus, the wage should be high enough to provide sustenance for the labourer (and his family).[83] Moreover, mere sustenance was not enough: the just wage should allow the labourer to make a decent living.

Of course, this is highly reminiscent of the cost-labour interpretation of Aquinas, which is however no longer generally accepted.[84] In any case, De Gryse seems to concur with Aquinas – consciously or not – on the requirement of a sustenance wage.[85]

His views are however slightly more nuanced. According to De Gryse, an employer is only under the moral duty to fully reimburse his labourers insofar he made a profit. If he did not make a profit or suffered losses, wages could be lower.[86] Although this point of view may sound neoliberal to modern standards, one must not forget that even the idea of a minimal wage was highly contested at the time. De Gryse even expressly rejected an unlimited application of the liberty of labour and openly attacked Dunoyer, who advocated an amoral (or perhaps even immoral) economy.[87] In the end, De Gryse may not have been a neo-Thomist, but in many aspects his views were closer to the *Summa* than those of his contemporaries. It should come as no surprise then

81 Chafuen, *Faith and Liberty*, 105-107. With regard to the question to what extent Aquinas' views support a pure market theory, I refer to the relevant subsection discussed above. See in particular: Langholm, "Thomas Aquinas", 11 and Decock, *Theologians and Contract Law*, 423. For very strong views on this issue, see: Frémeaux and Noël, "Qu'est-ce qu'une juste rémunération?", 84-85.

82 Unlike Charles Dunoyer for example who recognised that the unlimited liberty of labour was mainly beneficial to the wealthy and created poverty and inequality, but this – he believed – was natural and not a problem that could be attributed to the liberty of labour itself. See: Dunoyer, *De la liberté du travail*, 408 and 412-436.

83 De Gryse, *Notre Droit National*, 249-251. De Gryse was in favour of a family wage (*salaire familial*) determined *in abstracto* on the basis of the necessities of a family of one man, one woman and two children. Although he did not oppose government intervention, he feared the state to be inefficient in enforcing these requirement. This of course emphasises the progressive position of De Gryse. Again, he does not support his views with Aquinas, but by referring to Adam Smith and Pellegrino Rossi, two economists (De Gryse, *Notre Droit National*, 251-253).

84 Nureev and Petrakov, "Doctrine of Fair Price by Thomas Aquinas", 20.

85 Of course, this does not mean Aquinas promoted the idea of a minimum wage in the modern sense of the word. For Aquinas on the sustenance wage: cf. *supra*.

86 De Gryse, *Notre Droit National*, 244.

87 Ibid., 246 and 259-260.

that he inspired – and supported! – many progressive neo-Thomistic scholars (cf. *infra*).

Victor Brants: La lutte pour le pain quotidien (1888)

Victor Brants (1856-1917) was one of the most influential Belgian Catholic minds of his time, a proto-neo-Thomist and a leading figure concerning political economy.[88] A pupil of both Charles Périn and Francis de Mogne de Franeau (1836-1907), Brants soon found himself drawn into conservative Catholicism and ultramontanism.[89] From 1882 onwards, Brants was influenced by Frédéric Le Play (1806-1882) and he adhered to a more moderate, nuanced – some would argue realistic – position.[90] Moreover, after 1885 he would also dedicate a great part of his work to the social question in particular. Gradually, Brants left the ideals of his former mentor Périn and alienated himself from the Catholic circles to which he had belonged early in his career.[91]

Crucial to Brants' thinking on the social question and the just wage in particular, is his work *La lutte pour le pain quotidien* (hereafter: *La lutte*), published in 1888. For the first time, Brants developed a consistent theory on the labour and wages, which he explicitly based on Thomistic ideals.[92] Moreover, *La lutte* is pivotal with regard to his views on state intervention. In his early works, he excluded the possibility of any governmental action, whereas in 1885 he finally accepted it as "a sad necessity".[93] Nevertheless, Brants was no revolutionary. In many ways, *La lutte* remains the work of a 'moderate conservative' and a fine example of an intermediate position between two competing factions and interpretations of Thomistic ideas.

In *La lutte*, Brants promotes a duty for the rich, as a social authority, to share their wealth with the poor, an opinion for which he was much lauded.[94] Much like De Gryse, he believed wages were to be determined by market

---

88 For an extensive overview of his life and work, see his autobiographical work: *Notes et souvenirs de Victor Brants (1856-1917)*. A critical review was made as part of an unpublished master's thesis (Casteleyn, *Notes et souvenirs de Victor Brants. Tekstkritische uitgave van een autobiografische reflectie geschreven tijdens de Eerste Wereldoorlog*). Also see: Meerts, "De Leuvense hoogleraar Victor Brants: een brugfiguur in het sociaal-katholicisme (1856-1891)", 197-233 and Id., "De Leuvense hoogleraar Victor Brants: sociale ideeën tussen katholieke romantiek en realisme (1856-1891)", 101-130.

89 Meerts, "De Leuvense hoogleraar Victor Brants: een brugfiguur in het sociaal-katholicisme", 200-202 and 205-207.

90 Id., "De Leuvense hoogleraar Victor Brants: sociale ideeën tussen katholieke romantiek en realisme", 108-109.

91 Ibid., 114.

92 For example, he expressly defines the very notion of 'wage' by referring to Aquinas (Brants, *La lutte*, 142).

93 Van Dievoet et al., *Lovanium docet*, 182 and Meerts, "De Leuvense hoogleraar Victor Brants: sociale ideeën tussen katholieke romantiek en realisme", 113.

94 du Sart de Boulan, "La lutte pour le pain quotidien", 8-10.

principles, but he also acknowledged the social issues this line of thinking created.[95] Therefore, he sought to find a solution in Christian morality and looked for an absolute law, dictated by justice to establish a minimal wage.[96] Interestingly, this makes Brants' position far more rigid than that of Aquinas, for whom a estimation *in concreto* sufficed (cf. *supra*).[97] Much like De Gryse, Brants found this minimal wage in the sustenance wage.[98]

However, for Brants, this minimal sustenance wage sufficed. Indeed, this also clarifies his distinction between 'poverty' and 'misery'. 'Poverty' meant someone had difficulties to make ends meet, which was regrettable but acceptable. Only 'misery', i.e. the situation where someone could not sustain himself, was unacceptable.[99] Similarly, Brants refused to take an explicit position in the debates on the just wage. He acknowledged the existence of a lively debate in a neutral fashion. On the one hand, he recognised the position of those pleading for a substantial minimum wage that not only allowed the labourer to survive, but also to make a decent living (thus preventing 'poverty').[100]

On the other hand, he acknowledged the views of those that believed the only just wage was the wage on which parties had agreed, regardless of economic coercion.[101] In general, Brants avoids all controversies in *La lutte*. He promotes a minimal wage, but does not give it much content. He recognises the duty to pay a sufficient wage, but remains suspicious towards government intervention to enforce such a wage.[102] He would also later confirm these views in his book *La lutte contre l'usure dans les lois modernes*.[103] In *La lutte,* he expressly refers to Aquinas, but in many ways his views are more symptomatic of sixteenth-century scholasticism. Indeed, Brants remains loyal to Aquinas, only insofar as Aquinas' views may be equated with market principles.[104] Nevertheless, Brants undertook a laudable attempt, being tutored in very conservative circles, to reconcile two inherently conflicting ideas: that of the liberty of labour and that of the just wage. In doing so, Brants tried to be a bridge between two rivalling factions.

95   Brants, *La lutte*, 146-147.
96   Ibid., 147-148.
97   Compare: Aquinas, *Summa* II-II Q77(1) reply to the first objection.
98   Brants, *La lutte*, 147 and 154.
99   du Sart de Boulan, "La lutte pour le pain quotidien", 8-10.
100 Brants, *La lutte*, 157. Moreover, Brants argued against De Gryse, believing the priest did not account for economic reality.
101 Brants, *La lutte*, 156-157.
102 As stated above, he would come to accept it as a 'sad necessity', but that does not make him a great supporter of government intervention either, see for example also: Brants, "Economie des échanges: juste prix", 87.
103 The chapter in which he discusses the just wage is mainly a reprise of the corresponding chapter in *Le salaire usuraire devant la loi et les juges allemands*. In itself, both chapters mostly confirm the ideas expressed in *La lutte*.
104 See for example the absence of the recognition of economic coercion.

The Third Congress of Liège and the debates on the just wage (1890)

The Congresses of Liège were symptomatic of the struggle between compet-ing factions within the Catholic movement and had a great influence on the formation of a progressive Catholic front, both from a national and an inter-national perspective.[105] They would also serve as a source of inspiration for the – almost mythical – encyclical *Rerum novarum*, discussed below.[106]

With regard to the issue of the just wage, particular attention must be given to the Third Congress of Liège. Not only did this Congress expressly deal with the issue (albeit indirectly, cf. *infra*), but it did so with the approval and encouragement of the Holy See.[107] Moreover, the Congress was clearly divid-ed by conservatives and progressives, who directly interacted with each other and directly refuted each other's arguments. Therefore, the Third Congress provides a 'practical' overview on how the debate on the just wage was carried on prior to the interpretation of *Rerum novarum*. The contributions of both Abbé Antoine Pottier (1849-1923) and Francois de Kuefstein (1841-1918) will be discussed here.

Antoine Pottier on the just wage

Antoine Pottier, professor of theology at the seminary of Liège, was a con-troversial figure in his days. Being the public face of progressive Catholicism in Liège, he often provoked the establishment. Thanks to the support of his direct superior the bishop of Liège, Mgr. Doutreloux, Pottier evaded public condemnation (unlike his Flemish spiritual counterpart, Adolphe Daens).[108] The life, work and importance of Antoine Pottier is discussed extensively else-where by Mgr. Delville.[109] Therefore, in this research only his essay published at the occasion of the Third Congress, "Ce qu'il y a de légitime dans les reven-dications ouvrières" (hereafter: "Ce qu'il y a de legitime"), will be discussed.

Pottier's contentious essay opens with an overt accusation of the Catho-lic bourgeoisie. In his view, they paved the way for socialism by colluding with capitalism.[110] Consequently, Pottier demands that the bourgeoisie pay a just wage and contribute to the general interest.

105 Gérin, *Les origines de la démocratie chrétienne à Liège*, 97 and Id., "Sociaal-katholicisme en christen-democratie", 65. Indeed, Charles Woeste even suspected a plot in the choice of rapporteurs to the Congress to unite progressive Catholics and pave the way for legislative intervention (Woeste, *Mémoires*, 421).
106 Ibid., 74-76.
107 Leo XIII, "Lettre du Pape Léon XIII", 10-11.
108 He was however forced to refrain from further political intervention in 1898. In 1913 he became a domestic prelate to Pius X, which can be seen as a kind of rehabilitation (Gérin, "Sociaal-katholicisme en christen-democratie", 73).
109 See the contribution of Jean-Pierre Delville in this book.
110 Pottier, "Ce qu'il y a de légitime", 20.

For this purpose, he also explains what he understands to be a just wage. For him, an employer does not act justly by merely paying the wage that has been agreed upon.[111] Justice requires an equality of performances, which is reminiscent of the ideal of justice in exchange and the *iustum pretium*-theory of Aquinas (cf. *supra*), although Pottier also relied on Adam Smith and economic theory.[112] Like Aquinas, Pottier believed a just wage should enable the labourer to sustain himself (and his family)[113] so that they make a decent living, because of the nature of both labour and private property.[114] Indeed, he considered labour to be private property of the labourer and taking this labour without just remuneration thus equalled theft.[115]

Pottier however was aware of the predominant interpretation of Aquinas at the time and – seemingly – nuanced his position. Citing arguments from later Thomists and scholastics, such as Luis de Molina (1535-1600), Leonard Lessius (1554-1623), Francis de Lugo (1580-1652), Martin Bonacina (1585-1631) and Anaclet Reiffenstuel (1642-1703), he accepted that a wage below the sustenance level is not unjust by definition *if* the labourer freely chooses to accept such a lower wage.[116] Yet at the same time, he asserts that labourers have no true freedom of choice because they are forced by economic coercion. Consequently the argument of free choice still holds, but is inapplicable in these particular circumstances.[117]

Taking everything into account, Pottier advocated in "Ce qu'il y a de légitme" a theoretically moderate position, whilst being radical (for his time) in practice. Although he had his supporters, amongst which De Gryse, his reputation as a troublemaker and his overt accusations against the establishment meant his work was not discussed at the Congress, but merely added afterwards as an essay. Nevertheless Pottier's influence on the debate and the development of the progressive faction in general, cannot be underestimated.[118]

---

111   This of course is a clear deviation from the liberty of labour and the views of later scholastics (Chafuen, *Faith and Liberty*, 105-107).

112   Pottier, "Ce qu'il y a de légitime", 21-22, 25-26. Some argue Smith himself was inspired by Aquinas (or at least a modern interpretation of Aquinas). The two are consequently not irreconcilable, although it remains doubtful their theories can be equated.

113   Again, the extension to a 'family wage' cannot be inferred directly from Aquinas, but it can be justified.

114   Pottier, "Ce qu'il a de légitime", 29 and 45. In my view, Pottier enlarges the Thomistic notion of a just wage to a concept that does not only allow the labourer to survive, but also allows him to make a decent, comfortable living. Of course, it can be expected that this interpretation is in line with the intent of the *Summa*.

115   Pottier, "Ce qu'il y a de légitime", 112-113.

116   Ibid., 34-35.

117   Ibid., 37. Pottier's view is quite similar to that of Saint Antoninus of Florence and de Vitoria (Chafuen, *Faith and Liberty*, 106-109 and Langholm, "Voluntary Exchange and Coercion in Scholastic Economics", 8).

118   Gérin, "La démocratie chrétienne", 267.

Count de Kuefstein and the debates of 8-9 May 1890

Count François de Kuefstein, a member of the Union of Fribourg, was considered to be an authority in the field of societal issues at his time.[119] In 1890 he was appointed as one of the rapporteurs to the Congress, much to the chagrin of Charles Woeste.[120] Unlike Pottier's 'banished' essay however, the report by Count de Kuefstein on the duration of labour was not only included, but also ferociously debated at the third Congress. Despite its main topic being labour-duration, Count de Kuefstein touched on the question on the just wage as well.[121]

Referring to the *Summa*, he first asserted that a just wage should be construed as a family wage (*salaire familial*), i.e. a wage sufficient to provide in the living of the labourer and his immediate family *in concreto*.[122] This view directly contradicts the idea of a just wage *in abstracto*, regardless of the needs of the labourer, contrary to what had been argued by – for example – De Gryse (cf. *supra*).[123] Secondly, de Kuefstein connected the wage level to his view on the duration of labour: a just wage should be determined on the basis of the duration of the labour for which it is supposed to be a compensation.[124] Although de Kuefstein's view is not particularly revolutionary from today's perspective, his propositions were heavily contested at the Congress. His main opponents are discussed in the following paragraphs.

Albert Poncelet (1861-1912)[125] adhered to the traditional liberal theory of the liberty of labour. For him, a just wage was nothing else than the wage upon which parties had agreed in their contract.[126] The view that a labourer was not free in practice to agree or refuse the contract was considered to be nonsensical.[127] Poncelet was supported in this view by Auguste Roussel (b. 1844)[128], who added pragmatic reasons to oppose a just minimum wage as proposed by de Kuefstein.

---

119 Massard, *L'œuvre sociale du Cardinal Mermillod*, 118-119.
120 Woeste, *Mémoires*, 421.
121 de Kuefstein, "Réglementation de la durée du travail", 56.
122 From that point of view, de Kuefstein's position is similar to that of De Gryse and Pottier and in line with the general progressive reading of Aquinas (cf. *supra*; see also fn. 19).
123 Ibid., 57.
124 Ibid., 58. This seems to suggest de Kuefstein was in favour of a cost-labour interpretation of Aquinas.
125 Albert Poncelet was born in Liège and studied theology in Leuven. He was a Jesuit and Bollandist (see: Joassart, "Ursmer Belière et les bollandistes Albert Poncelet et Hippolyte Delehaye", 135). Although it is not entirely certain 'A. Poncelet' refers to Albert Poncelet, he is the most likely candidate to fill the role.
126 Poncelet, "Réponse à M. le comte de Kuefstein", 99-100.
127 Ibid.
128 Auguste Roussel was one of the most uncompromising students of Mgr. Pierre-Louis Parisis (1795-1866), bishop of Langres. He was a journalist of *l'Univers* at the time and would later found *La Vérité (française)* in 1893. He should not be confused with his namesake Auguste Roussel (de Méry) (1817-1880), a poet.

Indeed, guaranteeing such a minimum wage would lure good men from the countryside, while there was a clear shortage of labourers at the farms. Thus, according to Roussel, the solution was not to guarantee any wage. Otherwise there was a risk of "labour drain" from the countryside to the cities.[129]

Gustave Théry (1836-1928) was the third major opponent of de Kuefstein and also the fiercest.[130] Moreover, it is particularly interesting to look how he used Thomistic theory to support his view. Like many neo-Thomists, he used the theory of the just price to develop a theory on the just wage. However, Théry made a distinction between a desirable wage and a just wage. A desirable wage allowed a family to live in relative comfort and benefits society as a whole.[131] A just wage however, was nothing more than the sum agreed between employer and employee.[132] Therefore, a just wage could be considerably lower than a desirable wage. The desirable wage was only due on the basis of charity, which was the domain of the Church (albeit supported by the state).[133] For Théry, this was the obvious intent of the *Summa*, although this is clearly not the case (cf. *supra*). Indeed, there is no basis in the *Summa* for the aforementioned distinction.

Despite the fierce opposition against de Kuefstein, he also had some supporters, the most important of which was Michel Levie (1851-1939)[134], who repeatedly tried to force the Congress into taking position on the matter of the just wage. Not only did he criticise the fact that only foreigners stood up for Belgian labourers who could not make ends meet, thus referring to the German descent of Count de Kuefstein and a brief intervention by the bishop of Nottingham (cf. *supra*), but he also attacked the aversion of Roussel and Théry against government intervention.[135] Indeed, he argued, they refuted state intervention to aid the labourer, but if a labourer were to steal a loaf of bread to

---

129 Roussel, "Réponse à M. le comte de Kuefstein", 105.
130 Gustave Théry was a lawyer and co-founder of the University of Lille. He was also the son of the famous politician Antoine Théry (see Bibliothèque Nationale de France: <https://catalogue.bnf.fr/ark:/12148/cb103353381>).
131 Théry, "Réponse à M. le comte de Kuefstein", 108.
132 Ibid.
133 Ibid, 110-111.
134 Michel Levie was an attorney and one of the leading figures of the progressive Catholic movement (i.e. the Christian democrats) in Hainaut. Eventually, he would become Minister of Finance (1911) and a special secret emissary of the Belgian Government during the First World War. In 1918, he became Minister of State. Levie would also be a great support to Prime Minister Delacroix in this time (see: Gérin, "Sociaal-katholicisme en christen-democratie", 73. For a full account on the live and work of Michel Levie, see the biography written by his son: Levie, *Michel Levie (1851-1939)*).
135 Levie, "Réponse à M. le comte de Kuefstein", 101.

survive, they would know where to find the force of the law and the state to seek compensation for themselves.[136]

Levie's furious plea was however interrupted by the bishop of Treves, who had the Congress close the debate on the just wage and had it banned from any further discussion. Although the Congress of 1890 refused to take a stance on the subject-matter, the debates of 1890 would influence Leo XIII and echo in his encyclical *Rerum novarum*, which was – in part – meant to silence the debate in Belgium (and elsewhere) once and for all.

The just wage in *Rerum novarum* (1891)

Leo XIII's encyclical *Rerum novarum* is well known and has acquired a near-mystical status as *the* Catholic social charter.[137] It contains Leo's view on the social issues of the late nineteenth century and the corrupting influence of socialism and includes guidelines for Catholics (especially Catholics in a position of power).[138] Considering its international fame, *Rerum novarum* needs no further introduction, so that only the issues directly related to the theory on the just wage need to be discussed here.

With regard to the just wage, *Rerum novarum* remains relatively loyal to the Thomistic ideals on which it is based, although it obviously contains original ideas not found in the work of Aquinas. One of those core ideas was the dual characterisation of 'labour'. According to the encyclical, labour was both personal and necessary. Personal, because labour (and the products generated by it) were the exclusive property of the labourer.[139] Necessary, because

---

136 Levie, "Réponse à M. le comte de Kuefstein", 127. This argument is somewhat reminiscent of the arguments of Aquinas in *Summa* IIa, IIae Q66 (7). Much like Aquinas (Langholm, *Economics in the Medieval Schools*, 218), Levie argues there is no crime in case of theft out of necessity. A similar argument will be developed by de Lantsheere in *Le pain volé* (cf. *infra*).

137 Walsh, "The Myth of *Rerum Novarum*", 156. Of course, *Rerum novarum* is not the beginning of Catholic social thinking. Several authors had already written about the subject and in 1890 Leo attended a congress in Berlin (Crawford, *The Church and the Worker*, 30-31). Nevertheless, *Rerum novarum* remains pivotal; subsequent social encyclicals always refer to it (e.g. *Quadragesimo Anno* by Pius XI and *Centessimus Annus* by John Paul II). Moreover, they are also inspired by *Rerum novarum* substantially (see: Bigo, *La doctrine sociale de l'Église*, 314-329).

138 Pope Leo XIII was well-acquainted with the conditions in which labourers had to work in industrial Europe. In 1843 he was named papal nuncio to Brussels and travelled many European cities, giving him first-hand experience (see: Obradovic, "Pope Leo XIII's *Rerum Novarum*", 96). His experience should not be overestimated either, however. *Rerum novarum* was largely written by two Jesuits (Mazella and Liberatore) and a Dominican (Zigliara) (see: Astier and Disselkamp, "Pauvreté et propriété privée", 212).

139 This idea does not stem from the *Summa*, but is implied in the liberty of labour and the economic doctrines of the nineteenth century (cf. *supra*).

one had to labour to survive.[140] Theoretically, both characteristics exist in their own right. In practice however, they cannot be separated from each other.[141] Because labour is both necessary and personal at the same time, freedom to contract (the corollary of the personal nature of labour) cannot infringe on labour's role as a means of sustenance.[142]

Consequently, no division can be made between a 'just wage' agreed upon by the labourer and the employer and a 'desirable wage' which enables the labourer to make a living.[143] It follows employers have a duty to pay a wage which enables the labourer and his family to survive in decent conditions (i.e. the idea of a family wage, *salaire familial*).[144]

This interpretation of the just wage seems at first sight relatively progressive and in line with the position of Levie, de Kuefstein and Pottier. Yet, *Rerum novarum*'s progressive tendencies should not be overestimated. Just as with Thomas Aquinas himself, the concept of just wage can only be properly understood in combination with the concept of private property, on which *Rerum novarum* takes a far more conservative position. Indeed, unlike the *Summa* (cf. *supra*), *Rerum novarum* considers private property to be part of natural law, the ultimate purpose of labour and therefore the yardstick to determine what a just wage entails.[145]

In the long run, a just wage should enable labourers to put some savings aside and become owners with an interest in the protection of private property.[146] In the *Summa*, private property remained conditional and subject to the external ultimate purpose of labour: sustenance (cf. *supra*). *Rerum novarum* however, made it unconditional, sacred and a purpose in its own right, an idea which is more resembling of the theory of Locke than of

---

140 Leo XIII, *Rerum Novarum*, §44. It is easy to see the similarity here with Aquinas (Aquinas, *Summa* II-II Q187(3), resp.): *Unde si quis absque manducatione posset vitam transigere, non teneretur manibus operari* (see fn. 17).

141 Leo XIII, *Rerum Novarum*, §44.

142 Ibid.

143 Ibid., §43-44. This of course, contradicts the views of amongst others Théry at the Congress of Liège.

144 Crawford, *The Church and the Worker*, 39. A *caveat* is warranted. *Rerum novarum* seems to equate a 'just wage' with a (familial) sustenance wage. However, as discussed above a mere sustenance wage is not necessarily a just wage according to Aquinas; there still seems to be a difference. One way to solve the tension is by reading *Rerum novarum* in a way it internalises the factors to determine a just wage when it deals with the wage that allows a labourer to sustain himself and his family. Indeed, the official translation of the encyclical suggests as much (Leo XIII, *Rerum Novarum*, §46, "comfortably").

145 Leo XIII, *Rerum Novarum*, §8-9. Compare with Aquinas, *Summa* II-II Q66(2), resp. and reply to the first objection (see also: Langholm, *Economics in the Medieval Schools*, 210-211 and Höpfl, *Jesuit Political Thought*, 296).

146 Leo XIII, *Rerum Novarum*, §22 and §45 and Tideman, "The Justice and the Economies of *Rerum Novarum* on Land", 131-132.

Thomas Aquinas.[147] This clear shift from the ideals of Thomism is all the more remarkable since (1) *Rerum novarum* explicitly claims to be in line with Thomistic theory and (2) an earlier draft of the encyclical, written by the Jesuit Matteo Liberatore, actually remained loyal to the original ideas of Thomism. Only in a later stage of writing *Rerum novarum* departs from the Thomistic concept of private property as man-made law.[148] The rationale behind this change is not entirely clear; it is possible that this reversal made the contrast with socialism more clear and denounced socialist views on private property as 'unnatural'.[149]

Of course the fact that *Rerum novarum* tried to be a faithful successor to Aquinas and deliberately deviated from his teachings at the same time, did not improve the coherence in neo-Thomistic circles. On the contrary, the dual message of *Rerum novarum* only added fuel to the already heated discussion between progressive and conservative Catholics (in Belgium), since both parties found a confirmation of their views in the encyclical.[150] Conservatives, like Charles Périn and the Jesuit Auguste Castelein adhered to a minimalist interpretation of the encyclical and a confirmation of the *status quo*.[151] Progressives however, would point out the responsibility of the employers to back up the demands for fixed higher wages.[152]

Taking this into account, it comes as no surprise that the interpretation of *Rerum novarum* would remain a breakpoint between conservatives and progressives until the start of the First World War.[153] The discussion also put the Belgian episcopate between a rock and a hard place. Since the Belgian bishops did not want to estrange either side of the discussion (and the ruling Catholic Party in the government), they were *de facto* prevented from commenting too much on the subject.[154] The diversity of interpretations however, forced the bishops to react. Yet even the most progressive of bishops, most notably the bishop of Liège, Mgr. Doutreloux, had to remain careful not to cause too

147 Astier and Disselkamp, "Pauvreté et propriété privée", 209-211.
148 Walsh, "The Myth of *Rerum Novarum*", 160.
149 Leo XIII, *Rerum Novarum*, §17.
150 Verdoodt, "Roma locuta, causa nondum finita", 254.
151 Ibid., 16-17. The strong confirmation of private property was fully in their advantage, but it was already a common theory at the time. Moreover, many progressive Catholics also adhered to this theory and used it for their own advantage by considering the 'property' of labour (e.g. De Gryse, Pottier etc.). Therefore, it can be expected conservatives did not perceived *Rerum novarum*'s confirmation of private property as the victory of conservatism it actually was. Rather, they focused on the aspects of the just wage which were clearly disadvantageous to them and contrary to the absolute liberty of labour they had adhered to (and found in Aquinas, as they saw him).
152 Verdoodt, "Roma locuta, causa nondum finita", 15-16.
153 In 1895 the pope would intervene to prevent a political fragmentation of Catholic votes between the Catholic Party and Christian Party. This discussion however is outside the scope of this research.
154 Ibid., 48-52.

much controversy in his pastoral letters.[155] This, of course, illustrates the highly contentious nature of *Rerum novarum* and its explosive influence on Belgian politics and society.

The just wage after Rerum novarum (1891-1914)

The issuing of *Rerum novarum* paved the way for a stream of interpretations and claims, invoking not only the encyclical, but also its 'mythical' source of inspiration. In the following paragraphs, the most influential authors are discussed, at least insofar they wrote on the just wage. First, a minimalist interpretation promoted by Charles Périn and Auguste Castelein is dealt with. Second, the essay of Léon de Lantsheere, *Le pain volé*, is worth mentioning, both for its widespread influence and its loyalty to the original ideas of the *Summa*. Finally, the view of Mgr. Waffelaert, bishop of Bruges is discussed. Although he is far less known than his Liègeois counterpart, Waffelaert's essay is a quintessential example of the intermediate position of the Belgian episcopate, navigating between a progressive Scylla and a conservative Charibdis.

The minimalist interpretation: Périn and Castelein

Charles Périn: *Note sur le juste salaire d'après l'encyclique Rerum novarum* (1892)

Charles Périn belonged to the intellectual core of conservative Catholicism.[156] He had been an attorney, a professor and dean of the Law Faculty in Leuven for several years.[157] By the time *Rerum novarum* was issued in 1891 however, Périn was already 77 years old and past his heydays.[158] Ten years prior, he had been forced to retire from public life after a scandalous publication.[159] Nevertheless, Périn remained influential in his later years. In 1892 he published a brief note on *Rerum novarum*, which he subsequently added to the last publication of his major work *Premiers principes d'économie politique* in 1896.[160] Interestingly,

---

155 See: Doutreloux, *Lettre pastorale*. The work of Mgr. Doutreloux, though interesting, is not discussed in this essay. Again, I refer to the contribution of his successor, Mgr. Delville in this book.
156 This, however, does not mean he lacked social empathy. Indeed, Périn was aware of the circumstances of the proletariat and actively sought to improve their situation. He however could not accept any such intervention by the state and sought improvement via the moral duties and charity of the bourgeoisie (Van Dievoet et al., *Lovanium docet*, 161.
157 See the contribution of Joeri De Smet in this book.
158 Van Dievoet et al., *Geschiedenis van de Leuvense rechtsfaculteit*, 162.
159 Ibid. and the contribution of Joeri De Smet in this book.
160 This work is better known under the title of the original publication of its first edition in 1861: *Richesse dans les sociétés chrétiennes*.

the question on the just wage is one of the few elements in Périn's work which shows a hint of evolution throughout the years.[161]

In his earliest work, Périn only accepted the market principles of supply and demand. In 1886 he denounced claims to regulate wages as dangerous to the social order and incompatible with the nature of labour agreements.[162] Of course, this view was supported by conjuring the dreaded phantom of social-ism.[163]

Yet Leo XIII's encyclical forced Périn to reconsider. According to Périn the factual circumstances of the economy had to be taken into account.[164] This meant one had to delineate what part of a product was created by the labour-er and what part was made by the employer (who invests capital) in order to decide on what a 'just wage' entails.[165] In principle this meant that a labourer was entitled to a just wage which enabled him to make a living.[166]

However, for Périn, there were many circumstances that justified a lower wage. Economic crises diminished the usability of labour and could lead to a reduction of wages. If not, an employer would be forced to relinquish part of his property, which – according to Périn – could only be considered a form of charity, not of justice.[167]

Whether such circumstances justifying reduced wages actually occurred, was a factual matter, not to be discussed in his work.[168] It is clear that no such circumstances can be found in Aquinas' work (cf. *supra*) or in *Rerum novarum*. Indeed, by allowing the just wage to go below the level of a sustenance wage, Périn alienates himself from the most basic ideas of *Rerum novarum*. Never-theless, his express reference to the *Summa* is – once more – an illustration of the open-ended nature of Aquinas' work and the large array of possible interpretations.

Auguste Castelein: *Le problème social et l'encyclique Rerum novarum* (1892)

Auguste Castelein, Jesuit and professor in Leuven and Namur, is considered to be one of the more influential neo-Thomists together with Désiré Mercier (1851-1926), Louis de San (1832-1904) and Antoine Dupont (1836-1917).[169] His

---

161 Michotte, "Un économiste belge: Charles Périn", 259.
162 Ibid.
163 Ibid.
164 Périn, *Note sur le juste salaire*, 4.
165 Ibid.
166 Michotte, "Un économiste belge: Charles Périn", 259.
167 Périn, *Note sur le juste salaire*, 6. Périn would later be reproached for using an inconsis-tent concept of charity and justice and mixing the two together (see: Damoiseaux, "Un économiste catholique belge", 183-186).
168 Périn, *Note sur le juste salaire*, 7-8.
169 Verlinde and Heyrman, "Auguste Castelein".

work was much appreciated, amongst others by Victor Brants. Castelein made a reputation as a staunch conservative and a critic of the Catholic social teachings, making him one of the main representatives of the minimalist interpretation of *Rerum novarum*, which he tackled in his work *Le problème social et l'encyclique Rerum Novarum* (hereafter: *Le problème social*).[170]

Quite cleverly, Castelein attacked the encyclical with praise.[171] Castelein argued that the social problems of his time could only be solved by a return to Christian values.[172] This was exactly what *Rerum novarum* did. Moreover, he emphasised the parts of the encyclical on private property as a natural right, which is – as stated before – a reflection of the liberal concept of ownership and directly contrary to Aquinas' views. Castelein went even further however: not only was private property natural, but so was inequality.[173] Therefore, he argued, a harmonious society should not try to eliminate inequality, but rather accept and respect it. This inequality creates duties for both employers and employees (labourers). At this point, Castelein concluded that one of the duties of the employers was to pay the just wage, which in his view should only allow the survival of the labourer, regardless of familial issues.[174] In other words, Castelein interpreted both *Rerum novarum* and the *Summa* in the strictest possible way, equating the just wage with a sustenance wage (*sensu stricto*).[175] By doing so, Castelein managed to reconcile these works with the interests of the bourgeoisie. Although he is considered to be one of the great neo-Thomists of his time, his relationship with Thomistic teachings seems to have been ambiguous at best. Castelein's interpretation was perhaps in line with the textual basis provided by Aquinas (and Leo), but it is doubtful it was in line with the intent of their teachings.

Léon de Lantsheere: Le pain volé (1897-1898)

Léon de Lantsheere was a true *homo universalis*, with an interest in history, philosophy, maths and languages.[176] In 1891 he had already obtained the degrees of doctor in laws and philosophy and was a member of parliament, all before the age of thirty.[177] Later he would become minister of Justice, professor

---

170 Verdoodt, "Roma locuta, causa nondum finita", 38.
171 Castelein, *Le problème sociale*, 7.
172 Ibid., 12.
173 Ibid., 18. On this issue, Castelein completely concurs with the ultraliberal standpoints of Charles Dunoyer (cf. *supra*: Dunoyer, *De la liberté du travail*, 408).
174 Castelein, *Le problème sociale*, 20-22.
175 See on the interpretation of just wage versus sustenance wage fn 25.
176 Descamps, *Léon de Lantsheere*, 1.
177 Ibid., 1-20 and Vinck, "Léon de Lantsheere".

and dean of the Law Faculty in Leuven, before his untimely death in 1912.[178] As a member of the 'Jeune Droite' he found himself on the progressive side of the Catholic front as an early Christian democrat. De Lantsheere wrote a great number of works, but with regard to the question on the just wage, De Lantsheere's main contribution was his well-received and widely acknowledged essay "Le pain volé", which was published in two parts in the *Revue Sociale Catholique*.[179]

"Le pain volé" opens with a quote of Victor Hugo's *Claude Gueux*, immediately catching the attention of the audience. De Lantsheere – citing Hugo – wrote: "Un hiver, l'ouvrage manqua. Pas de feu ni de pain dans le galetas. L'homme, la femme et l'enfant eurent froid et faim. L'homme vola... De ce vol, il résulta trois jours de pain et de feu pour la femme et l'enfant, et cinq ans de prison pour l'homme."[180] Although Hugo wrote fiction, de Lantsheere made it no secret that these kind of situations were very real in his days: the immediate cause for de Lantsheere's essay was the heavily contested acquittal of a woman stealing bread to feed her child by the French court at Château-Thierry.[181] More conservative authors complained the court had acted *contra legem* and violated the principles of property law (a legalistic perspective), while others praised the court for the humanity of its decision and the audacity to put aside the law if need be (a moralistic perspective).[182]

De Lantsheere took an intermediate position, reconciling both views. He referred to article 64 of the French *Code Pénal* (i.e. the contemporary article 71 of the Belgian Criminal Code) which states that there is no crime when the otherwise criminal act was imposed by an irresistible force.[183] Although the ingenuity of the solution is remarkable, it is not the main point of de Lantsheere's essay. Indeed de Lantsheere sought not to justify a crime, but wanted to discuss the higher moral law that took away every sense of illegitimacy of the contested act.[184]

178 A brief, but relatively complete overview of de Lantsheere's life and work can be found in the eulogy written and pronounced on the 14th of November 1912 by baron Edouard Descamps: Descamps, "Léon de Lantsheere".
179 Defourny, "Léon de Lantsheere", 344.
180 de Lantsheere, "Le pain volé", 193.
181 Ibid.
182 Defourny, "Léon de Lantsheere", 344.
183 de Lantsheere, "Le pain volé", 196. The superior court at Amiens would reform the judgement of the court in Château-Thierry in this way as well. Sadly, these cases still exist today. For example, the Italian Supreme Court (Corte Suprema di Cassazione) ruled in its judgement on 13 February 2017 (!) in favour of a defendant who had stolen cheese and bread to feed himself. The Court held there was no crime, because of a 'state of necessity'. Moreover, the court specifically referred to public morals and the general feeling it would be unjust to punish the thief in this case ("la coscienza collettiva sente come ingiusto il ricorso alla sanzione penale"). *Nihil novi sub sole*, indeed... (see: Italian Supreme Court 17 February 2017, ECLI:IT:CASS:2017:6635:PEN).
184 de Lantsheere, "Le pain volé", 201.

At this point, de Lantsheere reveals himself to be a true neo-Thomist. He maintained the baker could not invoke property law against the thief stealing out of hunger, because all goods are meant to sustain humanity and private property is only a conditional addendum of man-made law to this natural law.[185] Private property was meant as a means to fulfil this ultimate purpose in a more efficient way. The wealthy had a moral duty to share with the poor, but retained the freedom to do so in a way they see fit.[186] Situations of emergency however limited this freedom of choice, so that the poor did not only commit no crime if they stole out of need, but they *could not* commit a crime since the emergency situation undid the very right to private property.[187]

In support of these views, de Lantsheere referred to the relevant passages of the *Summa*.[188] Of course, by doing so, de Lantsheere also contradicted the 'new ideas' of *Rerum Novarum* on private property.[189]

What conclusions can be inferred from this with regard to the just wage? De Lantsheere does not talk about a just wage directly, but – considering his relative accurate representation of de *Summa* – it is reasonable to assume de Lantsheere would accept the views of de *Summa* as well. As stated above it is not possible to discover a conclusive view on the just wage in Aquinas' work. However, it can reasonably be argued that private property can only be maintained insofar a sufficiently high (just) wage is paid (cf. *supra*). At least de Lantsheere seems to accept this.[190]

Gustavus Waffelaert: Animadversiones (1901)

Unlike many others discussed above, Mgr. Gustavus Waffelaert (1847-1931) was of modest descent. Given the chance to study at Leuven, Waffelaert became a doctor in theology and, like De Gryse, started teaching at the seminary of Bruges. As bishop of Bruges he was concerned about the unity of the Catholic movement and rejected the 'revolutionary' Daens, but he supported the Christian labour movement.[191] Waffelaert took up the topic in 1901 when he wrote a brief contribution in the *Collationes Brugenses*[192], which led to praise

---

185 Ibid., 264.
186 Ibid.
187 Ibid., 265.
188 Cf. *supra*. See in particular: Aquinas, *Summa* II-II Q66(7) resp. and Langholm, *Economics in the Medieval Schools*, 218. Indeed, de Lantsheere is probably the only author discussed in this essay who kept so true to the Thomistic teachings, certainly with respect to the just wage.
189 Leo XIII, *Rerum Novarum*, § 8-9.
190 By way of a reasoning *a contrario*: if no sufficiently high wage is paid, private property ceases to exist.
191 Debruyne, "Gustave Waffelaert".
192 A journal founded by him.

from – amongst others – Simon Deploige, who otherwise did not write on the topic himself.[193]

In the past, Waffelaert had been supportive of initiatives in favour of higher and more secure 'just' wages. Pottier felt that they were on the same line[194], yet Waffelaert was no revolutionary. Unlike some of his more radical colleagues, again mostly the bishop of Liège, he opposed the idea of taking action against the conservative frontman of the Catholic Party, Charles Woeste.[195] Instead, he wrote down his ideas in his "Animadversiones quaedam de justa mercede seu justo salario opificum; de salario, ut adjunt, familiali, etc." (hereafter: "Animadversiones").[196]

Waffelaert's view was based on three pillars. First, he believed a labourer was entitled to a wage that represented the value of his labour, regardless of the wealth of the labourer or his employer.[197] Fluctuations on the market need not influence wages, but neither could a wealthy employer be expected to pay higher wages simply because he could afford it. Similarly, Waffelaert discarded the needs of labourers as a relevant criterion: "La mesure propre, directe et universelle du juste salaire n'est pas la somme des besoins de l'ouvrier".[198]

How can this statement be reconciled with the *Summa* and the – for that time relatively recent – message of *Rerum novarum*? For Waffelaert, the key to understanding lay in the spirit of his time. Where the Angelic Doctor and his immediate successors only envisaged their own premodern societies, *Rerum novarum* applied their teachings to a modern, industrial context. This would form the basis of his second principle: the natural duty of man is to sustain himself. Since labour was the only way a labourer could sustain himself, they should sell their labour to a price (wage) that enabled them to do so.

In other words, it was not up to employers to pay a wage that meets the demands of their labourers; it was up to labourers to find a job that corresponds to a sufficiently high wage.[199] If this proved to be impossible, Waffelaert believed government intervention should find a solution. At this point, Waffelaert clearly distances himself from more conservative authors for whom

193 Deploige, "Pensées d'un évêque sur le juste salaire", 55-56. Waffelaert himself would not write much about it either; his academic work is mainly concerned with a more mystical approach to theology.

194 Pottier, "Ce qu'il y a de légitime", 37.

195 Verdoodt, *Het loon van de werkman*, 50.

196 Waffelaert also wrote an extensive commentary on *Rerum novarum* in which he discussed the nature of private property *in extenso*. However the question on the just wage was not dealt with, although Waffelaert proves himself to be a true neo-Thomist in this work; see: Waffelaert, *Exposé sommaire des Principes Généraux*, 124-145.

197 Waffelaert, "Animadversiones", 15-16. Waffelaert seems to have followed to a cost-value interpretation of Aquinas, independent of the needs of the labourer.

198 Ibid., 16.

199 Ibid., 17.

government intervention was not only unthinkable but often even diaboli-cal.[200] Finally, Waffelaert declared himself in favour of a wage high enough to sustain a family, independent of the question whether a labourer actually had a family.[201] In other words, the just wage for him, was a family wage *in abstracto*.

Final remarks

Key to this essay was the question to what extent nineteenth-century neo-Thomists were true to the Thomistic ideals they claimed to follow. By us-ing the subtopic of the just wage as a guideline, I have tried to provide a solid (yet necessarily inexhaustive) overview of the key players in the Belgian de-bate and to compare them with the original source material in the *Summa*. Although this essay is far too brief to allow for definite conclusions, some pre-liminary findings can be maintained.

First, with regard to the question on the just wage, the gap between con-servatives and progressives diminished at the end of the (long) nineteenth century. Before 1891 there was a clear rift between the conservative and pro-gressive factions in religious, political and intellectual Catholic circles. Con-servatives had embraced the liberty of labour as a Christian value, while pro-gressives strived for a minimum wage in favour of labourers. The issuing of *Rerum novarum* in 1891 led to an open strife between those in favour of a min-imalist interpretation (Périn, Castelein) and those that gave a more substan-tive interpretation to the encyclical (Doutreloux, de Lantsheere, Waffelaert). At the end of the nineteenth century, the latter interpretation seemed to have prevailed, although the emancipation of labourers was still in an early stage. Nevertheless, several key questions remained unanswered, for example with regard to the exact amount that constituted a just wage (is the mere survival of the labourer sufficient or is more warranted), the family wage (*in abstracto* or *in concreto*) and the legal basis for a 'just' wage. The answers to those ques-tions however, were all sought in Thomistic morality and its transformation in early modern scholastic theology by the then dominant Catholic intelligentsia.

Second, despite its interest in Thomism, neo-Thomism seems to have distanced itself in practice if not in name from the original Thomistic ideals. Both conservatives (Périn) and progressives (De Gryse) mixed liberal econom-ic views with Christian morality. For them, a just wage was first and foremost decided by market principles of supply and demand that were – to a lesser or greater extent – tempered by Christian morality. *Rerum novarum*, widely

200 This of course because it was symptomatic of socialism, which was considered a direct attack on religion in general and Christianity in particular.
201 Waffelaert, "Animadversiones", 21-22.

considered to be the guideline for Catholics with regard to the social question, purposely deviated from the *Summa*. Rather than defending the Thomistic idea of private property, neo-Thomists adhered to economic liberalism as promoted by John Locke and Adam Smith under the guise of Catholicism (with the notable exception of Léon de Lantsheere). Another key element in the modern interpretation of Thomism in general and *Rerum novarum* in particular was the creation of several distinctions that did not exist in original Thomistic theory (e.g. the distinction between a just and a desirable wage). Consequently, the neo-Thomistic movement seems extremely fragmented. Apart from the rift between conservatives and progressives, there seems to be a different reading of Thomism for each individual member of one of these groups. Indeed, many of the aforementioned authors appear to have almost nothing in common except for the topic on which they express themselves. Consequently, one might argue that the 'neo-Thomistic movement' was neither Thomistic nor a movement.

Some nuances must be made however. First of all, Aquinas did not develop a full theory on the just wage (or economics in general) in its own right. Consequently, every so-called 'Thomistic' theory on the just wage is only an interpretation *ex post*. Since Aquinas' work is in many ways 'open-ended' it is only to be expected that a great diversity of interpretations exists.

It would be far more remarkable if this had not been the case. Moreover, time is an important factor as well. Indeed, the gap between Aquinas (thirteenth century) and neo-Thomism (nineteenth century) cannot be underestimated. For centuries, there had been an interpretative tradition or *Umdeutung*, reshaping Thomistic teachings. Furthermore the societal and economic context of both periods cannot be compared, necessitating a modern approach to the source material. The mismatch between 'true' Thomism – insofar it ever existed – and neo-Thomism should therefore be explained as the difference between two shackles in a chain of interpretation, rather than as a misrepresentation of a consistent theory.

Moreover, three defining criteria may be derived from the combined work of the neo-Thomists that unite their views in one 'agenda'. First, all of the so-called neo-Thomists shared a great fear and aversion for socialism. The socialist threat to the social order was crucial to the development of Catholic social theory and neo-Thomism.

Thus, neo-Thomism is essentially a countermovement, aimed at distinguishing itself from other competing models of social organisation such as socialism and – to a lesser extent – liberalism. Second, neo-Thomists shared the desire to develop positive law in accordance with natural law, as perceived by Thomas Aquinas. From that perspective, neo-Thomism also appears as a Catholic countermovement against legal positivism. Finally, all neo-Thomists referred to Aquinas and Thomistic teachings. Even if their views did not correspond entirely with the ideals of the *Summa* or each other, they all belonged to the same *Diskursgemeinschaft*, setting them apart from other (socialist or liberal) thinkers, who did not belong to this 'community'.

In conclusion, the general feeling on neo-Thomism seems confirmed, albeit with nuances. Neo-Thomism was perhaps not really a movement in its own right. Nevertheless it was a *counter*-movement opposing alternate solutions to the social issues of the late nineteenth century on the one hand and a perspective on the law that gave no prominent position to morality on the other hand. Moreover, despite its obvious differences from its source material, neo-Thomism sought to be true to Thomistic ideas. From that perspective, it is exactly as its name suggests: New Thomism.

BIBLIOGRAPHY

Astier, Isabelle and Annette Disselkamp. "Pauvreté et propriété privée dans l'encyclique *Rerum Novarum*". *Cahiers d'économie politique*, 2 (2010) 59, 205-224.

Bigo, Pierre. *La doctrine sociale de l'Église: recherche et dialogue*. Paris: Presses Universitaires de France, 1966.

Blanpain, Roger. *Hebben de vakbonden nog een toekomst? De vrijheid van vakvereniging naar internationaal, Europees en Belgisch recht*. Bruges: die Keure, 2012.

Brants, Victor. *La lutte pour le pain quotidien*. Leuven: Peeters, 1888.

Brants, Victor. *La lutte contre l'usure dans les lois modernes*. Leuven: Peeters, 1907.

Brants, Victor. "Economie des échanges: juste prix". *Revue d'histoire ecclésiastique*, 13 (1912) 1, 84-89.

Caracausi, Andrea. "The Just Wage in Early Modern Italy: A Reflection on Zacchia's *De Salario seu Operariorum Mercede*". *International Review of Social History (IRSH)*, 56 (2011), special issue, 107-124.

Castelein, Auguste. *Le problème social et l'encyclique Rerum Novarum*. Brussels: Société belge de librairie, 1892.

Casteleyn, Davy. *Notes et souvenirs de Victor Brants. Tekstkritische uitgave van een autobiografische reflectie geschreven tijdens de Eerste Wereldoorlog*. Unpublished master thesis, KU Leuven, 2012/2013.

Chafuen, Alejandro. *Faith and Liberty: The Economic Thought of the Late Scholastics*. New York: Lexington Books, 2003.

Crawford, Virginia. *The Church and the Worker*. Oxford: Catholic Social Guild, 1936.

Damoiseaux, Maurice. "Un économiste catholique belge". *Revue Sociale Catholique*, 1897-1898, 181-186.

Debruyne, André. "Gustave Waffelaert". In: ODIS. <www.odis.be/hercules/search2.php?-searchMethod=simple&search=Waffelaert>.

Decock, Wim. *Theologians and Contract Law: The Moral Transformation of the ius commune (ca. 1500-1650)*. Leiden: Nijhoff, 2013.

Decoene, Alberic. *Doctor Edward De Gryse, deken van Kortrijk: zijn leven, zijn werk*. Bruges: Groenys, 1944.

Deferme, Jo. *Uit de ketens van de vrijheid: het debat over de sociale politiek in België 1886-1914*. Leuven: Universitaire Pers Leuven, 2007.

Defourny, Maurice. "Léon de Lantsheere". *Revue Sociale Catholique*, 1911-1912, 343-350.

De Gryse, Eduard. *Notre droit national et la Révolution*. Roeselare: De Meester, 1885.

De Kuefstein, François. "Réglementation de la durée du travail". In *Congrès des Œuvres sociales à Liège. Troisième session, 7-10 septembre 1890*. Deuxième section. Liège: Demarteau, 1890, 53-78.

de Lantsheere, Léon. "Le pain volé". *Revue Sociale Catholique*, 1897-1898, 193-201 and 257-267.

Deploige, Simon. "Pensées d'un évêque sur le juste salaire". *Revue Philosophique de Louvain*, (1901) 29, 55-57.

De Roover, Raymond. "The Concept of the Just Price: Theory and Economic Policy". *Journal of Economic History*, 18 (1958) December edition, 418-434.

Descamps, Edouard. *Léon de Lantsheere*. Leuven: Van Linthout, 1912.

Dewaele, Kwinten. "Het neothomisme in België en het rechtvaardig loon (1879-1914)". *Jura Falconis*, 54 (2017-2018) 2, 307-345.

Doutreloux, Victor-Joseph. *Lettre pastorale de Sa Grandeur Mgr. Doutreloux, Evêque de Liége au clergé de son diocèse sur la question ouvrière suivie de l'encyclique Rerum Novarum et de plusieurs documents pontificaux*. Liège: Dessain, 1894.

Dunoyer, Charles. *De la liberté du travail ou Simple exposé des conditions dans lesquelles les forces humaines s'exercent avec le plus de puissance*. Paris: Guillaumin Libraire, 1845.

du Sart de Boulan, Raoul. "La lutte pour le pain quotidien". *Magasin Littéraire et Scientifique*, 1886, 5-15.

Frémeaux, Sandrine and Christine Noël. "Qu'est-ce qu'une juste rémunération? Ce que nous enseigne la conception du juste salaire de Thomas d'Aquin". *Revue Management en Avenir*, 8 (2011) 48, 76-93.

Gaddis, John Lewis. *On Grand Strategy*. New York: Penguin Press, 2018.

Gérin, Paul. *Les origines de la démocratie chrétienne à Liège*. Brussels: La pensée catholique, 1958.

Gérin, Paul. "La démocratie chrétienne dans les relations Église-État à la fin du XIXe siècle". In Gaston Braive and Jacques Lory. *L'Église et l'État à l'époque contemporaine. Mélanges dédiés à la mémoire de Mgr. Aloïs Simon*. Brussels: Facultés Universitaires Saint-Louis, 1975, 255-287.

Gérin, Paul. "Sociaal-katholicisme en christen-democratie (1884-1904)". In Emmanuel Gerard, ed. *De christelijke arbeidersbeweging in België*. Vol. 1. Leuven: Universitaire Pers Leuven, 1991, 56-109.

Heirbaut, Dirk. *Een beknopte geschiedenis van het sociaal, het economisch en het fiscaal recht in België*. Ghent: Academia Press, 2013.

Hirschfeld, Mary. *Aquinas and the Market: Toward a Humane Economy*. Cambridge: Harvard University Press, 2018.

Hollander, Samuel. "On the Interpretation of the Just Price". *Kyklos*, 18 (1965) 4, 615-634.

Höpfl, Harro. *Jesuit Political Thought*. Cambridge: Cambridge University Press, 2004.

Joassart, Bernard. "Ursmer Belière et les bollandistes Albert Poncelet et Hippolyte Delehaye". *Analecta Bollandiana*, 131 (2013) 1, 134-153.

Koehler, Benedikt. "The Thirteenth-Century Economics of Thomas Aquinas". *Economic Affairs*, 36 (2016) 1, 56-63.

Langholm, Odd Inge. *Economics in the Medieval Schools*. Leiden: Brill, 1992.

Langholm, Odd Inge. "The Medieval Schoolmen (1200-1400)". In Stanly Todd Lowry and Barry Gordon. *Ancient and Medieval Economic Ideas and Concepts of Social Justice*. Leiden: Brill, 1998, 439-501.

Langholm, Odd Inge. "Thomas Aquinas". In Jan Pell and Irene van Staveren. *Handbook of Economics and Ethics*. Cheltenham: Edward Elgar Publishing, 2010.

Langholm, Odd Inge. "Voluntary Exchange and Coercion in Scholastic Economics". In Paul Oslington, ed. *The Oxford Handbook of Christianity and Economics*. New York: Oxford University Press, 2014.

Lapidus, André. "Norm, Virtue and Information: The Just Price and Individual Behaviour in Thomas Aquinas' Summa Theologiae". *Journal of the History of Economic Thought*, 1 (1994) 3, 435-473.

Leo XIII. *Aeterni Patris*. Consulted via: <Enghttp://w2.vatican.va/content/leo-xiii/en/encyclicals/documents/hf_l-xiii_enc_04081879_aeterni-patris.html>.

Leo XIII. "Lettre du Pape Léon XIII. In: *Congrès des Œuvres sociales à Liège. Troisième session, 7-10 septembre 1890*. Séance d'ouverture. Liège: Demarteau, 1890, 10-12.

Leo XIII. *Rerum Novarum*. Consulted via: <http://w2.vatican.va/content/leo-xiii/en/encyclicals/documents/hf_l-xiii_enc_15051891_rerum-novarum.html>.

Levie, Michel. "Réponse à M. le comte de Kuefstein". In: *Congrès des Œuvres sociales à Liège. Troisième session, 7-10 septembre 1890*. Deuxième section. Liège: Demarteau, 1890, 97-132.

Levie, Jean. *Michel Levie (1851-1939) et le mouvement chrétien social de son temps*. Leuven: Société d'études morales, sociales et juridiques, 1962.

Massard, Cyrille. *L'œuvre sociale du Cardinal Mermillod: l'Union de Fribourg, d'après des documents inédits*. Leuven: Uytspruyt, 1914.

Meerts, Kristin. "De Leuvense hoogleraar Victor Brants: een brugfiguur in het sociaal-katholicisme (1856-1891)". *Bijdragen tot de geschiedenis*, 65 (1982), 197-233.

Meerts, Kristin. "De Leuvense hoogleraar Victor Brants: sociale ideeën tussen katholieke romantiek en realisme (1856-1891)". *Bijdragen tot de geschiedenis*, 66 (1983), 101-130.

Michotte, Paul-Lambert. "Un économiste belge: Charles Périn". *Revue Sociale Catholique* (1904-1905), 240-264.

Noell, Edd. "Bargaining, Consent and the Just Wage in the Sources of Scholastic Economic Thought". *Journal of History of Economic Thought*, 20 (1998) 4, 467-478.

Noell, Edd. "In Pursuit of the Just Wage: A Comparison of Reformation and Counter-Reformation Economic Thought". *Journal of the History of Economic Thought*, 23 (2001) 4, 467-489.

Nureev, Rustem and Pavel Petrakov. "Doctrine of Fair Price by Thomas Aquinas: Background, Laws of Development and Specific Interpretation". *Journal of Institutional Studies*, 7 (2015) 1, 6-24.

Obradovic, Goran. "Pope Leo XIII's *Rerum Novarum*". *Zbornik Radova Pravnog Fakulteta U Nisu*, 55 (2016) 2, 92-104.

Périn, Charles. *Note sur le juste salaire d'après l'Encyclique Rerum Novarum*. Mons: Desguin, 1892.

Périn, Charles. *Premiers principes d'économie politique*. Paris: Lecoffre, 1896.

Poncelet, *Albert**. "Réponse à M. le comte de Kuefstein". In *Congrès des Œuvres sociales à Liège. Troisième session, 7-10 septembre 1890. Deuxième section*. Liège: Demarteau, 1890, 97-132.

Pottier, Antoine. "Ce qu'il y a de légitime dans les revendications ouvrières". In *Congrès des Œuvres sociales à Liège. Troisième session, 7-10 septembre 1890. Deuxième section*. Liège: Demarteau, 1890, 20-48.

Roussel, Auguste. "Réponse à M. le comte de Kuefstein". *Congrès des Œuvres sociales à Liège. Troisième session, 7-10 septembre 1890. Deuxième section*. Liège: Demarteau, 1890, 97-132.

Scholl, S.H. "Werkstakingen en organisaties". In S.H. Scholl. *150 jaar katholieke arbeidersbeweging in België (1789-1939). Vol. 2: De christen-democratie (1886-1914)*. Brussels: De Arbeiderspers, 1965, 205-397.

Théry, Gustave. "Réponse à M. le comte de Kuefstein". In: *Congrès des Œuvres sociales à Liège. Troisième session, 7-10 septembre 1890. Deuxième section*. Liège: Demarteau, 1890, 97-132.

Thomas Aquinas. *In libros Politicorum exposition*. Translated by Richard Regan. Consulted via: <https://static1.squarespace.com/static/58d6b5ff86e6c087a92f8f89/t/5913d17a9f-7456878ba52cfb/14943>.

Thomas Aquinas. *Summa Theologiae*. Translation Dominican Fathers. Consulted via: <https://dhspriory.org/thomas/summa/>.

Tideman, Nicolaus. "The Justice and the Economics of *Rerum Novarum* on Land". In Jürgen Backhaus et al. *On the Economic Significance of the Catholic Social Doctrine: 125 Years of Rerum Novarum*. Cham: Springer International Publishing, 2017, 125-134.

Van Dievoet, Guido et al, eds. *Lovanium docet. Geschiedenis van de Leuvense Rechtsfaculteit 1425-1914*. Leuven: KU Leuven, Faculty of Law, 1988.

Van Ommen Kloeke, Wilhelm. *De vrijheid van beroep en bedrijf*. Groningen: Gebroeders Hoitsema, 1945.

Verdoodt, Frans-Jos. *Het loon van de werkman. Christenen en Katholieken in België ten tijde van Rerum Novarum*. Ghent: Perspectief Uitgaven, 1991.

Verdoodt, Frans-Jos. "Roma locuta. Causa nondum finita. Christelijk-sociaal denken in België in de negentiende eeuw". In Gerrit-Jan Schutte. *Een arbeider is zijn loon waardig*. The Hague: Meinema, 1991, 242-257.

Verlinde, Patrick and Peter Heyrman. "Auguste Castelein". In ODIS. <www.odis.be/hercules/search2.php?searchMethod=simple&search=auguste%20castelein>.

Vinck, Sharon. "Léon de Lantsheere". In ODIS. <www.odis.be/hercules/search2.php?searchMethod=simple&search=L%C3%A9on%20de%20Lantsheere>.

Waffelaert, Gustavus. *Exposé sommaire des principes généraux de la science sociale devant servir d'introduction à l'intelligence de l'encyclique Rerum Novarum sur la condition des ouvriers*. Bruges: Beyaert, 1894.

Waffellaert, Gustavus. "Animadversiones quaedam de justa mercede seu justo salario opificum; de salario, ut ajunt familiali, etc.". *Collationes Brugenses*, 1901, 15-23.

Walsh, Michael. "The Myth of *Rerum Novarum*". *New Blackfriars*, 93 (2012) 1044, 155-162.

Wils, Lode. "België in de negentiende eeuw: religieus, politiek en sociaal". In Emmanuel Gerard, ed. *De christelijke arbeidersbeweging in België*. Vol. 1. Leuven: Universitaire Pers Leuven, 1991, 18-54.

Wilson, George. "The Economics of the Just Price". *HOPE*, 7 (1975) 1, 56-74.

Witte, Els et al. *Nieuwe geschiedenis van België*. Vol. 1: *1830-1905*. Tielt: Lannoo, 2005.

Woeste, Charles. *Mémoires pour server à l'histoire contemporaine de la Belgique (1859-1894)*. Brussels: Librairie A. Dewit, 1927.

The identity of this author is not entirely certain.

AUTHORS

Philippe Chenaux is full Professor of Modern Church History at the Pontifical Lateran University. He is a specialist of the history of Catholicism and the papacy in the 20th century. Among his main publications: *Pie XII. Diplomate et pasteur* (2003); *L'Eglise catholique et le communisme en Europe (1917-1989). De Lénine à Jean-Paul II* (2009); *Paul VI. Le souverain éclairé* (2015). He is a member of the Pontifical Committee of Historical Sciences.

Wim Decock holds the chair in Roman Law and Legal History at the University of Louvain in Louvain-la-Neuve. He is the author of the prize-winning books *Theologians and Contract Law: The Moral Transformation of the Ius Commune (c. 1500-1650)* (Leiden/Boston: Brill/Nijhoff, 2013), and *Le marché du mérite. Penser le droit et l'économie avec Léonard Lessius* (Brussels: Zones Sensibles, 2019).

Jo Deferme holds the degrees of doctor in history and licentiate in Germanic philology. He has worked as a researcher and lecturer at institutions such as KU Leuven, HUBrussel, Erasmushogeschool Brussel and Drew University. His main area of expertise are the history of sociopolitical policy and theory.

Jean-Pierre Delville is professor emeritus in History of Christianity at the Université Catholique de Louvain (UCLouvain). In 2010, he was director of the *Revue d'histoire ecclésiastique* and president of the research institute Religions, Spiritualités, Cultures, Sociétés (UCLouvain). He published on the history of exegesis in the 16th century, the history of the papacy and on contemporary social history. He was ordained bishop of Liège in 2013.

Joeri De Smet read law in Leuven (Bachelor of Laws, 2016; Master of Laws, 2018) and Oxford (Magister Juris, 2019). He joined the Faculty of Law at KU Leuven as a doctoral researcher in September 2019 and has been a fellow of the Research Foundation Flanders (FWO) since November 2020. He is writing a dissertation on systemic risk in the financial sector. Outside the realm of financial regulation, he remains interested in Roman law and legal history, conflict of laws and corporate law.

Kwinten Dewaele graduated in 2019 from KU Leuven as Master of Laws with a specialisation in economic and private law. As an FWO-research fellow of the Institute for Contract Law at KU Leuven, he currently prepares a PhD under the supervision of Bernard Tilleman, Johan De Tavernier and Quentin Michel (ULg).

Vincent Genin holds a PhD in contemporary history and is FWO postdoctoral researcher at KU Leuven and *post-doctorant* at the École Pratique des Hautes Études (Sciences religieuses, Paris), GSRL. Recently, he published *Avec Marcel Detienne* (2021). His postdoc focuses on Max Weber - *L'Ethique protestante de Max Weber et les historiens français (1905-1979)* (2021) - and secularism in the 19th and 20th century. His habilitation à diriger des recherches (EPHE) focuses on french laïcité as social science.

Peter Heyrman is a historian and head of Research at KADOC, the Documentation and Research Centre on Religion, Culture and Society at KU Leuven. His research and publications deal with the multifold impact of religion on 19th- and 20th-century society, this with a particular interest in social policy, civil society, social security, small and medium-sized business and entrepreneurship.

Emiel Lamberts is professor emeritus at KU Leuven and has done extensive research in the field of modern political and religious European history. His most important publications include *Christian Democracy in the European Union (1945-1995)*, *The Black International (1870–1878)*, the co-edited *History of the Low Countries* and *The Struggle with Leviathan (1815-1965)*.

Faustino Martínez Martínez obtained his PhD in Law at the University of Santiago de Compostela. Since 2009, he is full professor at the Universidad Complutense de Madrid. He authored several books and numerous articles and papers dealing with various aspects of legal history from an international-comparative perspective. His latest research focuses on Spain's constitutional history and on 19th-century political thought. Recently he wrote an essay on Juan Bravo Murillo, a Spanish mid-19th-century conservative politician.

Bart Raymaekers is professor in moral philosophy and philosophy of law at the Institute of Philosophy, KU Leuven. His research and publications are focused on Kant's philosophy and the intersection between ethics and law. From 2017 through 2021 he was the vicerector for Humanities and Social Sciences at KU Leuven.

Erik Sengers is a sociologist of religion and a Church historian. He is affiliated to the Tilburg School of Catholic Theology as a guest researcher. Furthermore, he is a deacon of the diocese of Haarlem-Amsterdam and a board member of the Dutch Centre for the Social Teachings of the Church (www.cslk.nl). In addition to his biography of Joannes Aengenent, he published on the role of the Dutch Norbertine fathers in the Dutch Catholic social movement (2019).

Jakub Štofaník holds a PhD in History and is affiliated to the Department for Modern Political and Intellectual History of the Masaryk Institute and Archives of the Czech Academy of Sciences in Prague. His research focuses on social and religious history of the first half of the 20th century, all this from an international-comparative perspective. His last monograph deals with working-class religiosity in the Czech lands.

Cinzia Sulas. After graduating in Philosophy from La Sapienza University of Rome in 2011, she was a research fellow at the European School of Religious Sciences Giuseppe Alberigo of the Institute for Religious Sciences in Bologna for four years. In 2020, she obtained a PhD in European History and became a postdoctoral fellow at the Deutsches Historisches Institut in Rome. Her research focused on the relationship between scientific knowledge and Catholic doctrine, on State-Church relations in the modern and contemporary ages, on the history of the restored Society of Jesus, and on religious associationism. These themes particularly come to the fore in her biographical study of the Jesuit Luigi Taparelli d'Azeglio and her dissertation on the history of the Amicizia Cristiana.

Kasper Swerts is currently researcher at ADVN|Archive for National Movements in Antwerp and a postdoctoral researcher at the Centre for Political History at the University of Antwerp. He obtained his PhD at the Department of Social and Political Science at the University of Edinburgh in 2018 with a thesis titled *Vetera Novis Augere: Nationalism, neo-Thomism and Historiography in Quebec and Flanders 1900-1945*, focusing on the link between neo-Thomism and national(ist) historiography.

INDEX OF PERSONS

COLOPHON

FINAL EDITING
Luc Vints

COPY EDITING
Lieve Claes

LAY-OUT
Alexis Vermeylen

KADOC-KU Leuven
Documentation and Research Centre on Religion, Culture and Society
Vlamingenstraat 39
B - 3000 Leuven
www.kadoc.kuleuven.be

Leuven University Press
Minderbroedersstraat 4
B - 3000 Leuven
www.lup.be